THE MASTER
SWING TRADER

THE MASTER SWING TRADER

Tools and Techniques to Profit from Outstanding Short-Term Trading Opportunities

ALAN S. FARLEY

McGraw-Hill

New York   Chicago   San Francisco   Lisbon   London   Madrid
Mexico City   Milan   New Delhi   San Juan   Seoul
Singapore   Sydney   Toronto

Library of Congress Cataloging-in-Publication Data

Farley, Alan S.
   The master swing trader : tools and techniques to profit from outstanding short-term trading opportunities / by Alan S. Farley.
      p. cm.
   Includes bibliographical references.
   ISBN 0-07-136309-2
   1. Speculation.   2. Stocks—Charts, diagrams, etc.   3. Stock price forecasting.   4. Day trading (Securities)   I. Title.

HG6041.F35 2000
332.64'5—dc21

00-062222

McGraw-Hill

A Division of The McGraw·Hill Companies

17 18 19 20 21 22 23   DOC/DOC   1 4 3 2 1 0

ISBN 0-07-136309-2

Printed and bound by R.R. Donnelley & Sons Company.

McGraw-Hill books are available at special quantity discounts to use as premiums and sales promotions, or for use in corporate training programs. For more information, please write to the Director of Special Sales, Professional Publishing, McGraw-Hill, Two Penn Plaza, New York, NY 10121-2298. Or contact your local bookstore.

To John Yurko
Market Wizard, Selfless Teacher, and Ancient Soul

CONTENTS

Chapter 3

Analyzing the Market   69

Chapter 6

Understanding Time   219

PART TWO

THE 7-BELLS: TOOLS TO LOCATE OUTSTANDING OPPORTUNITIES

Chapter 7

Mastering the Setup   243

Chapter 8

Dip Trip   261

Chapter 11

Hole-in-the-Wall   313

Conclusion

Thirty Rules for the Master Swing Trader   423

F O R E W O R D

With explosive growth of the Internet and major changes in the financial markets, a new breed of speculators has evolved. Armed with high-tech tools, these new traders access Wall Street via their home computers in a search for the Promised Land. Although the art of speculation in all of its forms has existed for centuries, the financial media label these online traders as common gamblers who missed the bus to Atlantic City.

The use of skill rather than luck separates profitable speculation from gambling. Now that the gates to Wall Street are open to all who wish to compete, smart speculators will hone their trading skills and apply the right tools as they attempt to become masters of their profession. Education is the essential element in building success in any discipline, and trading is no exception. Fortunately, you are already on the right path if you are reading these words. You are seeking your trading education from one of the best instructors in the industry today.

My dear friend Alan Farley teaches traders across the globe how to master the art of high-probability short-term trading. He founded Hard Right Edge (http://www.hardrightedge.com), an excellent website for short-term traders and a comprehensive online resource that provides thousands of traders with educational materials on a daily basis. Alan is also an active message board participant, generously answering challenging questions from both new traders and market professionals. He has a true passion for teaching the beginner how to avoid the mistakes and pitfalls associated with short-term trading. When I asked Alan how he finds the time to answer all of those questions, he told me that he makes the time because new traders depend on veteran traders to give them good advice. "If I manage to save only one new trader from making a costly mistake, then it is well worth my time," Alan said.

Alan is determined to provide high-end education and has joined me on several occasions as we took center stage to teach at national online trading events. Although our compensation is small, I always look forward to spending time with him because he has true character and a great sense of humor. The greatest thing about his success is the fact that he has done very well just being himself. He is an asset to the trading community, and I am proud to be his friend.

Trade Smart!

Tony Oz
President, StockJunkie.com
Author of *Stock Trading Wizard: Advanced
Short-Term Trading Strategies and The Stock Trader:
How I Make a Living Trading Stocks*
June 2000

ACKNOWLEDGMENTS

Many friends and associates helped in the creation of *The Master Swing Trader*. I will fondly recall their invaluable assistance for many years to come. Writing any book is a hard task even for an accomplished writer. Writing a good book that may help thousands of swing traders beat the game is far more difficult. The following individuals should take pride in knowing that they played an important role in raising the bar of swing trading knowledge.

Special thanks to Tony Oz for many hours of late-night discussion about the modern trading press and its many complications. His mentoring and friendship are greatly appreciated. Also, warm, personal thanks to Tim Bourquin, Jim Sugarman, Joe Bettencourt, and Hillary Marks for allowing a new voice to speak at national trading Expos. These dedicated individuals represent the bright future of trading education, and their influence on the financial world should persist for decades to come.

A very grateful acknowledgement to Ross Ditlove and the MB Trading team in El Segundo, California, for a Townsend Real Tick account that allowed me to produce high-quality illustrations for the book. MB Trading presents a professional direct-access broker choice. They also offer readers $5.00 trades for the first 60 days after a new account opens. Call them at 1-888-790-4800 for details.

I must acknowledge David Singerman, a graduate of my online trading course and very nice guy, for his endless hours reading and commenting on the book manuscript. His eye for small details goes well beyond my capabilities, and his efforts are greatly appreciated.

Thanks for the special guidance of other professional traders and their ability to teach me new things each day. Perish the thought that all there is to know about the financial markets has already been written. It certainly has not, and these are the brilliant individuals who will continue to offer inspiration in the coming years: Mark Seleznov, Eric Patterson, Joe DiNapoli, Michael Turner, Teresa Lo, Rogan LaBier, Oswald Castillo, Linda Bradford Raschke, Michael Williams, Chris Wheeler, Geoff Mott, Steve Bell, Brandon Frederickson, Toni Hansen, and Vadym Graifer.

A special thank you to members of the media and website community for making online trading one of the most powerful financial forces of the new century and allowing Hard Right Edge to be part of that juggernaut: Mark Etzkorn, Frank Kollar, Michelle Riley, Todd Switzer, Noble Ershad, Dave Huff, Tom Nelson, Teresa Carey, Gary Smith, Tom Perry, Angela Alaimo, Dennis Shepherd, Chuck Thompson, and Josh Friedman.

Finally, warm acknowledgement to two Californians who talk me down whenever the trip gets really strange: Steve Moebius and Steve Sando.

INTRODUCTION

Market knowledge comes from the most unlikely places. In March 1983 I spent a week learning Native American survival and tracking techniques at a very cold farm in western New Jersey. Our class spent restless nights on a freezing barn floor and days investigating scat, nests, sounds, and a thousand little secrets that changed our way of viewing nature. We mastered some practical skills by the end of that grueling week. We could read the outcome of a sudden battle through a chaotic set of footprints. Owl vision focused our sight to the animal's point of view instead of our own. And we could sneak up on prey with a quiet fox walk without alerting them to our hungry intentions.

As my interest in the financial markets grew, I quickly realized that successful trading requires these same natural talents. The price chart takes the place of animal tracks but still demands our inner knowledge to interpret the endless conflict. We sense opportunity when we see through the eyes of the emotional crowd and measure its members' greed or fear. And we build consistent profits when we quietly sneak up behind them and empty their well-filled pockets.

Many traders never fully understand the nature of competition in the markets. We are taught in Sunday school or by well-meaning spouses to be nice to others in all of our daily activities. This makes its difficult to build the predatory instinct that leads to successful trading. Recognize our single purpose when the market opens each morning. We are there to take other people's money before they take ours. The only way to accomplish this task is to exercise a market point of view or trading edge that defeats this competition.

BIRTH OF THE PATTERN CYCLES

I remember the first time that I saw Bollinger Bands. I was amazed that such a thing could exist. My technical analysis skills were still very young, and simple stock charts were hard enough to understand. But these elastic bands went far beyond the patterns and indicators that I was reading about. They seemed to predict the future quickly and efficiently in an almost mystical way. This made no sense at all.

I spent weeks just staring at them. I would print out a stock chart and hold a piece of paper over the action. Then I would guess the location of the next price bar and move the paper over to see if I was right or wrong. Sometimes I knew exactly where the stock was headed, but other times I didn't have a clue. After awhile my predictive skills started to grow and my guesses became more and more accurate. I was certain that I had found the secret key to market success. Then I met John Yurko.

John was a staff member on the popular Compuserve Investors Forum. Before the days of the Net, this was the online place to chat with market professionals, traders, and other novices. One July 4 holiday weekend I saw John's brilliant comments on the board's technical analysis section and decided to ask him about Bollinger Bands. This simple inquiry started a fascinating relationship that lasted several years until his untimely death.

This amazing technician offered a wealth of market knowledge that I've never found on a financial bookshelf. He explained during our long chain of messages that I wasn't really predicting the future with Bollinger Bands. I was actually using the chart to read the past, and this was how I could see what would happen next. While Bollinger Bands improved my vision, the underlying patterns and trends within the bands were telling me where price was about to go. John also suggested that this complex world of chart patterns was really built upon a single unified structure. He never described its appearance, but it became clear to me that this master pattern might explain price movement through all time frames. I became fascinated with this intriguing concept and decided to learn more.

I looked for this master market pattern everywhere but could only find pieces of it. I noticed that stock charts would print the same old formations over and over again. There were triangles, wedges, and reversals from the classic books by John Murphy and Edwards and Magee. I saw more evidence through the big W in market bottoms and the five-wave decline in major selloffs. I discovered Fibonacci and Elliott but couldn't understand how all the pieces fit together.

It appeared to me that popular gurus were faring no better in their quest for true market knowledge. They would talk endlessly about a trading method or strategy but would rarely discuss the underlying mechanics that create opportunity in the first place. They would allege ownership of a common chart pattern and charge a fortune to those willing to pay for its secrets. And they would feed ruthlessly off their uninformed disciples with a few simple techniques they learned through actual market experience.

Finally, two brilliant traders opened my vision to this master pattern. Linda Bradford Raschke saw John's world and vividly describes it as a musical piece in her interview in *The New Market Wizards,* by Jack Schwager. She uses this clever analogy to illustrate how both sides of the brain must work together to visualize and interpret the broad range of price patterns. Stan Weinstein uncovers these same powerful mechanisms through classic trading strategies that rely on stage analysis in his book *Stan Weinstein's Secrets for Profiting in Bull and Bear Markets.*

The Traders Wheel was slowly brought to life through their powerful insight. In early materials that first appeared at Compuserve, the Wheel describes how markets move relentlessly from bottom to top and back again through all time frames. This first crude theory evolved over time and branched out into many different trading tactics. I later renamed it "Pattern Cycles" to acknowledge that these shifting market stages repeat in an orderly process. These broad concepts now form the core of my lecture materials and the Hard Right Edge (http://www.hardrightedge.com) financial portal.

In the beginning I didn't realize just how efficiently markets cycle through repeating price patterns. The original materials have grown well beyond my initial expectations. They now encompass all market movement and provide a simple definition for how price gets from one place to the other in a predictable manner. They also offer many powerful tools for swing traders to gain a needed edge over their competition.

Pattern Cycles describe the machine language within market opportunity. They reveal the origin of the trade setup and how to capitalize on inefficiency through every phase of bull and bear conflict. They show swing traders where to find consistent profits and offer natural methods to shift tactics quickly as conditions change. Above all else, this master pattern accurately predicts the impact of the emotional crowd on trend, range, and price development.

WHO SHOULD READ THIS BOOK?

This book describes an original trading methodology that relies heavily on classic technical analysis and pattern interpretation. It offers dozens of specific trading strategies and setups that include reward, risk, and stop loss considerations. It presents concrete tips, concepts, and workflows for readers to make informed choices at all stages of short-term trading development. It looks specifically at brokers, execution styles, and stock characteristics to offer advice on how to match personal lifestyle with trade management. Readers will note a highly original market view throughout the text that offers the journeyman trader extensive support on the road to consistent performance.

Enthusiasts at all levels of experience will appreciate this book's broad content and trading strategies. But it does assume knowledge of basic market mechanics and technical analysis. Take the time to build a core understanding of the financial world before attempting to absorb this text. Professional traders and other market insiders will find this book of great value for expanding their skills and improving their bottom line. And market timers will discover that technical analysis still has fresh ideas to offer after several centuries of noble service.

What does "swing trading" really describe in our modern markets? For decades, this expression referred to a futures market strategy that held positions from 1–3 days in order to capitalize on cyclical swings in buying and selling behavior. This classic concept now describes any execution method that avoids the hyperactivity of day trading. But this generic definition narrows the utility of this powerful art. In reality, swing trading characterizes a time frame-independent strategy that executes single, direct price movement. In this era of massive market liquidity, the swing trader may find excellent opportunities on both 5-minute and weekly charts.

The swing trader should read this book. But so should the day trader. And let's not leave out the position trader or technically-oriented investor. Day traders can discover short-term tactics that don't rely on scalping or frantic news releases. Mutual fund holders can improve their timing with these classic principles and swing their investments into a higher return. Is it unusual for one trading concept to have such broad applications? Not when that view includes all of the price patterns that markets can draw.

WHAT'S IN THIS BOOK?

The text begins with a detailed background on Pattern Cycles and the trend-range axis. It takes swing traders step by step through preparation, analysis and strategic considerations for each trade setup and execution. The middle section illustrates dozens of specific trading applications that include extensive discussion of profit and loss targets as well as position management. Take adequate time to read the first section before studying these examples and case studies. The text introduces many original terms, concepts and strategies into the trading workflow.

The book organizes information so that the swing trader first masters Pattern Cycles, advanced technical tools, and time management. It then demonstrates how to use these powerful forces to locate and execute outstanding short-term profit opportunities. The final section studies execution techniques and system choices that each reader must manage to access the modern market environment. Pay close attention throughout the text to the attitude of the successful swing trader and how the crowd becomes the source of profit at each turn.

CHAPTER 1: TRADING THE PATTERN CYCLE

Learn why the markets print repeating patterns over and over again. Discover the trend-range axis and see how it impacts every trade execution. Find out how swing trading differs from momentum trading. Begin the task of mastering the trade through knowledge of key market influences.

CHAPTER 2: PREPARING FOR THE MARKET DAY

Start the new day at the closing bell and get ready for the next market session. Build a solid database of promising stocks to watch for short-term profit opportunities. Learn the secrets of 3D charting and how the pattern points to reward and risk. Find out how market polarity continuously shifts internal trading mechanics between two active states.

CHAPTER 3: ANALYZING THE MARKET

Follow Pattern Cycles as they build new bottoms, eject into strong rallies, stall at major tops, and decline into painful selloffs. Study the secrets of this master pattern and see why it works through all markets and time frames. Learn how to apply volume tools that read the crowd and signal emotional peaks and valleys.

CHAPTER 4: BUILDING A SWING TRADING STRATEGY

Develop the edge that leads to consistent market profits. Measure the risks of momentum trading and master tactics that succeed in strong and weak market environments. Learn how to stand apart from the crowd at all times and use its mindless behavior for personal gain. Apply effective short sale strategies at every opportunity and manage advanced risk techniques to stay in the game for the long term.

CHAPTER 5: MASTERING THE TOOLS

Add dozens of highly effective technical tools to the trading arsenal. Find out how they work and when they should be ignored. Study a new proprietary indicator that signals major reversals and breakouts well ahead of the crowd's participation. Master morning gaps and quickly separate those that will fill right away from those that will never fill. Learn the secrets of pattern failure and how to trade popular technical patterns against the herd. Use multi-time frame Fibonacci retracements to locate turning points within a single tick.

CHAPTER 6: UNDERSTANDING TIME

Watch the market clock and see how it impacts the trading day. Identify specific times of day that show bullish or bearish tendencies. See how the 90-minute S&P alternation cycle impacts buying and selling behavior each day. Master trading strategies through the first and last hours as high volatility shakes out weak hands.

CHAPTER 7: MASTERING THE SETUP

Study the differences between classic and original chart patterns. Find out why original patterns provide more dependable results. Learn how to use whipsaws for personal gain. Develop perfect timing to enter promising trade setups at the lowest risk. Study original patterns that represent little-known profit opportunities.

CHAPTER 8: DIP TRIP

Learn to trade the pullback in all of its forms and incarnations. Use Fibonacci retracements to pinpoint reversals before they happen. Recognize bull flags as they print and see how to focus on their natural breakout levels. Review detailed case studies to gain an edge over the competition.

CHAPTER 9: COILED SPRING

Trade breakouts from the narrow range price bar. Build strategies to capitalize on this versatile pattern regardless of which way the market goes. Find out the differences between dull sideways markets and those about to explode into a new trend. Review pattern variations that appear over and over again in diverse market conditions.

CHAPTER 10: FINGER FINDER

See how one-bar candlestick reversals offer important swing trading signals. Learn to use multi-time frame analysis to build profitable setups that respond to dojis, hammers, and harami candles. Find these patterns in the intraday markets to pinpoint turning points and profitable opportunities. Add three original candle setups to the swing trader's toolbox.

CHAPTER 11: HOLE-IN-THE-WALL

Study a new gap that generates promising setups and dependable profits. See why other authors and traders missed it for decades. Build diverse strategies to take advantage of price action after the gap occurs. Learn how to predict future trend after the crowd responds.

CHAPTER 12: POWER SPIKE

Predict how heavy volume will impact subsequent trading activity. Use high-volume events to execute a variety of trading tactics that take advantage of Pattern Cycle stages. Recognize the differences between climax volume and breakout volume. Find out how to trade pullbacks after big-volume breakouts.

CHAPTER 13: BEAR HUG

Master the short sale and pinpoint the best times to avoid the short squeeze. Find markets in bear rallies that have run out of fresh buyers. See how narrow range bars signal impending selloffs and invite low-risk short sale opportunities. Recognize the market patterns that signal imminent declines and study detailed examples of successful short sale strategies.

CHAPTER 14: 3rd WATCH

See why triple tops offer tremendous profit opportunities. Learn many variations of the classic cup and handle breakout. Find frequent low-risk entry points with high reward potential. Recognize this classic setup on many intraday charts. Identify specific stop loss and profit targets that take advantage of the pattern. Use the third rise into any type of resistance to locate a short-term trade.

CHAPTER 15: PRECISE TRADE EXECUTION

Apply Pattern Cycle analysis to execution tactics and increase profits. Manage diverse intraday tools to master the market environment regardless of short-term conditions. Find out how to filter impending setups through the Level II screen or ticker tape to reduce risk. Discover when ECNs work and when they invite danger. Choose an execution system and broker to match a specific trading style or personal plan. Find out how the markets tell lies through every session and how to play with the liars.

CONCLUSION: THIRTY RULES FOR THE MASTER SING TRADER

Review key concepts that build outstanding profit performance. Step into the shoes of the master swing trader.

HOW TO USE THIS BOOK

This book will immediately benefit both active market participants and part-time trading enthusiasts. Keep a charting database or website close at hand through the study of each chapter. Find fresh examples of the trading concepts through current market action or favorite stock picks. *The Master Swing Trader* describes a visual universe that requires personal experience to be fully understood. This presentation does not represent an isolated market occurrence. It forms an inner structure that guides the development of all chart patterns and indicators.

The best results will come when the reader practices these original strategies through actual trade execution. Experiment with the new concepts and add them slowly into the trading toolbox. An immediate improvement in market vision will provide the first benefit. Take extra time to internalize the dozens of case studies and examples throughout the book. They will open up fresh tactics and build confidence when taking a position ahead of, behind, or against the restless crowd. But don't stop there.

The detailed illustrations enable the reader to visualize a new market reality. This unsuspected world offers intense feedback on the current trading environment. Pattern Cycles also present a dynamic system that digests price change and updates the charting landscape in real-time. This allows the swing trader to master a powerful execution strategy that few others will ever see.

PART ONE

THE GATEWAY TO SHORT-TERM TRADING

1 CHAPTER

TRADING THE
PATTERN CYCLE

THE PATH TO TRADING POWER

Swing traders must compete against the best-informed crowd in history. Financial institutions spent decades building expensive barriers to keep their middlemen in the seat of power. The Net revolution collapsed this unfortunate scheme and opened the markets to the average investor. Now anyone with a computer can access breaking news, execute a low-commission trade, and witness the immediate result. Technical analysis has come to the masses as well. The Web ensures that everyone knows their highs from their lows and can identify popular patterns as soon as they appear on their favorite stock charts.

Managing information and finding opportunity grow more difficult each day. Common knowledge of any market condition closes the system inefficiency that allows easy profit. But the masses respond slowly and continue to throw money at losing strategies for some time. Swing traders succeed when they recognize changing conditions and stay one step ahead of this restless crowd. This simple task requires great discipline because they must constantly abandon winning strategies and trade fresh ones as soon as the herd charges in their direction.

The markets have grown enormously complex over the past century. Look back at Charles Dow's revelations on trend and reversal in *The Wall Street Journal* or read the fascinating accounts of Roaring 20s trader Jesse Livermore in Edwin LeFevre's *Reminiscences of a Stock Operator*. The middlemen of that day pocketed such a large piece of the trading action that only the well-greased elite could profit from most market fluctuations. Imagine a world with no electronic communications networks, derivatives markets, or talking heads.

Yet the core elements of swing trading and technical analysis have not changed in decades. Stocks still go up or down with many pullbacks to test support and resistance. New highs continue to generate greed that carries price well past most rational expectations. And modern traders face the same emotional crowd that Livermore did when he played the bucket shops early in the last century.

Today's aspirants often confuse execution with opportunity. Rapid placement tools and fast connections promise a level playing field for any individual interested in the markets. Add some high-tech software, and the home office may even rival a glass tower financial house. But these complex systems can short circuit the most critical requirement for consistent profits: market timing that relies on accuracy rather than speed. And the tremendous ease of execution generates instant karma for errors and washes out traders at the fastest rate in history.

When new players first enter this fascinating world, they run quickly to bookshelves and absorb the trading masters. But Murphy, Elder, and Schwager reveal an organism that can only be digested in small bits and pieces. Neophytes must move slowly and protect capital until experience finally awakens knowledge. Over time, trade rewards and tragedies condition the mind to develop the instincts needed for long-term survival. Only then will the journeyman trader finally discover what works and what doesn't in this challenging game.

Seasoned traders often carry a flawed and incomplete market reality as well. They limit execution to a few classic setups rather than build understanding of the entire complex mechanism. When the market fails to offer perfect conditions for their limited strategies, tactics demand that they stand aside and wait. But if they lack strong discipline, the restless mind fills in the missing pieces and encourages bad positions. These narrow tactics may end careers in other ways. If the masses discover their well-worn game, it could stop working completely and leave them with no source of income.

The daily demands of trading are so intense that many borderline participants just grow lazy and evolve a self-destructive style. Fatigue sets in as the mind struggles to organize this complex world and many valuable shades of gray resolve into black and white illusion. In this dangerous view, stock positions become all-or-nothing events and wish fulfillment distorts vital incoming signals. As hope replaces good judgment, another market loser washes out and looks for a safer hobby.

Trading at all skill levels evokes emotions that generate great illusions. Sudden gains convince us that we are invulnerable, while painful losses confirm our ugly imperfection. We then externalize and turn to others who will comfort us as they parrot our point of view. Or we try to blame external systems for our failure. After all, everyone knows that market makers steal our money through evil tactics while bad connections and buggy software keep us from reaping fortunes.

The path to modern trading power must allow participants to adapt quickly

F I G U R E   1.1

Parallel price channels offer a classic breakout pattern favored by many experienced traders. But the setup may fail when the crowd sees it coming. Note how buyers of the early May 3Com gap never had an opportunity to profit before the stock reversed. Even those that bought the first pullback to the upper channel paid the price if they held the position overnight.

to new inefficiencies, offer profit opportunities throughout changing conditions, and allow fast, accurate analysis of all system input. It must be powerful enough to short circuit both mental and emotional trader illusions. This market knowledge must be simple to understand but provide continuous feedback through all time frames. And it must present a broad context to manage trade setups, risk, and execution through a variety of strategies, including day trading, swing trading, and investment.

THE HIDDEN MARKET

The vast majority of destabilizing and supportive market energies remain hidden from individual traders. Insiders quietly manipulate news to protect options positions. Analysts push stocks so their trading departments can unload inventory. Operating failures pass through accounting magic and disappear. As a result, market knowledge has limited value unless it meets one important test: it must stand alone as a complete fractal image of all hidden and known information about that market.

Traders and investors study markets through price charts. These powerful visual tools offer a common language for all equities, derivatives, and indices. The simplest chart just draws a time-price axis and adds each day's closing price as a single point or vertical bar. The connected data points then plot a series of oscillating highs and lows that participants study to predict whether price will move up or down over time.

Pattern analysis begins with the simple observation that all market activity reflects itself in the fractal properties of price and volume. These small bits of information create a profound visual representation when tied together into a continuous time series: a display of both current and past outcomes for all interactions of infinite market forces as seen through the eyes of all participants.

In contrast to the cold discipline of fundamental analysis, the pattern analyst's world reeks with lust and intrigue. The markets are about money. No other controlled substance brings out the best and worst of humanity with quite so much intensity. The markets become our lovers, our bosses, and the bullies who beat us up when we were young. As assets shrink or swell, emotions flood in and cloud reason, planning, and self-discipline. Chronic fight-flight impulses emerge to trigger unconscious (and often inappropriate) buying and selling behavior.

Actions initiated through emotional impulse generate oscillations in both price and time that print clearly on charts. The skilled pattern reader observes this unstable behavior and visualizes impending price movement. But successful trade execution requires both accurate prediction and excellent timing. Fortunately, chart patterns work without crystal balls or divine intervention. As a detailed map of all market forces, patterns identify exact trigger points where the swing trader can exploit the emotional crowd.

Patterns simplify and condense a vast universe of market interplay into easily recognizable setups. The subsequent analysis actually evokes the subjective right brain processes rather than the cold analytics of the orb's left side. Correct interpretation requires that the swing trader focus intuition on crowd impulses evident within each price chart. Those who divine correctly and apply that knowledge to obtaining profits are truly artists at their core, not masters of science.

Edwards and Magee did not invent patterns for their 1948 classic *Technical Analysis of Stock Trends.* They observed an order within price movement as ancient as the auction place. They also recognized the existence of cyclical crowd behavior throughout all time frames and all markets. Although the individual components are simple and easy to understand, these repeating formations offer the most intriguing predictive methods in the entire financial world.

PATTERN CYCLES

The U.S. stock exchanges trade over 9,000 issues each day. Add to that many thousands of emerging exchanges and companies worldwide. On any given day, every bull and bear condition, from euphoria to panic, exists somewhere on the planet. Buried within this universe of volatility and price movement, perfect trade setups wait to be discovered. But how can the speculator consistently tap this deep well of profit without being crushed by information overload or burnout?

For many decades, technical traders learned chart interpretation through the concepts of Dow Theory. Or they studied Edwards and Magee and faithfully memorized the characteristics of familiar price patterns seen daily on their favorite stocks or futures. These speculators were a minority within the investment community, and their size allowed them to execute effective strategies that capitalized on these little-known patterns when they appeared.

Net connectivity revolutionizes public access to price charts. They no longer require an expensive subscription, and most market participants can view them quickly in real-time. Now everyone reads the charts and believes that he or she understands the inner secrets of technical analysis. As noted earlier in this chapter, common knowledge of any market condition closes the system inefficiency that allows easy profit from it. Triangles, flags, and double tops now belong to the masses and are often undependable to trade through old methods.

Fortunately, the popularity of chart reading opens a new and powerful inefficiency for swing traders to manipulate. They can use the crowd's limited pattern knowledge for their own profit. The new disciples of technical analysis tend to focus on those few patterns that have worked well over the past century. Skilled traders can place themselves on the other side of popular interpretation and fade those setups with pattern failure tactics. More importantly, they can master the unified structure that underlies all pattern development and awaken the skills required to successfully trade dependable setups that have no name or adoring crowd.

Pattern Cycles recognize that markets travel through repeated bull and bear conditions in all time frames. Trends uncoil in a predictable manner, while constricted ranges print common shapes. Measurable characteristics distinguish each opportunity phase from uptrend to downtrend and back again. Most participants see these changes as the typical top, bottom, and congestion patterns. But a far richer trading world exists.

The twin engines of greed and fear fuel the creation of market opportunity. Through their power, the crowd reacts in a predictable manner at every stage of price development. Prices fall and fear releases discounted equities into patient value hands. Prices rise and mindless greed bids up hot shares into the pockets of momentum players. On and on it goes through all markets and time frames.

Rising prices attract greed. Paper profits distort self-image and foster inappropriate use of margin. The addictive thrill of a rally draws in many participants looking for a quick buck. More jump on board just to take a joyride in the market's amusement park. But greed-driven rallies will continue only as long as the greater fool mechanism holds. Eventually, growing excitement closes the mind to negative news as the crowd recognizes only positive reinforcement. Momentum fades and the uptrend finally ends.

Falling prices awaken fear. The rational mind sets artificial limits as profits evaporate or losses deepen. Corrections repeatedly pierce these thin boundaries and force animal instinct to replace reason. Negative emotions build quickly as pockets empty. Personality flaws invade the psyche of the wounded long while sudden short-covering rallies raise false hopes and increase pain. The subsequent decline finally becomes unbearable and the tortured shareholder sells, just as the market reverses.

The emotional crowd generates constant price imbalances that swing traders can exploit. But successful execution requires precision in both time and direction. Fortunately, this chaotic world of price change masks the orderly Pattern Cycle structure that generates accurate prediction and profitable opportunities through all market conditions. This inner order frees the mind, provides continuous feedback, and empowers spontaneous execution of rewarding trades.

Swing traders capitalize on the emotions of others after they control their own. Pattern Cycles caution them to stand apart from the crowd at all times. In the simplest terms it represents the attractive prey from which their livelihood is made. And just as a wild cat stalks the herd's edge looking for a vulnerable meal, the swing trader must recognize opportunity by watching the daily grind of price swings, volume spikes, and market noise.

Prices trend only fifteen to twenty percent of the time through all equities, derivatives, and indices. This is true in all charts, from 1-minute bars through monthly displays. Markets spend the balance of time absorbing instability created by trend-induced momentum. Swing traders see this process in the wavelike motion of price bars as they oscillate between support and resistance.

Each burst of crowd excitement alternates with extended periods of relative inactivity. Reduced volume and countertrend movement mark this loss of energy. As ranges contract, so does volatility. Like a coiled spring, markets approach neutral points from which momentum reawakens to trigger directional price movement. This interface between the end of an inactive period and the start of a new surge marks a high-reward empty zone (EZ) for those that can find it.

Prior to beginning each new breath, the body experiences a moment of silence as the last exhalation completes. The markets regenerate momentum in a similar manner. The EZ signals that price has returned to stability. Because only instability can change that condition, volatility then sparks a new action cycle of directional movement. Price bars expand sharply out of the EZ into trending waves.

Swing traders use pattern recognition to identify these profitable turning points. Price bar range (distance from the high to low) tends to narrow as markets approach stability. Skilled eyes search for a narrowing series of these bars in sideways congestion after a stock pulls back from a strong trend. Once located, they place execution orders on both sides of the EZ and enter their position in whatever direction the market breaks out.

Paradoxically, most math-based indicators fail to identify these important trading interfaces. Modern tools such as moving averages and rate of change measurements tend to flatline or revert toward neutral just as price action reaches the EZ trigger point. This failure reinforces one of the great wisdoms of technical analysis: use math-based indicators to verify the price pattern, but not the other way around.

Volatility provides the raw material for momentum to generate. This elusive concept opens the door to trading opportunity, so take the time to understand how this works. *Technical Analysis of Stocks and Commodities* magazine describes volatility as "a measure of a stock's tendency to move up and down in price, based on its daily price history over the latest 12 months." While this definition fixes only upon a single time frame, it illustrates how relative price swings reveal unique characteristics of market movement.

Rate of change (ROC) indicators measure trending price over time. Volatility studies this same information but first removes direction from the equation. It stretches waves of price movement into a straight line and then calculates the length. Volatile markets move greater distances over time than less volatile ones. But this internal engine has little value to swing traders unless it can contribute to profits. Fortunately, volatility has an important characteristic that enables accurate prediction. It tends to move in regular and identifiable cycles.

As prices ebb and flow, volatility oscillates between active and inactive states. Swing traders can apply original techniques to measure this phenomenon in both the equities and futures markets. For example, 10- and 100-period Historical Volatility studies the relationship between cyclical price swings and their current movement. And Tony Crabel's classic study of range expansion, *Day Trading with Short Term Price Patterns and Opening Range Breakout,* predicts volatility through patterns of wide and narrow price bars.

TREND-RANGE AXIS

Markets cycle between constricted ranges and directional trends through all time frames. Congestion reflects negative feedback energy that invokes price movement between well-marked boundaries but does not build direction. Rallies and selloffs reflect positive feedback energy that invokes directional price movement. Congestion breakouts shift market force from negative to positive feedback. Climax events shift market force from positive to negative feedback. Profit opportunity rises sharply at all feedback interfaces.

Momentum generates great force as increasing volatility resolves into directional price movement. It quickly awakens the positive feedback state that invokes chart bar expansion out of congestion. The crowd takes notice of this new, dynamic condition and participation rises. This fuels an escalating momentum engine and generates further price change. This dynamic mechanism continues to feed on itself until a climax finally shuts it down and forces a reversal into new congestion.

Trend marks territory as it spikes through relative highs and lows within all time frames. This signature behavior appears through all markets and in all historical chart activity. Trends print rising or falling prices over time. A series of lower highs and lower lows identify downtrends while uptrends reverse this sequence with higher highs and higher lows. Individual markets reflect a powerful trend relativity phenomenon when viewed through different time frames. The same stock may exhibit an uptrend on the daily chart, a bear market on the weekly, and sideways congestion when seen through 60-minute bars.

Quiet periods characterize most market action. Strong directional movement requires an extended rest to absorb instability. Long sideways or countertrend ranges after trends reflect lower participation while they establish new support and resistance. Volatility slowly declines through this congestion as price action recedes. As noted earlier, these dull markets finally invoke conditions that encourage the next trend leg. Price reaches stability and momentum quickly returns to start a new round of activity.

Price patterns represent dynamic trend or range systems that invoke measurable outcomes. Each setup formation exhibits a directional probability that reflects current internal and external conditions. Swing traders execute positions to capitalize on the pattern's highest-odds tendency. They also measure risk and apply defensive techniques to exit their trades if the pattern fails to respond according to expectations.

Different tactics capitalize on each stage of the trend-range axis. But many participants misinterpret their location and apply the wrong strategy at the wrong time. Or they limit execution to a narrow trading style that fails through most market stages. Swing traders avoid these dangerous pitfalls when they learn diverse strategies that apply to many different conditions and environments. But first they must understand the complex mechanics of the trend-range axis:

- Price movement demonstrates both directional trend and nondirectional range.
- Range motion alternates with trend movement.
- Trends reflect a state of positive feedback where price movement builds incrementally in a single direction.
- Ranges reflect a state of negative feedback where price movement pulses between minimum and maximum points but does not build direction.

- Trends reflect an upward or downward bias.
- Trends change and reverse at certain complex points of development.
- Ranges reflect their repeating patterns, bias for continuation or reversal, and the trend intensity expected to follow them.
- Movement out of ranges continues the existing trend or reverses it.
- Range volatility peaks at the interface between a trend climax and the inception point of a new congestion pattern.
- Range volatility ebbs at the apex point just prior to the inception of a new trend.
- High range volatility = wide range bars, high volume, and low price rate of change.
- Low range volatility = narrow range bars, low volume, and low price rate of change.
- Congestion pattern breakouts reflect a shift from negative feedback to positive feedback.
- High volatility associated with the end of positive feedback induces nondirectional price movement.
- Low volatility associated with the end of negative feedback induces directional price movement.
- Negative feedback registers on oscillators as shifts between overbought and oversold states but does not register on momentum gauges.
- Positive feedback registers on momentum indicators as directional movement but gives false readings on oscillators.

The pendulum swings endlessly between trend and range. As a market completes one dynamic thrust, it pauses to test boundaries of the prior move and draw in new participants. Price finally absorbs volatility and another trend leg begins. This cyclical movement invokes predictive chart patterns over and over again through all time frames. Profitable trade execution arises through early recognition of these formations and custom rules that capitalize on them.

Markets must continuously digest new information. Their future discounting mechanism drives cyclical impulses of stability and instability. Each fresh piece of information shocks the common knowledge and builds a dynamic friction that dissipates through volatility-driven price movement. In its purest form, volatility generates negative feedback as price swings randomly back and forth. But when focused in a single direction, positive feedback awakens to generate momentum into a strong trend. Proper recognition of these active-passive states will determine the swing trader's success or failure in market speculation.

Pattern Cycles organize trading strategy along this important trend-range axis. When breakouts erupt, follow the instincts of the momentum player. Buy high and sell higher as long as a greater fool waits to assume the position. But quickly recognize when volume falls and bars contract. Then focus to classic swing trading tactics and use price boundaries to fade the short-term direction.

FIGURE 1.2

Markets alternate between directional trend and congested range through all time frames. After a rally or selloff, stability slowly returns as a new range evolves. This quiet market eventually offers the right conditions for a new trend to erupt. Notice how the end of each range exhibits a narrow empty zone interface just before a new trend suddenly appears to start a fresh cycle.

Daily   (Right) AFCI - ADVANCED FIBRE COMMUNIC   Bar

SWING VS. MOMENTUM

Fast-moving stocks attract attention and awaken great excitement. Many neophytes catch gambling fever with these hot plays and never explore any other methods of speculation. The financial press reinforces their dangerous illusion with frantic reporting of big gainers and losers. But momentum profits require great skill and discipline. When the emotional crowd ignites sharp price movement, greed quickly clouds risk awareness. Many participants react foolishly and chase positions into major reversals. For most traders, momentum devours equity and destroys promising careers.

Price seeks equilibrium. When shock events destabilize a market, countertrend force emerges quickly to return a stable state. This inevitable backward reaction follows each forward impulse. Novices fail to consider this action-reaction cycle when they enter momentum positions. They blindly execute trades that rely on a common but dangerous strategy: long side entry on an accelerating price thrust. Reversals then appear suddenly to shake out the weak hands. The typical momentum player lacks an effective risk management plan during these sharp countertrends and tries to exit with the herd. Bids dry up quickly on the selloff and force an execution well below the intended price.

The momentum chase chews up trading accounts during choppy markets as well. This popular strategy requires a strong trending environment. As noted earlier, periods of directional price change last a relatively short time in relation to longer sideways congestion. But rather than stand aside, many participants fall prey to wish fulfillment and see trends where they don't exist. They enter small price swings on the false assumption that the action represents a new breakout. While these errors may not incur large losses, they damage equity and confidence at the same time.

Survivors of the momentum game begin to appreciate the market's complexity and realize that trading mastery requires many diverse skills. As price cycles through regular phases, strategy needs to adapt quickly to capitalize on the current crowd. Swing trades that execute right near support or resistance offer one powerful alternative. This classic execution style demands more precise planning than momentum, but allows measurable risk and highly consistent rewards.

Trend-range alternation spawns different trading styles. When markets ignite into rapid price movement, skilled momentum traders use the crowd's excitement

T A B L E   1.1

Momentum vs. Swing Characteristics

Trade	Momentum	Swing
State:	Positive feedback	Negative feedback
Strategy:	Reward	Risk
Basis:	Demand	Supply
Chart:	Trend	Range
Impulse:	Action	Reaction
Purpose:	Thrust	Test
Condition:	Instability	Stability
Indicator:	Lagging	Leading
Price Change:	Directional	Flat-line

to pocket large gains. The inevitable rollover into defined support and resistance marks the dominance of precise swing trading techniques. But neither category actually stands apart from the other. The need to adapt quickly to changing market conditions requires that all successful traders apply elements of both strategies to earn a living.

Swing traders seek to exploit direct price thrusts as they enter positions at support or resistance. They use chart pattern characteristics to locate and execute short-term market inefficiencies in both trending and rangebound markets. This classic strategy closely relates to position trading tactics that hold stocks from 1 to 3 days or 1 to 3 weeks. But swing trading actually represents a time frame-independent methodology. Modern practitioners may never hold a position overnight but still apply the exact same strategies as longer-term participants.

The origin of the swing stems from George Taylor's *The Taylor Trading Technique,* a classic commentary on the futures markets first published in the 1950s. His 3-Day Method envisions a cycle that classifies each day as a "buy," "sell," or "sell short" opportunity. At its core, the narrow swing tactic buys at support and sells at resistance through congested markets. It fades the short-term direction as it predicts that a barrier will hold and reverse price. Modern trading expands this concept to locate the swing through many other market conditions and broadens the tactics that build profits.

The equity markets present a natural arena for the swing trader. The symbiotic relationship between futures and equities ensures that cyclical buying and selling behavior crosses all markets. Equities have the advantages of massive liquidity and time frame diversity. In other words, participants can scalp the same market at the same time that institutions take positions for multiyear investments.

Classic swing trading concepts must adapt to unlock their power in today's markets. The revolution in high-speed trade execution opens swing strategies that last for minutes instead of days. Dependable price patterns appear on charts in all time frames. As modern traders work with real-time charting, intraday swing setups offer the same opportunities that appear daily on longer-term charts.

The ability to trade through diverse conditions marks successful careers. Swing trading provides a natural framework to identify changing conditions and apply new methods to exploit them. This exposes another outdated concept for this versatile approach. At its core, swing trading is not the opposite of momentum trading. During those times when strong price movement characterizes a market, disciplined momentum strategy becomes the preferred swing trade. In this way, modern swing traders can apply the principles of risk management and price boundaries to the manic world of the speculator—and use momentum's greed to their advantage.

TIME

Pattern Cycles oscillate equally through all time frames. Trade setups remain valid in every chart view, whether they print on 1-minute or monthly bars. Each chart length attracts a specialized group of participants that interacts with all other groups through the universal mechanics of greed and fear. This dynamic 3D process results in trend convergence-divergence through different time lengths. Swing traders improve performance when they adjust their chart view to match the chosen holding period. As Table 1–2 illustrates, modern swing tactics encompass both the world of the day trader and the position trader.

Successful trade execution aligns positions through a multidimensional time view. First choose a primary screen that reflects the holding period and matching strategy. Then study the chart one magnitude above that period to identify support-resistance and other landscape features that impact reward:risk. Finally, shift down to the chart one magnitude below the primary screen and identify low-risk entry points. Alexander Elder defined many elements of this strategy in his Triple Screen system in *Trading for a Living*. The time has come to expand his classic concepts to accommodate the faster fingers of the modern high-speed markets.

Evaluate a trade setup through all time frames that may affect the position. The view just above and below the intended holding period may not capture important trendlines, gaps, or patterns. Study that market's multiyear history before execution as time permits to identify large-scale swing pivots. If the trade target passes through major highs or lows that are several years old, give those levels adequate attention. Other players will see the same chart features and may use them for entry or exit. But keep in mind that the importance of old price extremes decays over time. Consider the current emotional intensity of the crowd before dismissing trades based on old obstacles.

Time frame analysis above and below the current setup chart will identify opportunity and risk in most cases. For example, when a promising setup appears on a 5-minute chart, the swing trader checks the 60-minute chart for support-resistance but uses the 1-minute chart to time execution to the short-term flow of the market. This multidimensional approach works through all time levels. Even mutual fund holders can benefit when they locate a potential investment on a weekly chart but use the daily and monthly to time entry to the highest probability for success.

Market participants routinely fail at time management. Many never identify their intended holding period before they enter a trade. Others miss major support-

T A B L E   1.2

Trading Style and Related Price Chart

Participant	Price Chart
Scalpers	1-minute
Day traders	5-minute
Position traders	60-minute
Investors	Daily
Institutions	Weekly

resistance on the daily chart when they execute on the 60-minute bars. Some sit on nonperforming positions for weeks and tie up important capital while excellent opportunities pass by. In all cases, time works as efficiently as price to end promising careers.

Time of day, week, and month all display unique properties that enhance or damage the odds for profit. Market insiders use the volatility of first-hour executions to fade clean trends and empty pockets. Options expiration week can kill strong markets or force flat markets to explode. Thin holiday sessions offer dramatic rallies or selloffs in the most unexpected issues. And many Fridays begin with government statistics that ignite sharp price movement.

Every profit opportunity arrives with a time shadow hanging over it. Learn to focus attention on important feedback at the exact time that the information will likely impact that market. It may flag an execution window that closes in minutes or offer an exit that should be taken without question when it arrives. Recognize the impact of time on reward:risk before position entry and update conclusions as each new price bar prints.

Swing traders must manage time as efficiently as price. Calculate the expected holding period for each new position based on the distance to the next high-risk zone. Use both price and time triggers for stop loss management. Time should activate exits on nonperforming trades even when price stops have not been hit. Execute only when time bias improves the odds for profit, and stand aside frequently.

TREND RELATIVITY

Trends validate only for the time frame in which they occur. A trend in one time frame does not predict price change in the next lower time frame until the shorter period intersects key levels of the larger impulse. Pattern Cycles in time frames larger and smaller than the current trend are independent and display unique attributes of the trend-range axis. This interrelationship continues all the way from 1-minute through yearly chart analysis.

Swing traders must always operate within this 3D trend relativity. The most profitable positions will align to support-resistance on the chart above the trade and display low-risk entry points on the chart below. But trend relativity considerations do not end there. Price evolves through bull and bear conflicts in all time frames. When ongoing trends don't fit neatly into specific charting periods, trade preparation may become subjective and dangerous.

Hard work yields promising setups that align to the swing trader's holding period. But these opportunities must fit into a larger market structure for the positions to succeed. With trends in motion less than 20% of the time through all markets, odds do not favor a confluence of favorable trading conditions through three time frames. The perfect opportunity rarely exists. An exciting breakout on one chart may face massive resistance on the longer-term view just above a planned entry level. Or a shorter-term chart may display so much volatility that any entry becomes a dangerous enterprise.

Few executions align perfectly with the charting landscape. Successful trading requires a careful analysis of conflicting information and entry when favorable odds rise to an acceptable level. When faced with a good setup in one time frame but marginal conditions for those surrounding it, use all available skills to evaluate the overall risk. If reward:risk moves into a tolerable range, consider execution even if all factors do not favor success. That's the nature of the trading game.

Support-resistance priority parallels chart length. Use this hierarchy to locate high-probability entry levels and avoid low-reward trades. For example, major highs and lows on the daily chart carry greater importance than those on the 5-minute chart. As the shorter bars drift down toward the lows of the longer view, strong support exists for a significant bounce. These 3D mechanics also suggest that resistance in the time frame shorter than the position can safely be ignored when other conditions support the entry.

Profit opportunity aligns to specific time frames. But many participants never clearly define their targeted holding period and trap themselves in a destructive strategy flaw. They see their trades in one time frame but execute them in another. This trend relativity error often forces a new position just as the short-term swing turns sharply against the entry. Neophytes fall into this trap with great frequency. They feel pride when they see an impending move on their favorite chart and recklessly jump on board. The action-reaction cycle then kicks in and shakes them out as price tests support before heading higher.

Trend relativity errors rob profits on good entries as well. No one wants to leave money on the table. So marginal players may freeze as soon as a new position moves in their favor. But inaccurate price targets can measure one trend while the initial entry springs off another. Natural wave motion then whipsaws the flawed position sharply and sends the trade into a substantial loss well before reaching a reward target.

Visual information seeks to reduce noise and increase signal as it travels from the eye to the brain. The rational mind sees large trends but may conveniently filter out the many obstacles along the way. Or the marginal participant manipulates the chosen holding period and curve fits the opportunity to match the current plan. Most players should never change their holding period without detailed preplanning. Specific time frames require unique skills that each swing trader must master with experience. This noble effort should not begin trying to rescue a loser from bad decision-making.

Compensate for this mental bias through precise trade management. Begin with a sharp focus on the next direct move within a predetermined time frame. Prepare a written trading plan that states how long the position will be held and stick with it. Establish a profit target for each promising setup and then reevaluate the landscape that price must cross to get there. Consider the pure time element of the trade. Decide how many bars must pass before a trade will be abandoned, regardless of gain or loss.

FIGURE   1.3

Three different time frame charts paint very different pictures of the same price action. Atmel breaks through major horizontal support and pulls back to test resistance on the daily view. But that important test hides from the 60-minute chart where price draws a tight symmetrical triangle. Meanwhile the day trader only sees a breakout and bull flag on the 5-minute screen. Finding opportunities in one time frame but trading them in another leads to costly trend relativity errors.

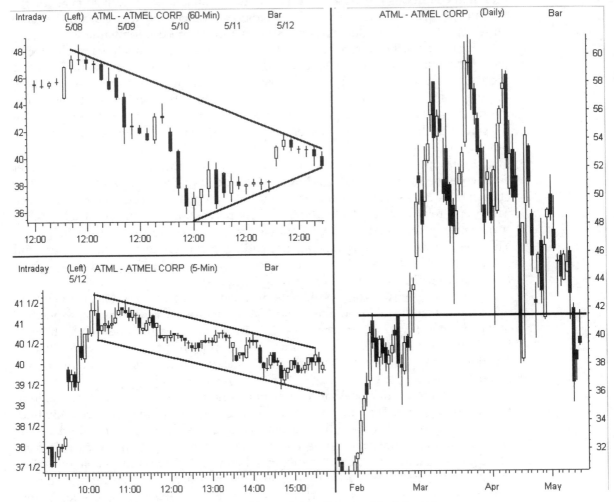

VOLUME

Emotional forces shape trends through all market conditions. New uptrends build crowd enthusiasm, which attracts waves of greedy buyers. Gaming mentality slowly overcomes good judgment as prices push higher and higher into uncharted territory. The frantic rally finally cools and the herd turns nervous. As the market rolls over, fearful selling replaces greedy excitement. The decline gathers force and continues well past rational expectations. Panic replaces fear, but just as pain becomes unbearable, value players jump in and end the correction. Price starts to form a bottom and a new Pattern Cycle springs to life.

In a turbulent marketplace, distorted expectations characterize both long and short positions. Price destabilizes and crowd participation swells as bulls and bears swing through emotional battles. Although these constant waves of accumulation and distribution appear chaotic, they often conceal an axis of directional movement. To measure this underlying tendency, study the emotional imprint of buying and selling behavior.

Two simple pieces of data unlock the mysteries of emotional markets: price and volume. While technicians manipulate price through many patterns and indicators, the best volume analysis arises from the simple histograms offered through most charting packages. These spikes and valleys in the lower pane of the price chart often tell swing traders all they need to know about the current crowd.

Common histograms display volume through a single hue or color-code the action based on the price bar's closing direction. The two-color (red for down and green for up) version offers a powerful view of that market's trend-range axis and uncovers complex insight into crowd direction. Once this is detected, watch for opportunity as the indicator tracks the interplay between buying-selling behavior and directional price movement.

Volume rarely reveals accumulation-distribution in a straightforward manner. Bursts of emotional buying or selling may dictate price direction over short periods of time, regardless of the underlying trend. Effective longer-term analysis requires filtering mechanisms to distinguish between these pockets of frantic volatility and significant participation that will eventually guide prices higher or lower.

A hidden spring ties together volume and price change. Accumulation-distribution may lead or lag trend. As one force steps forward, tension on the spring increases. The leading impulse pauses until a release point strikes and the other surges to join its partner. This tension measurement between price and volume offers an important signal for impending market movement. Since positive feedback requires synchronicity between both elements, volume leadership predicts price change.

Classic technical indicators provide continuous accumulation-distribution readings. Lesser-known techniques measure the tension on the price-volume spring itself. Like water brought slowly to a boil, volume reflects latent energy that releases itself through trend. Accumulation-distribution and histograms measure the power of this emotional force.

Analysis of crowd participation through volume has little value unless it accurately predicts price change. Profitable setups arise through recognition of climax volume events and identification of emotional force building at key breakout and breakdown points. Human nature swings greed and fear between stable boundaries most of the time. The master swing trader can identify those narrow conditions where volatility will spike and destabilize crowd behavior toward its emotional extremes.

Accumulation-distribution reaches into herd behavior better than any other form of technical analysis. It also requires great effort to filter out meaningless data and focus on key crowd interactions. Markets generate volume for many non-emotional reasons, such as secondary offerings or block trade reporting. But these technical events never move trends the same way as greed or fear. In most cases, successful trade execution belongs to those who can consistently read the paranoid mind of the markets.

CROSS-MARKET ANALYSIS

Market action spins off both internal and external Pattern Cycles. Swing traders must consider both factors before executing their positions. The complex interplay of world markets works its way downward into individual stocks and futures on a daily basis. But accurate prediction of the exact impact during any given session requires a detailed understanding of macroeconomic forces and arbitrage between different entities.

Consider the influence of the credit and futures markets before entering an equity position. A sudden selloff in either of these exchanges can have an immediate effect on stock prices. Arbitrage between equities, futures, and credit also leads to intraday oscillation that runs through all exchanges. Observe this rhythmic movement on TICK registers and in the cyclical price swing that runs through all major indices. Swing traders can use this well-known phenomenon to time executions that synchronize with these larger forces.

Local influences change quickly from day to day. The markets constantly seek leadership. In the absence of larger forces, that role can shift at any time from the S&P futures to Nasdaq to the Dow 30 Industrials. A major sector can suddenly move into the limelight and carry other markets higher or lower with little warning. These fluctuations may or may not affect any individual position. The swing trader must determine the potential impact quickly and shift strategy when required.

Cross-market influences shift between local and worldwide forces. During quiet periods, simple arbitrage generates primary influence. But world events or broad currency issues may rise to the surface and shock American markets. Always defend active positions by staying informed and planning a safe exit in the case of an emergency. Avoid overnight holds during very volatile periods and think contrary at all times. The best opportunity may come right after the crowd jumps for the exits.

Follow the charts of the major indices and S&P futures on a daily basis. Intraday traders should watch their real-time movement throughout each session. Keep track of the current bond yield and identify major support-resistance levels. Identify market leadership as early in the day as possible. Then use that price action to predict the short-term flow of the market. When a macroeconomic event appears, consider taking the day off unless a clear strategy emerges to capitalize upon it.

Promising setups often fail badly on these days because they can't find the crowd to carry them.

REWARD:RISK

Swing trading requires a serious commitment to skill, knowledge, and emotional control. Treat it as a business at all times. Prepare a personal trading plan, carefully evaluate risk capital, and set attainable goals for the future. If personal bias expects this discipline to earn quick wealth, find another hobby immediately or just take up gambling. The markets have no intention of offering money to those who do not earn it. And always remember this valuable wisdom: attention to profit is a sign of trading immaturity, while attention to loss is a sign of trading experience.

Show a willingness to forgo marginal positions and wait for good opportunities to appear. Prepare to experience long periods of boredom between frantic surges of concentration. Expect to stand aside, wait, and watch when the markets offer nothing to do. Accept this unwelcome state as all successful participants do. The need for excitement makes a very dangerous trading partner.

Careful stock selection controls risk better than any stop loss system. Bad timing does more damage than sustaining large losses. Make wise choices before position entry and face less risk at the exit. Watch out for secondary gains that have nothing to do with profit. Trade execution will release adrenaline regardless of whether the position makes or loses money. Always face your true reasons for swing trading the markets. The primary motivation must be to aggressively take money out of someone else's pocket. Rest assured, the skilled competition will do their best to take yours at every opportunity.

Every setup has a price that violates the pattern. The measurement from this breach to the trade entry marks the risk for the position. When planning execution, look for levels where price must move only a short distance to show that the trade was a mistake. Then expand this measurement to find the reasonable profit target and apply this methodology to every new opportunity. Limit execution to positions where risk remains below an acceptable level and use profit targets to enter markets that have the highest reward:risk ratios.

Each swing trader carries a different risk tolerance. Some find comfort flipping NYSE behemoths, while others play low float screamers. Follow natural tendencies and remember that swing strategies use discretionary entry. The trader alone must decide when to enter, exit, or stand aside. Test overall results by looking at profit and loss at the end of each week, month, and year. Good results make money, while bad results lose it.

MASTERING THE TRADE

Consistent trading performance requires accurate identification of current market conditions and the application of appropriate strategies to capitalize upon them.

Pattern Cycles provide an effective method for price discovery through all charts and time frames. This expanded concept of swing trading offers diverse tools to uncover profit opportunities through continuous feedback, regardless of bull, bear, or sideways markets.

But information does not equal profit. The markets have a limited number of opportunities to offer at any given time. Price charts evolve slowly from one promising setup to the next. In between, they emit divergent information in which definable elements of risk and reward conflict with each other. At times this inconsistency yields important clues about the next trade. More often it represents noise that must be ignored at all costs. The ability to tell the difference between the two marks an important passage on the road to trading success.

Trading noise occurs during both positive and negative feedback. It simply represents those periods when participants should remain on the sidelines rather than jump into the action. Account capital has limitations and should only commit to the most promising setups. While effective strategies book profits, many participants experience anxiety between positions and tend to pull the trigger prematurely. Remember that longevity requires strict self-discipline. Swing traders unconsciously seek excitement in the place of profits during quiet market periods. Allow boredom to bring down the emotional level and wait patiently for the next real thing.

Both negative and positive feedback conditions produce rewarding trades, but confusion between the two can lead to major losses. Classic swing strategies work best during negative feedback, while positive feedback supports profitable momentum entry. Avoid the danger of choosing the wrong strategy through consistent application of the expanded swing methods. Regarding of market phase, use this simple, unified approach for all trade executions: enter positions at low risk and exit them at high risk. These mechanics often parallel the buying at support and selling at resistance exercised in classic swing tactics. But this expanded definition allows entry into the realm of the momentum trader with safety and precision.

Swing traders study both action and reaction when evaluating setups in the momentum environment. This demands complex planning and detached execution that aligns positions to the underlying trend but against the current crowd emotions. This strategy naturally favors execution against traditional momentum tactics. Countertrend reactions provide excellent swing entry levels in momentum markets. Once filled, these positions find a comfortable exit on the next accelerating thrust just as new participants jump in from the other direction.

Highly experienced players can use more sophisticated techniques to locate less obvious low-risk trade entry and enter into accelerating momentum. These high volatility positions require tight trailing stops that protect risk capital. But successful exit strategy remains the same through diverse entry tactics. Look for acceleration and feed the position into the hungry hands of other participants just as price pushes into a high-risk zone.

Execution must synchronize with momentum action-reaction or it will yield frustrating results. Every player knows the pain of executing a low-risk entry, riding a profitable trend but then losing everything on a subsequent reaction. Clearly de-

FIGURE   1.4

The continuous momentum cycle forms a timing core for swing traders to align profitable executions. Trend surges forward against the friction of countertrend weight. Momentum slows and price falls backward to test prior boundaries. As it reaches stability, the primary trend finally reasserts itself and ignites new momentum. Use repeating chart patterns to uncover these pullbacks and enter long or short positions in harmony with the larger impulse.

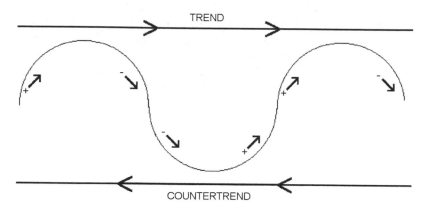

fined swing exit tactics will avoid this unpleasant experience. Multi-trend technical analysis and cross-verification techniques identify probable reversal points well in advance of the price action. Unfortunately, most market participants do not visualize their exit when they enter a new position and allow greed to overpower analysis as soon as it moves into a profit. The master swing trader always locates natural escape routes and major profit levels before new execution.

Manage risk on both sides of the trade. Focus on optimizing entry-exit points and specialize in single direct price moves. Remember that execution of low-risk entries into mediocre positions allows more flexibility than high-risk entries into good markets. Avoid fundamental analysis of short-term trading vehicles. Mental bias from knowledge of a company's inner workings can distort the message of the price chart just when opportunity knocks.

Swing trading allows many methods to improve profitability. Try to adjust position size, manage time more efficiently, or slowly scale out of winners to retain a piece for the next price thrust. But careful trade selection does more to build capital than any other technique. Enter new positions only when signals converge and send a clear message. Standing aside requires as much careful preparation as entry or exit and must be considered before every execution.

Winning is a tough game. Each swing trader must compete against all other participants to take their money. House rules ensure that the insiders always retain an advantage. Market makers and specialists use proven techniques to frighten small players and shake them out of positions. Exercise original strategies while controlling emotions with strong mental discipline to find that needed edge over the crowd.

Use technical analysis and drill swing prices into memory. Target acceptable dollar and tick losses. Remember that the average position gain must be significantly higher than average loss or survival will depend upon a winning percentage well above 60%. Improve results by reducing losses first and increasing profits second. Keep current and accurate trading records. The mind will play cruel tricks when results depend on memory.

Consider the real impact of available capital and leverage. The well-greased competition can overcome their transaction costs by trading large blocks. But small equity accounts must watch trade size and frequency closely. Frequent commissions and small capital will eventually end promising careers in speculation. When trying to grow a small account, lengthen holding period and go for larger profits per entry. And use any drawdowns as a major signal to lighten up and slow down.

PREPARING FOR THE MARKET DAY

THE CLOSING BELL

The closing bell signals the start of preparation for the next market day. Use this valuable time to measure current cycles and find winners for the next session. Probe markets for the best new opportunities and apply price chart techniques to identify the likely trading conditions. Take a look back and critique actions taken during the preceding session. Adjust watch lists to remove lost opportunities and add new stocks that show promise for the future.

Update the personal trading plan and current strategy after reviewing the events of each session. Make small strategic adjustments on a daily basis, but do significant editing only after weeks of data mining and personal introspection. Look back at the day with complete honesty. Were exits taken when offered? Did hope replace good judgment? Were personal rules followed, and did that make a difference in the profit and loss statement? Make sure to revise all trading records daily to avoid a backlog of old tickets and account statements.

Every market of interest generates new feedback as the trading day comes to a close. Trendlines break and shock gaps change important assumptions. Significant news may dictate new strategies or establish a fresh bias on short-term direction. Review specific issues that will likely move the markets when the new day begins. How has sentiment changed and what impact will it have on the crowd? Quickly categorize the current market and refresh tactics that will respond to it.

Review the economic calendar for important government reports. Exercise greater caution on Fridays that release the unemployment report or unwind options positions. If volatility will surge sharply due to unpleasant news or conditions, don't hesitate to take the day off and let the competition assume the risk. The market will still offer many opportunities after others get caught in sharp whipsaws or take dramatic profits.

Avoid information overload. Set aside a reasonable time for preparation and limit analysis to focus on key stocks and indices in detail. Reduce watch lists, news, and charts until they conform to a healthy personal lifestyle. Get recreation, eat right, and get plenty of sleep before the new market day begins. Exhausted swing traders make terrible decisions.

Use the quiet hours to locate and evaluate trade setups. Hurried analysis of new opportunities during the market day invites danger. Important charting features go unnoticed and the pulse of the Level II screen becomes difficult to ignore. The swing trader also faces many chores that interfere with clearheaded reward: risk evaluation during the active session. Prior preparation frees the schedule so that the active session can receive full attention.

When the market opens, be prepared to respond to a flood of fresh data quickly and without hesitation. Apply original 3D chart skills that quickly filter opportunity and manage risk. Use new twists on classic strategies to place each issue within its Pattern Cycle and generate continuous feedback through all conditions. Watch the ticker closely to defend against external influences, and exercise tactics that swing against the crowd to book consistent profits.

SUPPORT-RESISTANCE

Support-resistance (S/R) organizes the charting landscape into well-marked levels that predict swings and breakouts. Price action at these important boundaries depends on their unique characteristics and specific locations within the trend-range axis. Stocks can swing back and forth across a central S/R pivot rather than find a floor or ceiling. Support-resistance may present an absolute barrier that cannot be crossed or exhibit elasticity that can be stretched but not broken. In common horizontal S/R, resistance becomes support when price mounts it and vice versa when it falls through. Swing traders earn their livelihoods as they find and execute setups along S/R interfaces.

Diverse S/R boundaries print on every chart in all time frames. Most carry a unique load factor and will break when buying or selling intensity exceeds it. Once price pierces a level, it normally expands toward the next S/R barrier. This mechanism provides the source for many profitable strategies. The classic swing trade buys at support and sells at resistance. Therefore, these levels define both reward and risk. Look to buy support when the nearest resistance is far above, and look to sell resistance when the nearest support is far below. But make sure the landscape hides no dangerous obstacles. A single overlooked level can have disastrous results.

Profitability depends on accurate prediction at S/R interfaces. The skilled eye must quickly locate these points and evaluate their impact on every setup. Begin with a dense chart template that layers all types of S/R boundaries directly on price. Then study the individual elements and how each affects reward:risk. Start with highs and lows in the longest applicable time frame and work down to recent price action. Pay special attention to shock events that may produce significant S/R in a single bar. For example, strong gaps can stay unfilled for many years.

Apply a simple hierarchy that rates the importance of each S/R feature. Horizontal levels that persist over time carry more weight than those from shorter periods. Major highs and lows provide stronger S/R than moving averages or other price derivatives. Hidden levels offer cleaner opportunities than well-known ones that invite whipsaws and fading strategies. S/R strengthens when many barriers converge at the same price and weakens when a single obstacle blocks the progress of price movement.

TYPES OF S/R

Horizontal price marks the most common form of S/R. These important highs and lows reveal scarred battlegrounds between bulls and bears. They carry an emotional shadow that exerts lasting influence whenever price returns. Markets tend to draw bottom support on high volume and then test it repeatedly. Over time these become significant floors during future corrections. Alternatively, tops that print during frantic rallies may persist for years. Failed tests at these levels reinforce resistance and generate a pool of investor supply that must be absorbed before the uptrend can continue. In both cases, horizontal S/R levels should be obvious at first glance of a promising new setup.

Look for price to fail the first test of any significant high or low horizontal S/R level. But then expect a successful violation on the next try. This classic price action has the appearance of a triple top or bottom breakout. The popular cup and handle pattern offers a clear illustration of this dynamic process. Also watch closely where the first test fails. If price cannot reach the horizontal barrier before rolling over, a second test becomes unlikely until the pattern breaks sharply in the other direction.

Swing traders must evaluate many price restraints beyond simple floors and ceilings. These lesser-known pivots provide superb entry and exit when located. The crowd often misinterprets price action at these levels and triggers opportunity on the other side of the trade. As noted earlier, common knowledge tends to undermine the dependability of technical setups. Alternatively, the markets reward original vision and strategy. Consider the substantial benefits when classic S/R mechanics combine with contrary entry.

Trending markets emit their own S/R fingerprint. Rising or falling moving averages routinely mark significant boundaries. Popular settings for these versatile indicators have found their way into the financial press, technical analysis manuals and charting programs. The most common calculations draw lines at the 20-day, 50-day, and 200-day moving averages. These three derivative plots have wide acceptance as natural boundaries for price pullbacks. Two important forces empower

FIGURE   2.1

Swing traders scan the charting landscape to identify horizontal support-resistance and major moving averages that uncover natural reversal levels. While this process appears simple, price action generates many complex variations that baffle execution planning. Try to combine as many forms of price convergence as possible to pick out high-odds setups.

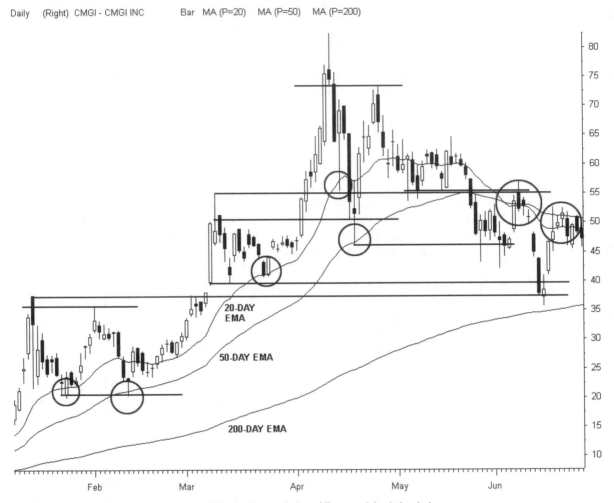

Daily   (Right) CMGI - CMGI INC   Bar MA (P=20)   MA (P=50)   MA (P=200)

these classic averages. First, they define levels where profit and loss taking will ebb following strong price movement. Second, their common recognition draws a crowd that perpetrates a self-fulfilling event whenever price approaches.

The S/R character of moving averages changes as they flatten and roll over. The turn of a specific average toward horizontal signifies a loss of momentum for that time frame. This increases the odds of a major line break. But don't confuse

T A B L E   2.1

Moving Average Settings and Related Trends

Moving Average	Trend
20-day	Short-term
50-day	Intermediate-term
200-day	Long-term

this condition with an extended sideways market in which several averages flatline and draw close to each other. In this dead market, price will most likely swivel back and forth repeatedly across their axis in a noisy pattern. Swing traders find few opportunities in this type of environment.

Trendlines and channels signal major S/R in active markets. A useful charting line prints from any vector drawn across two relative highs or lows. But these simple features have little staying power. Look for three or more points to intersect in a straight line. Then extend out that trendline to locate important boundaries for price development. As with other landscape features, long-term lines have greater persistence than shorter ones. Strong trendlines may even last for decades without violation.

Draw valid lines above three or more highs and below three or more lows, regardless of whether the market prints an uptrend or downtrend. Two or more sets of trendlines that lie parallel to each other form price channels. Their construction requires at least four points: two at support and two at resistance. Aggressive participants can build price channel projections with only three points and extend out estimated lines for the missing plots. But use these extensions only to predict turning points and be very reluctant to wager the account solely on their results.

Many swing traders assume that violation of a trendline or channel signifies the start of a new trend. This is not true and leads to inappropriate strategies. Trendline breaks signal the end of a prior trend and beginning of a sideways (range-bound) phase. A market can easily resume a former trend after it returns to stability. Shock events that combine with line breaks can start immediate trends in the opposite direction, but these happen infrequently. Hole-in-the-wall gaps (see Chapter 11) provide a powerful example of this phenomenon.

Trendline and channel breaks should induce immediate price expansion toward the next barrier. When this thrust does not occur, it can signal a false breakout that forces price to jump back across the line and trap the crowd. Whipsaws and pattern failures characterize modern markets. As common knowledge of technical analysis grows, insiders routinely push price past S/R just to trigger stops and volume. These gunning exercises end only after the fuel runs out and induces price to drop quietly back into its former location.

Mathematical statistics of central tendency study the esoteric realm of divergence from a central price axis. Analysts use these calculations every day as they explore standard deviation of market price from an expected value and its eventual

F I G U R E   2.2

Trendlines and parallel price channels print throughout the charting landscape. Note how Cisco's 60-minute candlesticks set up multiple channels over this short 9-day segment. Channels often generate harmonic levels that invoke additional parallel lines between major boundaries.

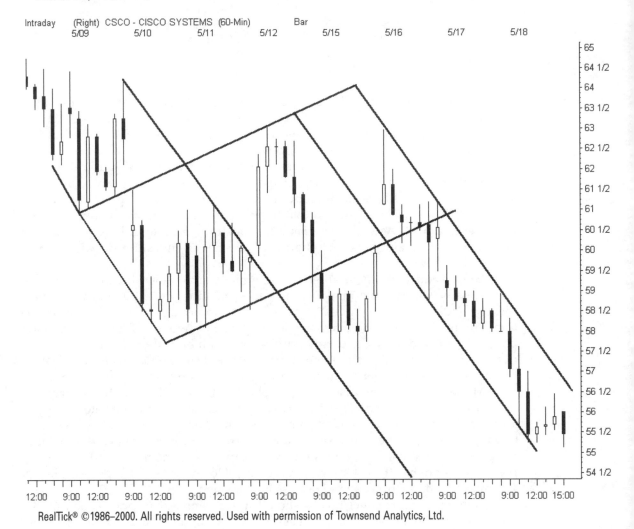

regression back to the mean. Broad concepts of overbought and oversold conditions rely on proper measurement of these complex variables. Swing traders depend on this arcane science to identify powerful standard deviation resistance through Bollinger Bands and other central tendency tools.

Each market leaves a fingerprint of its historical volatility as it swings back and forth. Central tendency defines how far price action should carry before an elastic effect draws it back toward the evolving center. Like a rubber band that stretches to its limit, price should spring back sharply when expanding force releases. These unique tools also measure flat markets better than any other method. As price change contracts to the low end of its expected range, values often converge toward a single point that triggers a violent move, which raises volatility back toward its expected mean.

Central tendency provides excellent trading opportunities but take the time to understand its mechanics. Extreme conditions often last well beyond expectations and shake out contrary positions. They may trigger trend relativity errors when elastic extremes don't line up through different time frames. This powerful tool supplements other classic pattern and S/R measurements but doesn't replace them. Use central tendency to uncover ripe trading conditions but then shift to other indicators to identify low-risk entry levels and proper timing.

Volume establishes important S/R boundaries. When markets print very high volume, they undergo significant ownership change that exerts lasting influence on price development. The frantic event may occur in a single bar or last for several sessions. The volume action must rise well above that issue's historical average in either case. These power spikes invoke special characteristics that may yield frequent trading opportunities. But the event will leave a long-lasting mark on the charting landscape whether or not it produces an immediate profit.

Crowd accumulation and distribution (acc-dis) define hidden volume boundaries. Buying or selling pressure often leads price development. When acc-dis diverges sharply in either direction, price will routinely thrust forward to resolve the conflict. Divergence itself induces the S/R mechanics. For example, a stock may drop sharply but remain under strong accumulation as it falls. The buying behavior not only slows the decline but also signals that the issue will likely print major support and bounce quickly.

Few swing traders understood Fibonacci retracement S/R before modern charting programs offered simple tools for this fascinating study. Fib math calculates how far a rally or decline will likely pull back before reversing. Retracement analysis intimidates many participants. Some even believe that it represents a form of market voodoo rather than science. And others just can't understand why stocks stop falling for no reason at apparently random levels.

Fibonacci math works through crowd behavior. A rally builds a common structure of participation. When it finally ends and starts to unwind, shareholders try to predict how far price might fall before the underlying trend resumes. The unconscious mind first sees the proportional one-third retracement as a good reversal point. New buyers do emerge here, but the subsequent bounce often fails and the issue falls through the prior intermediate low. This terminates the crowd's greed phase and begins a period of reason. The concerned eye now sees the halfway retracement as support and the issue again bounces on schedule.

Pullbacks can strike diverse S/R boundaries at any time and shift direction. But corrections routinely retrace at least one-third to one-half before support begins a new rally phase. Many active trends pull back all the way to two-thirds before the primary direction reasserts itself. These deep dips have a strong effect on the

F I G U R E   2.3

Central tendency tools respond to short-term shifts in volatility and direction. They also signal when price movement exceeds historical boundaries. These 13-period, 2 std dev Bollinger Bands accurately track Qualcomm's progress through a sharp rally and topping reversal on the 5-minute chart. Always pay close attention to changing band angles as bars approach. Horizontal bands point to hidden resistance that can quickly reverse price movement.

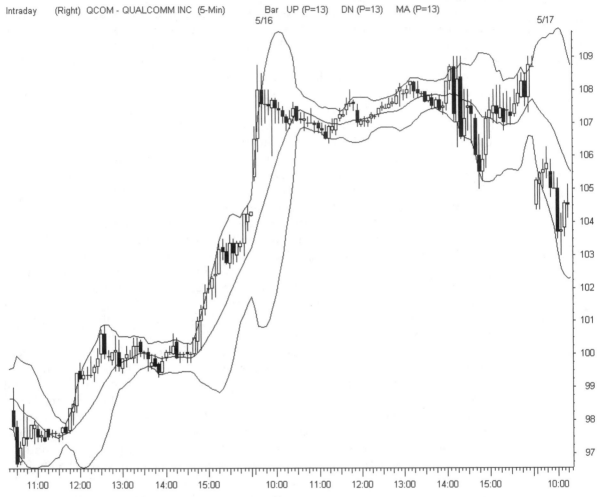

crowd. The break of halfway support terminates reason and awakens fear. The threat that the prior trend will completely reverse triggers sharp selling through this last level until a final shakeout ends the decline.

Downtrends work through emotional mechanics similar to those of rallies. The math and proportional elements remain identical. However, pullbacks from selloffs begin with fear that evolves into a period of reason at the same retracement levels.

F I G U R E   2.4

High-volume events often deplete the available crowd supply and trigger important reversals. Good news ignited a stampede into new WebMD positions during a dramatic 25-million-share day. Just 3 days later, the stock printed a major top that eventually rolled over into a painful bear market.

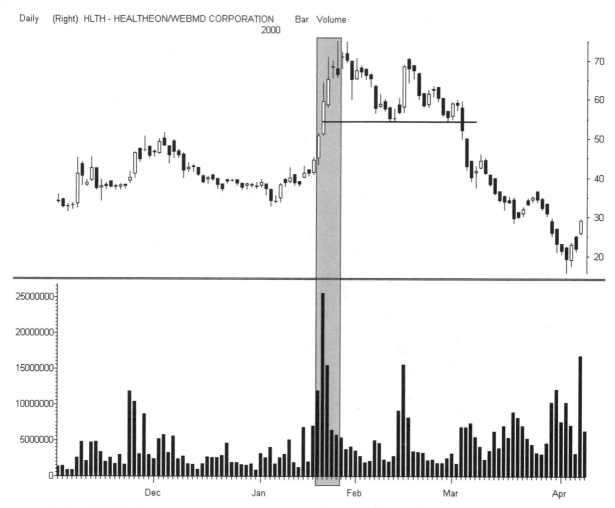

Daily   (Right) HLTH - HEALTHEON/WEBMD CORPORATION   Bar Volume
2000

This gives way to hope if the retracement pushes toward the two-thirds barrier. Gravity also influences how these bear rallies turn back toward the primary downtrend. Rollovers often occur violently here after price reaches an important resistance target.

Modern markets hide boundaries more esoteric in nature than retracement science. Round numbers affect trend development through all time frames. S/R intensity increases as zeros add onto price. For example, stocks that approach 100

F I G U R E   2.5

Price pullbacks through this dynamic JDS Uniphase rally mask an underlying Fibonacci order. Note how the dips end at classic retracement levels before igniting into new trend legs. The middle Fib range between 38% and 62% often exhibits congested price movement and sharp swings as the crowd shifts through emotional barriers.

Daily   (Right) JDSU - JDS UNIPHASE CORP   Bar

face more significant resistance than those that reach under 10. Whole number S/R tends to peak according to multiples of 10. In other words, 10, 20, 30, etc. represent natural barriers. And look for further S/R at divisors of 10 such as 5, 15, and 25.

Market participants deal with whole number phenomena every day. Investors spent months watching the Dow battle 10,000 for the first time. Many position traders take profits as stocks approach 50 or 100. Day traders exercise scalping strategies as the Level II screen bids teenies back and forth across a single number. This fascinating S/R builds from the buy and sell orders that congregate at round numbers. Both investors and traders tend to focus execution targets and stop orders at these lazy levels.

CROSS-VERIFICATION

The complex interplay between different chart elements baffles many swing traders. They fail to evaluate all of the important S/R influences that predict directional price movement. The rational mind naturally rebels against detailed analysis as it reduces incoming data into manageable pieces. This works against the swing trader's interest and may contribute to poor preparation. A lazy mind can catch a single S/R level but miss a minefield of obstacles that a new position must face.

Cross-verification searches the charting landscape to locate the primary signposts of trading opportunity. Common sense dictates that multiple crowd influences favor certain price levels over others. Swing traders can identify these setup intersections when they uncover those points where different S/R types and time frames converge with each other. For example, a single level that points to a major high, a 50% retracement of a larger trend, and the 50-day moving average strongly implies that certain important events will occur when price strikes that point.

Prepare for the market day through a complete S/R analysis that looks for convergence at specific price levels. The more elements that intersect through a single boundary, the higher the probability that this chart feature will support or resist price change. Four or more cross-verification points may appear at a single S/R intersection and signal an excellent profit opportunity. But don't let fewer cross-points discard promising trades. Many good setups exhibit less convergence but display one significant entry with few barriers or points of interest in between.

Trade execution at or near new highs raises special S/R considerations. The high itself presents the only resistance barrier within the larger time frame. If shorter charting periods don't reveal smaller obstacles, the only required strategy decides whether to buy, sell, or maintain an active position on a test of that high. Of course, analysis of risk must also locate an easy escape route if the trade turns sour.

Focus trade preparation on cross-verification to locate promising setups and measure reward:risk. Look for price close to substantial support to identify low-risk long trades. Look for price close to substantial resistance to find low-risk short sales. Measure the distance between the entry and the next barrier within the holding period for the trade. This points to the intended exit and reasonable profit target (PT). Measure the distance between the entry and the price that confirms that the setup was wrong. This points to the unintended exit and reasonable failure target (FT). Execute only those trades with high PT and low FT distance.

3D CHARTING

Successful swing trading begins with original tactics and accurate prediction. Excellent timing then enters a position just before bar expansion and exits as the crowd

F I G U R E   2.6

Multiples of 10 measure Seibel's progress as it pushes toward 100. These classic round numbers elicit common S/R behavior with price breaking through resistance but then pulling back to test new support. Also note how price bars expand sharply as they pierce the horizontal barriers for the first time.

Daily   (Right) SEBL - SIEBEL SYSTEMS   Bar

loses control. Careful planning guides the enterprise through every phase and plans an escape route just in case things go sour. Trade time, price, and safety. Profits will quickly follow.

Accurate forecasting requires the ability to see price movement in more than one dimension. Investors and institutions can often accomplish this task with a single price chart. Swing traders need more information and must watch the mar-

Cross-verification finds promising setups at key intersections of price and time. Notice how chart elements converge to produce an excellent Broadvision short sale: 1. Price falls through support of the prior high at 65. 2. The same bar breaks the 2-month trendline. 3. The same bar also breaks the 50-day moving average. 4. Price gaps below support, the trendline and the moving average. 5. The bottom Bollinger Band expands to suggest lower prices ahead.

Daily   (Right) BVSN - BROADVISION INC   Bar MA (P=50)   UP (P=20)   DN (P=20)   MA (P=20)
                    2000

kets using 3D charting techniques. Identify three time frames that correspond to the chosen holding period. Find one segment above and one below the position focus. For example, many intraday traders rely on 1-minute, 5-minute, and 60-minute charts while many position traders manipulate 60-minute, daily, and weekly combinations.

Not sure how long to maintain a position? Most swing traders should choose a specific holding period that reflects their lifestyle and not change it until thoughtful planning presents an alternate strategy. The rational mind will turn poorly defined time frames into major losses. Trades become investments and ex-traders become humbled investors. As strategies evolve, slowly experiment with different time frames. During these phases, prepare to answer the time question clearly before each trade execution. Write it down and stick to it or success will not come easily.

THE CHARTING LANDSCAPE

Greed resists adequate trade planning and precise time execution. But consistent discipline pulls attention back to center as it marks the divide between success and failure. A neophyte may build false confidence by throwing money at hot stocks and flipping nice gains. Guess what? Short phases of the broad Pattern Cycle allow this strategy to work. But their reckless approach fails quickly as soon as momentum fades and swing traders empty their pockets with powerful 3D charting techniques.

Three-dimensional charting forces the swing trader to recognize trends through different time frames and evaluate how their interaction will affect price movement. Landscapes of support and resistance reveal hidden swing levels ripe for profitable trade entry. 3D charts pack layers of complex information into very small spaces to reveal these hot spots quickly. Through visual analysis, the trader finds where moving averages, retracements, price bands, bar patterns, and trendlines cross or converge with each other. These isolated time/price zones provide the playground for profitable entry.

Each element of the charting landscape has a distinct appearance. Take time to learn the special message that each one displays as these diverse forces interact with each other. Also become sharply aware of their limitations. The most memorable trades come when an indicator's message can be confidently ignored and informed instinct guides position management.

T A B L E   2.2

Holding Period and Chart Correlation

Trade Type	Holding Period	3D Chart Combination
Scalpers	Seconds to minutes	1-minute 5-minute 15-minute
Day traders	Minutes to hours	1-minute 5-minute 60-minute
Position traders	Hours to days	60-minute daily weekly
Investors	Days to weeks	Daily weekly monthly
Institutions	Weeks to years	Weekly monthly yearly

Toggle between arithmetic (linear) and logarithmic (geometric) charts frequently. Log charts examine percentage growth. The visual length between increments decreases as prices move higher. Linear charts examine price growth. The visual length between increments remains constant as prices move higher. Trendlines can form on either log or linear charts. If uncertain which view will yield the best information, apply this helpful rule for quick analysis: stick with log charts for low-priced stocks or stocks that experience significant price change over short periods of time, and rely on linear charts for higher-priced or slower-moving stocks.

Information panes below price bars serve a single purpose: to assist the investigation of the top pane. Use indicators to support the pattern analysis and not the other way around. Many market participants search so hard for mathematical perfection that they lose their ability to see. Above all else, technical analysis is a visual art. Always start trade preparation with a peek at the price bars first. If something catches your eye, then check the lower pane to find out whether it confirms or refutes the observation. Less-experienced players must cast out opportunities when lower-pane measurements don't support objective observations. But after experience grows with lower-pane indicators, judiciously ignore them when the pattern tells a different story.

BUILDING THE ROAD MAP

Markets give away their secrets to swing traders who take the time to look carefully. Building a detailed landscape on each chart reveals trend and pattern powerpoints where important crowd forces will converge. These focused time/price zones target the hidden points primed for reversals and breakouts. When the participant has a clearly defined plan of what to do when price hits one of these hot spots, they've learned the art of swing trading.

Watch these points in real time whenever possible to decide whether or not the tape action supports the message of the pattern. Pull the trigger at or near the predetermined low-risk entry price after confirmation. The path to perfect trade entry is reached by thoroughly understanding each component of the 3D road map. Every convergence event triggers a different physical reaction. Experienced technicians measure the relative impact of each individual force and make consistently accurate predictions of subsequent price movement.

Develop precise visual skills and don't rely on a toolbox of complex math-based indicators. Swing trading teaches discretionary execution based on convergence of time and price but does not require mechanical models or systems. Realize that most indicators arise from very simple building blocks. Learn these basic components well and hone that needed edge over the skilled competition.

Pay attention to new forces at work within the charting landscape. Markets evolve to close off opportunities as quickly as they appear, and dependable S/R levels will fail as new dynamics work to defeat the majority. Long-term profit requires quick adaptation to new conditions as old methods fail. Use the power of

Pattern Cycles to identify and test fresh strategies that respond to major market changes.

MOVING AVERAGE RIBBONS

Build the charting landscape with moving averages (MAs). These classic momentum tools define both trend and natural pullback levels. Use them in all charts through all time frames. MAs respond to specialized settings that reflect the prevailing crowd within any holding period. So take great care to choose appropriate values. Averages must align with the current swing trading strategy or they will generate poorly timed executions.

Moving averages provide highly visual information as they interact directly with price. Indicators that fit into a separate lower pane force the eye to filter out large quantities of noise to manage information. Unfortunately, the filtering process also discards important data. Moving averages emit continuous signal without noise because they plot within the price pane. They print real-time patterns that interact with other S/R features to reveal profitable convergence levels.

Identify convergence-divergence between price and MAs. Because price always moves toward or away from an underlying average, each new bar or candle uncovers characteristics of momentum, trend, and time. This same process works just as well in relationships between two or more MAs. For example, the classic MACD (Moving Average Convergence-Divergence) indicator applies this technique to measure trending markets.

Use exponential moving averages (EMAs) for longer time frames but shift down to simple moving averages (SMAs) for shorter ones. EMAs speed and smooth the action as they give more weight to recent price change. SMAs view each data point equally. While intraday markets trigger bursts of meaningless data, SMAs allow the swing trader to spy on other participants. Most keep their settings at these simple levels because they don't recognize the advantage of EMAs. Good intraday signals rely more on understanding how the competition thinks than they do on the technicals of the moment.

Swing traders access a powerful information tool when they add multiple MAs into 3D charts and build a complete multi-time frame trend system. Tie these MA ribbons (MARs) together through a mathematical relationship that mimics time. One classic combination for a daily chart utilizes 20, 50, and 200 periods. Notice how each segment approximates three to four times the preceding one. These ratios tend to narrow in the shorter intraday averages, but the purpose remains the same. They provide an effective framework to investigate and trade three distinct periods of trend: short, intermediate, and long-term.

MA ribbons emit continuous trend feedback. For example, they signal a bear market when they flip over on the daily and the 200-day MA stands on top. The bull reawakens when the shorter averages cross back above the longer ones and each lines up in order again. Expect choppy price action during phases when the averages criss-cross out of sequence. Price can bounce around like a pinball several times before breaking free when it gets caught between inverting averages.

Use standard settings of 20-50-200 for the daily time frame or speed them up to 18-50-150 for an aggressive view. Popular daily averages provide an easy framework for quick digestion of a large number of stock charts. Watch them to measure the opposing crowd. Focus on the common belief that short-term trends pull back to the 20-day MA while intermediate and long-term impulses find support at the 50- and 200-day MAs.

Intraday chart views must be faster because participants tend to react very quickly and trend changes can take place in minutes rather than days. Five, 8 and 13 period settings for 1-minute, 5-minute, and 60-minute charts tune to the swing of the short-term market. These Fibonacci numbers correspond to dynamic, routine, and weak trend action within individual equities, indices, and derivatives, and they interact powerfully with short-term central tendency tools such as Bollinger Bands.

MARs generate layers of convergence-divergence feedback. Instead of price interaction with averages, the averages now interact with each other. Classic crossover strategies evolve into complex patterns with many unique formations. Ribbons reveal subtle relationships among price, time, and trend. Major averages tend to print S/R behavior with each other. Swing traders use this mechanism to generate original execution when other price action verifies opportunity. This behavior also assists precise timing because MAs lag price movement. They reduce whipsaws and false breakouts as they turn slowly to meet new conditions. Complex math indicators will often point right to entry where major moving averages converge. MA ribbons ease the swing trader's work through their visual simplicity and their unique spectrum analysis.

Trending markets echo characteristic price behavior over and over again. Measure this fractal fingerprint in the depth that an issue corrects after each impulse of a trend. MARs allow quick examination to locate classic retracement levels to use for entry on the next pullback. These can be very pleasant times for swing traders. Watch closely how price penetrates the ribbon. The depth it reaches before emerging often reflects a level that the trend will repeat over and over again. When price undergoes a sudden shift in direction, ribbons twist and mark clear signposts for awakening volatility. Each of the averages requires a different time period to absorb price change and roll over. This emits a broad range of rainbow patterns that have obvious predictive power.

MARs slowly invert to accommodate changing conditions as price shock induces a new trend. Manage positions using these visual interrelationships. Execute short-term swing trades when criss-cross MARs predict pivoting price movement. Once inversion completes, shift to momentum entry that takes advantage of the new convergent environment. Spreading MARs signal accelerating momentum when layered through adjacent time periods.

The practice of technical analysis often lacks simplicity. Many swing traders believe that they cannot succeed without complicated sets of math input to predict price change. On the contrary, many earn their living through simple elements of

FIGURE 2.8

MA ribbons mark Amazon's progress after a major selloff on the 60-minute chart. This versatile tool offers continuous feedback on relative momentum through many time frames. Watch how deeply price penetrates the ribbon column and the unique types of patterns that the interaction creates. Note how AMZN price bars move up one major average at a time before falling back to retest the lows.

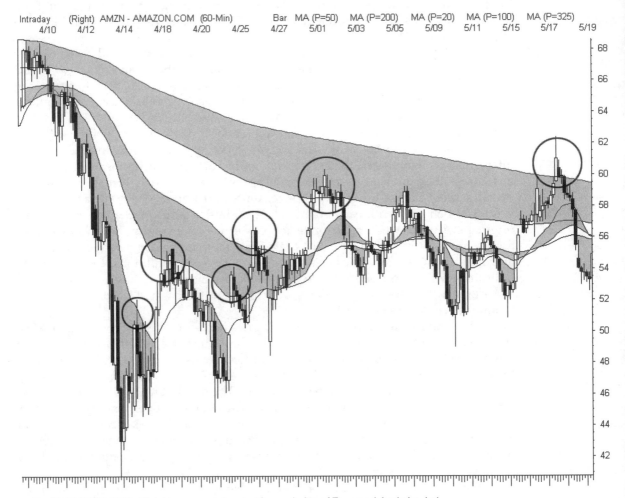

price and volume, packaged with moving averages. These primary indicators provide the essential link among time, price, and trend, and these natural building blocks easily tie together into powerful visual trading systems.

CANDLESTICKS

Candlestick history goes back much further than standard price bars. Japanese traders used them in the 18th century to forecast rice prices. According to legend, one local speculator executed over 100 consecutive winning positions by applying this simple tool. The military names for many candlestick formations arise from that era's feudal system. The pattern names that compare trading sessions to battles and blood remain valid 300 years later.

Candlestick charts condense far more information than standard bar plots. They separate price range extremes within a chosen period from the central opening and closing values. The candlestick real body represents the core price action, measured from open to close. Upper and lower shadows mark the range outside this boundary. Candlesticks illustrate intrabar conflict between bulls and bears. They reveal price action in the time frame below the one measured by the chart.

Color-coding of intrabar price movement adds another dimension to candle study. When the open prints above the close, the real body will usually appear hollow and designate upward change. Alternatively, the body will fill with black, red, or any other color when the open lies below the close. The interplay of hollow and filled candles reveals very short-term swing conditions as well as surges in volatility. It also uncovers hidden gaps that fill by the bar's close. While most Western charting ignores these important failures, swing traders can examine many hidden levels with candlesticks and locate significant S/R.

Candles print numerous predictive patterns with only one to four bars of data, making them an outstanding tool for short-term trading. Candle prediction depends on the location of the pattern within the charting landscape. Two identical formations at different S/R boundaries will generate unique outcomes. Consider abandoning plain vanilla price bars and trading with candles exclusively.

Use candlesticks for all charts in all time frames, but exercise caution on very short-term views. Extremes of intraday candles (shadow zones) generate inaccurate information created by bad ticks. Mentally filter price extremes to avoid executing positions based on faulty data. Act only on candles that print with length and volume both well above the average of the previous bars and those precisely located at major S/R pivots. Avoid all signals based on patterns in low-priced or thin issues.

Candlesticks illustrate reversal patterns better than any other technical tool. Many changes in trend originate within the time frame below the primary view of the swing trader. Common formations such as shooting stars, hammers, dojis, and haramis provide early warning to prepare strategies against the crowd. But all signals must work within the context that the candles print.

F I G U R E   2.9

Candlesticks work well in conjunction with Bollinger Bands and other central tendency tools. Look for reversal patterns when price pushes outside of the top or bottom band. Candle action at Apple's central band signals several intermediate swings that precede sharp thrusts back toward the band extremes. Notice that many of these reversal patterns also correspond with key highs and lows as well as pullbacks to support after breakout movement.

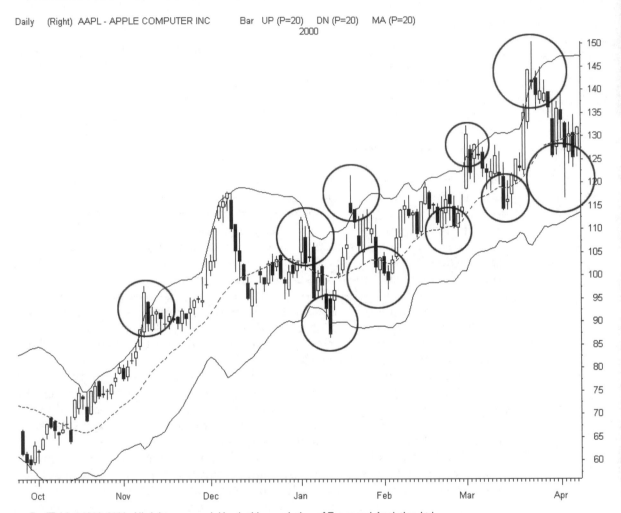

Daily   (Right) AAPL - APPLE COMPUTER INC   Bar   UP (P=20)   DN (P=20)   MA (P=20)
                                                              2000

Locate S/R convergence through cross-verification before relying on any interesting pattern. Japanese candlesticks work very well in conjunction with classic Western technical analysis. Watch for their appearance along moving average barriers in trending markets. Look for high-volume reversal candles at tests of tops and bottoms, major zones of S/R, and standard Fibonacci retracements.

Stop loss raids cripple trendlines drawn from standard price bars, but candle charts survive these short-term violations of known S/R. While the bar chartist concludes that support has broken and moves on to the next opportunity, the candle chartist knows that the same level still remains intact. Candle construction permits trendlines both at the shadow extreme and the real body's edge. This allows a powerful contrary view in an environment where everyone knows the basics of technical analysis.

Manipulation at major S/R generates frequent price violations and increased risk. Candles provide a perfect tool to adapt in this noisy environment. Doji and hammer reversal patterns reach across many S/R barriers, only to close back within support. Both their location and appearance signal that the boundary's support remains well intact. These important levels generate interesting contrary strategies and improve timing. (See Chapter 10).

Forget most standard candle pattern definitions found in modern financial books. Concentrate on the few major formations that consistently point to crowd conflict and resolution. Every setup acts differently, depending on location, volume, and trend. See the truth whether it confirms or disputes popular opinion. Undocumented patterns with strong predictive power appear every day. Learn to read the message of the candles even if they don't carry a warrior identity. Most hidden archetypes of crowd excitement, panic, and reversal arise in the unconscious mind and can be understood through trader intuition as well as analysis.

BOLLINGER BANDS

Swing traders must investigate central tendency in every promising opportunity. Market action should spring back toward a center of gravity after extending sharply in either direction. This axis tends to support price from below and resist it from above during active markets. In flat rangebound periods, price action commonly oscillates back and forth across the pivot until volatility triggers a new directional impulse.

Bollinger Bands (BBs) focus analysis of central tendency in real-time. As markets evolve, this powerful tool draws upper and lower channels that predict extremes based on price's relationship to the most recent action. To use the bands effectively, apply a central moving average that tunes into the expected holding period. Choose this important value carefully. Longer averages will lead to later signals, while shorter ones will generate whipsaws. Pick shorter settings for intraday charts such as 5-minute and 60-minute bars. Swing traders can't afford late information when playing in this frantic time frame. Expand to longer averages for daily or weekly charts to uncover broad market cycles and emerging trends.

Set standard deviation (std dev) parameters to regulate how far price will stretch before striking a band. Most technical analysis sources advise 2 std dev as the common setting. Shorten this length to speed up signals but face the same whipsaws encountered with moving average manipulation. Most swing traders should start with the most popular parameters for each time frame and adjust them to the volatility of their favorite markets. Price should rarely exceed upper or lower boundaries in average trends when Bollinger Bands are set at 2 std dev. But parabolic rallies and selloffs can exceed bands set all the way to 3 std dev and above.

Don't try to find perfect settings. Learn how imperfect ones work and when they flash false signals. Similar bars may repeatedly pop through certain bands but

FIGURE   2.10

Standard deviation predicts how far price will stretch before it reverses. Bollinger Bands set to a 20-bar moving average and 2 std dev will enclose most market swings within its boundaries. But when volatile stocks start to exceed these common settings, expand outward toward 3 std dev. This adjusts to peak volatility and will work in most parabolic markets.

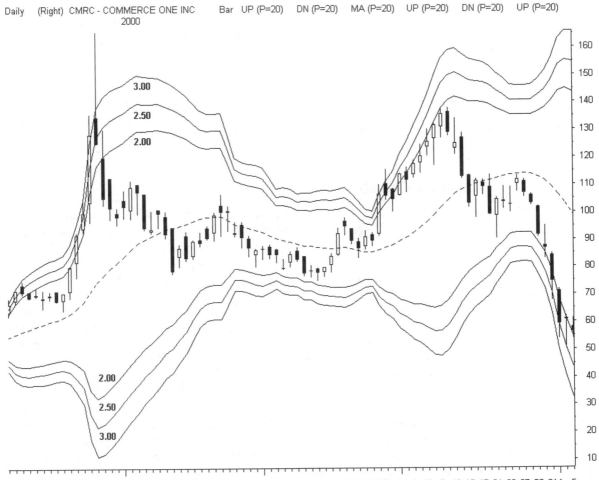

still offer valuable feedback on impending reversals. Predictive BB patterns print on all charts regardless of inputs and reward entry with great accuracy. When in doubt about which settings to use for a specific market, create a BB ribbon by layering multiple deviation levels on a single chart. Then see how that market responds to the bands through different trend phases.

Most charting programs default to the popular 20-bar, 2 std dev settings. Pull up this common view frequently to eavesdrop on how the crowd views its positions. This standard BB promotes simple tactics that align to common herd reactions. Enter fade positions when price strikes horizontal top or bottom bands that hold firm after the collision. Look for bands to tighten around a dull market in expectation of a sharp breakout move. In active markets, congestion often forms as price nears the center band and persists until bars expand sharply through the barrier or reverse in a failure. Enter positions in the direction of the expansion or place entry stops at both extremes of the congestion. Consider new short sales when price pops more than 50% out of the top band and new longs after the same violation of the bottom band.

Swing traders require faster signals than investors. Consider a 13-bar, 2 std dev setting for most intraday charts. This more sensitive input captures trend activity and breakdown better than the 20-bar. All BBs work best in combination with other moving averages placed over the bands. Add 5-bar and 8-bar SMAs to create a 5-8-13 combination. This Fibonacci number set consistently picks up major intraday swings and reversals. Use the 5-bar for S/R on dynamic trends, the 8-bar for pullbacks, and the 13-bar to locate trend change and reversal.

Bollinger Bands identify subphases within the current trend. Price enters a bull phase when it rises above the center band. That central axis now supports price on pullbacks. When crossed, price tends to move all the way to the top band before any major reversal takes place. This pattern supports long swing entry when confirmed by other landscape features. The center band becomes resistance when price breaks below it. Odds favor price falling all the way to the bottom band when the central pivot breaks. This pattern supports short swing entry when confirmed by other landscape features.

Bollinger Bands combine the sophistication of complex mathematics with the simplicity of pattern recognition. A strong trend in either direction prints bar patterns that appear to cling to the top or bottom band like curtain rungs. Often they display a series of small pullbacks that never reach the center band before resuming the trend. These sharp moves may climax when more than 50% of the price bar reaches outside the end of a band. This signals an overbought or oversold state that triggers sharp resistance and pulls price back within its limits. But trade timing with this phenomenon can be tricky. Very strong issues may overcome this strong central tendency for a number of price bars before fading back into the boundaries.

Bollinger Bands add horsepower to analysis of multiple time frame events. Toggle from weekly through intraday bands without changing any of the settings. This exercise reveals a 3D view with excellent predictive power. It may even uncover hidden S/R and pinpoint reversals to within a single price bar. A similar

The 5-8-13 Bollinger Bands offer intraday traders a powerful analysis tool. Use them on 1-minute, 5-minute and 60-minute charts to track very short-term market oscillations and opportunities. Note how Applied Materials pulls back repeatedly to the 8-bar MA during the big rally from 69 to 83. The 5-8-13 will often signal low-risk entry to within a single tick.

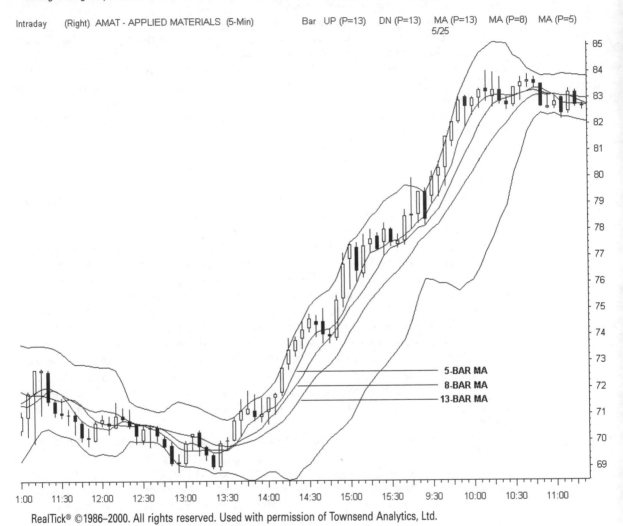

method builds a simultaneous three-chart display that tracks market progress through different time frames. Apply Elder's Triple Screen strategy with either method to align entry to the relative bull/bear price positions within the bands.

Someday another Charles Dow or Edwards and Magee will come along to categorize the great variety of band/price patterns and assign effective trading rules for them. Until then, apply these simple band concepts to daily market preparation:

1. Location and direction determine trading phase:
   - *Upper vs. lower action:* Location of price bars determines the strength of the current phase. Price within the upper band signifies power while price within the lower band signals weakness.
   - *Price direction:* Direction of price within the band identifies convergence-divergence with the current trend. Divergence prints when price rises within the lower band or falls within the upper band. Convergence prints when price rises within the upper band or falls within the lower band.
   - *Trend testing:* The lower, center, and upper bands represent S/R for the trend. Reversal off any band increases odds that price will expand in the reversed direction and return to the last band crossed or touched.
2. Penetration through the center band increases directional momentum:
   - *Crossing from below center to above:* Uptrend increase in strength. Observe directional movement of the upper band as price approaches.
   - *Crossing from above center to below:* Downtrend increase in weakness. Observe directional movement of the lower band as price approaches.
3. Bands open in response to awakening trend:
   - *Climbing the ladder:* If the angle of the upper band rises in response to approaching price, expect a series of upward price bars, each riding higher along the top band. This is an uptrend in progress.
   - *The slippery slope:* If the angle of the lower band falls in response to approaching price, expect a series of downward price bars, each pushing lower along the bottom band. This is a downtrend in progress.
4. Bands flatten in response to awakening trend:
   - *Head in ceiling:* If the angle of the upper band flattens in response to approaching price, expect price bars to pierce the band and reverse. This will likely end an upward swing and start a downward one. But watch if price pulls back slowly while the band then opens. This will signal an impending breakout.
   - *Foot in floor:* If the angle of the lower band flattens in response to approaching price, expect price bars to pierce the band and reverse. This will likely end a downward swing and start an upward one. But watch if price pulls back slowly while the band then opens. This will signal an impending breakdown.

Bollinger Bands define natural extremes in trend development. As bands are hit, price often bounces backward until sufficient strength can push the band out of the way. Congestion will likely develop just below the top band or above the bottom band if the overall pattern supports increasing momentum. This will continue until the band turns and opens away from price, indicating that resistance has been overcome. Price may then eject into a sustainable trend and cling to the band's edge. But keep in mind that ultimate movement will depend on all S/R boundaries and not just those associated with BBs.

F I G U R E   2.12

The 5-minute Lucent landscape prints common Bollinger Band patterns while classic S/R converges at important band turning points: 1. Head in ceiling reversal appears at short-term double top. 2. Price action retests the high while upper band turns away from price to signal an impending breakout. 3. The new uptrend climbs the ladder into another top. 4. Price rises into a sharply declining band that signals another downward swing and break of the 2-day trendline. 5. Price action retests the low in a descending triangle while the lower band turns away from price to signal an impending breakdown. 6. The new downtrend slides down the slippery slope.

Intraday   (Right) LU - LUCENT TECHNOLOGIES (5-Min)   Bar   UP (P=20)   DN (P=20)   MA (P=20)
                        5/17   5/18

CHART POLARITY

Interpreting the endless variety of patterns, indicators, bands, and lines can seem overwhelming. Fortunately, the market simplifies this process through its native polarity. Price action shifts movement between two polar states or flattens it toward a neutral middle. This underlying axis characterizes almost all market phases, conditions, and indicators. For example, prices can only rise or fall with directionless periods in between. This signals the existence of bull, bear, or sideways markets.

BULL-BEAR

Effective swing trading begins with identification of the current market phase. But strategies require more detailed information before trade execution. Start with the following questions: How quickly are conditions changing? Do they represent broad or narrow events? How will volatility affect the trading environment? The answers may mark the difference between a simple price correction and a market crash.

Bull markets represent periods in which strong buying pressure characterizes price movement. Bear markets represent periods in which strong selling pressure characterizes price movement. These graphic images have no correlation to a specific time frame but commonly represent action on daily charts. The most popular view establishes the 200-day moving average as the interface between bull and bear markets within individual equities.

Swing traders can apply this concept to any time frame by establishing an appropriate bull-bear axis. Fibonacci retracement provides a more powerful tool for this purpose than standard moving averages. First establish the major uptrend or downtrend that guides the trade setup. Then draw a Fib grid over the extremes. During relative uptrends, avoid short sales when price remains at least 38% above the low. Through relative downtrends, avoid long entry when price remains at least 38% below the relative high. Alternatively, look at a violation of any 62% retracement as a shift through the bull-bear axis.

This simple concept may confuse at first glance. Trends and bull-bear sentiment actually represent separate forces. An uptrend can exist within a bear environment and vice versa. In fact, early phases of new trends often travel in a hostile atmosphere and without recognition by the crowd. Trend relativity also allows strong contrary movement in smaller time frames than the major bull-bear interface. Use this polarity to prepare pullback entry strategies. Identify the current sentiment and active trend within the market of interest. Watch for countertrend pullbacks when both forces line up. Follow price until it reaches a strong S/R level and then execute a position as it realigns with the primary force. The active trend should reassert itself quickly and carry price back in the other direction.

TREND-RANGE

Trend-range polarity underlies all swing trade preparation. Align execution properly with this primary axis or profits will vanish. Trends rarely move in a straight line. As price surges forward, it pauses frequently to test, retrace, and rest. This countertrend pull shakes out profit takers, losers, and disbelievers. It lowers volatility and allows new participants to jump on board in hopes of a new price surge. Fresh positions require excellent timing in these conditions. Early execution subjects

Bulls live above the 200-day MA while bears live below. When trading within this time frame, align general strategies to conditions that favor the right side of the market. For example, stay long when price moves above the average and sell short when it goes below. Shorter-term traders must understand how large-scale bull or bear pressure can affect the performance of their individual trading vehicles. But they must align positions with smaller-scale buying and selling pressure to book profits.

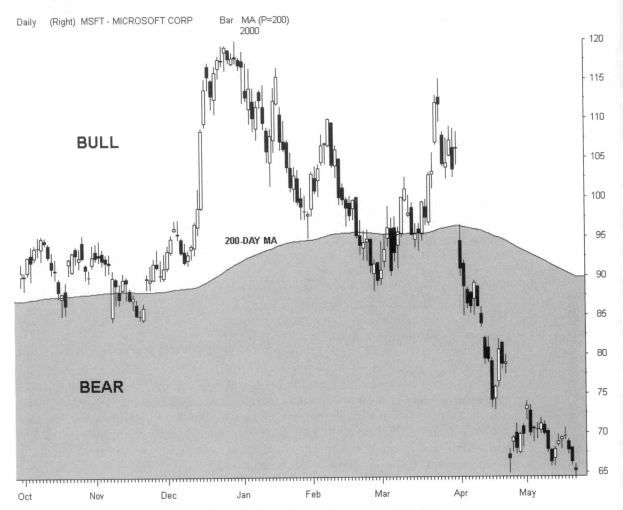

Daily   (Right) MSFT - MICROSOFT CORP   Bar   MA (P=200)
                                                       2000

BULL

200-DAY MA

BEAR

Oct   Nov   Dec   Jan   Feb   Mar   Apr   May

the swing trader to whipsaws while late entries miss the move and face increased risk. Ranges also carry a high probability for trend relativity errors. Participants trap themselves into narrow price movement while fixated on a broader trending market. Although the range limits losses, tied-up capital misses other opportunities.

Focus trading strategies on the trend-range axis but build timing on the swing-momentum cycle that underlies it. Positive feedback (directional movement) tends to surge in waves. These momentum thrusts carry all the rewards that swing traders seek. Negative feedback (nondirectional movement) sets the stage by providing the conditions needed to generate profitable entry points. Coordinate these two impulses to execute with perfect timing. Enter positions when the range nears primary S/R and then watch for momentum in the next lower time frame to carry the trade to a profit. As the position starts to run, align an exit to momentum in the same time frame as the entry to maximize the gain.

Identify trend-range through pattern recognition and indicator support. Trends print as sharp-ramping price bars. They force price rate of change (ROC) and directional movement indicators (ADX) to rise sharply. Ranges appear as pullbacks, price constriction, or sideways action. Look for volume and rate of change to drop off as ranges develop. They force moving averages to flatline according to their period length. Oscillators such as Stochastics swing back and forth quickly through small shifts in range direction. Watch the indicator jump to one extreme and stay there when the trend takes over.

Use repeating chart patterns to uncover important swing points. Classic triangle, flag, and pennant formations locate trade setups with clearly defined entry and risk levels. Constricting price bars, lowering volatility, and range placement signal the end of one swing and beginning of a new impulse. Align long or short positions in harmony with the expected movement but watch out for a better trade in the opposite direction should pattern failure emerge.

EXPANSION-CONTRACTION

Price bars demonstrate orderly expansion-contraction polarity as the swing-momentum cycle evolves. Bars tend to expand rapidly into a climax through rallies and selloffs. Then congestion sets in and volatility drops as bar range contracts along with price rate of change. This negative feedback characterizes progress until tight congestion signals an impending price movement that again releases into expanding bars. Pattern readers have a trading advantage here because these entry points capture the eye's attention. Conversely, many math indicators hit neutral zones in this environment and show nothing of interest.

Swing traders must pay special attention to these overlooked neutral conditions. Quiet balance points trigger the most powerful and profitable opportunities throughout the markets. Empty zones have little sponsorship or interest. They draw their initial power in a state of low volatility and resolve it through directional movement and high volatility. They signal high-reward, low-risk entry levels that allow swing traders to step in front of the crowd. Because narrow range bars characterize this opportunity, adverse movement after entry permits a fast stop loss exit with little slippage.

Expansion-contraction ties closely into reward planning. Odds increase greatly that the next few bars will contract when expansion bars thrust into known S/R. For this reason, the appearance of wide range bars often signals the need for caution. Look at the chart landscape again, identify all obstacles, and reexamine the intended holding period. The odds favor a pullback that will draw down profit substantially before ejecting into another move.

For most trades, plan to exit when price expands into S/R. This strategy tracks the old wisdom that advises us to "enter in mild times but exit in wild times." Also consider closing the position when the market prints a wide range bar that departs substantially from the routine price action but does not occur at a breakout point. These often mark short covering moves, stop runs within smaller time frames, and countertrend climaxes.

The swing trader seeks profit from single, direct price thrusts except when highly favorable conditions demand greater flexibility. When momentum cycles align through several time frames, and positions already show a profit, try to capture a series of expansion bars. But recall that markets trend only fifteen to twenty percent of the time. Odds favor accepting the gift of a few bars and moving on to the next trade. Only seasoned trading skill can consistently select the right path to take with any particular setup. Learn to watch opportunity in three dimensions and take a giant step toward this wisdom.

LEADING-LAGGING

Most technical indicators rely upon simple price/volume inputs. When these data points shift back and forth, they also generate chart polarity in derivative math calculations. This interrelationship explains why the swing trader should not seek the perfect indicator. The restless crowd drives price change, but mathematics only interprets the residue of their participation. The eyes see emerging trends long before the numbers signal their presence. For this reason, always use technical indicators to support the pattern, not the other way around.

Apply popular price indicators to examine chart polarity that leads or lags shifting cycles. Oscillators look forward to locate major swing reversals. Stochastics and Wilder's Relative Strength Indicator (RSI) both watch the changing axis of overbought-oversold conditions to identify turning points. Trend-following indicators look backward to examine price development. Plot MA ribbons or use the classic MACD Histogram to measure the trend-range axis and pinpoint the current phase of the swing-momentum cycle.

A finite pool of buyers and sellers participates in each market at any point in time. Rallies and corrections feed on this supply until it dissipates. The stronger the rally or weaker the correction, the more quickly a stock will reach the bottom of its fuel supply. Oscillators measure this important gauge through overbought-oversold

F I G U R E   2.14

All markets cycle endlessly between contraction and expansion. But congestive phases use up many more price bars than trending moves. This suggests why making money in the markets can be so difficult. A trend may already be over by the time most participants see a sharp rally or selloff. At the least, risk escalates dramatically as advancing price can reverse or enter new congestion at any time. The swing trader tries to enter a low-risk position just before price bar expansion, whenever possible, and let the breakout crowd push it into a quick profit.

Daily   (Right) EBAY - EBAY INC   Bar

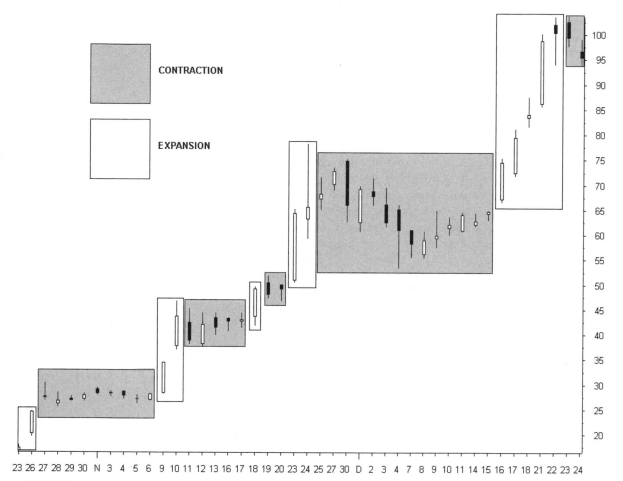

polarity. These forward-looking indicators tend to hover near extremes and then swing sharply toward the opposite pole. Swing traders anticipate where this shift will occur in both entry and exit strategies.

Markets can tap fresh crowds as prices move. New participants may quickly replace depleted supplies. This self-feeding trend mechanism allows extreme buying and selling conditions to continue long after measurements suggest that reversals should take place. Oscillators reflect this when they move to one extreme and just stay there. For this reason, don't rely on these indicators in trending markets. They work best within constricted ranges where natural cycles allow regular shifts in supply and demand.

Forward-looking indicators oscillate back and forth between 0 and 100 or swing through a central axis. Popular interpretation suggests that price reaches overbought levels near the top value and triggers selling pressure. This same reasoning dictates that oversold conditions exist near the lows and invite longs to consider new positions. Over time, chartists have defined intermediate values where plot crossovers signal the start of the related phase. For example, RSI commonly uses levels of 30–70 to signal oversold-overbought states.

Trend-following indicators measure directional polarity. Moving averages fit right into the price pane while many other plots draw separately. Some print common patterns that uncover new trends and pinpoint trade timing. But trend-following indicators lag most chart action. In other words, they will turn up or down after price movement and not before it. They identify directional cycles over many different time elements. For example, half the averages may point up and the other half point down at the same time in a typical MA ribbon.

Use these lagging measurements when oscillators stop working. Trend-following indicators offer a better road map in directional markets and identify lower-risk entry triggers. They pinpoint a stock's location on the trend-range axis and reveal natural pullback levels. Apply them to momentum strategies that capitalize on strong trending conditions. Also let them signal the start of a new range. Then pull up some oscillators to reexamine the changing environment.

CONVERGENCE-DIVERGENCE

Successful trade execution relies upon correct interpretation of the convergence-divergence (C-D) axis. This powerful concept defines relationships between price and all other aspects of the charting landscape. Indicators that trend in a different direction than price signal divergence. They converge when their movement corresponds with price direction. Divergent conditions mark negative feedback, while convergence aligns with positive feedback. One market can also converge or diverge with another. When S&P 500 goes up and Nasdaq 100 goes down, the two indices diverge. Bonds and index futures converge when they both rise.

Swing traders must decide which forces will prevail as divergent conditions resolve. For example, when falling price bars move against a rising MA, one will eventually rotate to track the other. Common technical wisdom dictates that indi-

F I G U R E   2.15

Oscillators pick up market turns faster than trend-following indicators. Notice how the Stochastics swings quickly in response to each Cisco reversal while the slower MACD Histogram responds incrementally to each price bar. Use oscillators in choppy markets but switch to trend-following measurements during sharp breakouts and breakdowns.

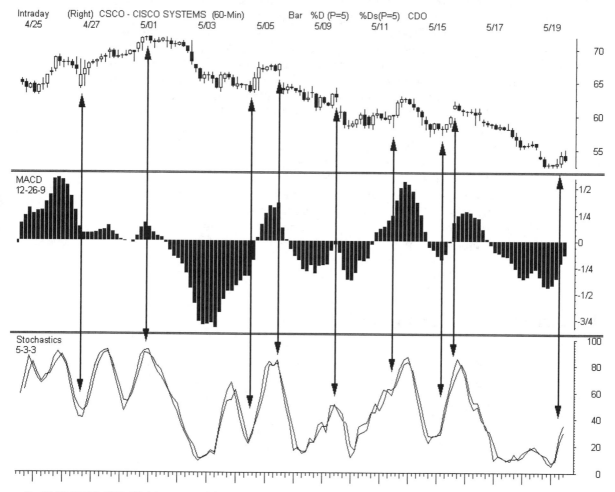

cators define an underlying trend more accurately than price over short periods of time. But this logic often fails and wayward indicators obediently turn to confirm the price action.

Apply a logical strategy to evaluate divergence and avoid very bad executions. Start with a recognition that every market will exhibit numerous C-D relationships. Limit detailed analysis to those elements that will support or interfere with the planned setup within the chosen holding period. Locate the major C-D themes and filter out the smaller ones. Some divergences tend to resolve more quickly than others. Accumulation can lag price for a long time before stopping a rally. But a declining moving average could have a dramatic effect on price as a short-term rally strikes it.

Apply cross-verification techniques to C-D trade analysis. Look for many discontinuous forms of convergence that support the promising pattern. Compare these with the elements that diverge to reach a logical conclusion about the next price direction. When convergence aligns repeatedly through a single price point, odds increase dramatically that an important breakout or reversal will occur right there. Couple this knowledge with well-marked S/R information and execute with confidence. S/R exerts a greater influence on price development than C-D. When a market builds a bullish pattern in the face of declining indicators, subsequent price action will more likely confirm the pattern than the divergent mathematics.

Identify other conditions that support or conflict with current price development before making the trade. Determine how seasonality or time-of-day bias affects the odds for the predicted move. Consider the limitations of the indicator or landscape feature that exhibits the divergence. Oscillators in trending markets and trend-following indicators in flat markets both trigger many false signals. When in doubt, step to the sidelines and wait for a better opportunity. The most profitable trades will exhibit major convergence between many chart elements.

READING MARKET SENTIMENT

Successful swing traders start each market day with a thoughtful analysis of current conditions. Identify larger cycles, external influences, and important news that will likely drive price action. Then look at the most promising setups and decide whether they properly align with those complex forces. Evaluate any special risk associated with trading that day and decide how to alter execution strategy to adjust to the new environment. Should position size be increased or decreased? Should the first hour be avoided or aggressively traded? Are conditions ripe for a major rally, selloff, or reversal?

Review current sentiment, important numbers, and technical indicators. Define what types of unexpected factors will tighten or relax current trade management tactics. Write down those parameters to avoid getting fooled, if required. Then execute according to the predetermined boundaries. Watch how the first hour action alters or adjusts this initial analysis. Then shift the active strategy to accommodate real reversals, breakouts, or breakdowns as they exert their influence. But beware of costly trend relativity errors. Make certain that important market shifts occur within the time frame of interest before adjusting the trading plan to accommodate them.

AVOIDING THE MOMENTUM TRAP

Success depends on overall market strength or weakness and how well positions capitalize on the changing environment. Individual entries can act against sentiment and yield good profits, but over time, the odds for success decrease when positions do not track movement in the larger indices and market cycles. Swing trading produces better results when riding the wave and not drowning in it.

Markets tend to correct for many months at a time. But most participants focus on relatively brief periods of strong upside momentum where they hope to pocket big gains. Unfortunately these exciting times also awaken greed and weaken risk management. Participants violate personal rules, chase dangerous positions, and develop an unhealthy sense of invulnerability. They also forget that the momo environment will disappear quickly and without warning.

Strategies that work well in hot markets destroy trading accounts during cool ones. Most players carry a long-side momentum bias into topping markets and corrections. This triggers inappropriate positions, leads to missed opportunities, and empties the same pockets that filled so easily during parabolic rallies. Avoid this common trap as experience grows. Learn to read the broader market and adapt quickly to changing conditions. Build personal cycle measurements that bypass the financial press and stock board chatter. Use common sense to anticipate and test new profit strategies that the crowd may never see.

Combine market sentiment and Pattern Cycles to locate the best opportunities of the moment. Broad forces align well with different setups on individual stocks. First gauge current conditions and then decide what types of trades will work best in that environment. Make certain that strategies correspond to the same time frame as the analysis. When major indices converge, trade the same phase as their current Pattern Cycle whenever possible. When they don't, choose positions that support general sentiment and current risk. Use S/R barriers on both stocks and broader indices to time profitable exits.

Swing traders must sell short as easily as they go long. This challenges the investor bias that most neophytes carry into modern markets. Many participants still don't understand many aspects of this classic trading practice. The financial establishment discouraged retail customers from learning about short sales for many years. The uptick rule made entry difficult, while Wall Street told practitioners that they were hurting the American economy so that they could keep this profitable strategy for themselves. Times have changed. Direct access execution systems now allow short sale entry as quickly as long positions. Learn to use them without delay.

Pattern Cycles require a broad range of execution strategies in both directions. Be prepared to adapt quickly to changes in market sentiment by learning simple ways to recognize new broad-scale conditions. All sincere efforts will be greatly rewarded. The easiest trades always come early in a trend before the crowd notices them. Profit from momentum markets, but don't fall in love with them. Increased risk always follows increased reward. Work to broaden execution skills and learn to trade anything that offers a good opportunity. Market players who hit many singles will last longer than those who knock a few home runs but strike out the rest of the time. Be consistent and make a good living through both up and down trends.

THE BIG PICTURE

Swing traders must digest a vast amount of market information to reach simple conclusions about opportunity and risk. Start with cross-market analysis and decide whether local or world influences will more likely move the price action. Stay aware of news or fundamental conditions that will impact the markets, but stay focused on the patterns and numbers. Except for shock events, markets will follow the technicals because insiders already trade most hidden news in advance of the public.

The interplay among debt, currency, and commodities can dramatically affect the U.S. equity markets. These broad forces trigger arbitrage between index futures and debt that move stock prices and rob profits. Fortunately, most significant shifts between these world markets occur slowly. Swing traders can adequately prepare for their substantial impact through a few well-chosen news articles or weekly index chart analysis.

Stay informed. Today's excitement won't move tomorrow's markets. Learn to recognize the big picture and anticipate leadership through background study of economics, the media and world politics. Once grounded in the basics, just follow the financial news and the most important message of the day will become obvious. Modern markets have a self-fulfilling mechanism that pushes the most emotional issues right to the top of the trading heap. Study these central themes first and decide how serious or long lasting their impact may be.

Identify the leaders and laggards of the U.S. indices. Look at the Pattern Cycles for each index to find the current trading phases. Are they rangebound or trending? Are oscillators rising or falling? Do they converge or diverge? Each index has characteristics that affect and distort daily results. Take the time to learn their construction and how individual stock movement can generate lopsided information. For example, a Microsoft rally or selloff on certain days in 1999 accounted for most price change in both the Dow 30 and Nasdaq 100.

Follow those indices and measurements that impact daily decision-making. Nasdaq Composite, Nasdaq 100, S&P 500, and the Dow Industrials provide most of the data required to participate in the American markets. Swing traders can isolate many subsector rallies and selloffs through these major influences. Also follow the bond futures or bond yield and add smaller markets that generate special interest. But discard information quickly if it doesn't improve the bottom line.

Many equity traders now keep active futures data on their real-time screens. The decline of Chicago Merchantile Exchange (CME) fees and birth of the S&P E-

F I G U R E   2.16

Index relative strength indicators measure current trading conditions and cycles. A spread between Nasdaq and the SP-500 contrasts the activity of growth stocks against the safety of blue chips. Market bottoms tend to print when Nasdaq takes over leadership from the other indices. A 14-week RSI reveals long-term Nasdaq buying and selling pressures. Smooth the average by 5 to 7 periods and few whipsaws will occur once the plot starts to roll over. Swing traders improve performance when they align long and short tactics to broad market sentiment.

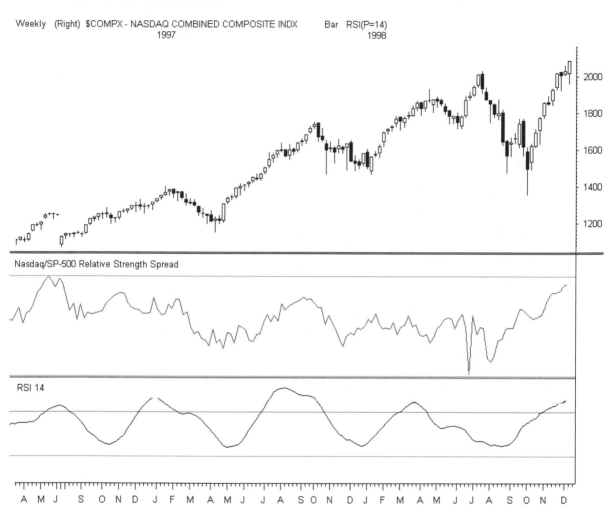

Mini index futures contract allow retail participants to view derivative markets that were hidden to the public just a few years ago. Start to examine futures by replacing S&P 500 Index quotes with the popular E-Mini. Then view the interplay between that market and equities. This daily tug and pull explains much of the short-term price oscillation that appears as noise to most observers. With a little practice, swing traders can build strategies that carefully time execution to these fluctuations.

The S&P futures crowd has a higher percentage of professionals than equities. Swing traders can see their participation on the intraday charts. Major fades follow almost every wide bar movement. This gives an odd porcupine appearance to the flow of price action. Use this phenomenon as a noise filter for execution of equity positions. Real breakouts and breakdowns will thrust past these fade points while false moves terminate at them. Pay attention and learn to stand aside when others get caught in small intraday price ripples that bleed trading accounts.

DOW THEORY Y2K

Update and apply Dow Theory for modern American markets. Those experts who still use the Dow Transportation and Utility Averages to predict broad intermediate trends don't deserve our attention. Market interplay now revolves around the Dow Industrials, S&P 500, and Nasdaq Composite. Swing traders can evaluate the character of most major rallies and corrections by using these three indices. Also consider the growing dominance of the Nasdaq market as the world shifts from the industrial into the information age. In a few years even the Dow Industrials may no longer capture anyone's interest.

Leader-laggard relationships among the big indices define most current market conditions. When Nasdaq leads the blue chips, it signals a retail-driven, speculative technology phase with sharp price change and increased volatility. The ascent of the S&P 500 or Dow points to a flight to safety, with big institutional money moving the markets. Their leadership signals a period of lower volatility and a high probability for a quieter sideways pattern.

Nasdaq has several quirks very unfriendly to traders, although it attracts most retail attention. Three separate subsectors comprise this dominant market: behemoth mega-techs, middle technology/service, and a large universe of small caps. Evaluate Nasdaq price action only after inspecting the current performance of each sub sector. Frequently, the four largest Nasdaq stocks will account for most price change in the index. Other times, lethargy in these same mega-stocks masks small cap rallies or selloffs.

Verify that actual market conditions support the chosen swing strategies. Mega-caps trade like small indices and often require little external analysis. But positions in thinner issues can depend on the right index subsector acting in a supportive manner. Most swing traders should follow the broad Nasdaq Composite and a small cap index to filter out distortions. Add the Nasdaq 100 or individual mega-stocks to track the impact of these behemoths. Always take a peek at their movement just before entering an intraday position whenever possible.

A tendency toward rally or correction drives the major market averages at almost all times. The emotional pull between bullishness and bearishness practically ensures that prices will swing too far toward whatever directional bias exists at the moment. This broad market inefficiency invokes a profound mechanism that underlies all swing trading profit: when directional force places an object in motion, it tends to remain in motion until another force intercedes.

Capitalize on directional bias by watching for follow-through days. After wide range index bars, markets tend to surge in that same direction the next morning. This may occur as a large gap move or a just a slow grind. In either case, overnight positions use this tendency to increase profits. One popular strategy takes a closing position in a trending stock that prints a wide range bar and ends the day near its high or low. The swing trader then grabs a quick exit in the pre-morning action or early in the first hour before price discovery steals the profit.

Positions held after this first morning surge face increased risk. An opening gap often marks a short-term trend climax. Since markets require very strong trends to print two wide directional bars in a row, indices often reverse sharply right after wide range movement. Swing traders recognize this tendency and watch the volatile morning action very closely. They search their watch lists in advance for new setups that may benefit if a sudden reversal appears. Then they confidently time their execution to the broad indices when the market turns.

FINDING WINNERS

Work hard to find fresh opportunities in the equity markets. Start by throwing out most stocks as unsuitable for trading. These include REITs (Real Estate Investment Trusts), closed-end funds, ADRs (American Depository Receipts), and utilities. Then eliminate the bottom half to two-thirds of all stocks sorted by average daily volume. Seek liquid stocks that allow low slippage entry and exit. This narrows down choices to about 2,000 issues. At any given time, 90% of these higher volume stocks lack the required characteristics to pocket a reasonable profit. So a daily scanning strategy must search for the 10% that hide decent setups and opportunities. And most times yesterday's stocks won't match tomorrow's promising plays. So new scans must refresh an active list as old choices are discarded.

NEEDLE IN THE HAYSTACK

Swing traders have two ways to locate good setups: find the stocks themselves or have someone else do it for them. Chat room picks and website scans offer great opportunities when they match individual trading styles and pose serious dangers when they don't. Always perform a personal analysis and never rely solely on someone else's opinion for any stock pick. Long-term success will not come from setups identified by someone else. That website operator, newsletter guru, or stock board promoter has a different holding strategy and execution method than any individual market participant.

A daily planning routine should identify promising Pattern Cycle setups, measure reward:risk and locate appropriate execution levels in advance. Build an automatic filtering process that evaluates every stock pick or scan objectively for these characteristics. The right workflow will uncover setups that support all three considerations. Realize that a single major flaw that doesn't fit into the trading plan will negate an opportunity. For example, avoid a well-formed triangle breakout if potential reward doesn't offer good profit or the pattern conflicts with other landscape features.

Watch out for the tendency to see something that isn't there. Detailed review through scanning or chart study often uncovers the basic elements of a successful setup but offers no attractive entry. Unfortunately, this analysis process can induce a form of secondary reinforcement. It relaxes, puts the brain into game theory mode, and soothes the ego that sees all those past setups that could have been entered with perfect hindsight. This unconscious enjoyment encourages the mind to fill in the missing pieces on questionable new patterns. Always exercise rigid self-discipline when asking the eyes to look for opportunity.

The most urgent preparatory task throws out almost everything that looked great the first time around. Know when a setup has no potential and be willing to move on to the next opportunity. Nightly preparation must uncover stocks that show so much promise that the swing trader just can't wait for the next session. But before the new day finally begins, take a second look at every setup that rang the dinner bell just the night before. Good prospects should not lose their luster in the morning glare. Remember this golden rule for finding consistent winners: If you have to look, it isn't there. Forget your college degree and trust your instincts.

OPPORTUNITY COSTS

Consider an offline charting package and take the leap away from canned indicators. Use the package to find fresh opportunities that match the personal trading style. Software allows far more customization than the most sophisticated websites. It also offers the ability to modify the machine language behind popular calculations and bend numbers to individual needs. Don't confuse chart analysis packages with database programs. Software that focuses on intensive market scanning often provides a basic set of indicators that can easily be duplicated online. Charting programs will scan markets, but their strength lies in heavy numbers crunching.

The Net still provides a great place to find fresh scans, picks, and opportunities. Build a filtered list of stocks in promising setup positions. Then examine their charts in detail through multiple time frames at the best online services available. Construct a second stock watch list to review each day regardless of short-term opportunity. Become highly familiar with how their prices change, how their spreads move, and how they react to general market conditions. While some active markets will offer a few good setups over time, search for those issues that generate bread-and-butter trades week after week.

Avoid trading the most liquid short-term stocks. Seasoned professionals actively compete against each other in Dell Computer (DELL), Intel Corp (INTC), Cisco Systems (CSCO), and Microsoft Corp. (MSFT). These stocks will crush most participants who lack extensive skill or experience. Note that the current trading style may not support their volatile price action. These high-volume stocks often move in price channels rather than simple lines. Any strategy that includes these behemoths must also address the drawdowns associated with this type of chart behavior.

Every broker and execution system provides fast fills for some issues and slow ones for others. Make sure to trade only what responds quickly and avoid what doesn't. Direct-access issues must have deep representation through ECNs or they will trigger heavy slippage. Discount brokers have order flow arrangements with wholesale market makers that favor certain stocks over others. Some may even fill as fast as ECN matching orders. Use this general rule for trade entry and exit: the longer the holding period, the less urgent that instant execution becomes. For example, big Nasdaq market makers spend so much time shaking out scalpers that 1–3 day swing traders can easily fill low-risk positions below this radar and turn consistent profits.

Opportunity relates directly to the amount of time set aside for market analysis. Pick only one or two issues and follow them exclusively if trading time is limited to a couple of hours per week. Several hours per day presents the minimum commitment to successfully swing trade a variety of stocks. Increase the watch list size as dedicated time expands. Success comes more quickly trading 2 or 3 well-analyzed stocks than chasing 20 or 30 poorly understand ones.

The ability to watch the markets in real-time determines the appropriate trading strategy. Lengthen the holding period to multiple days when positions can't be followed tick by tick. Use both physical stops and limit orders to control risk. Real-time systems work best for the intraday swing trader and scalper. The vast majority of market participants have a wide range of unrelated interests that take substantial attention during each session. Don't rely on snapshot quotes or Net utilities hiding under the primary work window to manage trades. The boss will be standing right at the terminal just when the market really starts to move.

Stock boards offer great places to chat with friends but do terrible damage to a trading account. Almost everyone on the Net has a hidden agenda, and all information must be treated with suspicion. Successful swing trading requires little knowledge about a company's underlying fundamentals. Chances are that participation on a board will only reinforce underlying bias. Be prepared to understand the truth regardless of whether it helps or hurts an active position. Technical traders don't believe in companies. They believe in the numbers.

Only price, time, and risk should trigger trading actions. Know the charts inside and out without looking at them. Pinpoint the exact location of price within each chart's Pattern Cycle. Search for that S/R level where the crowd will jump in or where a falling knife can be caught with safety. Finding winners requires a level of emotional detachment that most individuals find very uncomfortable. Discomfort and profit often stand side by side.

BUILDING WATCH LISTS

Modern technology offers fast access to short-term stock watch lists. Free online services scan markets in real-time and output leaders/laggards in many categories. But over time, swing traders find that these listings don't address their growing needs, and they start to build their own custom databases. These valuable tools rapidly organize market information and scan for impending setups, often in real-time. Scans provide an efficient method to uncover subsets of the market universe that match individual risk tolerance. Experience develops an affinity for stocks at defined sectors, liquidity, and volatility. Scan filters target these unique quirks and do an excellent job focusing on specific information needs.

Most CD and online market databases now contain entire exchanges of individual issues. Create a subset of this total stock universe to isolate all of the major categories and sectors of interest. Many database services let users define custom scans that include technical strength rankings and filter output through volume, market capitalization, and price/earnings growth. But avoid too many rules and filters. That beaten-up sector in today's market could become liquid and volatile in a relatively short period of time. So program the scans to capture these gems when they finally wake up from the dead.

Carefully evaluate how trading account size will impact the watch list. In general, available capital will rule out positions over or under certain price levels. Small retail traders may avoid issues over $100, while many professionals won't look at stocks valued under $30–40. Small accounts should avoid the tendency to trade very low-priced stocks in the false belief that this will overcome undercapitalization. High relative spreads on these issues negate their greater percentage price movement. Bigger fortunes grow in small accounts that control risk than in those that chase quick rewards.

Scan by exchange as well as individual stock characteristics. Nasdaq's popularity for short-term execution makes it the preferred choice for intraday traders. But position traders often conclude that the NYSE provides better opportunities for gain with controlled risk. Most participants can build effective watch lists through this simple method: retain the upper half of the NYSE but only the top one-third of Nasdaq. Avoid thinner Nasdaq stocks unless executing trades through a direct-access terminal that routinely fills between the spread. Without an execution advantage, illiquid stocks steal profits and ruin risk management. For long-side opportunities, consider an additional filter to sort low-volume issues by relative strength. Save only the best output from this group and add them to the universe of liquid stocks.

The 1,000–3,000 stocks that survive the first scanning process become the raw material for end-of-day trading analysis. Run these issues through custom criteria that create separate watch lists to target specific stock plays or setups (see Chapters 7–14). Remember that the best scans will build multiple filters on top of one another. The size of these subsequent output lists must match the time available for preparation. It makes no sense to uncover great setups that will never be traded.

Consider unique scan criteria to uncover promising short sales. Keep in mind that these issues require greater average volume to minimize the dangers of the short squeeze. They also take more effort to locate. While strong stocks usually make good long positions, weak stocks may not produce good short sales. Markets fall faster than they rise and with less warning. Custom scans must account for the fear-driven characteristics that produce quick declines.

Use scans to pick out emerging trends in addition to imminent setups. Create and manage a separate core group of 50–100 major issues to review nightly. Add active output from this list to the top picks from the specific setup groups. This produces a final hot list to focus the swing trader's attention during the following session. Try to follow these stocks on a tick-by-tick basis to catch the predetermined execution price. If this list outputs too much to watch during market hours, create an abbreviated group of 20–30 stocks and discard the rest. Alter the hot list each evening but keep the core group for months at a time.

WRITING SCANS

Look at a typical database scan that searches for characteristics of the classic MACD (Moving Average Convergence-Divergence) Histogram indicator with Worden's TC2000 EasyScan language. The scan applies the popular 12-26-9 settings as it moves step by step through a logical filtering process:

1. MACD starts with the difference between a short moving average and a longer moving average:
   SCAN: (AVGC12)-(AVGC26)
   TRANSLATION: Subtract a 26-day simple moving average of the closing price from a 12-day simple moving average of the closing price.
2. MACD then looks for this difference smoothed over 9 days:
   SCAN: AVG(AVGC12,9)-AVG(AVGC26,9)
   TRANSLATION: Subtract a 26-day simple moving average of the closing price over the last 9 days from a 12-day simple moving average of the closing price over the last 9 days.
3. MACD signals BUY based on UP histogram zero crossover:
   SCAN: (AVGC12.1-AVGC26.1)-(AVG(AVGC12.1,9)-AVG(AVGC26.1,9))<0
   AND (AVGC12-AVGC26)-(AVG(AVGC12.1,9)-AVG(AVGC26.1,9))>0
   TRANSLATION: Yesterday's MACD is below histogram zero line and current MACD is above histogram zero line.
4. MACD signals SELL based on DOWN histogram zero crossover:
   SCAN: (AVGC12.1-AVGC26.1)-(AVG(AVGC12.1,9)-AVG(AVGC26.1,9))>0
   AND (AVGC12-AVGC26)-(AVG(AVGC12,9)-AVG(AVGC26,9))<0

TRANSLATION: Yesterday's MACD is above histogram's zero line and current MACD is below histogram zero line.

This scan may appear complicated at first glance. But it just uses simple price inputs and looks back several days to compare the current action. Signals generate from crossovers at a key indicator level and adjust easily to user preferences. Fortunately, less math-inclined swing traders can locate many of these scans free and online at websites dedicated to the various database packages. More industrious technicians will find the scan languages easy to learn and highly versatile.

Keep in mind that scans serve two primary needs. First, they reach into broad databases and output a primary list that meets the swing trader's general specifications. Second, they perform narrow analysis on this remaining subset to uncover specific trading setups and patterns. Perform frequent maintenance on the primary list but don't rerun the entire database every day. Develop a sense of how often they clog with dead data and need a fresh spin. However, run setup scans nightly as each day's data become available. The markets change so quickly that the edge belongs to those who prepare fresh tactics for the opening bell.

3
C H A P T E R

ANALYZING THE MARKET

PATTERN CYCLES

Original market analysis must uncover high probability setups, point to exact entries and tell swing traders when they're wrong. It must apply to all time frames, be intuitive, and support accurate, real-time decision-making. This versatile tool must work through all markets, provide continuous feedback, and make trading simple yet profitable.

Pattern Cycles fulfill these demanding characteristics. They provide a complete, powerful method to locate opportunity regardless of market conditions. These classic stages evolve as the charting landscape repeats common and predictable elements. Since markets cannot travel upward to infinity or downward below zero, well-marked ranges evolve within each time frame. Trends slowly awaken at these narrow levels and shoot forward in emotional waves.

Stocks and their related charts cycle through a finite number of bull and bear conditions. Price bars shape common patterns over and over again through impulses that may last only a few seconds or persist for decades. When swing traders recognize the separate stages of this market evolution, their skilled vision awakens to a world of low-risk opportunity. Learn the well-marked steps of Pattern Cycle development and discover the hidden language of the master pattern.

Chart polarity appears everywhere in the financial markets. Pattern Cycles feed off this axis to simplify decision-making. Use their mechanics to register market trends quickly and see profit setups at logical interfaces. They offer a potent visual tool that unites left and right brain functions. The pattern-trained eye intuitively sees natural execution levels that can then be verified through objective measurement. No complex or math-driven trading system will respond more quickly to changing price in real-time market conditions.

Pattern Cycles evolve through the engine of greed and fear. The emotional crowd acts in a predictable manner through chart patterns. This herd behavior translates into directional movement that offers a rich source for profits. But the swing trader must first define a competitive relationship with the crowd as part of every new analysis. This requires an understanding of how insiders may fade popular response to obvious trading opportunities.

Look for a low-risk execution target (ET) in each Pattern Cycle setup. This elusive trigger identifies the optimum price, time, and risk parameters for each intended entry. Find this important action level through analysis, experience, and common sense. Then determine whether the next few sessions should activate its specific criteria. If not, filter out the setup and move on to the next pattern. Never compromise an ET to force a position. Use it as a situational filter to avoid very bad timing.

BOTTOMS

Bottoms print as a direct result of Pattern Cycle physics. The natural movement of impulse and reaction dictates that two unique formations must develop at some point within each cycle. In an uptrend, a lower high will eventually follow a higher high and mark a new top. In a downtrend, the sequence of lower lows will finally end when price forms a higher low. This second event marks the birth of the double bottom.

Double bottoms draw their predictive power from the trends that precede them. Downtrends often accelerate as a series of lower lows prints on a bar chart. The trading crowd notices and develops a gravity bias that expects the fall to continue unabated. Then suddenly the last low appears to hold. The crowd takes notice and bottom fishers slowly enter new positions. Apparent price stability triggers more players to recognize the potential pattern and jump in.

Stock percentage growth potential peaks at the very beginning of a new uptrend. For this reason, being right at a bottom can produce the highest profit for any trade. But picking bottoms can be a very dangerous game. Swing traders must weigh all evidence at their disposal before taking the leap and exercise strict risk discipline to ensure a safe exit if proven wrong. Losses must be taken immediately upon violation of the prior low.

Double bottoms generate excellent swing trades when price first thrusts toward the last relative high (center peak), and after that level becomes a base of support for the next move upward. The Adam and Eve bottom illustrates the center peak's importance in the creation of this classic reversal. A very sharp and deep first bottom (Adam) initiates this pattern. The stock then bounces high into a center retracement before falling into a gentle, rolling second bottom (Eve). Price action

F I G U R E   3.1

Legato Systems draws a well-formed Adam and Eve reversal on the daily chart. Eve's rounded bottom takes longer to print than the sharp Adam spike. Look for volume to decrease as the stock heals and prepares for a new uptrend breakout. Adam and Eve patterns aren't limited to bottoms. Watch for their mirror image at the end of parabolic rallies.

Daily   (Right) LGTO - LEGATO SYSTEMS   Bar

finally constricts into a tight range and the stock breaks out strongly to the upside. Many times Eve's top prints a flat shelf that marks an excellent entry point. Shelf resistance typically develops right along the top of the center retracement pivot. The relationship between this center pivot and current price marks the important focal point as the swing trader closely watches the development of the suspected pattern.

Manage risk defensively—bottoms occur in downtrends. The greedy eye wants to believe the immature formation, and fast execution fingers may bypass better judgment. Even spectacular reversals offer little profit if price can't ascend back out of the hole it came from. Violation of the prior low presents the natural first choice for stop loss. Make certain the entry permits a safe exit for an acceptable loss at this location. Don't stick around long if the uptrend begins to fail. Price will gather downside momentum quickly at broken lows as it searches for new support.

Successful bottom entry requires a strong stomach. Highly negative sentiment infects these volatile turning points even when all S/R and other technicals line up. But the profit potential for these classic setups presents very high reward:risk. In addition to new longs ready to speculate on a good upside move, high short interest will fuel explosive impulses off these levels. Perhaps for this reason alone, swing traders must explore the secrets of double bottom execution.

Rounded bottoms also provide opportunity for patient traders. Enter a long position after momentum clearly shifts back toward the positive, but realize that it may take some time for a profit to grow. Better yet, use rounded bottoms to identify bear markets that wash out and gear up for a new bull leg. The formation supports a very stable base for price to move upward once the pattern completes.

The Big W reference pattern maps the entire bottom reversal process. This signpost identifies key pivots and flashes early warning signals. The pattern begins at a market's last high just prior to the first bottom. The first bounce after this low marks the center peak of the W as it retraces between 38% and 62% of that last downward move. This rally fades and price descends back toward a test of the last low. The swing trader then waits patiently for the first bell to ring. A wide range reversal bar (preferably a doji or hammer) may appear close to the low price of the last bottom. Or volume may spike sharply but price holds firm. Better yet, a 2B reversal prints where price violates the last low by a few ticks but then bounces sharply back above support. Focus attention on the potential second leg of this Big W when any or all of these events occur.

Initiate entry near the bottom of this second leg when multiple cross-verification supports the trade and conditions permit tight stop loss. The middle of the W now becomes the central analysis point for further setups. Price must retrace 100% of the last minor decline to jump to this level. This small move finally breaks the descending bear cycle. Enter less aggressive positions when this emerging second bottom retraces through 62% of the fall into the second low. But sufficient profit must exist between that entry and the top of the W center pivot for the setup to make sense. Longer-term participants can hold positions as price tries to mount this barrier but most traders should exit immediately.

Expect another upward leg after support establishes along the center pivot. The break of the downtrend invites many new players, and price has a high probability of rising further. Look for the next thrust to retrace 100% of the original downward impulse that pushed price into the first bottom. This final move completes both the double bottom and the Big W. The pattern may provide further opportunity on a quick pullback, but extended congestion can form in this area before trend pushes much higher. So assume a defensive posture and wait for the market to signal the next direction.

BREAKOUTS

Significant declines evolve into long basing periods characterized by failed rallies and retesting of prior lows. But as new accumulation slowly shakes out the last crowd of losers, a bear market's character changes. Price starts to rally toward the top of key resistance. Short-term relative strength improves and the chart may print a series of bullish bars with closing ticks near their highs. Finally, the issue begins a steady march through the wall marked by previous failures.

Stocks must overcome gravity to enter new uptrends. Value players build bases but can't supply the critical force needed to fuel strong rallies. Fortunately, the momentum crowd arrives just in time to fill this chore. As a stock slowly rises above resistance, greed rings a loud bell and these growth players jump on board all at the same time.

The appearance of a sharp breakout gap has tremendous buying power. But the swing trader must remain cautious if the move lacks heavy volume. Bursts of enthusiastic buying must draw wide attention that ignites further price expansion. The gap may fill quickly and trap the emotional longs when significant volume fails to appear. Non-gapping, high-volume surges provide a comfortable breakout floor similar to gaps. But support can be less dependable and force a stock to swing into a new range rather than rise quickly.

Moderate strength breakouts often set up good pullback trades. The uptrend terrain faces considerable obstacles marked by clear air pockets and congestion from prior downtrends. These barriers should force frequent dips that mark good buying opportunities. The swing trader must identify these profitable resistance zones in advance and be ready to act. Look for price to shoot past the top Bollinger Band just as it strikes a strong ceiling. This should define the most likely turning point. Then follow the price correction back to natural support and look for low-risk entry.

Price surges register on trend-following indicators such as MACD and ADX as momentum builds. Volatility quickly absorbs each new thrust and vertical rallies erupt. Abandon dip setups once this starts and try to catch these runaway expansion moves by shifting down to the next-lower time frame and finding small support pockets. Volume peaks as a trend wave draws to a climax while price expands bar to bar and often culminates in a final exhaustion spike.

Markets need time to absorb instability generated by rapid price movement. They pause to catch their breath as both volume and price rate of change drop sharply. During these consolidation periods, new ranges undergo continuous testing for support and resistance. To the pattern reader, these appear as the familiar shapes of flags, pennants and triangles. Relatively simple mechanics underlie the formation of these continuation patterns. The orderly return to a market's mean state sets the foundation for a new thrust in the same direction. Price pulls back with declining

F I G U R E   3.2

The Big W pattern provides swing traders with a powerful tool to locate low-risk bottom entry in all time frames and all markets. The center pivot may retrace 38%, 50%, or 62% of the selloff that leads into the first low. As the second bottom breaks the downtrend, look for a fast pullback to the top of the W center before the market moves higher. The pattern completes when price pushes through a 100% retracement of the last selloff.

Intraday   (Right) $COMPX - NASDAQ COMBINED COMPOSITE INDX (5-Min)   Bar
    4/17

volume but does not violate any significant support. The primary trend reasserts itself as stability returns.

Congestion tends to alternate between simple and complex patterns in a series of sharp trend waves. This odd phenomenon occurs in both range time and size. For example, the first pullback after a rally may only print 8–10 bars in a tight pattern while the subsequent congestion exhibits wide price swings through 20–25

F I G U R E   3.3

Very strong gap breakouts rise more quickly toward higher prices than simple resistance breakouts. Trading tactics that wait for a low-risk pullback may prove futile because the new uptrend often goes vertical. Extreme crowd enthusiasm ignites continued buying at higher levels and the market never needs a dip to locate more fuel. Use a momentum strategy to enter a long position in this environment and manage risk with absolute price or percentage stop loss.

Daily   (Right) AAPL - APPLE COMPUTER INC   Bar

bars. Always take a look back at the last range to estimate the expected price action for the new congestion. Trade more defensively if the prior pattern was both short and simple. Go on the offense after observing an extended battle in the last range.

Swing traders must pay close attention to proportionality when examining continuation patterns. This visual element will validate or nullify other predictive observations. Constricted ranges should be proportional in both time and size to the trends that precede them. When they take on dimensions larger than expected from visual examination, odds increase that the observed range actually relates to a broader trend than the rally just completed. This can trigger devastating trend relativity errors, in which traders base execution on patterns longer or shorter than the targeted holding period.

Evaluate all patterns within the context of this trend relativity. A constricted range exists only within the time frame under consideration. For example, a market may print a strong bull move on the weekly chart, a bear on the daily, and a tight continuation pattern on the 5-minute bars, all at the same time. A range drawn through one time frame does not necessarily signal swing conditions in the other periods that particular market trades through.

RALLIES

The cult of Elliott Wave Theory (EWT) intimidates the most experienced swing traders. But simple elements of this arcane practice add great insight to Pattern Cycle analysis. Strong trends routinely print orderly action-reaction waves. EWT uncovers these predictive patterns through their repeating count of three primary waves and two countertrend ones.

Wave impulses correspond with the crowd's emotional participation. A surging first wave represents the fresh enthusiasm of an initial breakout. The new crowd then hesitates and prices drop into a countertrend second wave. This coils the action for the rising greed of the runaway third wave. Then, after another pullback slowly awakens fear, the manic crowd exhausts itself in a final fifth-wave blowoff.

Primary wave setups require very little knowledge of the underlying theory. Just look for the five-wave trend structure in all time frames. While these price thrusts may seem hard to locate, the trained eye can uncover wave patterns in many strong uptrends. Trading strategy follows other types of swing tactics. Locate smaller waves embedded within larger ones and execute positions at convergent points where two or more time frames intersect. These cross-verification zones capture major trend, reversal, and breakout points. For example, the third wave of a primary trend often exhibits dynamic vertical motion. This single thrust can hide a complete five-wave rally within the next-smaller time frame. Locate this hidden pattern and execute a long position at the "third of a third," one of the most powerful wave phenomena within an entire uptrend.

Dynamic third waves often trigger broad continuation gaps. These occur just as emotion replaces reason, and they frustrate good swing traders. Many exit positions on the bars just prior to the big gap because common sense dictates that the surging stock should retrace. Use timely wave analysis and a strong stomach to anticipate this big move before it occurs. It often prints right after several vertical bars close near the top of their ranges. Look for the last bar to reach right into broad resistance. Price should jump beyond that level on the gap. Also watch for RSI and other strength indicators to rise to the middle of their plots just as the big event erupts.

Fourth-wave corrections initiate the sentiment mechanics for the final fifth wave. The crowd experiences an emotional setback as this countertrend slowly generates fear through a sharp downturn or long sideways move. The same momentum signals that carry the crowd into positions now roll over and turn against it. But as the herd prepares to exit, the trend suddenly reawakens and price again surges into a new wave.

F I G U R E   3.4

The greedy crowd ignites a powerful December rally in Amgen. Note the embedded five-wave pattern within the larger primary third wave. This potent time frame alignment appears frequently in surging trends and marks a significant profit opportunity. A third wave within another third wave (third of a third) signals the most dynamic momentum for an entire rally.

The crowd loses good judgment during this final, fifth wave. Both parabolic moves and aborted rallies occur here with great frequency. Survival through the last sharp countertrend (fourth wave) builds an unhealthy sense of invulnerability into the crowd mechanics. Movement becomes unpredictable and the uptrend ends suddenly just as the last greedy participant jumps in.

Analyze the specific wave landscape through this classic pattern's special characteristics. The bottom of the fourth wave should never touch the top of the second-wave. The second and fourth waves should alternate between simple and complex shapes. The fifth wave may exhibit a parabolic rally under the right circumstances but can also fail as soon as it breaks out of the fourth-wave range. Two of the three primary waves tend to print identical price change. The wave structure often exhibits very clean Fibonacci relationships. For example, two primary waves may print 38% each of the complete wave set.

Use volatile past action to identify effective trades when trend finally turns back through old price and begins a correction. Battles between bulls and bears leave a scarred landscape of unique charting features. For example, prior gaps can present excellent profit opportunities. Third-wave continuation gaps rarely fill on the first retracement, except through an opposing gap. Execute pullback entry in the direction of support as soon as price dips into a continuation gap, as long as the setup meets other reward:risk considerations. This pattern also generates good intraday setups because most major gaps occur overnight. But don't jump in without first recognizing the important differences between continuation gaps and other, less dependable ones. Some will fill easily and trigger immediate price expansion in the opposite direction.

Past breaks in support identify low-risk short sales as corrections evolve. The more violent the break, the more likely it will resist penetration. Head and shoulders, rectangles, and double top formations leave their mark with strong resistance levels. These patterns often print multiple doji and hammer lows just prior to a final break as insiders clean out stops near the extremes of the pattern. Use their descending tails to pinpoint a reversal target for short sale entry.

Clear air marks price pockets with thin participation and ownership. These volatile zones often print a series of wide range bars as trends thrust from one stable level to another. This rapid movement tends to repeat each time that price action passes its boundaries. Potential reward spikes sharply through these unique levels for obvious reasons. But watch out: reversals tend to be sharp and vertical as well. Use tight stops at all times.

The 3D charting landscape recognizes that important features may not be horizontal. What the eye resolves as uptrend or downtrend may contain multiple impulses that shoot out in many directions. Parallel price channels offer the most common example of this multipath phenomenon. These complex patterns also offer very clean trade setups. Fade one trendline with a stop loss just beyond the violation point. Book the profit and reverse when price swings to the other channel extreme.

HIGHS

Swing traders discover great rewards in uncharted territory. Stocks at new highs generate unique momentum properties that ignite sharp price movement. But these dynamic breakouts can also demonstrate very unexpected behavior. Old S/R battlegrounds disappear at new highs, and few chart references remain to guide execution. Risk escalates with each promising setup in this volatile environment. The final breakout to new highs completes a stock's digestion of overhead supply. But the struggle for greater price gains still continues. These strong markets often undergo additional testing and base-building before resuming their dynamic uptrends. Watch this building process through typical pattern development seen during these events.

New high stocks may return to test the top of prior resistance several times. This can force a series of stepping ranges before trend finally surges upward. Some issues go vertical immediately when they enter these breakouts. New high trade analysis faces the challenge of predicting which outcome is more likely. Let accumulation-distribution indicators and the developing pattern guide decision-making at these interfaces. Acc-dis consistently signals whether new highs will escalate immediately or just mark time. Price either leads or lags accumulation. When stocks reach new highs without sufficient ownership or buying pressure, they will usually pause to allow these broad forces to catch up. When accumulation builds more strongly than price, the initial thrust to new highs confirms the indicator signal. Odds then favor that the breakout will trigger a fresh round of buying interest and force price to take off immediately with no basing phase.

As stocks push into uncharted territory, examine the action through existing features of the pattern. The last congestion phase before the breakout often prints sharp initiation points for the new impulse. Locate this hidden root structure in double bottom lows embedded within the range under the breakout price. The distance between these lows and the top resistance boundary may yield accurate price targets for the subsequent rally. Barring larger forces, this new high should extend approximately 1.38 times the distance between that low and the resistance top before establishing a new range (see Figure 5.27).

A strong bull impulse can go vertical for an extended period after it finally escapes initial breakout gravity. Price action may even print a dramatic third wave for the trend initiated at the final congestion low. This thrust can easily exceed initial price targets when it converges with large-scale wave motion. In other words, when forces on the weekly, daily, and intraday charts move into synergy, trend movement can greatly exceed expectations. This explains why so many professional analysts routinely underestimate stock rallies.

Measure ongoing new highs with a MACD Histogram indicator. Effective swing trading of post-gravity impulses relies on the interaction between current price and the momentum cycle. Aggressive participants can enter long positions when price pulls back but the MACD slope begins to rise. Conservative traders can wait until the indicator crosses the zero signal line from below to above. Use the

FIGURE   3.5

Alternation predicts major trend waves with few retracements when complex basing occurs early in a dynamic uptrend. This CMGI parabolic move supports that theory. Note the extended range at the right shoulder of the inverse head and shoulders pattern. Inadequate accumulation stalled the stock just under the breakout high until fresh demand could push price through the barrier. Once the building process completed, price expanded through the old high, paused briefly, and ejected into an astounding rally.

Daily   (Right) CMGI - CMGI INC   Bar

descending histogram slope to exit positions and flag overbought conditions that favor ranges or reversals. Ignore the MACD when well-marked charting landscape features signal an immediate opportunity. For example, if an established trendline can be drawn under critical lows, key entry timing to that line rather than waiting for the indicator slope to turn up or down.

Avoid short sales completely when price and momentum peak, unless advanced skills can safely manage the increased risk. Remember that trying to pick tops is a loser's game. Delay short sales until momentum drops sharply but price sits high within a rangebound market. Pattern Cycle analysis will then locate favorable countertrends with much lower risk.

How long should a rally last when a stock breaks to new highs? Physics teaches that the star that burns brightest extinguishes itself long before one that emits a cooler, darker light. So it is with market rallies. Parabolic moves cannot sustain themselves over the long haul. Alternatively, stocks that struggle for each point of gain eventually give up and roll over. So logic dictates that the most durable path for uptrends lies somewhere in between these two extremes.

Overbought conditions trigger a decline in price momentum and illustrate one ever-present danger when trading new highs: stocks may stop rising at any moment and start extended sideways movement. Watch rallies closely to uncover early warning signs for this range development. The first break in a major trendline that follows a big move flags the end of a trend and beginning of sideways congestion. Exit momentum-based positions until conditions once again favor rapid price change. In this environment, consider countertrend swing trades if reward:risk opens up good opportunities. But stand aside as volatility slowly dissipates and crowd participation fades.

TOPS

No trend lasts forever. Crowd enthusiasm eventually outpaces a stock's fundamentals and the rally stalls. But topping formations do not end uptrends all by themselves. This stopping point may only signal a short pause that finally yields to higher prices. Or it may represent a long-term high just before a major collapse. Learn to evaluate topping ranges by understanding the psychology that drives them. Then get in the reversal door early and allow the herd to trigger sharp price expansion.

Classic topping formations take forever to issue their reversal signals. Head and shoulders and double tops draw complex distribution patterns as the crowd slowly loses faith. While the swing trader waits, the herd takes notice of the action and all stand together to wait for the eventual breakdown. Since common knowledge offers few good opportunities, access to early warning of trend change provides a needed edge for profit.

Use the first rise/first failure (FR/FF) pattern to target new ranges and reversals before the competition. This simple formation works through all time frames and applies to both tops and bottoms. FR/FF signals the first 100% retracement of a dynamic trend within the time frame of interest. Trends should find support during pullbacks no further than the 62% retracement, as measured from the starting point of the last wave that pushes price into an intermediate high or low. Healthy trends should base from this level and bounce toward a new breakout. The

market reverses within this specific time frame if price breaks through this important support.

The 100% retracement violates the primary price direction and terminates the
trend it corrects. Completion also provides significant S/R where swing traders can

F I G U R E   3.6

The familiar triangular shape of the first rise/first failure pattern quickly identifies potential reversals. The first retracement of a rally
through 62% ends the trend and sets the stage for a significant move in the opposite direction. Swing traders can often cross-verify
this break through other charting landscape features. Note how the strong trendline breaks on the same bar as the 62% violation
following this late 1998 Amazon explosion.

Daily   (Right) AMZN - AMAZON.COM   Bar

RealTick® ©1986–2000. All rights reserved. Used with permission of Townsend Analytics, Ltd.

initiate defensive bounce trades. From this important pivot, continuation trends may reawaken in the next-larger time frame if they push through the 38% (62% retracement level of the downtrend) S/R and continue past the 62% (38% retracement level of the downtrend) S/R, toward a test of the last intermediate high.

Long side entry at the 100% retracement offers good reward:risk when it coincides with a 38% or 62% retracement in the next-higher time frame. However, the setup may develop more slowly than anticipated. In other words, a successful position must pass expected congestion through the 38–62% zone before it can access a profitable retest of the old high and possibly move higher.

Allow for whipsaws at all major Fibonacci retracement levels before execution. Insiders know these hidden turning points and take out stops to generate volume. Also watch out for trend relativity errors. Bull and bear markets exist simultaneously through different time frames. Limit FR/FF trades to the time frame for which the retracement occurs unless cross-verification supports a broader opportunity.

Every popular topping formation draws its own unique pattern features. But all tell a common tale of crowd disillusionment. Whether it evolves through the loss of faith of the head and shoulders or the slow capitulation of the rising wedge, the final result remains the same. Price breaks sharply to lower levels while unhappy stockholders unload positions as quickly as they can.

Value and improving fundamentals attract knowledgeable holders early in a rally. But the motivation for new participants degenerates as an uptrend progresses. News of a budding stock rally creates excitement and attracts a greedier crowd. These momentum players slowly outnumber the value investors and price movement becomes more volatile. The issue continues upward as this frantic buying crowd feeds on itself well beyond most reasonable price targets.

Both fire and ice can kill uptrends. As long as the greater fool mechanism holds, each new long allows the previous one to turn a profit. But the right conditions eventually come along to force a climax to the upside action. A shock event can suddenly erupt to kill the buying enthusiasm and force a sharp reversal. Or the trend's fuel may just run out as the last buyer takes a final position. In either case, the stock loses its ability to defy gravity and stops rising.

Many swing traders mistakenly assume bulls turn into bears immediately following a dramatic, high-volume reversal. They enter ill-advised short sales well before the pattern physics rob the crowd's enthusiasm. These early sales provide fuel for the intense short covering rallies that most topping formations exhibit. Keep in mind that reversals only turn trends into sideways markets. Topping patterns must complete before they turn sideways markets into declines. Limit entry to classic fade strategies at the edges of S/R until the breakdown begins. Then initiate trend-following short sales to capitalize on crowd disillusionment and panic.

The descending triangle illustrates the slow evolution from bull market to bear decline better than any other topping pattern. Within this simple structure, examine how life drains slowly from a dynamic uptrend. Variations of this destructive formation precede more breakdowns than any other reversal. And they can be found doing their dirty deeds in all time frames and all markets.

REVERSALS

Why does the descending triangle work with such deadly accuracy? Most swing traders really don't understand how or why patterns predict outcomes. Some even believe these important tools rely on mysticism or convenient curve fitting. The simple truth is more powerful: congestion patterns reflect the impact of crowd psychology on price change.

Shock and fear quickly follow the first reversal that marks the triangle's major top. But many shareholders remain true believers and expect their profits will return after selling dissipates. They continue to hold their positions as hope slowly replaces better judgment. This initial selloff carries further than anticipated and their discomfort quickly increases. But just as pain begins to escalate, the correction suddenly ends and the stock firmly bounces.

For many longs, this late buying and short covering reinforces a dangerous bias that they were right all along. Renewed confidence even prompts some to add new positions. But smarter players have a change of heart and view this new rally as their first chance to get out whole. They quietly exit and the strong bounce loses momentum. The stock once again rolls over and draws the second lower top of the evolving pattern. Those still holding long positions then watch the low of the first reversal with much apprehension.

Prior countertrend lows draw scalpers and investors familiar with double bottom behavior. As price descends toward the emotional barrier of the last low, they step in and stop the decline. But the smart money stands aside and the subsequent bounce only draws in new investors with very bad timing. As the pattern draws its third peak, the last bullish energy dissipates from the criss-cross price swings. Price continues to hold up through this sideways action but relative strength indicators signal sharp negative divergence. Momentum indicators roll over and Bollinger Bands contract as price range narrows.

The scalpers depart and this final bounce quickly fades. Shorts now smell blood and enter larger positions. Fear increases and stops build just under the double low shelf. Price returns for one final test as negative sentiment expands sharply. Price and volatility then contract right at the breaking point. The bulls must hold this line, but the odds have shifted firmly against them. Recognizing the imminent breakdown, swing traders use all upticks to enter new short sales and counter any weak bull response. Finally, the last positive sentiment dies and horizontal support fails. As the sell stops trigger, price spirals downward in a substantial decline.

Stock charts print many unique topping formations. Many can be understood and traded with very little effort. But the emotional crowd also generates many undependable patterns as greed slowly evolves into mindless fear. Complex rising wedges will defy the technician's best efforts at prediction, while the odd diamond formation will burn trading capital as it swings randomly back and forth.

Avoid these fruitless positions and seek profit only where the odds strongly favor the predicted outcome. First locate the single feature common to most topping reversals: price draws at least one lower high within the broad congestion before violating the major uptrend. This simple double top mechanism becomes a primary

F I G U R E   3.7

Sharp, parabolic rallies often set the stage for dramatic topping formations. In this classic example, Infoseek sketches a perfect descending triangle reversal following a vertical 1998 price expansion. After the initial breakdown, price pulls back to the filled gap and offers a second short sale opportunity. Note how this triangle also draws a variation of the Adam and Eve pattern.

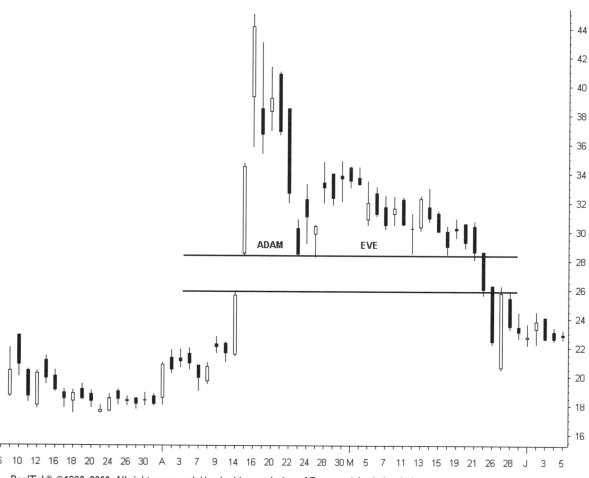

Daily   (Right) SEEK - INFOSEEK CORP   Bar

focus for short sale planning. Use this well-marked signpost to follow price outward to its natural breaking point and enter when support fails.

Flip over the Adam and Eve bottom pattern and find a highly predictive setup for topping reversals. This Adam and Eve top offers swing traders frequent high-profit short sales opportunities. Enter new shorts when price violates the reaction low, but use tight stops to avoid whipsaws and 2B reversals. These occur when sudden short covering rallies erupt right after the gunning of stops just below the failure.

Each uptrend generates positive sentiment that the topping formation must overcome. Adam and Eve tops represent an efficient bar structure to accomplish this task. The violent reversal of Adam first awakens fear. Then the slow dome of Eve absorbs the remaining bull impulse while dissipating the volatility needed to resume a rally. As the dome completes, price moves swiftly to lower levels without substantial resistance.

Observant swing traders recognize the mechanics of descending triangles and Adam and Eve formations in more complex reversals. The vast majority of tops display characteristics of these two familiar patterns. Crowd enthusiasm must be eliminated for a decline to proceed. Buying interest eventually recedes through the repeated failure of price to achieve new highs. Then the market can finally drop from its own weight.

Price draws a double top when it can't pass the resistance of the last high. The more violent the reversal at the initial top, the more likely the first attempt to exceed it will fail. The longer it takes for this test to approach the first top, the more likely it will fail. When both conditions support a double top failure, swing traders can sell short into the second rise if:

- They are willing to exit immediately if price violates the old high.
- The execution target stands at or just below the old high.

The third rise into a top should rarely be sold short. Markets can easily head to new highs when they turn and rally after pulling back from a first failed test. This first attempt washes out shorts and those that missed selling on the initial top. The third rise allows accumulation to build and sets up a classic cup and handle breakout pattern. It also traps shorts from the failed test and uses their buying power to build a new uptrend.

DECLINES

The same crowd that lifts price provides the fuel for a subsequent decline. Longs build false confidence after rally momentum fades and a topping pattern forms. As smart money quietly exits, the uptrend hits a critical trigger point: the bulls suddenly realize that they are trapped. They start to dump the stock in an attempt to salvage profits. Price breaks support and selling spirals downward through wave after wave.

Common features appear in most price declines. Volume repeatedly surges through waves of selling pressure while false bottoms print and then quickly fail. Violent covering rallies erupt to shake out poorly timed short sales and offer hope to wounded longs. Price carries well past rational targets, but just as panic builds, the stock finds a sustainable bottom.

The swing trader capitalizes upon this repeating market behavior through the same wave mechanics that guide strong rallies. But fear replaces greed during selloffs and invokes different setup considerations. When R. N. Elliott discussed primary trend waves in the 1930s, he noted the special characteristics of downtrends through the five-wave decline (5WD) pattern. This price correction structure remains as effective today as it was many decades ago. And swing traders can apply its power without understanding the broad Elliott Wave Theory, because it captures the fear of the emotional herd.

FIGURE   3.8

TOP-1-2-DROP UP: Use this simple count to identify the five-wave decline and accurately predict trend reversals. The three primary waves mark the Top-1-2 in the 5WD pattern. Connect the third (1) and fifth (2) waves with a trendline. The trendline can violate the first (TOP) wave in any way. The first bounce after the (DROP) may come close to that trendline but will rarely violate it.

The 5WD consists of three primary trend impulses and two reactions, just like its uptrend cousin. Direct waves push lower in this complex pattern between countertrend bear rallies. The middle wave often prints a downtrend continuation gap as dynamic as the uptrend version. The last impulse can reflect parabolic movement driven by intense fear. After this drop, the uptrend may resume immediately. But more often price forms a double bottom or similar pattern that provides a good base for a breakout above the downtrend line.

The first impulse (TOP) corrects the uptrend that carries an issue to a new high. This often prints a first failure retracement. It also initiates the price decline that completes the stock's technical breakdown through the third wave (1). Volume peaks sharply during this middle correction as shareholders recognize the ugly event. But the worst is usually reserved for last in major declines. As the third wave completes, a false bottom paints a comforting picture that slows the selling and brings in new value longs. The decline then suddenly resumes and accelerates into an emotional fifth wave (2) that violates popular targets and reasonable support zones. Note that the top of the fourth wave can reach up and touch the bottom of the second wave during the 5WD. This would violate common EWT rules if it occurred during a rally instead of a selloff.

The fifth wave panic extinguishes the selling pressure and bounces the stock. This rapid upward motion squeezes shorts and ignites the first impulse of a possible new uptrend. The strong rally then quickly fails. As longs brace for more pain, the prior low unexpectedly holds. A new crowd notices the support and steps in. Price builds back to the 1-2 trendline as a double bottom forms. The balance of power then shifts and the stock breaks out through that line into a new uptrend.

Orient the decline against broader uptrend movement to predict price evolution. Start with Fibonacci retracement analysis and measure the selloff against the prior trends. One simple 5WD structure draws the first wave to 38%, the second to 50%, and the final impulse to 62% of a larger uptrend. This predicts that price will eventually return to test the high where the decline originally began. But if the pattern corrects 100% or more of a major rally, the subsequent bounce could be very weak and the stock may eventually go lower. Expect price to break through the down trendline in these conditions but quickly pause and drop back below new support. Trade defensively and capitalize on the price swings. Then shift tactics quickly when the bottom appears ready to break.

5WD short selling requires great precision. The 1-2 trendline consists of only two points unless the TOP aligns perfectly with the next two impulses. So this important signpost doesn't really print until the second major selloff breaks to new lows. The first upward impulse after the climax marks a good short entry if price gets close enough to the trendline. But this setup carries a lower reward than the other downward moves and the position requires countertrend entry because price should eventually hold above the prior low.

The best short sales arise from natural breakdown points as impulses violate prior support. Avoid positions on the first impulse since this wave may complete with no technical breakdown. This first decline also faces a short squeeze danger and a large pool of potential longs. The second downward 5WD impulse (1) may begin close to the high of the TOP. This forms a classic double top pattern. Subse-

F I G U R E   3.9

Examine every decline within the context of larger price movement. After Tellabs rallied for 6 points on the 5-minute chart, it quickly pulled back to the 62% retracement in a clear five-wave decline pattern. It then formed a simple double bottom and broke out to the upside. Since the old uptrend remained intact, the first target should be a test of the old high at 62. Keep an eye out for TOP-1-2-DROP-UP in all time frames.

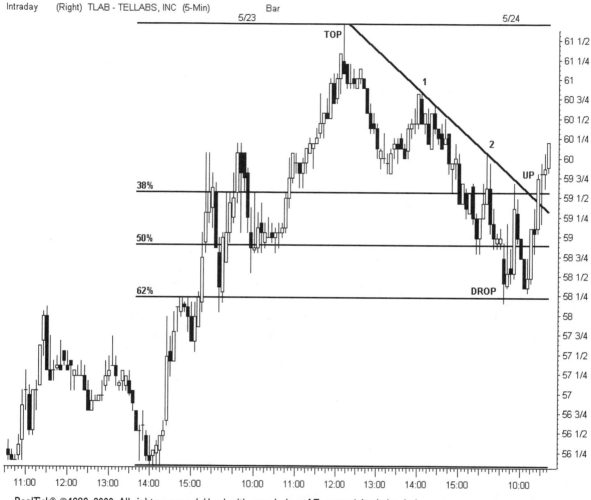

RealTick® ©1986–2000. All rights reserved. Used with permission of Townsend Analytics, Ltd.

quent waves present less danger to short positions as the bear mentality undermines price recovery. Locate logical entry points where weak rallies bounce into major resistance.

Experience teaches that downtrends do not easily give way to new uptrends. While a break of the 1-2 trendline marks the completion of the 5WD, subsequent price movement may not generate much momentum. Try to capture the expansion move across the trendline or the first pullback for a quick swing trade. Then exercise caution to see how the new uptrend develops. Remember the old adage: the bigger the move, the broader the base. Long declines need time to heal and the broken trendline may only yield to a sideways market. Price break momentum will be directly proportional to the distribution level during the previous decline. Recognize those times when price will likely rise at the same angle at which it originally fell, and watch out for those times when it won't.

The skilled eye will find 5WDs in all time frames. Some exhibit sharp vertical selloffs, while others move sideways and provoke far less attention. Both occurrences allow swing traders to focus attention on price correction and find low-risk entry on both sides of the market. Fit this volatile formation into its proper stage within the broad Pattern Cycles structure. Then watch how markets create opportunity through the evolution of the master pattern.

MARKET MECHANICS

Most Pattern Cycles trading occurs at key intersections. Prior action prints complex S/R barriers. Price discovery then tests these constricted zones, which must eventually hold or fail. Classic swing strategies depend on these barriers to stop and reverse price. Momentum tactics expect them to break. When they do, bars expand in the direction of the violation. This common trending mechanism also displays a fortunate side effect for sleeping traders. Price often revisits the original breakout level and permits low-risk pullback entry.

S/R takes many diverse forms. It may appear as a series of tops or bottoms, gaps, retracements, or a variety of other landscape features. Any straight set of three or more lines that extend outward yields a trendline that can stop price movement. When S/R methods intersect, they signal cross-verification and odds increase that the predicted trading event will occur. Train the mind to see unique S/R on each stock chart and then concentrate on the intersecting points. The next profit hides there and waits for discovery.

Bull, bear, top, bottom, breakout, breakdown, high, low. That's about it. Pattern Cycles continuously repeat the same stages through all charts and time frames. Successful swing trading requires little more than accurate recognition of a stock's current phase and waiting patiently for low-risk execution. Learn the characteristics of each stage and start to think in 3D. Consistent profits come from chart elements that align through several time periods. But concurrent trends often stand in conflict and yield unpredictable results. For example, many trading losses will come from buying one trend while another signals an immediate sale.

Above all else, Pattern Cycles recognize the difference between bull and bear markets. Trend mechanics operate very differently through rallies and declines. Collar the position to the bull-bear axis and filter trades in tune with the predominant cycle. Countertrend entry works well but requires advanced execution skills. Don't attempt it without extensive experience and careful planning. And avoid picking tops or bottoms in fast-moving conditions. The markets present much safer trades with equal rewards.

Try to execute positions just as countertrend movement ends and the primary trend reasserts itself. These pullbacks, dips, and bear rallies shift reward:risk strongly in the swing trader's favor. Trend mechanics exhibit frequent and predictable countertrend movement. The challenge during these times lies in emotional self-control. Success requires buying when fear says sell and selling when greed says buy. Profit at that critical moment depends on adhering to the prime directive of technical analysis: play the numbers and forget the story.

PATTERN CHARACTERISTICS

Congestion patterns swing between key S/R levels. They complete when a new trend leg breaks through this wall into directional price movement. This surge may be in the same or opposite direction as the previous one. A pattern between adjacent price moves in the same direction continues that trend. Alternatively, when a breakout turns backwards and retraces the last trend leg, that pattern reverses the prior move.

All range patterns display a tendency toward continuation or reversal. This underlying bias generates their predictive power. Reversal patterns take longer to complete than continuation patterns. Swing traders exploit this tendency when they locate other congestion zones within the same trend and compare the bar count. Learn to recognize patterns well before they complete, and choose entry points where price momentum will likely erupt. Always keep in mind that reversal patterns tend to be more dependable than breakout patterns.

Trend has only two choices upon reaching a barrier: continue forward or reverse. Pattern Cycles focus trading efforts toward the more likely result and point to low-risk execution levels that capitalize upon the event. But effective analysis must also consider that the opposite outcome could develop. Many times this pattern failure will yield a more profitable trade than the one originally planned. So always see if an execution in the other direction might make sense. Charts consistently offer early prediction of these events through unexpected behavior near common breakout levels.

Price acts differently at tops and bottoms. Bottoms take longer to form, and declines from tops tend to be more vertical than rises off bottoms. This phenomenon illustrates a known gravity principle within the markets. Price bars appear to have a weight that influences their trend development. This odd tendency generates an inappropriate gravity bias that inhibits the ability to visualize dramatic rallies before they occur. Fortunately, self-therapy for this condition will cure it. Take a chart and throw it on the floor. From above, walk circles around it until you don't know which way is up. The stroll confuses the mind and the bias will dissipate as hidden trade setups appear out of nowhere.

The big move hides just beyond the extremes of price congestion. Intermediate highs or lows within the boundaries of a range point to major breakouts when price violates them. They also locate major fade levels where the smart money recognizes that ranges persist longer than trends. First identify these important features through examination of the charting landscape. Then, rather than jump in with the crowd, wait for the herd's reaction to these pivots before deciding which way to make the trade.

UNDERSTANDING PRICE BREAKS

Trade new high breakouts differently than markets retracing old numbers. A special condition signals when stocks trend through new highs: no built-in supply of losers exists within that time frame. Price can easily go vertical when supply doesn't overhang the stock from a larger trend. Pullback strategies often fail in this environment. During these momentum markets, swing traders may need to enter near highs rather than pullbacks and manage risk without close support under positions.

One typical signal for a new high momentum trade prints a tight flag at the top of expanding price right after a breakout. This common pattern appears on both 5-minute and weekly charts. As trends jump to new highs, bars congest while price searches for the next crowd to carry it higher. Congestion near the top of the range generates strong demand that attracts the needed greed. Price pierces the top of the flag and ejects into a vertical move.

Breakouts and breakdowns attract many participants but require precise timing to turn a profit. Insiders know that these hot spots attract dumb money. They initiate whipsaws after each volume surge to shake out weak hands. This ensures that the majority enters positions just as the market reverses. Swing traders rarely run with the emotional crowd and never with these frantic momentum plays.

Effective momentum trading requires thorough analysis of the intended execution level before price strikes it. Plan to enter the position right at that number or pass up the trade. These volatile conditions may require breaking some of the rules that govern normal risk management. For example, a pre-open limit order might provide the best entry for a hot stock when many participants avoid this strategy at other times.

Swing traders can join the momentum club, get filled way above their comfort level, and still walk away with a nice profit. But this practice will crush their hopes of success over the long term. Breakouts and breakdowns consistently lack easy escape routes. This fast-paced environment will chew up participants that don't rely on flat stop losses. And glamorous momentum positions can trigger heavy losses but still maintain all the technicals of a good setup. That's a formula for disaster.

Flat percentage or dollar stop losses will avoid serious problems. But swing strategy depends on price pivot behavior against known S/R barriers. New high trends often display no simple price floors. Whenever possible, enter breakout trades close to the point that proves the setup was wrong if price violates it. And consider that markets offer tremendous opportunities that don't rely on strong momentum.

T A B L E   3.1

Pattern Play—Quick Tips for Successful Swing Trading

- No two patterns behave alike. Triangles and pennants are ideal shapes that rarely occur with perfection in the real world.
- Three strikes and you're out. Price should break out of a pattern no later than the third time a key price point is tested, to the upside or downside. Failure of price to reach the third test in either direction favors a breakout in the opposite direction.
- Use the rule of alternation to predict how a pattern will develop. Corrections should alternate between simple and complex shapes in a series of impulses.
- Every pattern has an underlying positive or negative appearance that represents the likely outcome. So if it looks bullish or bearish, it probably is.
- The sharp breakout above an ascending triangle often signals the climax of an entire series of rallies.
- Rising wedges can lead to very powerful upside breakouts, but they are too undependable to enter until the move is underway.
- Demand perfection on the inverse head and shoulders reversal. They attract attention only when every rule is fulfilled: the neckline must line up correctly, the two shoulder lows must be at the same price, and the breakout must pierce other known resistance (MAs, gaps, etc.) on high volume.
- Double triangles that form after strong rallies are very bullish for a new move of equal size to the one that occurred just before the first triangle.
- The contraction in price range and volatility that follows a new pattern seeks a natural balance point corresponding with the location of the new impulse. Use Bollinger Bands and rate of change indicators to identify this pivot in advance.
- Every pattern is a solvable puzzle defined by support, resistance, and volatility. Look for highs and lows to point to a natural exit spot in time. Volatility should decrease into this apex and expand out of it.
- Volume should dry up as each of the three rallies comprising the head and shoulders pattern uses up all the available bull power. The lower the volume on the right shoulder rally, the higher the odds that the neckline will eventually break.
- Excellent long trades on the head and shoulders can be initiated at the right shoulder neckline when accumulation diverges positively from the bearish pattern. Also watch closely when the neckline breaks but price immediately pops back above it and indicates that few stops were waiting.
- The deeper the downslope of the head and shoulders neckline, the greater the prospect for a bearish break. Stay away from ascending necklines completely. These patterns easily evolve into sideways motion.
- Calculate the Fibonacci relationship between the left shoulder peak and the head length of the head and shoulders pattern. If the left shoulder topped at a Fib retracement such as 62%, the right shoulder should go no higher and may be a good short sale entry point.

F I G U R E   3.10

Copper Mountain expands out of a channel break and gaps to new highs. It then forms a high, tight flag before adding 50% to price in a few weeks. Notice how the flag sits on the top of three vertical bars. It pulls back to test both the breakout gap and channel in a small hammer bar before leaping to higher ground.

Daily   (Right) CMTN - COPPER MOUNTAIN NETWORKS INC   Bar

Breakouts and breakdowns tend to occur in waves. Quite often each surge prints at a similar angle, duration, and extent to the one that precedes it. Use this tendency to predict when the break will occur and how many points that price will move when it ejects. Between each sharp thrust, price will often stop and congest until volatility winds down and stability returns. Trade analysis yields the greatest benefit right at this point. Study the prior waves and locate any trendlines or channels. Count the number of bars within prior congestion zones. Locate the S/R level where a violation will likely trigger the next trend wave. Look at price ranges for the last few bars or candles. Do they narrow or expand? Plan the setup now and decide what to do if the stock gaps through S/R on the next bar.

Price breaks often stop dead after the first surge and pull back very close to the original S/R barrier. This second chance provides an excellent entry point. Although momentum traders watch their profits drop as the market retraces, the underlying technicals actually strengthen and encourage new entry. Sometimes price will jump back through the barrier that ignited the original breakout and drop into the old range. But if the break occurred with good participation, pushed well out of old congestion, and volume dries up during the pullback, get on board fast. The countertrend will rebound quickly and with little warning.

Action speeds up as price breaks free of congestion. Expanding bars or candles reflect surging momentum, regardless of time frame. Expansion equals profit. Swing traders who enter the first pullback try to pocket a big piece of the next price thrust. This strategy becomes extremely important in exit planning. Natural bias assumes that the position should be held until momentum and price movement slow. But this exposes a large profit percentage to natural retracement. Protect the position by using bar expansion patterns to signal the exit. Combine this method with Bollinger Band resistance and grab a high profit exit just as the market turns against the crowd.

RECOGNIZING TRENDS

Markets alternate between constricted range and directional trend. Ranges emit negative feedback, a directionless state in which cumulative bars or indicators wobble between defined boundaries. Trends emit positive feedback, in which each bar or indicator builds on the previous one and clearly points in a single direction. This powerful axis overrides all other considerations for the swing trader. These opposing forces constantly battle to print the varied patterns that form the core of technical analysis.

This primary trend-range axis underlies price charts through all time frames and markets. Learn to recognize each element by watching how price reacts to important levels. Then focus on key relationships that effectively predict market movement through convergence-divergence over a small number of bars or candles. Remember to answer the three important trend-range questions in every setup analysis:

- What is the current trend or range intensity?
- What is the expected direction of the next price move?
- When will this move occur?

Trading profits depend on the trend-range axis. Individual stocks struggle through a constant cycle of synergy, balance, and conflict as trend intensity and direction shift alignment through different time frames. The most dynamic trends arise when multiple periods stack up into directional positive feedback. The most persistent ranges emerge when divergence generates negative feedback through many views and stalls price change.

Negative feedback initiates many of the classic chart patterns popularized in recent years. The head and shoulders, triangle, and wedge formations all reflect the discordant swings within a rangebound market. Swing traders must recognize new range conditions early and shift out of momentum strategies if they choose to remain in the game. Constricted price action requires selling strength and buying weakness at the extremes of the congestion.

The transition from negative feedback into positive feedback represents a high profit interface. Volatility, bar width, and volume all decline as a rangebound market nears its conclusion. Participation fades and many traders move on to other opportunities. But right at these quiet empty zones (EZs) the odds for price expansion sharply increase. The narrow bars encourage very low-risk entry where even a small move against the position signals a violation.

Examine the overall congestion pattern to identify which side of the trade to enter. The EZ rarely registers on technical indicators since most mathematics can't digest the flatline conditions. Use short-term bar range analysis to locate this interface. The NR7 (the narrowest range bar of the last seven bars) offers one classic method to find the elusive EZ. The next bar after a NR7 will often trigger a major breakout. If it doesn't, the appearance of a NR7-2 (the second NR7 day in a row) may ring an even louder bell. Odds then sharply increase for a major bar expansion event.

The trend-range axis offers all the signals needed to execute original intraday swing trades. Short-term cycles often carry across several days of trading. Prepare multiday views of 5-minute, 15-minute or 1-hour charts. Positive feedback in most markets tends to occur during the volatile first and last hours while negative feedback can persist throughout the rest of the day. Intraday planning remains the same as position trading: locate congestion boundaries and prepare to trade breakouts or fades against them. Remember that classic swing strategies require intraday ranges broad enough to permit decent reward. Range extremes should print at least 2 to 2 1/2 points apart to make the effort pay off.

Price bar expansion-contraction presents a simple visual method for the swing trader to evaluate volatility. Trends generally reflect expanding bars, while rangebound periods exhibit contracting ones. The highest profitability will come when entering a position at the end of a low-volatility period (contracting bar) and exiting on a volatility peak (expanding bar) just as the trend pulls back.

Learn to recognize the early warning signs for a trend change. The evolution from trending into a rangebound or reversing market forces a shift in trading strategies to capitalize on the new conditions. First rise/first failure provides one effective visual tool to beat the competition at this task. Get defensive when price gives up 100% of the last move. Then apply classic swing tactics until the intermediate high or low gets taken out.

TREND MIRRORS

Price remembers. Past battles between bulls and bears leave their mark long after the fight ends. As stocks pass through old price levels, they must continually navigate the trading debris generated by these prior events. These trend powerpoints mark their existence through dramatic S/R zones, sharp volume spikes, and runaway gapping thrusts. But rather than add confusion, this scarred battleground provides technicians with a trading map of incredible value.

Use trend mirrors (TMs) to interpret these volatile chart zones. Look horizontally at past action to predict where price bars should bounce or fail. Current movement will often mimic the angle and extent of past patterns. TMs locate S/R hotspots just as clear air targets bar expansion. When price action swings repeatedly off either side of a mirror, odds increase that bars will act the same way during the next pass. These chart memory levels can act as classic S/R or mark a swing axis for price to shift back and forth. Each type requires an appropriate trading response.

This intricate puzzle of time and price requires skill to solve. The TM landscape defines profitable execution points throughout the range from old low to new high. But an infinite variety of external forces can overcome a stock's natural tendency to reverse at exactly the same level it did in the past. Choppy action may repeat itself when price returns or one singular event may draw so much interest that other relative landscape features become undependable. Pass on low-reward conditions and seek TM levels that stand out dramatically as the current trend pushes towards them. Then seek cross-verification for the anticipated setup through moving averages, central tendency, and retracement tools.

Mirrors have a finite shelf life. As time passes, individual characteristics of prior trends reinforce or soften through subsequent price discovery. Common sense dictates that the more often that support holds through testing, the stronger it becomes. So when price finally breaks support, odds increase that it will break again on future swings. This testing creates a simple hierarchy that the swing trader applies to evaluate the strength of these price levels. Use it the same way as trendline analysis. In other words, place larger bets when levels hold for longer periods. Exercise caution on single past events and noisy patterns.

The combination of gaps, spikes, and surging volatility can overwhelm analysis. But beneath this complex landscape lies order and structure. Lay a Fibonacci grid across prior trend movement and many terrain features will stand out right at major retracement levels. Add moving averages to enclose the price activity within known S/R behavior. Draw trendlines and parallel price channels to cross-verify expected turning points. Opportunities should stand out at important price intersections after layers are applied.

Complex price action develops when trend breaks into levels where multiple swings took place in the past. The odds favor a new range of the same duration as prior passages through these zones. These offer excellent setups if they display clear horizontal S/R boundaries. Past persistence improves the odds for successful fades off each edge of the congestion. One quick way to measure the range's potential

F I G U R E   3.11

Trend mirrors build complex price action from the debris of prior bull-bear conflict. Although the puzzle appears difficult at first glance, it grows from simple elements of support and resistance. Start each TM investigation with prior gaps and horizontal price extremes. Then look for sideways congestion and volatile reversals. These key features should predict the most obvious course of events as price returns to test those levels.

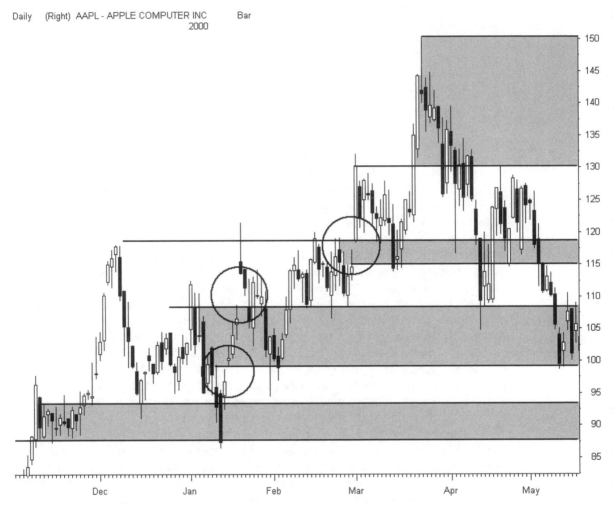

Daily   (Right) AAPL - APPLE COMPUTER INC   Bar
                                     2000

endurance is to count the number of individual swing moves in the past. The higher the total number of swings, the longer the fade strategy should work before price finally surges out of the congestion. The mirror also reveals which side of the swing contains the higher reward or risk. But make sure to look for other landscape features that might signal an earlier breakout from these profitable zones.

Trend mirrors can generate at many different S/R angles. Visible trend emerges from many small trendlets of divergent activity. Both upward and downward trendlets can contribute to price movement at the same time. And normal trendlines or channels may not fully contain these odd impulses. Trendlets will skip several crosses over a period of months or years but then reassert themselves just as everyone concludes that they no longer exist.

Past price action exerts a powerful influence on current price activity. But don't assume that each impulse will stop right at the tick where it did a year or two ago. Trend development combines many diverse forces to reach the printed outcome. But swing traders can still isolate key past influences on current price and make skilled judgments about where major reversals will occur.

Ride the trend coaster and appreciate the diverse elements that influence markets. Focus the eyes narrowly at the beginning of a major move and follow the price action bar by bar until the crowd emotions pop out of the chart. Better yet, page back through the charting program so that the beginning of the move is up against the hard right edge and then step forward one bar at a time. Discover that each trend has a different identity and emotional nature. This sentiment guides how greed and fear will interact to trigger reversals at important turning points. Study a market's TM history to examine these underlying emotions. New profit opportunities will suddenly appear out of the restless action.

CLEAR AIR

Profits depend on the relationship between price and time. When price moves a greater distance over a lesser period of time, individual chart bars and candlesticks expand in length. This phenomenon signals those points of greatest market opportunity. Swing traders enter positions to capitalize on these expansion events. Charting landscapes print many pockets of thin ownership even though trading volume may be high. When price moves into one of these well-defined levels, bars often expand sharply and trigger a surge toward the next barrier.

Clear air (CA) identifies TM price levels where this volatility should spike. The more violent the prior events, the more likely it is that rapid price change will print on the next pass. This tendency allows swing traders to locate outstanding reward through fast visual scans of their favorite stock charts. Search for CA zones through repeated expansion bars that print at the same levels in past price action. Prediction is simple: the more often expansion bars show up at these levels, the more likely that it will happen again.

Not all CAs offer tradable conditions. Some exhibit wild and unpredictable midstream bar reversals. Measure the pattern's dependability from review of the prior passage history. Past swings from one CA extreme to the other with few retracements suggests that the position will not face heavy whipsaws after entry. Target a position right near the zone's edge and plan to exit when price reaches the average number of bars required crossing that region in the past. Clearly defined horizontal extremes permit very profitable swing trades with simple exit strategies.

F I G U R E   3.12

Silicon Graphics paints a jigsaw puzzle of trendlines and channels. Trend mirrors reflect all angles of past price action. Market participants find ways to justify positions at almost every extension of two chart points. This can mask underlying directional movement and cloud effective prediction. Always concentrate on primary trend features but consider that these complex lines will introduce whipsaw and frustration into most setups.

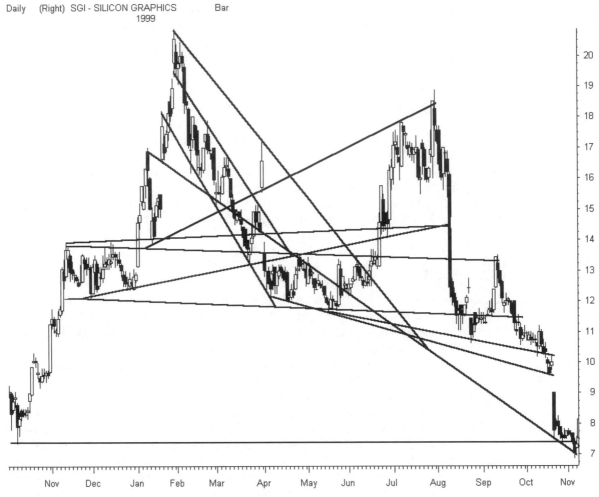

Daily   (Right)   SGI - SILICON GRAPHICS   Bar
                      1999

Congestion limits volatility. Range expansion offers the state of least congestion and greatest volatility. However, it also cautions the swing trader to manage risk closely as opportunity and danger stand side by side. Defense trading must be exercised in the active momentum environment. Clear air space can produce violent reversals. Utilize known S/R and Fibonacci retracement to predict natural swing

F I G U R E   3.13

Clear air pockets may persist for months. Lycos price action shot through this thin 17-point zone repeatedly in 1999. Note at least 16 quick swings of 10 or more points during the event. This chart also points out the danger of CA trades. Sharp and violent reversals characterize price movement, especially during the most volatile phase near the end of the prior trend.

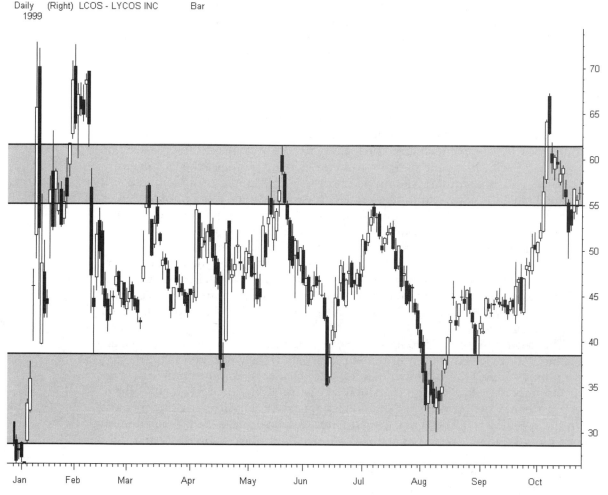

Daily   (Right) LCOS - LYCOS INC   Bar
1999

points in preexisting CA. Use detailed price/volume data from prior passages to target high-probability setups with natural entry and exit triggers.

Target new high CA with detailed Fibonacci projections. These major breaks often print few congestion and swing points that offer good S/R data. But skilled observation suggests that the last 38% of these rallies can exhibit vertical movement. Locate the base for the breakout in the last congestion under the new high and draw an extended Fib grid above the current rally to locate the final CA level. Keep in mind that this strategy requires great discipline since the method doesn't rely on prior passages.

Apply Fibonacci grids after the completion of a clear air series to examine hidden reversal zones not apparent during the event. This will assist planning for the next swing back into the zone. Try to place a grid over new expansion moves to anticipate where opportunities will emerge on next retracement. And always rely on the chart in the next-smaller time frame to pinpoint low-risk execution levels.

SIGNPOSTS

Trends evolve according to cyclic buying and selling behavior that the chart bottles into price bars. Market crowds act through predictable herd instinct at key moments within price development. Signposts identify where this mass crowd behavior should exert itself. Divergent market forces emit nothing but noise the vast majority of the time. Patience requires waiting for major impulses to intersect. Noise reduces and signal emits strongly within these small crossroads. When more impulses enter this convergent zone, signal gets even louder and noise can cease completely. That ringing bell is the sound of profitable opportunity for the swing trader.

The market tea leaves often require great skill to interpret. Fortunately, the swing trader can quickly evaluate each new setup by combining the right elements of trend and time. Signposts point to opportunity within the charting landscape. Double tops, gaps, and stage analysis join other 3D tools to awaken a complex world of market action. But it takes great skill to pick the right tools for each individual analysis.

This challenge can intimidate novices, but the market never reveals its secrets the same way twice. While an arithmetic chart shows a weak trendline, the log version may support the trade with strong price channels. Volume study may provide the important key to one execution but be safely ignored on many others. Rising price may say rally when the Bollinger Bands say selloff. Swing traders must learn the specific applications of each individual resource and develop the intuition to examine the most promising setups with the right ones at precisely the right time.

This vital process may appear complicated or confusing. Use the analogy of the traders' toolbox. Just as a woodworker relies on many different saws to build a cabinet, swing traders must apply the right set of tools to build successful positions. While the woodworker uses some items daily, others fulfill a special purpose that arises infrequently. The swing trader looks at similar chart features each day but must pull up special resources to answer difficult questions. In the end both skilled craftsman know when and how to use each individual tool to create their final work of art.

The charting landscape uncovers signposts through the convergence of two or more elements. This cross-verification (CV) process offers an objective method

F I G U R E   3.14

Signposts align through different charts to predict important price action. As Conexant undergoes a change of character, gaps from two time frames signal the swing trader's attention. The large hole-in-the-wall on the daily chart ends the powerful rally and sets up reversal conditions. Price retraces 50% to the gap wall and rolls into a long decline. Note the small breakout gap and double top on the 60-minute chart. Declining price violates the top support and fills this gap. This signals the end of the larger bear bounce. A pullback to the broken gap then allows a low-risk short sale before CNXT drops another 13 points.

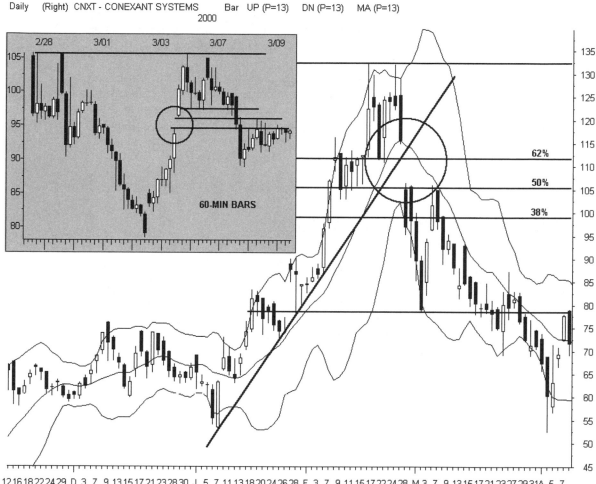

to determine the odds of success for any trade entry. CV power lies in this linear mechanism: the more intersecting points in a trade setup, the higher the trade probability. Study the landscape using the right tools to locate intersecting points within the evolving Pattern Cycle. At its core, this simple workflow sums up all the preparation and analysis required before the execution of a trade.

The novice typically misses many signposts, while a skilled trader may only require price to uncover that market's mysteries. Newer participants should rely upon checklists to ensure that their charts receive complete attention. Many software programs and online charting modules allow extensive customization. Use these tools to flip through many examination modes to find that needle in the trading haystack.

Price gaps mark powerful single-point signposts. They expose hidden S/R barriers when properly placed within a trend. Gaps come in many varieties, and swing traders must drill themselves in their various incarnations to avoid bad decision-making when it matters most. For example, intraday traders use opening breakout gaps to pinpoint momentum entry and exhaustion gaps to sell short when price retraces to test them. Mixing the two leads to unfortunate results.

VOLUME AND THE PATTERN CYCLE

Crowd action-reaction emits volume benchmarks at key price levels. Measure this unique past participation against current activity to determine the relative importance of fresh events. Regardless of holding period, watch these primary reference points when price returns to test key levels. But always examine volume within the proper context. A single bar's narrow impact may lead to poor interpretation of that market's underlying direction. Use volume history analysis to place the recent action into proper perspective within the recent trend.

The intermediate daily time frame provides a common basis for volume moving average computation. The 50- or 60-day VMA contrasts prior crowd participation with the current action for all liquid stocks through all exchanges. Use this simple measurement as a central tendency tool that gauges the crowd's emotional intensity in real-time. The crowd sends a significant signal when volume exceeds 150% of the daily average. If daily volume falls below 50% of the average, look for dull and directionless trading to characterize that market.

Volume peaks and valleys occur naturally within normal price evolution. They also tend to alternate in a cyclical pattern that parallels trend-range axis phases. Compare price placement within that axis against volume's central tendency deviation to identify impending feedback shifts. For example, expect lower than normal participation within extended range formations. When volume suddenly peaks well above average within these constricted zones, it often signals an imminent breakout into a new trend.

Don't be fooled by seasonal volume aberrations. January draws significant new cash into the markets as investors replenish mutual fund coffers. Summer trading limps through the lowest participation of the year. Insiders and institutions take off for the beaches during holiday markets throughout the year, leaving few movers and shakers on the scene. And options expiration triggers heavy position shifts the middle Friday of each month.

ACCUMULATION-DISTRIBUTION

Price movement generates through a value exchange between interested parties. As markets cycle through buying and selling pressure, transactions slowly reflect the willingness of participants to own stock at higher prices or dispose of it at lower prices. This poorly understood evolution defines an issue's accumulation-distribution (acc-dis). Acc-dis evolves continuously and often travels a different path than price development. For this reason, avoid the tendency to expect volume spikes to translate immediately into sustainable momentum.

Shareholders buy and sell stocks for many different reasons. Short-term crowds tend to focus much more on current price than long-term investors. They can also flip stocks very quickly. Institutions lack this retail liquidity and must build or eliminate large positions over a longer time frame. As the largest fish in the pond, their slow movement inhibits the sentiment evolution that drives other participants. This induces backfilling and testing of new trend movement. For example, watch how price swings back and forth repeatedly through a key emotional barrier (such as the 200-day moving average) while undergoing a long-term recovery from a bear market.

Acc-dis may lead or lag price rate of change. Often one measure will pull sharply ahead and then wait patiently for the other to catch up before proceeding on another leg. Swing traders build predictive indicators to capture this mechanism and track divergence between these two primary forces. As the slower element, acc-dis tends to pull price toward it rather than the other way around. In these divergent conditions, look for reversals just after price strikes overbought or oversold levels.

This tension assists trade analysis near tests of old highs and lows. These important zones respond better to acc-dis than other price levels. Both breakouts and breakdowns need crowd support to proceed. When a stock hits a new high, only significant participation will carry it higher. When a stock hits a new low, a fearful supply of sellers will generate further decline. For this reason, swing traders measure divergence near these extremes to choose whether to fade price or go with a momentum break. Expect a reversal as price barriers exert their influence if acc-dis indicators suggest weak participation.

Avoid decision-making based on very short-term acc-dis readings. The true nature of accumulation or distribution often remains hidden from all but the insiders. Large players, such as institutions and mutual funds, don't want to broadcast

F I G U R E   3.15

On Balance Volume presents a classic accumulation-distribution tool to examine new highs and lows. Over a month before Yahoo ejects into an astounding millennium rally, OBV pushes into uncharted territory and waits for its companion. By the time that price breaks through its old high, the strong accumulation allows an immediate burst to higher prices without further consolidation.

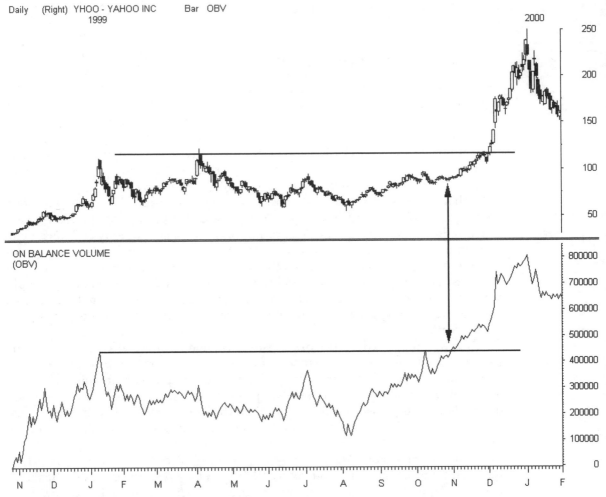

their intentions, for fear that the news will move the market before they complete their strategies. So they slowly unwind positions into strength or build them during weakness. This significant contrary activity clouds the interpretation and true meaning of short-term volume surges.

The trading flow may align with neither accumulation nor distribution during quieter phases. In a mixed fashion, bulls and bears evenly disperse the lower daily volume. Stocks rise or fall on broader market conditions in this environment. Mundane events can sharply affect trend without the shareholder's common voice. Try to avoid this noisy midrange between enthusiastic accumulation and fearful distribution when choosing short-term positions.

The best swing trading stocks have a float over 10-million shares and daily volume over 2-million. Volume-based indicators work extremely well with this broad participation. But be aware that Nasdaq double counts transactions, once on the buy and once on the sell. This can distort elements of crowd behavior. And always avoid acc-dis in the analysis of thin issues. Large holders try to manipulate the public view of such stocks to build a rosy picture that benefits their own pocketbooks.

TRENDS AND VOLUME

Expect volume to increase in the direction of the primary trend. Look for higher volume on up bars than down bars as prices rise during rallies. Reverse this during selloffs. In uptrends, more volume on sell-offs than rallies generates divergence that may foretell an impending change in trend. In downtrends, divergence again signals when volume shrinks on sell-offs and rises on rallies.

Volume can flash an early signal for an impending reversal when it deviates sharply from the VMA during an active trend. Declining directional volume suggests a loss of crowd interest. After awhile the stock may fall of its own weight. Alternatively, when volume peaks too sharply or quickly, it can short circuit and blow off movement in the prevailing price direction. These high-volume climax events wash out both buyers and sellers as efficiently as lack of interest. They often mark major tops or bottoms.

Moderate volume supports underlying trends for long periods of time. It often reflects participation very close to the VMA with few spikes or valleys. The flow of enthusiasm or discouragement generates price change that feeds on itself and allows one group after another to toss coins into the wishing well. Look for this phasing action on log charts that print rhythmic 45° patterns with repeated pullbacks to short-term moving averages.

New trends awaken with price or volume leading the emerging directional force. Better trading opportunities with fewer whipsaws appear if volume builds first. When crowd enthusiasm leads price, acc-dis should exert a strong pull on its twin. Like a coiled spring, price eventually snaps forward to relieve the tension. For obvious reasons, swing traders want to enter positions just before this happens. But precise timing can frustrate the most promising volume-based strategies. Acc-dis price divergence can persist for long periods without quick release.

New breakouts depend on volume support. Subsequent trend survival requires that price and volume move into convergence very early after the move. As price thrusts into all-time highs or pretraveled TMs, current acc-dis must support the next move. Fresh price levels place hidden demands on volume. New high breakouts require ample participation as well as alignment between acc-dis and

FIGURE   3.16

3Com collapses after a vertical high-volume blow-off event. Crowd frenzy reaches a peak as the technology behemoth spins off the Palm Pilot division. The new IPO starts to trade and no one remains to carry COMS higher. It falls quickly from its own weight and traps an overhead supply of bag holders that ensures a bumpy ride for months to come.

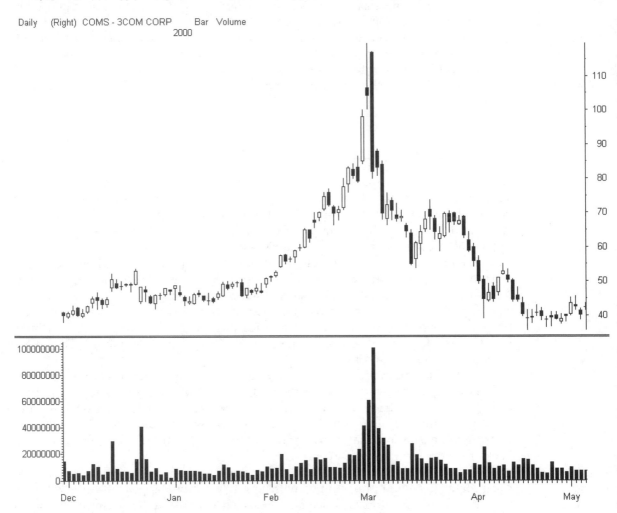

Daily   (Right) COMS - 3COM CORP   Bar Volume
2000

price. Breakouts into TM levels force volume to digest past supply and emotional scars. Divergence builds quickly and triggers sharp whipsaws when new participation at these levels can't absorb the resistance.

Volume often spikes well above short-term VMAs during major breakouts. Greed and fear drive participation as the crowd recognizes the active trend. Volume can quickly exceed historical levels and surge for many bars at new highs or lows.

Both strong uptrends and downtrends display similar volume signatures. High participation prints sharp gaps at emotional trend peaks, while short pullbacks exhibit declining interest. Few wish to exit trend-following positions in this active environment.

Swing traders watch closely for signs of a blow-off as trend advances. This important reversal reveals itself through volume that spikes well above recent action while related price bars expand and turn in failure. This climax event flags the end of the current trend and beginning for a new range period. Use candlestick patterns to quickly uncover these major reversals. Dark cloud cover, shooting star, and doji patterns all print frequently during blow-offs.

The trend's last phase reflects the most active crowd participation in a bull-bear cycle. This frantic action corresponds with Elliott's fifth-wave parabolic activity and sets the stage for the ensuing climax burnout. Once the event occurs, volume again surges when price approaches these levels from above or below. Extremes that print during blow-offs take great participation to violate. For this reason, fade early pullbacks to these climax bars through classic swing tactics. The reversal odds remain very strong as long as volume dries up on the move back toward the high or low.

CONGESTION AND VOLUME

New students of technical analysis expect to memorize well-known patterns and book quick profits when they locate them on their favorite stock charts. But flag and triangle formations don't fill wallets without considerable effort. Successful swing traders must study the chaotic swings within each congestion pattern to predict both direction and timing for the eventual breakout.

Volume characteristics change as markets swing between negative and positive feedback. Negative feedback generates much less interest from the crowd. These rangebound periods absorb recent price change volatility and prepare for new thrusting movement. Investors and traders take profits during these quiet conditions in an orderly manner that lowers the emotional fire that induces volume spikes.

Study histograms to reveal whether bulls or bears win small battles within a developing pattern. Profitable breakouts depend on accurate interpretation of these shifting crowd emotions. Short-term bursts of acc-dis within the confines of a constricted range often expose the underlying market tendency and required time for positive feedback to appear. Compare the small peaks of buying and selling pressure within the swings of the congestion pattern. When volume increases on short rallies and declines on dips, expect the bull's successful outcome. Alternatively, a series of lower bars with increasing volume reveals fear and often signals an eventual breakdown. But regardless of direction, expect volume to decline overall as a new pattern draws to a conclusion.

Volume should taper off and dry up as negative feedback builds. A trendline drawn above the volume histogram will downslope to reflect this declining condition. Near the end of range development, price and volume synchronize at the empty zone, that quiet terminus between negative and positive feedback. Participation reaches its nadir as the crowd turns away in boredom within this neutral interface. Watch closely from this center of apathy for evidence of the awakening trend. Use subsequent volume as one measure to locate an impending setup. When properly identified, participation on subsequent bars provides valuable feedback on the direction and strength for the impending move. For example, false breakout odds increase if price surges out of an apex without sufficient volume.

The crowd builds trend through volume. Hidden battles take place during negative feedback that impact the eventual market direction. Positions square out and a bias emerges that supports or diverges from the recent trend. Swing traders seek to uncover this prejudice through analysis of rangebound price bars. Begin by asking several important questions, as given in Table 3.2.

INTRADAY TRADING VOLUME

Avoid over-interpretation of intraday volume trends. Sixty percent or more of total daily participation occurs during the first and last hours. Swing traders design signals to trigger during favorable volume, but this intraday bias distorts output that applies to very short time frames. Limit most intraday examination to histo-

---

T A B L E   3.2

Uncovering Market Bias through Volume

Does volume increase or decrease at relative highs or lows?
  Range conditions generate small-scale trading patterns. Evaluate volume spikes as a stock swings back and forth to reveal small bursts of greed or fear within the crowd. One of these emotional forces will eventually ignite to ramp price toward the next level.
Is there a failed rally just outside congestion on higher volume than the rest of the range?
  Insiders often gun the buy stops to take out that side of the market. This reveals a bias toward taking the market down.
Is there a failed breakdown just outside congestion on higher volume than the rest of the range?
  Insiders often gun the sell stops to take out that side of the market. This reveals a bias toward taking the market up.
Do higher-volume days occur on narrow range or wide range bars and do bulls or bears win these days?
  Higher volume on wide bars suggests the market being pushed to generate transactions. Higher volume on narrow bars suggests accumulation or distribution that depends on the outcome of the bar.
Does a silent alarm signal appear?
  Certain volume events within ranges overcome all prior activity. Market character immediately changes when a massive volume day shows up.

---

grams. Also consider eliminating lower-pane volume indicators to focus attention on the time and sales ticker. This real-time oscillator provides all the crowd information needed to execute successfully within very short-term holding periods.

Routine intraday volume consistently displays a high noise-to-signal ratio for all but the most liquid stocks. Intermittent peaks and valleys on 5-minute histograms contain few predictive properties and fail badly when block trades pass through the system. These institutional blocks distort the trading picture since large transactions often scroll well after the actual execution takes place.

Noise decreases as liquidity increases. For example, the technology behemoths generate unique intraday volume properties as a massive crowd generates a virtual index market. Sufficient participation within each tick allows fluid data measurement and accurate price forecasting. The best volume signals in this liquid environment come at short-term tops or bottoms. Histogram spikes that converge with clear reversal bars trade as reliably as those that print on a daily or weekly chart.

Effective intraday trading studies the short-term impact of volume characteristics on the daily chart. This data identifies markets that are ripe for new opportunities as well as those best avoided. As current market price approaches past high-volume battle zones, intraday traders can expect a repeat performance. This advance warning allows them to watch specific markets for signs of increased volatility. Daily histograms also pinpoint developing breakouts and runaway trend moves that mark the most profitable of all intraday setups.

Many stocks become good intraday trading vehicles under the right circumstances. Sudden news events, warnings, or alliances can evoke several days of high-volume activity on relatively thin issues. Spreads narrow sharply as participants jump in and out of these temporary profit vehicles. Use watch list filters or online stock sites nightly to uncover and capitalize upon these temporary gems.

SILENT ALARM

A hidden market hotspot triggers the silent alarm (SA). This unusual zone reflects intense crossroads of buying and selling pressure. Emotional participation swells volume in a single bar, but a painful standoff develops between bulls and bears. Price sits still as friction reaches a boiling point. Swing traders who recognize the developing SA stand aside but then take positions in whatever direction that price finally ejects out of that bar's range.

Short-term volume may issue a powerful signal under special circumstances. The SA rarely occurs but flags a significant profit opportunity. The alarm sounds when price action meets three conditions:

- Volume exceeds 3 times to 5 times the average 50–60 bar VMA.
- Price bar range measures below the average of the last 7 bars.
- The price bar sits within congestion not broken by the volume event.

Alarms should not print a breakout through S/R. Price must remain trapped when the dust settles on that bar's activity. Verify prior emotional trading at the same price level through TM investigation. Also make certain the high volume doesn't reflect a prescheduled transaction such as a secondary offering.

READING THE CROWD

Volume breathes differently than price. Narrow action may yield sharp emotional behavior or an unexpected lack of participation. Each outcome carries different consequences for swing traders. This crowd-measurement tool works well on daily charts but consistently undermines intraday signals. It offers both early warnings and dead ends, often at the same time. Volume reflects a crowd psychosis that often makes little sense in the short term but turns highly predictable at key intersections of trend and time.

Successful swing trading requires skillful interpretation of the herd mentality that drives price change. Develop a seasoned understanding of volume's impact on the stock chart. Learn when to use it and how to ignore it when required. Always pay close attention to the evolution of crowd participation as well as the peaks and valleys. This often provides the clearest signals for major reversals and impending breakouts.

Opportunity arises from recognition of key volume events and correct interpretation of the odd crowd tension that builds around breakout and breakdown levels. Invoke both left- and right-brain functions to measure this complex struggle. Human nature channels greed and fear between stable boundaries most of the time. But the speculator's pocketbook depends upon those rare moments when crowd forces get thrown out of balance.

Many elements of the charting landscape read the emotional crowd and try to predict its next move. Volume addresses this difficult task better than any other tool. But keep in mind that profits depend on price change alone. Realize that price itself offers the best leading indicator for price change throughout the Pattern Cycle. As it rises, it predicts that further gains will follow. As it falls, odds increase that it will fall even further.

BEAR MARKETS

Modern participants have rarely faced severe bear market conditions. Most players wrongly believe that profits will continue even in a major decline as long as they just flip their long strategies upside down. But worldwide bear markets present difficult conditions for most short-side participants. Trend-following tactics often fail as sudden squeezes offer no escape and induce heavy losses.

A special personality marks each secular bear market. Inflation or oil prices may drive some while overheated economics or asset overvaluation awakens others. But bear markets all display one common characteristic: they make it much harder to turn short-term profits than typical bull markets. Swing traders should

F I G U R E   3.17

Dish Networks prints a silent alarm before jumping 15 points. The high-volume event ends with a small price range and the session never pushes DISH through resistance at 40. But the next morning the stock breaks out in a vertical rally that carries another three sessions.

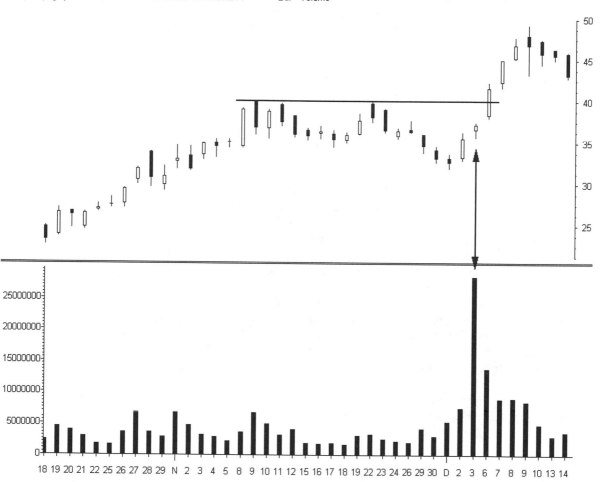

Daily   (Right) DISH - ECHOSTAR COMMUNICATIONS'A'   Bar Volume

prepare for the next downturn now so that they can survive and profit while waiting for better conditions.

Pattern Cycles suggest effective short sale tactics during individual stock bear markets. But volume drops sharply through most phases of a broad worldwide bear depression. This induces illiquidity and dangerous trading conditions. Spreads widen and slippage increases for both entries and exits. Opportunities vanish as good short sale inventories dry up at many broker-dealers. Reliable information disappears and good sources close up shop due to a lack of interest.

Bear markets appear through many time frames. They can represent grand bear markets, cyclical bear markets, intermediate-term corrections, or minor down-swings. Minor downtrends can last a few minutes or days. Longer ones may persist for several months. Grand bear markets can span decades and embed multiple cyclical bull-bear swings. These cyclical swings pose the greatest threat for modern swing traders. Historically this particular bull-bear cycle lasts about four years, with 25% (or one year) of that time spent in active bear conditions.

Bears shake out the market infrastructure and realign prevailing psychology. The actual price decline often takes up only a small percentage of the time that downtrend conditions persist. As with stocks, indices fall faster than they rise and the selling spasms tend to end quickly. The rest of the time the market meanders back and forth on low volume while it tries to heal. This offers another clue why trading during these times can be very difficult. The typical bear market doesn't end in the high-volume capitulation that marked volatile corrections in the 1990s. It slowly heals as value investors start to move back into positions. Many other participants will have little interest in the markets by that time.

The financial media condition traders and investors to believe that a simple 20% retracement off the index highs constitutes an active bear market. This comforts many participants, the small drop in their portfolios giving them battle credentials. But technical and psychological damage mark bear conditions with far greater ac-curacy than flat percentages. This type of pain has rarely been experienced over the past two decades.

A bear market corrects the excesses of a specific market uptrend. It retraces according to classic Fibonacci mathematics. When the prior rally displays a mod-erate advance, the bear market may not need a great pullback to correct the im-balance. But when market rallies extend to historical levels, conditions favor a very deep pullback that may take several years of basing before a new and sustainable rally can begin.

Swing traders should act defensively through cyclical bear market conditions unless the intraday charts signal opportunity. Rallies and selloffs that print at that level provide excellent short-term setups. Tighten the holding period and step into

T A B L E   3.3

Bear Market Severity

Bear Market	Percent Decline	Months to Recover
1973–1974	59%	48
1983–1984	31%	18
1987–1988	35%	20
1989–1990	33%	7
1998	29%	2

as many positions as the temporary market environment allows. Try to anticipate where short covering rallies will likely erupt. Get in along with the insiders and use the short seller's panic to turn a profit. Then find natural reversal levels and flip over to the short side after the squeeze completes. Follow the daily chart for key turning points but avoid being tossed around by the frequent tests of investor hope and fear.

Cyclical bear markets print according to the same mechanics as individual stocks and futures. Look for a double bottom or the Big W to signal the end of a major selloff. These emotional periods offer excellent longer-term profit for those with precise market timing. But as with other falling knives, entry requires execution against popular sentiment. Watch the technicals closely and act when cross-verification opens up the next bull phase.

4
C H A P T E R

BUILDING A SWING
TRADING STRATEGY

SYSTEMS AND METHODS

Swing traders must make the right choices to build an effective strategy. Seek original techniques that work in diverse market conditions and stand apart from the crowd's madness. Adopt a customized holding period that fits the personal lifestyle and permits careful position management. Spend more time controlling losses than seeking gains, and prepare to adjust everything as profits grow.

Opportunity depends on inefficiency. Price patterns expose inefficient markets that discharge their instability through rapid price change. Swing traders evolve fresh strategies to capture these events and build quick profits. But as high-odds tactics gain recognition, the crowd seizes them and inefficiency starts to close. Professionals then fade the setup and generate whipsaws that shake out many speculators. This intense competition for profit forces many swing traders to cut and run. They jump quickly to the next method that works, with the crowd always one step behind.

An effective market edge generates consistent trading profits. But most modern strategies must adapt continuously to the curse of common knowledge. Specialize on a single pattern for as long as it produces good results. But notice when unexpected outcomes start to undermine profitability. Stay focused and recognize immediately when the crowd discovers that pattern's virtues. Then have the confidence to move on quickly to the next original idea.

Emotional instability ensures that stock positions turn into surrogate spouses, bosses, and wayward offspring. Control your personal life first before taking a trade, or the market will do it for you. Keep in mind one disturbing fact: more swing traders will fail due to lack of discipline than lack of knowledge. Successful execution depends much more on the executioner than the strategy.

Profits require both effective risk management and emotional self-discipline. The greed-fear axis clouds the mind and opens the trading game to great danger. Use cold, objective rules to manage emotions and avoid the fatal traps that quickly end a career. Engage frequently in tactical role-playing and visualize appropriate responses to different market conditions. Hope for the best but always prepare for the worst with each new position. Both extremes will happen regularly over time.

MOMENTUM TRADING

Pattern Cycles generate powerful strategies to capitalize on changing conditions and major turning points. But most participants fall into the momentum game and never learn other tactics. While the greedy eye sees many rising trends with few pullbacks, most still lose money chasing a hot market. They realize too late that momentum demands precise timing and strict emotional control.

Greed-fear exerts tremendous force during dynamic price movement and clouds careful preparation. Ironically, initial gains can be dramatic for new momentum traders. Beginner's luck and fearlessness combine to make those first weeks or months very rewarding. But results often change quickly. Momentum traders at all levels lack sound risk management.

Focus on the big gain dulls awareness of the big loss. Market insiders adjust quickly to the momentum crowd and generate sharp whipsaws to shake out the weak hands. Confused participants start buying tops and selling bottoms with regularity. Or they abandon their rules and try to survive by holding old winners through violent selloffs and waiting for a decent bounce.

Sharp trends print wide range bars and many gapping moves. This volatility increases risk and inhibits safe entry-exit planning. Swing traders rely on S/R to define execution and reward targeting. Most momentum markets display few common landscape features. This requires entry without a clear violation level that proves that the setup was wrong. Only 3D charting or arbitrary stop loss keeps the speculator out of intense danger in this blind environment.

Momentum trading can be mastered. Three disciplines will break destructive habits and reprogram trading for success:

- *Abandon the adrenaline rush:* Forget the excitement. Profit depends upon detached and disciplined execution.
- *Learn the numbers:* The nature of price movement must be ingrained deeply enough to allow spontaneous decision-making during the trading day.
- *Cross-verify:* Objective measurements must filter unconscious bias.

Reduce momentum risk through 3D charting. Identify reward for the time frame of interest. Confirm that the stock shows no important divergences that may

FIGURE   4.1

The markets offer the momentum crowd many opportunities to fail. The neophyte sees continuous price change during this winter rally, but the active trends last only a short time. During one segment of this volatile move, Rambus prints 15 trend bars compared to 53 sideways range bars.

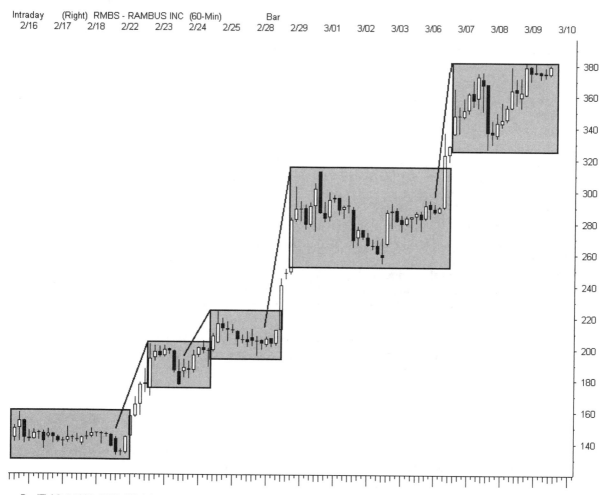

signal the end of the move or an impending reversal. Then guide execution and position management through the chart in the next-lower dimension. When a strong trend explodes on the daily chart, use the 60-minute bar to pick out lower-risk entry and define natural exit points. For intraday positions, control the 5-minute bar breakout by using a 1-minute chart to locate swing levels.

Successful momentum strategy requires solid tape reading skills. Demand on the time and sales ticker reveals the inner workings of rapid price movement. Both retail (small-lot) and professional (large-lot) traders need to participate in a sharp trend or it will fail. Watch the crowd's response to support numbers very closely. If the swing trader can't feel their urgency to get on board, perhaps it isn't there. Use round numbers to gauge demand when the action pushes into uncharted territory. Multiples of 10 often present strong resistance in place of classic S/R levels. Understand the motives of the big players that drive fast markets and ride their coattails to gain a needed edge. And if big lots start to move against a rally, be prepared to join them.

Time-of-day tendencies cultivate profit and danger zones. As the market opens, overnight imbalance and fresh retail cash trigger volatility that resolves through price change. Insiders guide stop gunning exercises and fade trends through the lunch hour's negative feedback. The final hour arrives, just in time to resolve many complex themes with sharp breakouts or breakdowns. And through it all, intraday buying and selling oscillates in an orderly 90-minute cycle.

Technical analysis uncovers momentum secrets as it exposes insider deception and herd behavior. Verify all fast markets through both patterns and indicators. Proper application will reduce failed entries because it invokes natural risk management. Always trade by the numbers and not the news. Use cold logic to painlessly exit marginal positions and move on quickly to the next opportunity.

Physics teaches that an object in motion tends to remain in motion. Momentum profits depend on this well-understood mechanism. Moving averages set to multiple time frames reveal trend velocity through their relationships with each other. Measure this acceleration-deceleration with a classic MACD indicator or apply MA ribbons and watch them spread or contract over different time periods. For obvious reasons, always seek acceleration cross-verification before momentum trade execution.

Swing traders apply original tactics to each phase of the Pattern Cycle. At new highs, they execute momentum setups that rely on sound risk management. When market conditions change, they move swiftly on to fresh ideas that reflect the new inefficiencies. Always opportunistic, they seek the next profit as a predator looks for a vulnerable meal.

Momentum strategies fail through most market conditions. Stocks trend only fifteen to twenty percent of the time. Constricted ranges bind price during the rest of its existence. Trading longevity requires diverse skills through both trending and congested markets. Be flexible enough to shift from one strategy to the other as feedback loops alternate between positive and negative. In other words, adapt tactics quickly to changing market conditions rather than wait for those limited times when the environment favors the hot stock.

COUNTERTREND TRADING

Constricted ranges dictate countertrend plays. This classic swing strategy uses clearly marked boundaries to buy weakness and sell strength. When S/R draws strong congestion, sell short as price tests resistance and go long when it falls into support. Use the charting landscape to guide low-risk execution levels. Keep in

F I G U R E   4.2

Short-term volatility shakes out intraday traders during these six hours of choppy Nextel action. Meaningless price swings of 2 to 2 ½ points mask the underlying downtrend, squeeze shorts and relieve weak hands of their stock positions. Many intraday trends respond to conflicting intermarket cycles that ensure a bumpy rise for the momentum crowd. Look for convergence between indices, futures, and equities when trading short-term momentum.

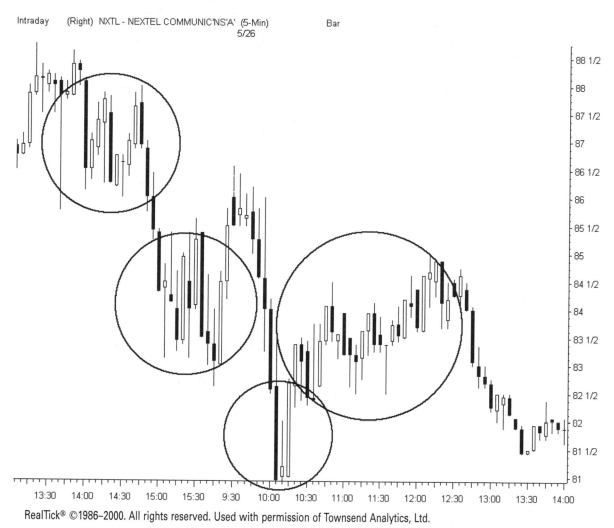

Intraday   (Right) NXTL - NEXTEL COMMUNIC'NS'A' (5-Min)   Bar
                                        5/26

mind that the first thrust into S/R usually offers the best fade position and that odds will deteriorate on repeated tests. And remember that swing entry is always very price-sensitive.

Focus the intended execution near a single price level and stick to it. Never chase entry and always maintain a tight stop loss. Countertrend trades must execute with minimum slippage right at or close to known S/R. The swing trader should stand aside if conditions don't allow for this narrow entry. These setups manage risk through small losses taken when positions violate specific S/R zones. A series of larger losses due to poor execution will eliminate a very good profit.

Target reward through examination of the local features. If possible, carry the position until price approaches the other extreme of the range. Broad congestion likely mirrors intermediate S/R that inhibits a quick price thrust across the pattern. Many swing traders find that single direct price moves without retracement provide the best conditions for a profitable exit. Consider getting out as price jumps into that first boundary. If this is the chosen style, the original reward:risk evaluation should confirm that this price target carries enough profit to make the trade worthwhile.

Buying bottoms and selling tops carefully applies countertrend strategies. Major highs and lows attract interest more than any other charting landscape feature. This ensures a large supply of participants but also invites more whipsaws and unexpected outcomes. Apply this primary rule at tests of prior highs and lows: fade the first test after a significant pullback but trade in the direction of the extreme on subsequent tests. Price tends to break out of ranges on the third try (second test of a high or low).

Use small reversal patterns in the chart below the holding period to fade entry near S/R extremes. Adam and Eve patterns and double tops/bottoms present simple formations that apply this 3D technique. Short sales depend on price violating the bottom of the smaller top pattern, while long positions signal when price surges through the top of the smaller bottom pattern. This original method allows low-risk execution close to the larger high or low in anticipation of a favorable price move.

Victor Sperandeo's 2B trade in *Methods of a Wall Street Master* and Raschke and Connor's Turtle Soup in *Street Smarts* both trap the crowd as it leans the wrong way right after price violates a high or low but reverses immediately. As smart traders adopt these contrary tactics, many price extremes face increased danger of a swift reversal after the initial breakout or breakdown. The safest 2B fade strategy lags the crowd before position entry. Let the price action break through key levels but don't execute in the opposite direction until it pops back across support or resistance.

Trade 2B setups defensively. The market may still want to break through the barrier. Ride the subsequent pullback to the first natural swing level and then exit. After a good reaction the trend can reassert itself quickly and take out the old extreme. This follows the wisdom to fade the first test of an old high or low but follow the trend on the second test. Apparent triple bottoms and tops often yield to significant breakouts or breakdowns.

Watch out when a new high or low retraces and forms congestion close to the price extreme. Simple continuation patterns can quickly ignite into new trend thrusts. Stay away from small pennants and short pullbacks when planning 2B entry. The best reversals for this pattern come when a sharp retracement occurs after the first high or low. The subsequent test should then print more price bars

F I G U R E   4.3

The 2B reversal (1) traps participants that sell short into a violation of the last intermediate low. This classic scenario also appears at double tops right after new highs. Enter the reversal as soon as price jumps back within the prior S/R. This Broadvision example also illustrates a clear stop gunning exercise just before the market moves substantially higher. Note how both (2) and (3) offer logical long side entry for the subsequent rally.

Daily   (Right) BVSN - BROADVISION INC   Bar
                 2000

than the decline that precedes it. Also pay close attention to lower-pane indicators as the event approaches. The trade cross-verifies when oscillators diverge from price direction just as the old high or low breaks.

Pullback entry into a strongly trending market represents a major category of swing tactics. This classic setup buys the first sharp decline into support or sells the first bear rally into resistance. Exit depends on many factors, including personal trading style, holding period, and available capital. Subsequent swings also offer safe entry, but risk increases as trends evolve and reach overbought-oversold conditions. In other words, each pullback after the first one has higher odds of being a reversal rather than a continuation pattern. Chapter 8 examines this bread-and-butter swing trade in greater detail.

Central tendency presents high reward: high risk opportunities at the extremes of price action. These tactics work best in congested markets or in the extreme volatility near climax events. The strategy fades price when a long bar thrusts out of a Bollinger Band extreme more than 50% of its entire length. In rangebound markets, odds for success improve substantially when the top or bottom band aligns horizontally just before the violation and price thrusts into known resistance (other than the band itself).

Consider this trade at the end of parabolic rallies and selloffs. The bands will turn close to vertical as these events progress. Look for an intense burst of energy that forces the bar to break halfway or more through the band. This signals the possible climax and invites countertrend entry. But successful execution requires both a skilled hand and excellent timing. Some blowoffs can issue a series of these bars before a violent reversal. Use cross-verification and tight stop loss to manage risk. And master other setups before attempting this dangerous trade.

TRADING TACTICS

Narrow range tactics enter positions in low volatility near the edge of S/R in anticipation of a breakout. Both range-based coiled springs and simple, well-placed congestion generate excellent reward:risk profiles. These unique opportunities may signal through the pattern alone, but look for volatility and price rate of change indicators to verify narrow conditions. Both plots should move toward flatline before a breakout occurs. This indicates that the pattern has a supportive environment but does not flag an impending move. Review coiled spring tactics in Chapter 9 to manage positions with this important contraction event.

Trends advance through major highs and lows after repeated attempts. When congested price tries to break S/R and subsequent bars narrow, they often signal impending breakouts and breakdowns. This tight congestion offers a very narrow execution window before price explodes through the barrier. These interfaces also signal low-risk failure when price rolls and expands slowly in the wrong direction. Focus sharp attention after a first test fades and retraces. The next attempt faces fewer whipsaws because most participants took their shot on the last try.

Many swing traders freeze at breakout interfaces and fail to execute these profitable positions. Because most opportunity relies on crowd participation, they wait too long for confirmation rather than accepting the pattern signal that flags the impending move. The narrow-range setup depends on execution ahead of the crowd and lets their fuel carry the position into a fast profit. Reprogram trading

F I G U R E   4.4

Overbought conditions and a long doji that prints well outside the top band signal a central tendency reversal trade. Stay out of these events in trending markets until extreme readings lower the risk. The shooting star that prints about 20 bars later offers a much easier profit opportunity. Note the horizontal top band and double top test that both raise the odds for a quick reversal. A few bars later, Vitesse finds a similar setup at the prior gap breakout and horizontal lower band. Finally, the stock moves downward and a 100% collapse through the trending lower band presents a final swing trade.

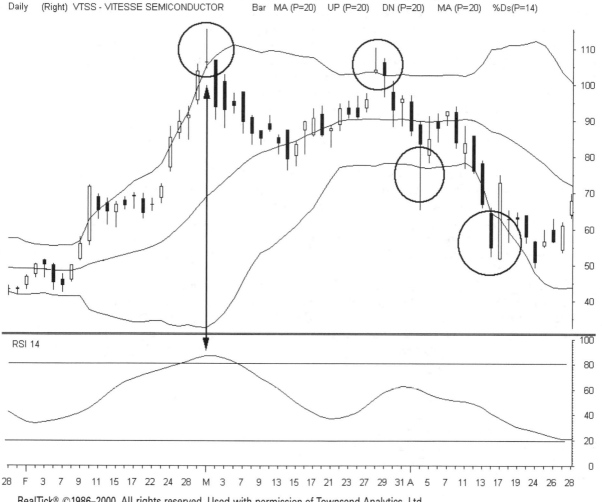

Daily   (Right) VTSS - VITESSE SEMICONDUCTOR   Bar MA (P=20)   UP (P=20)   DN (P=20)   MA (P=20)   %Ds(P=14)

RealTick® ©1986–2000. All rights reserved. Used with permission of Townsend Analytics, Ltd.

rhythm and watch these unique formations to capture trends just before they appear.

Setups work best when executions align with market conditions. Shorting rallies in hot markets or chasing trends in dull ones both empty trading accounts. It takes considerable skill to recognize the interface that separates a momentum market from a countertrend one. But this also allows a tactical shift that beats the crowd to the new dynamics. Changing conditions may not offer good setups right at the interface. A developing market trend may just shake up confidence and tell the swing trader to stand aside until opportunity shows up.

Learn to read market cycles before the crowd. Cycle analysis uncovers trends ready to tighten into congestion and offers another tool to locate impending breakouts into new trends. Apply a 14-day slow Stochastic or RSI and measure the longer-term swing between buyers and sellers. Or plot a five-bar slow Stochastic under a 5-minute chart and look for the 90-minute S&P alternation cycle. At potential turning points, watch for reversals at trendlines, channels, and other natural break levels. Align executions to these underlying cycles and place trades in tune with the market.

Study volatility through range bar expansion-contraction. Look for the range-bound NR7 and trending wide bars that reflect shifting crowd conditions. Apply Bollinger Bands to bar range study. Watch for constricting bands around price as volatility decreases and signals an imminent swing back into bar expansion. Measure how quickly they turn out and twist as price momentum builds. Or plot classic lower-pane volatility indicators that track the central tendency aspects of price change.

Volatility routinely increases through the early phases of a trend, decreases in the middle, and peaks as it climaxes into a sideways range. Friction and intense bull-bear battles characterize new breakouts and lead to wide range bars. The conflict eases as price ejects and the dominant crowd assumes control. Heavy cross-currents return near climaxes and participation surges again. Volatility decreases gradually through the congestion zone as volume dries up and price bar range narrows.

These peaks and valleys define points of swing trade opportunity. Frequent pullbacks after new breakouts offer low-risk countertrend entry. The dynamic third-wave trend environment favors momentum tactics as prices ramp bar after bar. Climax tops and bottoms invite central tendency trades at the extremes of overbought-oversold readings. Sideways congestion presents fade setups until the empty zone signals the start of a new trend.

MORE ON CROSS-VERIFICATION

Market participants have difficulty understanding the nature of opportunity. The pundits teach that a few well-marked patterns have secret triggers that lead to profit. In their logic, participants must find these quickly and take a seat before the

F I G U R E   4.5

A breakout beckons on Ciena's 5-minute chart. Price forms a clear ascending triangle and looks ready to explode upward. But overhead resistance can short circuit the most promising rally. Review all trade reward targets in advance and examine any intermediate barriers that price must mount to get there. Note how CIEN's 60-minute bars show clear sailing all the way to 110 before a prior high and descending Bollinger Band top both intervene. Right on schedule, the stock pops almost 5 points in 20 minutes but stops dead at the 110-resistance level.

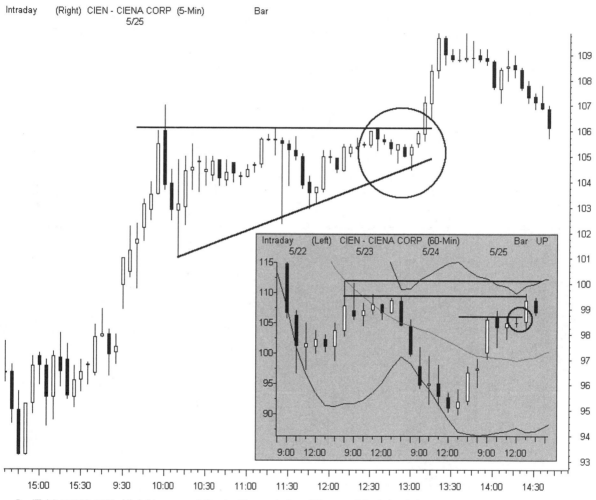

FIGURE 4.6

The 90-minute S&P alternation cycle rarely sets up perfectly in the real world. Atmel develops a rhythmic buy–sell swing that persists for well over a day. But a closer examination suggests that the cycle phase is closer to 1 hour than 90 minutes. Stay flexible and use cross-market tools to realign trade setups as required. The last two hours of the ATML chart also illustrate how intraday cycles shift timing when markets move from rangebound into trending periods. Keep one eye on the evolving pattern at all times while looking at short-term cycles.

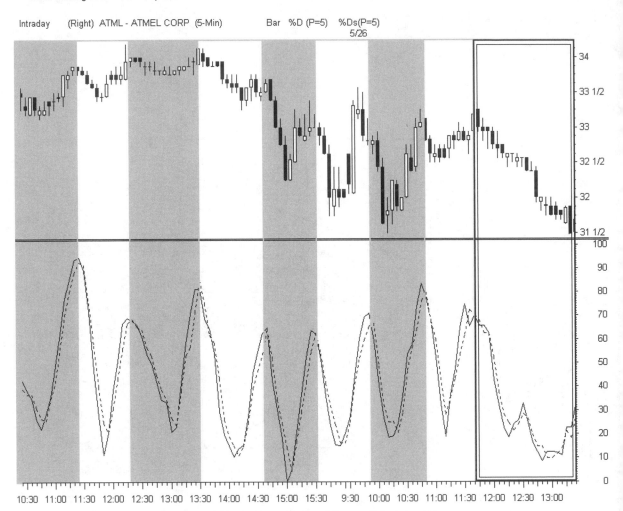

Intraday   (Right) ATML - ATMEL CORP (5-Min)   Bar %D (P=5)   %Ds(P=5)
                                                                5/26

blessed event. But effective strategy requires far more careful planning. Price emits continuous data about future direction. Each new piece of chart information can alter the likelihood that any specific outcome will occur. Execute the right bar and mediocre patterns may yield profits. Execute the wrong one and no textbook will save the position.

Directional probability falls through negative feedback and rises through positive feedback. But odds don't matter until setups appear. When they do, the charting landscape will filter opportunities with the highest odds for success. Predictive force peaks at certain crossroads on price charts. Odds for a specific outcome increase when discontinuous forms of S/R converge at a single price level. Apply this cross-verification (CV) mechanism to measure the setup's potency.

Each position generates a probability for success or failure. Enter a trade only when highly favorable odds support the setup. Measure probability by the actual number of converging S/R points. This simple analysis dictates that the more CV, the higher the likelihood that the position will produce a profit. When four or more levels intersect (CV4), entry into that setup at the low-risk execution target (ET) has the highest odds for profit. Keep in mind that trade probability must also align with favorable reward:risk. A move in the profitable direction does little when the potential gain remains small.

Understand the nature of the ET and its relationship to cross-verification. This important swing trade concept represents the price, time, and risk that trade entry must be considered. The best ET naturally occurs right at the strongest S/R. But the most promising CV4 setup offers no trade if it lacks an appropriate ET. The market's cruel nature generates many promising price expansion events with highly unfavorable entry points. Skilled participants must always manage execution as aggressively as opportunity to stay in the game.

Discontinuous information requires that different features exist independently of each other. Many types of S/R data actually derive from other calculations. For example, MACD Histograms arise from moving average data. Therefore, a setup does not cross-verify when MACD and MAs say the same thing. On the other hand, a hammer candle that strikes an old double top at the bottom of a horizontal Bollinger Band constitutes three unrelated elements that converge at a single point and suggest a major reversal. Take great care before accepting each CV point. Accidental combination of derivative measurements may carry substantial risk. The trade will inaccurately cross-verify and give false confidence to the position.

Cross-verification supports standard price convergence-divergence analysis. This method parallels the momentum cycle and confirms new trends. Multiple convergence improves the odds that the trend will continue. For example, when the Stochastics indicator moves sharply off a bottom, try to verify that observation with trendlines and pattern breakouts. Or when MA ribbons spread out, analyze the recent price bars to locate narrow range or wide range signals such as the NR7.

Fibonacci ratios offer excellent CV analysis. Stocks faithfully retrace certain percentages of prior movement before finally reversing or continuing the prevailing trend. These stair step levels identify significant setups when bottom pane indica-

F I G U R E   4.7

General Electric sets up a dramatic CV4 signal on the daily chart just before ejecting into a rally. Consider the high odds against these unrelated elements converging at the same price level: 1. Price pulls back to test the downtrend line. 2. Price pulls back to the 62% retracement of the last rally. 3. Price pulls back to test the Big W center pivot. 4. Price pulls back to the center Bollinger Band.

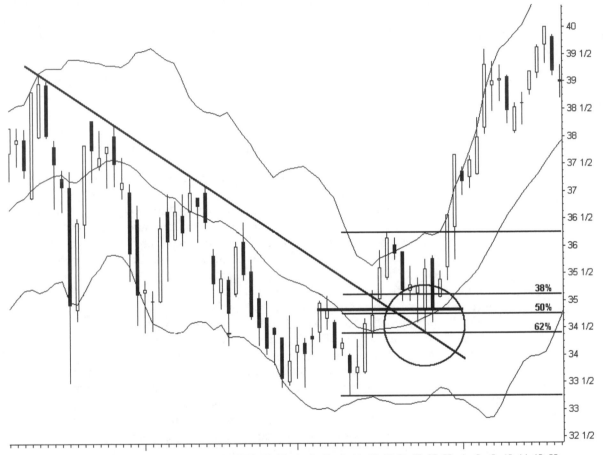

Daily   (Right) GE - GENL ELECTRIC   Bar   MA (P=20)   UP (P=20)   DN (P=20)

tors and landscape features converge to offer support. Apply a Fib grid to trend extremes and look for activity at the 38%, 50%, and 62% retracement levels. Price often bounces like a pool ball back and forth across this marvel of crowd mathematics.

TRADER vs. THE CROWD

Profits come from the other traders' pockets. While most participants realize that a winner stands next to every loser, few comprehend the true mechanics of this statement. The markets have never been a team sport. Swing traders must be predators ready to pounce on ill-advised decisions, poor judgment, and bad timing. Success depends on the misfortune of others.

Who exactly is the crowd? Swing trading tends to focus on short-term positions and the other market players who execute trades in this time frame. This total congregation exhibits predictable herd behavior in response to news events and S/R violations. The crowd reacts rather than acts when given the opportunity. It feeds on itself as members notice bursts of activity and fall into line, one after the other, until supply dissipates. Just as a stampeding herd suddenly reverses course upon reaching a barrier, the crowd may show little loyalty to a single price direction.

The trading core that acts on emotion rather than reason changes through every circumstance and defies accurate measurement. For obvious reasons, highly charged markets induce more herd instinct than quiet ones. Seek active conditions when looking for profit opportunities. Read the crowd's excitement through total volume and the time and sales ticker. Watch the trade rhythm as price strikes key S/R violation levels. Are the players tripping over themselves to get in or out of a position? How willing are they to execute well above or below the inside market? Their intensity tells the swing trader how long price breaks may last and the best strategy for that particular setup.

Trade ahead of, behind, or contrary to the crowd. Choose the strategy that aligns best with the current Pattern Cycles phase. Pick the ETs in advance based upon detached observation of the technical picture. Narrow-range executions work best to step in front of the crowd before a breakout. Stand behind the action on popular patterns such as the head and shoulders or symmetrical triangle and watch as insiders fade the masses that react to these well-known setups. Then look closely for the market's true intentions and execute after the crowd shakeout when the underlying direction finally emerges.

Never hesitate to go against crowd sentiment when the market telegraphs a reversal. But use careful timing and analysis before position entry. Crowds carry momentum that rarely allows instant directional change. Move down to the price chart below the time frame of interest and watch for small reversal patterns to print first. Then choose an ET that responds to that smaller pattern. Contrary tactics are not difficult to learn. Realize that greed-fear often motivates the crowd to act against its own best interests. Learn to recognize those profitable times and have a strategy ready to catch other traders' money as they let it go. Just mimic the insider's actions. Market makers take the other side of trades to ensure a liquid market. The swing trader should apply similar tactics when the crowd lines up on the wrong side at key reversal zones.

Use the crowd's excitement to exit trades on wide price bars before deep countertrends reduce profits. Reversals occur at peaks of crowd agitation. Sharp pullbacks trap players when they get greedy or wait too long for confirmation of a rollover. Safe exit requires that swing traders step in front of the crowd and close a position into its waiting hands. Get out quickly on bar expansion into major barriers such as prior highs or lows and Bollinger Band extremes.

Monitor personal stock board behavior closely. Don't identify with individual stocks or their related discussion groups. Board participants always have hidden agendas and will add a dangerous bias to detached execution. However, these virtual boiler rooms do fill an important data function: they assist in measurement of the crowd's emotional intensity for that stock. They also represent the pocket that the swing trader wants to pick.

Don't be an investor and swing trader on the same position. Investment represents a belief in a stock's underlying value or technical state. This bias will inhibit the ability to apply contrary strategies when the circumstances demand them. Investment relies upon wealth creation, while supply and demand drives trading. Don't confuse the two.

SHORT SALES

Price momentum builds strongly in both directions, but different crowd mechanics drive the underlying trends. Greed fuels stock rallies, while fear and pain guide selloffs. Each trend direction displays special chart characteristics that elicit different formation types. In other words, don't try to just flip a chart upside down to predict price movement in very active markets. But smaller thrusts through range constriction show less variation from uptrend to downtrend. Here the crowd behaves in a more rational manner as it moves in and out of positions. The smaller doses of greed and fear look alike through these zones.

Consider the difference between uptrends and downtrends in the development of trading tactics. Stocks tend to fall farther and faster than they rise. Volume builds rallies, but markets will fall from their own weight. Greed burns out faster than fear, which must be healed over time. Fear induces panic selling more reliably than greed induces panic buying. Momentum traders duck for cover quickly at new highs, but value investors routinely exercise great patience at new lows.

Many active traders never sell short. The upward price bias of the secular bull market teaches painful lessons to short sellers who don't apply defensive strategies. And the esoteric concept of selling stock before ownership confuses narrow logic although it follows common tactics that buy low and sell high. Many neophytes attempt a few short sales, get burned, and never look back. They fall into popular upside momentum strategies and never play any other setup.

Long-term market success depends on the ability to adapt to diverse trading conditions. Many Pattern Cycle phases signal profitable short sales opportunities. As with long positions, these setups align according to the trend-range axis. Classic strategies sell tests of old highs within ranges and use bear rallies to execute lower-risk entries in downside momentum markets. Smart short sellers also focus the ET through several time frames and build profits through 3D charting techniques.

Direct access execution revolutionizes short sale swing trading. For years, brokers relied on inefficient inventory handling that forced delays while excellent opportunities were lost. Short sellers had to overcome slow service and long phone calls to get permission to borrow shares. New interfaces now display available shares in real-time, and modern ECNs trigger fast executions when placing orders above the current inside bid. Once these are filled, swing traders can manage short positions as easily as long ones.

Swing traders must sell short within the context of the larger bull market. While the normal holding period will be short term, never underestimate the public buying power that drives modern markets. Always use 3D charting to examine major indices in the view above the intended execution. Avoid selling short near major market support levels. Also remember that indices tend to shift direction frequently as corrections build. An expanding selloff on a 5-minute Nasdaq chart rarely offers a safe environment for short sellers unless they operate through a very small execution window.

Trends depend on their time frame. Swing traders can safely sell short into corrections that last only a few bars or days. But these brief entries require very careful planning. Review other time frames to avoid trend relativity errors, and examine the pattern closely to pick the optimum entry points. Once a selloff is set into motion, buyers pull away and make execution more difficult. Wait for a pullback entry or get more consistent results by taking a position in narrow-range bars just prior to the break. Classic contraction against a S/R barrier offers a great tool to locate short sales as well as long positions.

Countertrend short sales require advanced trading skills. First build a profitable history of selling into downtrends and rangebound markets. Intermediate declines within uptrends can produce outstanding results. But the underlying buying power restricts safe execution to a few well-marked setups. Newer traders consistently sell short too early into these patterns and get ripped apart.

Experience builds the required patience to wait for the perfect countertrend opportunity. Sell breakdowns from one S/R level to the next. This requires defensive execution, precise measurement, and immediate profit taking. Use a Fibonacci line tool after a sharp uptrend thrust to identify the 38%, 50%, and 62% retracements. Cross-verify with time of day, horizontal S/R, and Bollinger Band extremes. Move quickly and without hesitation. At times these pullbacks will turn into larger trend changes. For example, a sharp thrust through the 62% retracement signals a possible first failure opportunity. If still short, keep the active position into the 100% level.

Bulls and greed live above the 200-day MA, while bears and fear live below. This popular reference level defines whether broad-scale strategies are trend or countertrend in nature. Rallies tap a larger pool of potential buyers above this important average, while corrections tap a larger pool of sellers below it. One-to-three day swing traders can execute long and short strategies through these broad conditions without special considerations. But longer-term position traders must exercise defensive tactics and precise execution if they choose to enter against this major average. Try instead to apply classic trend-following methods in this holding period. Sell the pullback, follow it down, and place cover stops to lock in profits during bear markets. Reverse strategy and direction in bull phases.

Short-term participants have few commonly agreed-upon alternatives to the 200-day MA. Rely on Pattern Cycles rather than moving averages to identify the market stage for the time frame of interest. Then apply first rise/first failure and Fibonacci retracements to pinpoint multi-trend bull-bear cycles. Simple 13- and 20-day MAs offer good trend analysis but don't mark long-term resistance when broken. Use the 50-day MA to signal intermediate resistance for declining stocks. This common setting triggers excellent short sales on the daily chart, and the shorter time period ensures many more tests than the broader 200-day MA.

Some stocks never participate in the market's broad upward movement and can be sold short all the way to oblivion. These natural position trades provide excellent opportunities for swing traders as well. The most obvious strategy awaits bear rallies in sustained downtrends. Allow the stock to reach overbought levels on a 14-day RSI. As it tops out, watch for a reversal pattern to print on the chart below the time frame of interest. If the trade arises on the daily chart, look for a double top or similar breakdown on the 60-minute view and use that level as the trigger for execution. Chapter 13 discusses these short sale tactics in more detail.

Short selling requires peaceful coexistence with the short squeeze. This time-honored practice relies on herd behavior. Position the sale ahead of, behind, or against the crowd to avoid these painful bear rallies. Squeezes erupt after downward price expansion invites latecomers with very bad timing to sell short. These volatile events end as quickly as they begin. They can carry further than routine pullbacks after upside breakouts due to the market's long-side bias. Keep in mind that short squeeze tops offer one of the best sale entry levels available. Shorts can fuel rallies up to a point in downtrends. Further price gains then require real demand.

Chasing downside momentum destroys trading accounts as efficiently as its long-side twin. Insiders generate squeezes very quickly to block natural trade exits and force serious damage. Participants who jump on board near the end of sharp selloffs have little experience and much fear motivation. Underlying retail optimism forces stomachs to turn more violently with ill-timed shorts than unprofitable long positions. They quickly cover in a panic that feeds on itself as price bars shoot skyward. Swing traders should capitalize on this popular insider shakeout and not suffer from it.

Enter short sales on pullback rallies to reduce risk and increase potential reward. Sell into the end of a short squeeze just as buying power fades. The squeeze alone will not force a 100% retracement of the last downward thrust most times. That takes real buying demand. They usually fail below 62% of the prior decline unless real longs emerge. Observe major S/R as the squeeze progresses, and watch for reversals near the 50% and 62% retracement levels of vertical rallies. These can uncover excellent short sales, and upticks will always be easy to find.

Channels and trendlines provide excellent short sale entry points as well. Draw a line across the top of declining lower highs to locate these important levels. Make sure to toggle between arithmetic and log scale—these lines appear on one

F I G U R E   4.8

This sudden @Home short-covering rally lasted only one hour but destroyed many trading careers. Price rose 11 points on an unsubstantiated rumor while insiders pushed the squeeze through several strong resistance levels. Only the continuation gap at 24 was finally able to contain the rocketship. Price dropped as quickly as it rose once the short fuel dissipated.

or the other but not both at the same time. Watch as price moves up toward the line. Does the level converge with other key S/R or major moving averages? Does price strike the top Bollinger Band while it turns downward? If so, cross-verification signals a potential short sale ET.

Intraday short sales require far more precision than longer ones. Fortunately, the time frame reduces the impact of investor participation. The swing trader can concentrate on S/R, TMs, classic patterns, and range bar examination. Find the best

F I G U R E   4.9

Parallel price channels and TMs fill the charting landscape to help swing traders locate low-risk short sale entry. Note how support becomes resistance after JDS Uniphase fails the late February gap at 120. Then the same thing occurs after violation of the earlier gap at 110. In both cases bear rallies push price into the declining channel top for a high-odds short sale.

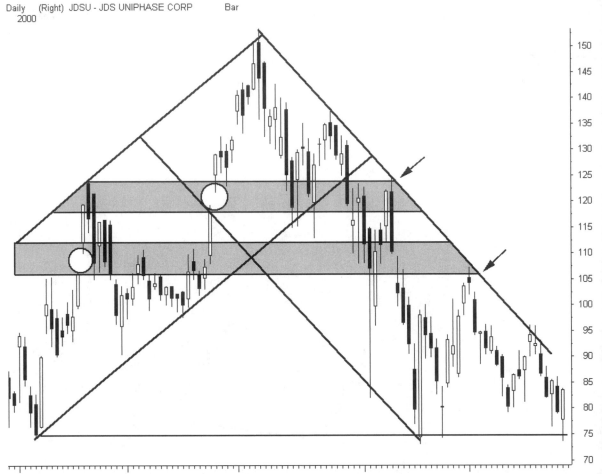

Daily   (Right) JDSU - JDS UNIPHASE CORP   Bar
2000

RealTick® ©1986–2000. All rights reserved. Used with permission of Townsend Analytics, Ltd.

short sale ET available but also control risk by pulling orders that do not fill immediately. Use multi-day intraday charts for 3D examination and exercise strong defense during the first and last hours. These time zones trigger the majority of intraday squeezes due to the heavy volume participation.

Cut losses immediately and recognize errors quickly when short. Use supplementary technical tools to choose wise exits. Thirteen- and 20-bar daily Bollinger

Bands point to clean cover zones when price strikes or violates the bottom band but the barrier remains horizontal. Hammer and doji reversal candlesticks predict that the next bars will go against the position. For intraday shorts, use a 5-8-13 (Fig. 2.11) and follow the same bar-expansion strategy that exits long-side trades.

TIME FRAME

Pick a holding period early in the game and stick with it until a better one comes along. Align all trades to this single time frame until self-discipline allows strict management of multiple strategies. Simultaneous positions that rely on different time frames raise the odds of trend relativity errors and allow weak-minded participants to turn trades into investments. Successful swing trading requires time specialization. Each Pattern Cycle subset marks unique trends and conditions. Learn the important characteristics for a chosen holding period and use them to improve performance.

Choose time frame wisely and for the right reasons. Swing trading must align with personal lifestyle or it can trigger very bad losses. Avoid intraday trading completely until advanced skills produce consistent profits through longer holding periods. Day trading hypnotizes many novices with sexy software, pretty colors, and subliminal advertising. But most market participants lack the time and resources to manage profitable intraday positions. Neophytes dream about the freedoms associated with day trading but forget to accept the risks. Ninety percent or more fail and lose large amounts of capital that could have attracted substantial profits in longer time frames.

Part-time intraday traders catch a few quick gains on their lunch hours and proclaim mastery of the art. Or they tap relatively brief momentum markets and believe their good times will last forever. If this sounds familiar, stop immediately and find an appropriate strategy that fits well with current responsibilities. Only time and commitment will lead to consistent performance. Very short-term positions require great effort to trade well, and successful players may spend 30 or more nonmarket hours per week examining new setups and tactics. There are no profit shortcuts in the modern markets.

Intraday Pattern Cycles produce more opportunities than daily ones. Swing traders can access setups in many small time frames throughout each session. But quick positions produce smaller average gains with higher transaction costs. Two strategies respond to this unpleasant characteristic. Shorten the time frame further and try to overcome very small reward through high-volume scalping techniques. Or lengthen the holding period to tap swing trade tactics that capture larger movement within this volatile environment. Both methods work well in the right hands and fail miserably in the wrong ones.

Intraday trading requires constant examination of range and range breakout. Success demands accurate prediction and precise timing. Learn to read the cycles and memorize the numbers in longer time frames before applying these skills to very short-term markets. Always enter trades in the direction of the highest odds at the time and exit immediately when proven wrong. Understand the narrow time window in which intraday traders must execute. Tiny whipsaws that few investors notice on daily charts incur sharp losses on 5-minute and 60-minute bars.

Level II access allows very short-term scalping strategies that work well with Pattern Cycles. In this time frame, classic ETs lose importance as players rely on observed order flow among market makers and ECNs. Few market participants should scalp. This risky strategy requires advanced skills and fast reflexes. Positions held between 30-minutes and 2 hours offer optimal profit conditions for most in-traday traders. Use this popular zone to apply classic tactics with highly predictive outcomes.

Two classic time frames attract most swing traders. The 1–3-day hold aligns positions to an underlying S&P futures buy-sell cycle. The 1–3-week hold parallels natural trend development on the daily chart. Both styles demand less time than intraday trading but offer dramatic profit opportunities with controlled risk. They also closely match common Pattern Cycle phases.

The 1–3-day swing measures an ideal holding period for many participants. The American markets tend to print 3-day mini-trends. Three strong bars often follow three weak ones. Three trending days precede 3 days of congestion. Find a recent reversal and count through swings to see how this natural pivot works under current conditions. This cycle expands and contracts as markets evolve. Instead of direct application, develop a sharp sense for natural market swing reversals and tune individual entries to these high-profit points.

Align positions correctly to this 1–3-day phase and catch large pieces of each move. This active style requires aggressive management and careful observation of open positions. Apply the same strategies as the intraday trader but use longer chart views to locate ETs and exit points. Sixty-minute and daily charts work well for these overnight positions. Trade frequently but control risk with tight stop losses that focus on primary chart landscape features.

The 1–3-week position aligns to a monthly buy-sell cycle that grabs a large price swing without aggressive position management. It fits well into a lifestyle not obsessed with the financial markets. Use the daily and weekly charts to organize profit opportunities and focus on closing prices. Ignore intraday volatility to avoid trend relativity errors. Manage profit and loss through physical stops. Protect gains with trailing stops that give positions adequate wriggle room. Then set stop losses based on natural breakdown zones and walk away.

Position traders have more time to consider promising setups and ideal strategies. They also seek higher individual profits, execute less frequently, and incur lower transaction costs. While intraday traders profit from single direct price thrusts, longer positions allow a greater variety of countertrend pullback strategies. Lock in a profit with a trailing stop and allow the stock to retrace when the charting landscape shows a strong trend. Then sit back and enjoy another sharp primary wave.

Consider time frame before every trade execution. Careful analysis must conclude that the setup works within the chosen holding period. This frustrating process will filter out many promising opportunities, but avoid chasing them. Successful tactics apply only to the swing trader's natural time tendency and can fail miserably if they miss their target. Market cycles exhibit polarity between adjacent trends. When holding periods compress or expand, they shift out of phase and can trigger opposite outcomes. Test new time frames slowly to ensure that proven tactics still function within the chosen cycle.

Look for setups that also work well in the time frame above the targeted holding period. These will exhibit few reward barriers, good support, and timing that converges with the smaller view. Follow larger-scale charts closely after execution and exit quickly if conditions change. For example, 1-minute scalpers follow important S/R features of the 5-minute chart while 1–3-day swing traders examine reward on the daily chart but execute patterns on the 60-minute bars.

Learn to decipher many subtle relationships between trends. Price movement occurs within short-term, intermediate, and long-term time frames. But these trends rarely synchronize with each other and often generate considerable friction. This flips price action through wavelike motion and may eventually force a reversal to relieve the stress. These volatile mechanics also create opportunity. Examine two adjacent trends and locate a good setup within the shorter one. Then add a lower dimension and time actual execution to price movement below the one that shows the trade.

Trading tools work through all time frames. Apply Bollinger Bands, Fibonacci retracements, and trendline channels to all chart views. Use this versatility to unleash tremendous predictive information. Toggle time frames to uncover tool convergence that cross-verifies promising setups. This confluence often locates major multi-point profit events. For example, when both daily and weekly Bollinger Bands converge at a single breakout number, odds increase that price will reverse right at that level.

Trend relativity errors steal more profits than any other trading mistake. An excellent position for one holding period often fails in the next larger or smaller time frame. Natural price waves that generate through multiple trends must align with reward targets and the chosen time frame. Make sure that strategies always focus on the right elements for that setup.

Investors make frequent relativity errors, but their broad position timing often forgives mistakes. Swing traders that miss their time frame will wash out of the markets quickly. Shorter holding periods spawn more critical time errors than longer ones. Short-term trends generate very noisy signals that trigger early positions. High transaction costs and lost opportunity also take their toll on these misinformed entries. Control this tendency through longer-term charts that capture broader price movement and filter errors.

LOADING THE GUN

Plan the trade; trade the plan. Swing traders must define a personal style, write it down, and update it frequently. Without one, they don't know what it is and will fail the next time their wallet really depends on it. The personal style defines trading

Different time frames tell different trend tales. Sun Microsystems stands on the brink of major decline during a severe correction on the daily chart. But the 5-minute chart shows the same stock ready to print a solid double bottom while the 1-minute view illustrates a pull back in a strong uptrend. Use the chart above the setup's time frame to establish reward:risk and the one below to fine-tune trade timing.

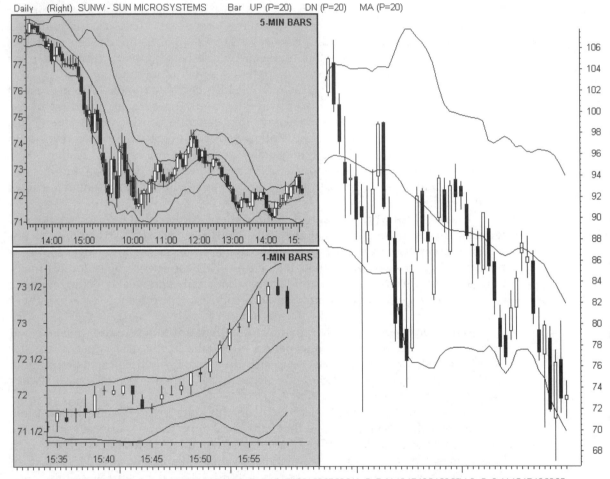

rules, holding periods, stock vehicles, execution criteria, and a series of filters that describe specific conditions under which to stand aside. Others may have good ideas on what belongs in each column. But only the swing trader's money is at risk, and no one else can make those important decisions.

Create a personal identity before the trade. Choose an appropriate holding period, since it defines so many other strategic considerations. This decision must look at both experience and available capital. Match positions to other lifestyle considerations and free time. New swing traders should also manage risk by applying longer time frames and smaller share commitments.

Review your major goals for participation in the financial markets. Is excitement or financial return more important? Must the profits pay household expenses or just the next family vacation? If no obvious goals appear, trade small until they do. The markets direct talented participants toward the trading styles that offer the greatest profits. Where they begin on that path may not be where they end up.

Trade small accounts wisely or they will disappear quickly. Avoid the tendency to overtrade a small amount of capital in the hopes of building it up quickly. Concentrate on applying the limited cash into promising opportunities rather than flipping it repeatedly and incurring heavy transaction costs. Decide whether or not to use the account's margin. Realize that margin increases both reward and risk. Trade with your head, not over it.

Define entry and exit rules. Start with reward:risk parameters and list conditions that must be met before taking a position. Many swing traders will not consider entry unless it shows a minimum 3:1 reward:risk. Short-term opportunities also depend upon the execution zone (EZ). This focal band surrounds the execution target and requires undivided attention as price bars move into it. Intermarket analysis and ticker interpretation then decide whether the ET warrants entry. Use rules to define exactly what must occur in the EZ before execution. Examine time of day, technical convergence, and underlying market sentiment to decide the minimum external support required for a position entry.

Focus on a specific price range for the current strategy. Then trade the right number of shares for each setup, regardless of account size. Opportunities that repeatedly cross-verify at a single point demand more shares than positions with

T A B L E   4.1

Typical Personal Trading Plan

- Trade price range > $12
- Holding period: 1–2 hours
- Enter: break of 2-day high
- Enter: S/R break
- Enter: Adam and Eve double bottom
- Enter: 62% retracement
- Exit: Touch of top Bollinger Band
- Exit: Break of 13-Bar MA on 5-minute chart
- Exit: Return into first hour range
- Filter: No entry on negative TICK
- Filter: No entry from 11:45am EST to 12:45pm EST

lower odds for success. Limit total shares to manage risk and always reduce share size when trying out new tactics or time frames. Decide whether or not to scale in and out of positions. Consider doing it for one side of the trade but not the other.

Will executions use limit or market orders? Will physical or mental stops decide trade exits? These important decisions may depend on the choice between a discount and a direct-access broker. Many direct systems don't allow placement of market orders or physical stops. They assume that participants will sit in front of their terminals at all times and guard positions. If lifestyle conflicts with this workflow, consider a less demanding system interface that allows automatic position management.

Modify personal style frequently as skills grow. Experience awakens fresh tactics that require new risk considerations. Since trading rules only represent guidelines to focus strategies, they should not strangle fresh ideas. Update them to incorporate your trading evolution and mark progress on the road to experience. One note of caution: review and adjust all prior tactics as necessary, but don't trade new styles first and document them later.

Decide where to place focus at the beginning of each market day. Time restraints force the elimination of many excellent opportunities in favor of those that appear more imminent through analysis. Choose wisely and setups will explode as predicted. Use personal trading style to define what will survive and capture the attention. Intuition plays a great part in this process. New setups that invoke excitement are more likely to ignite than those that draw fatigue.

Choose information sources wisely. How much chart analysis will be done each night? Will news as well as numbers trigger trade execution? Will positions remain active through major economic releases or will they close out in anticipation of shock events? Decide if a real-time news ticker will improve results and whether the TV set will stay on or off during market hours. Define clear relationships to stock boards and chat rooms. When will external opinions be shut out completely to prepare for the next entry?

Trading journals work well in conjunction with written rules. Compare the two frequently to determine how well decisions follow personal style and whether trading plans remain on target. Identify poor results and adjust tactics immediately. The game's complexity requires constant attention to stay focused on the goal. But avoid using a written journal to excuse failure. Confession only goes so far in healing emotions. Profits do a much better job.

DAY TRADING

Fast-execution systems popularize very short-term strategies that attack wide Nasdaq spreads. Direct-access broker-dealers teach their clients these tactics because many of them once worked the market floors and scalped for a living. Many financial professionals can't teach anything else—it's the only type of trade execution that they understand. As a result, many participants believe that day traders just scalp and do nothing else.

Scalping the spread should not be taught to neophytes. The quick-trigger environment requires a seasoned instinct and understanding of how markets move through buy-sell behavior. Scalping techniques teach players to capitalize on short swings in price and momentum. But most participants need years of practice to develop finely tuned reflexes that can jump quickly in and out of fast-moving stocks.

Veteran day traders have quietly flipped stocks for many years. Nightly Pattern Cycle review uncovered many opportunities with very short time triggers. Automatic speed dialers then rang brokers for quick fills as soon as ETs were struck during the next day's session. Although execution required a phone call rather than Net access, lower market volatility reduced slippage and permitted effective intraday strategies.

Successful swing trading does not rely on ECNs, SOES, BDs, MMs, and so on. It depends on accurate prediction of the market's next move. Participants book profits when they buy low and sell high. They lose money when they don't buy low and sell high. Common sense dictates that this elementary strategy becomes more difficult as the holding period shortens. Most successful day traders start with investing or position trading. They slowly move to the intraday arena after they master easier tactics and develop profound skills in the prediction of short-term market movement.

Position trading teaches all of the skills required for successful day trading but at a pace that the brain can easily assimilate. Day traders must apply instant market analysis and control risk in highly adverse conditions. This requires many years of experience for most participants. Jump into the day trading game with a lack of seasoned market-based skills and expect to be thrown into a meat blender.

Neophytes should seek classic technical training and avoid the video game suicide trap. Learn how, what, and when to buy and sell. Then use software systems and other tools to optimize strategies and improve results. Realize that the natural flow of opportunity often requires trade execution contrary to the crowd order flow that mindlessly chases small shifts in momentum.

RISK MANAGEMENT

Market participants have an amazing capacity to ignore risk management. Caught in the excitement of the game, no one wants to miss the next big thing. Each day we discover that everyone else makes money in the markets. Stock boards crow about huge gains but rarely admit big losses. Newsletters advise how to make a fortune but never how to avoid losing one. And our neighbors all bought hot stocks at the right time and are well on their way to retirement.

Swing traders fail when they don't manage positions. Long-term market survivors learn to control losses effectively before attempting to increase gains. Unfortunately, most neophytes don't have the required discipline to exercise this sound risk management. They chase positions with no safe exit as the lure of the big gain disables unbiased evaluation.

Greed attracts players to the strategies that have the highest failure rates. Danger increases significantly when trading in these high-volatility environments. Wide swings ensure that price moves a great distance in a very short time frame. These hot stocks offer few safe entry levels and many insider shakeouts. Borderline participants always see the upside but ignore the downside when they enter positions into crowd excitement. Whatever happens next is out of their control because they exercise no planning, reward targeting, or risk management.

Hot stocks build a sense of invulnerability as they move in the crowd's direction. Profit feeds the ego and strokes it as markets race higher. Large gains build and silence rational thought. Traders caught in this mindset quickly become investors and lose that predatory edge that finds consistent winners. If the stock turns, the ego says it will always come back. Entire gains vanish as these new investors insist on value instead of technical patterns. Or it can even ride higher and reinforce bad habits for the new conquering king.

Positions can move quickly against careless participants and generate strong fear. The charting landscape may offer few escape routes, and the trader freezes like a deer in the headlights as price takes off in the wrong direction. Survival instincts often kick in at this point, and flawed logic decides not to take the loss but ride it back to the entry level or a fresh profit. Anything can happen after that decision because all control has been abdicated to fate and ego. A trading account empties, or a miracle saves the day. In either case the speculator takes the next step toward washout and a safer hobby.

Neophytes should choose less volatile markets for their strategies. Look for stocks that move in slower motion and offer more opportunity to take appropriate safety measures. But even this calmer path will set participants on the road to failure if they build inadequate responses to dangerous conditions. Smaller gains in this environment also encourage more frequent trading. Transaction costs build quickly and bleed gains, while nonperforming positions waste capital and restrict other opportunities.

The most important rule of risk management requires little interpretation: never enter a trade without knowing the exit. Each ET choice generates a risk profile based on the distance between the entry and major S/R violation level. This level (failure target) determines the point where price action proves that the trade was wrong and should be abandoned. This distance must be acceptable before each trade entry.

This exit must not produce a loss in excess of the swing trader's predetermined risk tolerance. Target a permissible average loss as part of trading style and rule preparation. Smaller accounts must manage smaller losses than large accounts. Risk tolerance also aligns closely with reward measurement. The distance from the entry to the nearest S/R barrier in the direction of the trade (profit target) measures reward potential. Seek positions with reward targets that measure at least three times the calculated risk. Then estimate the actual dollar loss should the position fail and violate the risk level with the expected number of shares.

Many good positions should be avoided or exited quickly. Markets work well when setups yield profits, but trouble starts when they don't. Each promising trade has high odds for failure that must be considered before entry. Many participants fall into a gambling mentality when things go wrong. They rely on luck to get them past the risk and into a profit. Never follow this dangerous path. Do not execute a position unless the effect of being wrong matches the individual risk tolerance.

Slippage increases transaction costs. Actual trade fills may fall far from expected execution prices. Swing traders can exercise more slippage control on entries than exits by using limit orders. Exits must often be taken quickly and through any door available. This leads to losses that consistently exceed risk measurements. Slippage and increased transaction costs must factor into reward:risk calculations. One easy method just pulls a half-point off the ratio. For example, the final number won't exceed 2.5:1 if the original setup measures 3:1 reward:risk before real-world impact.

Seek low-risk entry whenever possible. Find setups with ET levels very close to S/R or look for deep pullbacks in well-established trends. Narrow-range bars offer safer entry than expansion moves. Spreads narrow and permit swift execution at specific prices in a quieter environment. Filter time as well as price. The first and last trading hours carry sharp volatility and higher risk. Avoid execution through discount brokers during this time or face high slippage and late fill reports that defeat loss management. And always consider the quiet lunch hour to enter positions for afternoon rallies.

WINNING AND LOSING

Swing trading success depends on the chosen path to profit. Some push hard for the big gain but risk big losses when the action suddenly turns against them. Others slowly build each profit and watch defensively for a quick exit when wrong. Choose the focus that matches your trading personality but prepare to deal with the consequences of the decision. You have to be very, very good before you allow yourself to be bad.

Measure ongoing performance using win–loss calculations. The simple %WIN ratio compares winners to losers and tracks the success of new strategies. Average winners (AvgWIN) and losers (AvgLOSS) measure results against risk tolerance. These calculations look at trades in the following manner:

%WIN = winners/total trades

AvgWIN = total profits/winning trades

AvgLOSS = total losses/losing trades

Example: The swing trader books profits of $300, $350, and $400 and one loss of $175 is recorded. Profits come from three out of four trades:

%WIN = 3 winners/4 trades

%WIN = 75%

AvgWIN = ($300 + $350 + $400)/3 winners

AvgWIN = $350

AvgLOSS = $175/1 loser

AvgLOSS = $175

Different strategies emit different risk profiles. Scalpers tend to exhibit high %WIN and low AvgWIN, while position traders reflect low %WIN and high AvgWIN. Strong momentum markets incur high AvgLOSS. Momentum players must compensate for this increased risk through higher %WIN if possible, but that often fails. Swing markets increase %WIN but limit both AvgWIN and AvgLOSS. Swing traders can impact results through time frame and strategy choices more than any other market player. They may wind up at either extreme, depending on their risk approach.

Trade risk shifts dramatically through small changes in %WIN, AvgWIN, and AvgLOSS. High-%WIN traders can absorb much higher dollar losses than low-%WIN traders and still profit. Many markets limit AvgWIN by the nature of their inefficiencies, but swing traders can often narrow AvgLOSS through careful risk management practices. Consider how AvgLOSS impacts performance from the 25% to 75% %WIN levels. And here's the kicker: most professional traders have a %WIN under 50%. Guess how they got to be professionals?

The markets offer only three ways to improve profitability, regardless of trading style: raise the %WIN, raise the AvgWIN, or lower the AvgLOSS. Intraday traders have fewer profitability options than position traders. Price tends to move away from entry as a function of time. So intraday profits (AvgWIN) tend to be smaller than longer-term gains. Very short-term time frames also frustrate attempts to raise %WIN because short-term traders must demonstrate perfect timing while position traders can wade through many whipsaws to get to their profit.

Intraday traders can control losses more efficiently than position traders. Price-time tendency now works to their advantage. In other words, incurred losses will be smaller on average because positions are held for a shorter time period. This allows loss distribution closer to zero than position trading. But frequent intraday executions often wash out this advantage through higher transaction costs.

Loss-side management increases profits more quickly than chasing gains. Take what the market gives and move on to the next trade. Successful participants know when they're wrong and execute a well-rehearsed exit plan. Learn this skill quickly because most traders lose more often than they win during a typical career. Enter every position with an exit door close to the entry to cut losses when wrong. Keep another just behind advancing price to protect gains when right. Expect some frustration along the way. Many stocks will whipsaw through S/R and shake out good positions just before taking off sharply in the right direction. Experience will reduce these unpleasant events but will never eliminate them completely.

T A B L E   4.2

Three Ways to Make a $10,000 Profit

%WIN	Trades	AvgWIN	AvgLOSS	Profit
75%	100	$800	$2000	$10,000
50%	100	$800	$ 600	$10,000
25%	100	$800	$ 133	$10,000

Seek liquidity at all times. Swing traders need fast execution with low slippage, and that won't happen unless there's an active crowd flipping the stock. Less liquid issues also carry higher transaction costs and erratic movement that will undermine sound risk management. Avoid stocks with volume less than 500K to 1M shares/day for 1–3-day positions. Intraday traders should focus on issues that trade 2M shares or more each session. Special conditions will change these guidelines. High-level shock events turn thin stocks into excellent swing trading vehicles for short periods of time. Shocked stocks that trade 3–5M shares or more produce excellent profits with low transaction costs.

STOP LOSSES

Avoid physical stops as long as positions can be managed in real-time. This reduces stop gunning exposure and allows a progression of natural exit points. As price evolves, so does exit planning. Swing tactics implement discretionary (voluntary) rather than system (automatic) trade execution. This flexibility extends through the exit from each active position. Terminate the trade when movement in the intended direction reaches a natural barrier that may impede further price change. Also get out when movement against the intended direction violates a natural barrier that may accelerate price change.

Focus on trailing S/R to locate appropriate stop loss for the intraday trade. Build a grid around advancing price with MA ribbons and Bollinger Bands. Apply the 5-8-13 settings and watch the averages closely. Exit on a break of the 8-bar that follows a very strong trend. Watch the 13-bar in moderate conditions and depart on a break of that level. Failure through this center point raises odds that price will expand sharply toward the other band extreme. The interplay among price, MA, and BB frequently points to a low-risk exit several bars before a serious reversal occurs. Consider an exit before the MA violates if price starts to roll sideways along the edge of the average.

External stop losses manage large cycle reversals. Individual stocks will turn and follow volatile intermarket conditions such as program selling or index breakouts. Mental stop preparation must identify external conditions that will terminate active equity positions. When unexplained reversals trigger sharp expansion on futures or index charts, close positions first and ask questions later. Don't wait for a response on the individual stock chart. Use that short interval to escape before others take notice of the event.

T A B L E   4.3

Market Liquidity in the Year 2000

Volume	Nasdaq	NYSE/ASE	All
Top 10%	417	361	778
Top 20%	895	663	1558
Top 30%	1400	1159	2559

F I G U R E   4.11

A series of low-risk channel trades appear during three hours of Immunex price action. Each promising setup generates a natural band (shaded area) that violates the chosen strategy. This marks a price level that signals the setup has failed and should be exited. Try to place stop loss orders within these bands to maintain sound risk management. Avoid the trade completely if a band cannot be drawn close to the intended entry level.

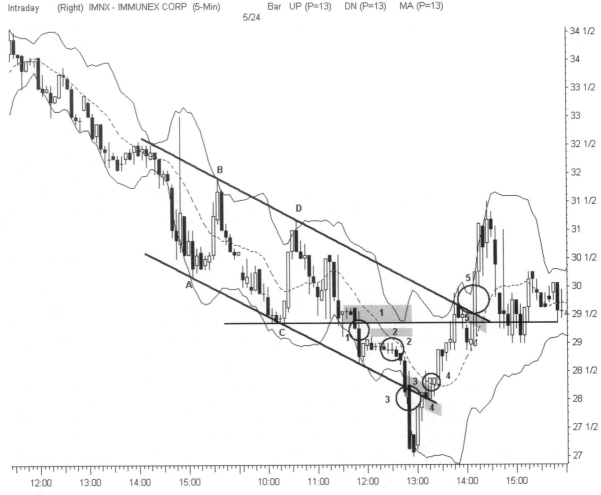

Intraday   (Right) IMNX - IMMUNEX CORP (5-Min)   Bar UP (P=13)   DN (P=13)   MA (P=13)

Swing traders consistently recognize impending failure as Pattern Cycles knowledge grows. Don't wait for the crowd to depart a failing position. Lead them out the exit door and move on to the next opportunity. A pullback will often follow the first violation of well-marked S/R in strong markets. One advanced strategy holds the position through the swing break and bids into the bouncing market to exit. While good discipline always grabs the first exit door, use this second chance when caught off guard.

Place an arbitrary stop to keep the trade within risk tolerance if momentum offers no obvious exit. Enter with the market in motion and place the exit order at any price that yields an acceptable loss. Better yet, bid into the market several times and place stops very close to the purchase prices. Then take a series of small losses in the effort to catch a major price thrust. Keep in mind that if a momentum market turns sharply, no stop loss will offer real protection.

Physical stops provide a convenient tool for part-timers that can't actively manage their open positions. Enter the sell stop as soon as the trade produces a new fill report. Place the limit order on the other side of known S/R within the risk parameters for the position. Add reasonable wriggle room to avoid whipsaw exits. If the position survives the session, reexamine the stop that night and adjust as necessary. Continue to review nightly and push the exit door closer to current price as soon as it moves into a profit. Adjust it even closer as the price target approaches or time reaches the intended holding period. And consider a quick windfall exit after any sharp bar expansion in the right direction.

CAPITALIZATION

Small accounts must maintain strict risk parameters to swing trade. The lower transaction costs and tight spreads of modern markets allow $2,000 to $5,000 of capital to earn a profit. But any impatience will lead to a quick account decline. Keep position size and trade frequency to a minimum. Execute longer-term strategies and allow gains to build over time. Choose lower beta issues that exhibit all of the Pattern Cycle phases but move in slow motion. The markets will still be around next week and next year.

Active swing traders should start with minimum capital of $10,000 to $25,000. This size permits good position management without the use of margin. Trade the highest-priced stocks that fit comfortably into the account and avoid buying low-priced issues. Buy or sell the right number of shares for each setup and keep free money aside for unexpected opportunities. Transaction costs still take a bite out of profits at this level. Increase risk through more volatile issues and position size rather than trade frequency.

Trading for a living requires at least $50,000 to $100,000 and a pool of savings that ensures the account will not be tapped for daily expenses. This size allows multiple positions in volatile stocks at all price levels and manages results through real-time systems that respond immediately to changing conditions. The professional treats swing trading as a business and commits sufficient time to match the high financial stakes. This commitment level should not be attempted until a consistent track record demonstrates significant talent and a stable personality for the occupation.

Professional day traders need larger accounts than swing traders as higher transaction costs and lower AvgWIN impact profitability. Smaller intraday movement requires larger position size to tap profits and losing trades must be exited quickly when they jump the wrong way. Account drawdowns will tend to be higher than swing trading, but shock events will do less damage. Consider the good reasons to reduce trade frequency and apply swing tactics instead of scalping or very short-term day trading.

Many players find it difficult to manage several open positions at one time regardless of account size. Avoid the urge to increase position size to compensate for a thin portfolio. Each trade has a risk level that matches the number of shares put to work. As experience grows, consider the addition of multiple time frames into a single account. Longer-term positions tap available cash but require less active babysitting. This strategy works well after the swing trader learns the risks of trend relativity errors and manages them efficiently.

Establish a solid performance record before incorporating margin into a personal trading plan. Increased buying power exaggerates both gain and loss. Margin can generate an unhealthy sense of power that introduces a gambling mentality into trade tactics. It can quickly wipe out a promising career through overtrading or excessive position size. Consider margin a powerful tool in the right hands and a dangerous weapon in the wrong hands.

RECORDS AND RESULTS

Most market participants lose more money in bad positions and have a lower %WIN than the conscious mind admits. Besides strong discipline, maintain objective and current records of all position activity. Let a spreadsheet or software program determine success, not the biased and ambitious mind. Never allow the broker-dealer to maintain the only trading account record. Broker-dealers make frequent recording errors, usually in their own favor. Realize that earned interest will distort loss reporting. Filter this out of personal records.

Format records to conform with tax reporting requirements. This will save much aggravation during filing times and display profit-loss in the same way as the government sees it. Always add transaction costs into basis and sale prices. Commissions can hide significant losses, especially on smaller accounts. Consider separate records to see how these fees impact different strategies or track the spread lost through each execution to estimate the impact of overtrading.

Broker records and trade slips don't offer full analysis of how well different tactics work. Review the trading plan and decide what additional information to track from day to day. Input these supplementary data into a spreadsheet that will average and compile performance over time. Actual holding period, share size, and win-loss streaks make perfect additions to standard %WIN, AvgWIN, and AvgLOSS statistics.

Assemble daily data important to survival but avoid too much information. Profit alone decides the swing trader's fate. Application of knowledge and discipline determines profit. Detailed records can uncover weaknesses and optimize strategies, but they won't stop poor execution. If information serves no purpose, ditch it and focus on major performance issues. Stay flexible. New strategies introduce new challenges that require a fresh look and objective feedback. Keep the spreadsheet loaded and ready to examine major concerns as they arise.

INNER TRADER

Are you ready for the truth about your current obsession with the markets? While exact figures remain closely guarded by the industry, the swing trading failure rate likely stands well over 70%. So chances are good that new participants will eventually lose all or part of their equity accounts and be forced to move on to less stressful hobbies. To avoid this fate, take the pursuit very seriously and find an original trading strategy that takes full advantage of the unique characteristics of the short-term markets.

The trading fascination lies in the favorable time/profit curve. Short-term markets generate sharp price swings that capture the public's attention. This encourages experienced investors to abandon buy-and-hold strategies and concentrate on these quick turns. But they soon realize that short-term profits depend on highly effective time management. This critical demand requires far more skill than most new traders anticipate and they wash out quickly.

Neophytes see market speculation as an exciting way to make money and break out of the business world. The discipline routinely attracts over-40 white males with professional backgrounds in other occupations. They believe that their financial success in one career will quickly translate into trading profits. These well-capitalized participants apply the same ambition that works so well in the business world's pecking order. But testosterone can't force money from the markets, and quiet introspection builds better strategies than bravado. Those who finally survive the game all tell a common tale: this fascinating pursuit was the hardest challenge they ever faced.

Aspirants must commit many hours to market study or avoid trading entirely. Develop a predatory instinct, avoid greed, and view this occupation as a lifelong quest. Work hard to complete every analysis in detail, and don't cut corners. Part-timers can succeed but must specialize on a few strategies and skip broader study. Match execution with effort or pay the price. Highly trained market professionals stand ready to empty careless wallets, and only adequate preparation will uncover the secrets that produce consistent profits.

Watch the clock and become a market survivor. Develop an intuitive sense of how positions will react to intraday cycles. Learn to coordinate trades so they align with these underlying tendencies. For example, don't buy weakness in the last hour if price is below support. Time-of-day favors further declines for these issues near market close. The first and last hours attract most participants. But they carry higher risk than any other time period. Avoid this excitement until specific strategies can address the increased risk. Early opportunities disappear quickly and trap unskilled players. Highly profitable setups appear throughout the middle hours. Use this quieter time to build up trading skills and avoid the crowd.

Develop an original style that avoids the most volatile stocks. Markets generate small-scale inefficiencies all the time. Learn to recognize the odd daily quirks that produce high-probability setups. Notice strange behavior and apply simple techniques to capitalize on it. Give up the excitement of chasing parabolic stocks and find quiet opportunity that books higher profits with less stress. In any case, always travel a different path than the restless crowd.

Focus on optimizing entry and exit. Work out a detailed strategy before each trade that accurately measures reward and risk. Write it down if possible and don't stop until consistent performance proves mastery of the game. Play single direct price thrusts, stay defensive, and manage size to control risk. When buy signals don't line up perfectly, skip the trade or enter a smaller position. Profit depends on discretion and wise execution. When one opportunity passes, another will appear like magic. And remember that precise entries on mediocre positions make more money over time than bad executions on good ones.

Apply cross-verification to all trading decisions. Technical convergence through identical levels greatly enhances the odds for success. Use it for both analysis and position management. Enter setups when S/R points repeatedly to an obvious ET level. Compare upper- and lower-pane indicators to measure the trend-range axis. When Fibonacci retracements, MA ribbons, and trendlines all work together, load the trading gun and take profits with confidence and ease.

AVOIDING SELF-DESTRUCTION

The markets provide the perfect mechanism to confirm just how screwed up someone's life really is. Money represents power in modern culture. Swing traders seek to master this force and become true wizards of the game. But the subconscious mind often has its own agenda. Many participants don't really want to succeed in market speculation, so they project hidden inadequacies into their trading performance, all the while thinking, "Yes, I'm bad and don't deserve the good things that trading will bring me."

The business world forces employees to perform a laundry list of duties for an extended period of time before rewarding them with a paycheck. This rat-in-the-maze mentality deeply affects our view of money. It trains us to believe that our financial fates are in the hands of a powerful third party who controls wealth. But successful swing traders must recognize their own power in the creation of capital. Learning this simple skill may take a lifetime of effort to undo years of bad programming.

The markets require a level of discipline that most fail to achieve in the rest of their lives. So why should it be any different with trading? Stock positions offer endless opportunities to break rules and ignore danger. Wise participants recognize non-market limitations and deal with those before proceeding on the path to profit.

Losing weight, quitting smoking, and exercising regularly all improve the odds for trading longevity. Add stress reduction and watch performance improve faster than taking a weekend stock course.

Swing trading frustrates those who find great achievement in other walks of life. Few other disciplines require constant loss to reach their goals. The pain of losing money stands beside profit throughout the road to success. Accept this unpleasant fact and prepare to deal with the emotional rollercoaster. Both winning streaks and drawdowns test rational behavior and trading strategies. Stay focused and stick to the plan. Participants who lose concentration face a gambler's paradise. And just like all games of chance, expect to leave the bright lights with very empty pockets.

Greed and fear bring out the extremes in human behavior. But swing traders can control the impact of emotion with solid rules and strict self-discipline. Rules must apply to all circumstances, regardless of how it feels or the short-term financial impact. Few can maintain this discipline perfectly, and most find themselves in dangerous situations. At those critical times, decide quickly how to steer the boat back into the harbor before it gets sunk.

See the setup with both sides of the brain. As skills evolve, an accurate inner voice adds a powerful new dimension to reasoned analysis of the price chart. Growing knowledge internalizes the market swing and tunes into natural opportunity. Go ahead and follow those trade instincts unless solid reasons dictate another path. But don't confuse intuition with impulse. High levels of frustration and excitement can push bad trades without good reasons. Fall back on the numbers when in doubt.

Promising stock opportunities turn into disasters. Time works against the swing trader when conditions turn dangerous, and waiting to be right is the best way to be wrong. Those who hesitate in the face of doom get taken out of the action for a very long time. Fortunately, most patterns warn of impending shocks. Sharp reversals rarely occur in a single bar, and well-marked signposts scream the need for a fast exit. Always protect the trading account and listen to the chart's message regardless of what it says.

Many participants seek excitement from the markets. They get a sharp adrenaline rush every time they execute a new position. Unfortunately the same rush comes whether they win or lose. This builds operant conditioning that rewards loss as well as gain. Getting high on the markets draws a quick path to failure. Successful swing traders kill the thrill and practice inner detachment through each execution. They experience long periods of boredom but don't use mediocre setups to escape the monotony.

Never marry a stock position. Don't bother to find out too much about the trading vehicle beyond basic sector analysis. Swing traders understand that stocks represent numbers and nothing else. Remember that message board surfers don't seek the truth. They seek validation for their point of view. Participants find easy support for distorted beliefs that make it more difficult to exit a loser when it's time to get out. Get away from the boards for weeks or months at a time and realize that only one point of view really counts when it comes to the markets.

F I G U R E   4.12

Impending price shocks may offer little warning. Lucent violates a rising trendline and breaks through a double top only two bars before a 20-point, overnight gap down. Swing traders must act quickly on early danger signals to avoid being crushed by the crowd.

Daily   (Right) LU - LUCENT TECHNOLOGIES   Bar   Volume

5

MASTERING THE TOOLS

PATTERNS VS. INDICATORS

Swing traders apply both art and science to uncover market mysteries. The subjective mind studies chart patterns and looks for common shapes from times past. The practical mind rarely trusts the eyes and seeks truth in the cold, hard numbers. Effective trade preparation combines these diverse tasks into a single, well-organized plan. The cooperative brain first digests vast amounts of information to arrive at probabilities regarding the direction of price movement. Then it organizes this output into vision and tactical planning.

The mind plays tricks on what the eye perceives. The human brain attempts to construct order from visual chaos and sees promising patterns even in random data. Unfortunately, this false order may tranquilize the eye but lacks truth or predictive power. And it bleeds trading accounts until effective filters stop this noise from passing into the system.

Technical indicators apply truth serum to endless chart patterns. They bypass distorted vision and output simplified plots that draw important conclusions about current price activity. Profitable setups depend on seeing reality rather than illusion. Mathematics cross-verify odd chart formations and predict what to expect next. The lower pane reveals hidden characteristics through convergence or divergence with bar information. Some even measure relative position to a cyclical axis.

Market mathematics churns blocks of price and volume into well-digested summaries. Swing traders then apply time restraints and compare output to observable price development. This taps a market's unique 3D mechanics. Use specific time intervals to identify unique trends and conditions within that period alone. Then compare this information to similar statistics from other intervals and conclude what market action will likely do next.

Technical indicators flash many false signals. Simple price input often elicits dangerous output. Promising results may point to opportunities that apply to the wrong time frame. Bad exchange or vendor data generate indicator peaks and valleys with no truth. These quirks and limitations frustrate sincere efforts to uncover market clarity. Above all else, learn when indicators offer the keys to the kingdom and when even Bozo the Clown should pass on the revelations.

Chart patterns and technical indicators are not created equally. A highly skilled technician can trade successfully using only a bar chart. But the most powerful set of market indicators has little value when viewed in the absence of price. Just try this simple exercise: buy a stock at oversold or sell it at overbought without looking at price. Not a good way to make money.

Chart patterns reveal quirks of crowd greed-fear behavior. They represent universal fractals that repeat over and over again through all time frames. Best of all, they point to exact locations for low-risk trade opportunities. But neophytes should never rely on patterns alone for trade execution. Triangle and flag reading takes little effort, while technical indicator interpretation requires serious study. So many borderline participants walk the easier path and fail miserably when their profit depends on precise application of these powerful tools.

MANAGING TECHNICAL TOOLS

Physics teaches that energy sources leave telltale signatures in the form of exhaust or radiation. Similarly, chart patterns with true predictive power emit evidence that mathematics can detect and measure. When trading signals converge through both types of analysis, odds sharply increase that the opportunity will produce a valid result.

Understand two common indicator quirks and shorten the learning curve. First, well-known authors publish endless variations of the same few technical studies. Stick with the classics until they stop working or limit personal trading style. Second, all technical indicators suffer from the same limitation: they only work through certain market phases and not others. Identify primarily conditions in advance of setup analysis to avoid false readings.

Beware of the overbought-oversold trap. This convenient terminology implies a trading response when oscillators push into extreme territory. But this questionable strategy robs profits in trending markets. For example, common wisdom says to sell when Stochastics punches above 80 or to buy when it drops below 20. But this response fails during major breakouts and breakdowns. Always look to the pattern first before trying to interpret a technical indicator, and remember Martin Zweig's classic advice that "the trend is your friend."

F I G U R E   5.1

Average directional movement (ADX) signals the end of Qualcomm's record-breaking rally more than 2 weeks before the daily price bar trendline breaks. Well-tuned technical indicators pick up important changes in crowd behavior well in advance of price patterns. Use them to filter trade setups through convergence-divergence feedback and their unique charting landscape features.

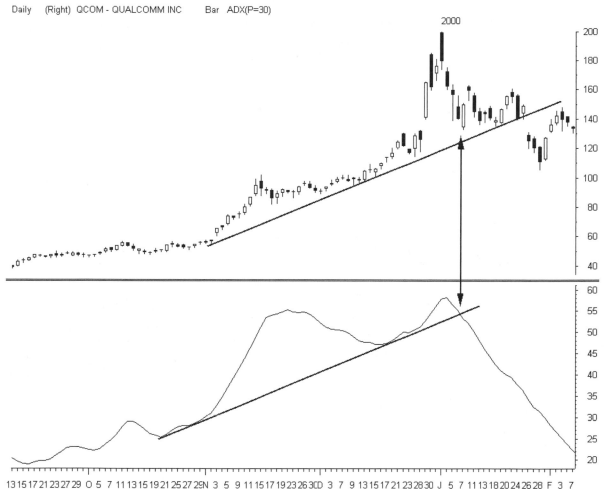

Daily   (Right) QCOM - QUALCOMM INC   Bar ADX(P=30)

Use both pattern analysis and technical indicators to predict future price movement. But the indicator must support the pattern rather than the other way around. Patterns handle reward:risk measurements as well as price targets and identification of the optimum execution target. Apply indicators to uncover hidden divergence and flag impending reversals. For example, don't buy congestion in

F I G U R E   5.2

Oscillators work well in flat markets but lose their power during strong trends and emit false signals. Classic trading wisdom advises to sell stocks when the Stochastics indicator reaches over 80 into overbought territory. But that would have been bad advice during this intraday Oracle rally. The indicator struck 80 but the stock continued to rise for another 3-1/2 points. Notice how the indicator double top offered a much better sell signal as a sideways market took over the action.

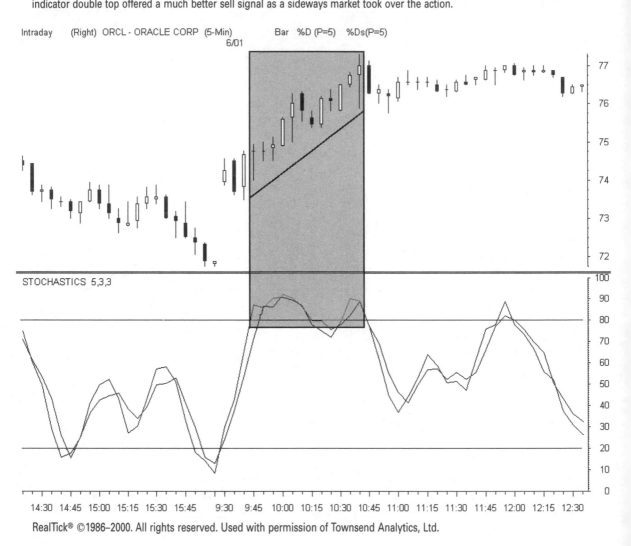

Intraday   (Right) ORCL - ORACLE CORP (5-Min)   Bar   %D (P=5)   %Ds(P=5)
6/01

STOCHASTICS 5,3,3

14:30 14:45 15:00 15:15 15:30 15:45   9:30   9:45   10:00 10:15 10:30 10:45 11:00 11:15 11:30 11:45 12:00 12:15 12:30

anticipation of a breakout when Stochastics rolls over sharply from an overbought state. Or avoid short sales in bear markets when RSI turns up from an oversold state.

Trading tools must address both numbers and emotions to locate promising setups. While state-of-the-art software builds very complex buy-sell signals, most indicators miss the emotional tension that ultimately drives price change. Turn to the visual examination of recurring price and volume patterns for this essential task. Effective pattern analysis uncovers crowd behavior as it finds signal within the random noise of stock charts. Classic formations contain response fractals that predict how volatility and price movement will evolve over time. A seasoned pattern reader can often ignore mathematics (and fundamentals) when underlying price development paints a sharp picture. But most swing traders still need to apply math-based indicators to verify important observations and filter bias.

Recognize the unique appearance of each technical indicator. Many print characteristic patterns, while others oscillate between two extremes. For example, On Balance Volume (OBV) can display a head and shoulders formation with the same predictive power as its better-known cousin. But even the most effective indicators emit both signal and noise. Learn when to listen to their distinctive message and when to ignore them.

Every good analysis should validate current conditions through both forward (strength) oscillators and backward (momentum) indicators. Popular oscillating tools, such as RSI and Stochastics, identify overbought-oversold markets. Moving averages and MACD look back and measure momentum change. Or swing traders can just draw simple trendlines and channels in all time frames and use those instead as primary momentum tools.

Build custom settings to address specific styles and personal goals. Modern trading software features dozens of prepackaged indicators that study different aspects of market behavior. Learn how these common tools respond to changing conditions, and then examine their calculations in detail. Slowly adjust settings and look at the resultant shift in output. Over time, small changes will add considerable horsepower to profit performance.

Apply analysis tools equally to all time frames. But adjust indicator settings to the special characteristics of each holding period. Many strategies work best when the math aligns to the common crowd view. This taps its herd behavior and allows the swing trader to anticipate its next move. For greater flexibility, toggle between popular and custom settings to review the differences in signal output.

Pack indicators into 5-minute and 60-minute charts to track the intraday markets. Fill both upper and lower plots with layered information so that a single glance effectively captures current conditions. Apply 5-8-13 Bollinger Bands to identify short-term trends and intraday S/R. Place a smoothed five-bar stochastics under candlesticks to measure oscillation between buying and selling behavior. Then plot a classic 12-26-9 MACD histogram beneath the 60-minute bars to visualize broad intraday swing cycles.

Apply classic 20-day Bollinger Bands to track crowd behavior for swing positions from 1 day to 3 weeks. Plot a 14 day, smoothed RSI beneath price to measure longer-term overbought-oversold conditions. If possible, observe daily volume with a color-coded histogram that marks up days in green and down days in red. Place a 60-day volume moving average right across the spikes to signal when individual

Look at the same Oracle chart as the last illustration with a trend-following MACD histogram under the price action instead of Stochastics. Simple MACD tactics that buy a break above the –0- line and sell the first down histogram would capture about 2/3 of the rally. Trend-following indicators work very well in rising or falling markets but emit false signals in sideways ranges.

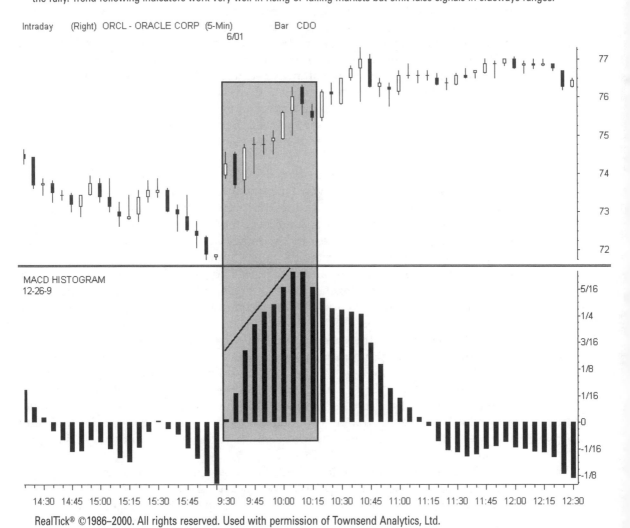

RealTick® ©1986–2000. All rights reserved. Used with permission of Townsend Analytics, Ltd.

sessions draw unexpected interest. And always toggle between daily and weekly views for all indicators to view broad cycles that may affect position management.

PRICE, TIME, AND VOLUME

Build indicator knowledge through study of the core elements of price, time, and volume. Large-scale technical analysis requires highly complicated math inputs to

FIGURE 5.4

Layered indicators through multiple time frames build a 3D landscape of short-term trends, cycles, and congestion. Both the 5-minute and 60-minute Nextel charts feature 13-bar Bollinger Bands with 5- and 8-bar simple MAs. A trend-following MACD histogram under the 60-minute chart tracks momentum while the oscillating Stochastics under the 5-minute chart measures short-term buying and selling cycles. The best trades arise when features through different time frames come into perfect alignment.

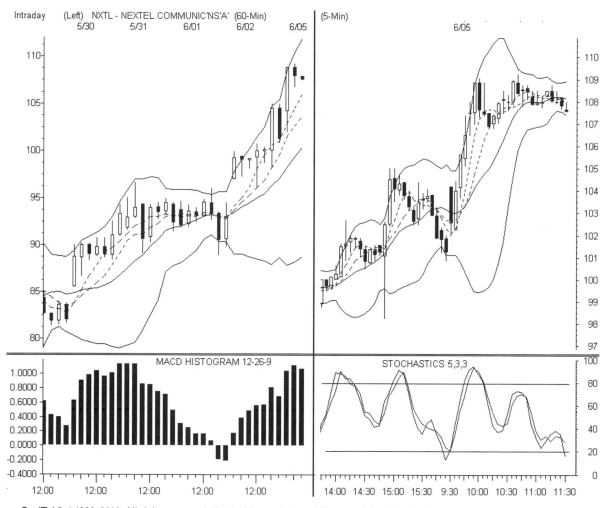

gauge public sentiment and broad cash flows. But common data bits effectively measure individual stocks. The vast majority of popular indicators use only simple snapshots of price and/or volume over specified points in time.

Many oscillators measure the distance between a bar's closing price and range high to predict underlying buying power. Price itself represents the ultimate leading indicator with these simple tools. But keep in mind that derivative calculations always emit slower information than the data itself. While this smoothing process benefits swing traders who tend to act too quickly, it can also generate late signals.

Time invokes an indicator's power as it compares key values and marks developing trends. Period-based snapshots sum up this price-volume activity and quantify relative movement. Fresh calculations then examine each new piece of data so the swing trader can make informed predictions about future price direction. Indicator time frames destroy the best tool's effectiveness when they don't align properly with current cycles or holding period. Alternatively, resonant time readings with mediocre tools will generate startling accuracy in prediction.

Study of market volume has two primary functions. First, it attempts to measure actual levels of accumulation and distribution hidden under the massive flow of the ticker tape. Second, it gathers up the crowd's divergent impulses and evokes graphic images of their herd behavior. Volume indicators comprise a significant subset of all technical analysis. But they offer far less useful information than most price-based tools.

The lack of a simple linear relationship between volume and price change frustrates attempts to make accurate predictions. Volume leads the crowd as often as it lags, and it always seems to make perfect sense in hindsight. Timing trades to volume signals alone yields very poor results. Always combine volume study with price action before making important decisions. Swing traders should apply a simple histogram and accumulation-distribution overview to most charts. But move on quickly to more urgent matters unless the emotional crowd demands a more detailed examination.

BUILDING CUSTOM INDICATORS

Most technical indicators tune to preadjusted settings by the author, charting software or website. Use these canned inputs to track crowd behavior, but set them aside when growing skills demand original strategies. Trends and opportunities exist throughout all time frames. Proper choice of both indicators and their related settings requires considerable attention. Common parameters can misalign with particular tactics and trigger execution decisions that depend on false information.

Vary time frame to track cyclical price behavior and build a 3D trend model. Place one custom set above and below a central study that correlates with the chosen holding period. This may require plotting different indicator types for each length chart. For example, to track faster signals on intraday holds between 1 and 3 hours, try a 6-17-9 MACD histogram on a 60-minute chart, 5-3-3 Stochastics on the 5-minute, and watch the broad daily action with 8-day Bollinger Bands.

Many indicators apply smoothing averages to their raw calculations. These slow down choppy output and filter individual data to emit fewer false signals. Swing traders apply these moving averages in different ways to remove inherent bias from the classic formula. Exponential MAs offer the most common variation. This measure applies greater weight to more recent input and filters the double count tendency of simple MAs. Experiment with alternative MA calculations when indicators require a smoother appearance. The varied output may improve a particular tactic or method. Use this custom technique to speed up, slow down, or filter out certain levels of data.

When a classic analysis method gains popularity with the masses, price adjusts to undermine its most common outcome. An indicator may stop working entirely when the trading majority bases decisions on that price examination. This popularity forces constant reevaluation of indicator effectiveness and choice of parameters. Common knowledge focuses upon specific time periods and smoothing averages. Swing traders adjust by phasing their parameters ahead of or behind those of the crowd. This capitalizes on the herd instinct and uses its behavior to build trading profits.

Canned indicators never answer all of the important questions for each promising setup. Because this limitation adversely affects performance, develop customized views of market activity that reflect and support unique strategies. Start with pieces of popular tools already in existence. More importantly, learn to articulate exactly what new information will support evolving tactics. Identify the question first and then compose an original way to answer it.

Test many variations of a new math application before moving on to the next step. Once in place, find optimum smoothing averages through trial and error. Then run this new indicator through a systems testing program such as TradeStation. These heavy number-crunching software programs take complex data sets and evaluate them through numerous markets to measure how well they signal primary buy and sell zones.

PATTERN TOOLS

Apply price pattern tools before beginning any other chart analysis. They provide the core knowledge required to execute original and profitable trading strategies.

T A B L E   5.1

Core Elements of Popular Indicators

Indicator	Element
ADX	Bar Range
Chaikin oscillator	Volume
Commodity channel index	Price deviation
HIstorical volatility	Price deviation
MACD histogram	Price moving average
McClellan oscillator	Daily breadth
MoneyFlow	Up closes vs. down closes
Rate of change	Price
RSI	Up closes vs. down closes
Stochastics	Bar close vs. bar range

TRENDLINES

Trendlines reflect hidden market order as well as self-fulfilling prophecy. Because many market participants watch straight-line extensions of two prior highs or lows, odds increase that any extended line will support or resist price when struck. Trendlines grow stronger after each successful test. Some may persist for years, while others may break in minutes. An individual trendline will print on the arithmetic or log scale chart, but not both at the same time. Always toggle between chart types to uncover these important S/R barriers.

Trendlines have many applications beyond their well-known uses. The indicator plots average momentum for the trend that forms the line. The rate of price change up or down the line always remains constant. Therefore, these straight lines reflect momentum convergence-divergence when compared with other price inputs. For example, momentum increases when price expands away from a trendline and decreases when it rolls toward the line. Also monitor the distance between trendlines and major moving averages. This oscillation provides significant timing feedback when used in conjunction with Pattern Cycles.

Trendlines often print in a psychotic manner. This odd phenomenon occurs through many scenarios. For example, important lines or channels may vanish for no apparent reason and then reappear unexpectedly months or years after their departure, still exerting major influence. Or an apparently normal trendline may suddenly act as a price swivel, rather than support or resistance. Price strikes it once, and the line holds but then breaks on a second test. Price thrusts through, pulls back, and tests successfully from the other side, but then fails once more and jumps back to the original side. The line becomes a central pivot axis that drives swing traders crazy.

Legitimate trendline breaks display common price mechanics. Bars expand sharply away from the violation point on greater-than-average volume. Pullbacks occur, but not until price prints a good distance away from the break point. Volume then declines on a slow reversal back toward the former barrier. When price breaks a trendline on low participation and doesn't expand quickly, an immediate jump back across S/R often occurs. This behavior triggers an excellent pattern failure signal in the opposite direction. Watch for price to draw a miniature reversal pattern right across the trendline. Use these small double tops and bottoms to signal a low-risk fade entry.

The relationship between trendlines and the charting landscape shifts relative to the time frame of each element. The swing trader must properly tune time to explore different aspects of momentum. Make certain the time inputs match holding period for the intended execution. For example, the plot of a 6-month trendline has little meaning for intraday trading unless price touches it that day. But the return of a 5-minute candlestick to a 3-hour trendline may pinpoint a profitable entry zone.

The first break in a major trendline does not signify a reversal. It flags the end of a move and beginning of sideways congestion. Take the time to understand the difference between that phenomenon and an actual trend change. Congestion represents an important feature of the underlying trend. It often leads to a new price

F I G U R E   5.5

Three variations of a 20-day moving average can produce very different results. The linear weighted MA logs the fastest overall signals on this Verticalnet chart, while the simple MA lags far behind. Notice how the distance between the simple and linear weighted averages exceeds 10% through some volatile periods in VERT's price development. Choose moving averages that correspond with temperament and timing. For example, aggressive traders can respond quickly with faster MA signals while defensive traders avoid whipsaws with slower ones.

Daily   (Right) VERT - VERTICALNET INC   Bar   MA (P=20)   MA (P=20)   MA (P=20)

LINEAR WEIGHTED

EXPONENTIAL

SIMPLE

thrust in the same direction as the previous one. Sometimes congestion evolves into a legitimate reversal, but other conditions must support the change first.

Price action rings a profitable buy signal when it remounts a broken trendline. This occurs after a pullback that follows the breakdown. Momentum reverses in

F I G U R E   5.6

Siebel Systems builds a series of stepping trendlines while momentum sharply increases. Each trendline generates a constant rate of price change for that segment of the rally. As it approaches parabolic movement, SEBL collapses back into a substantial correction. Note how price returns to test the prior trendlines, which now define clear stages of declining momentum.

Daily   (Right) SEBL - SIEBEL SYSTEMS   Bar

2000

the direction of the trendline, and significant participation spikes price back through the line. Support from this new floor should be strong and eventually push the growing rally into another breakout move. Look for price waves to print a series of rising trendlines that arc upward above the original remount level.

Charting landscapes may print conflicting trendlines within the same time frame. This adds considerable noise to any trade analysis. Each intersecting force

F I G U R E   5.7

Adobe enters a vertical rally after remounting a broken trendline. Whipsaws right at the line after the initial break suggest a lack of conviction as price rolls over and drops through 55. The violation also occurs within a bull flag that declines at a mirror angle to the prior rally. Note how price first gaps up out of the flag and then uses the next bar to climb the trendline.

Daily   (Right) ADBE - ADOBE SYSTEMS   Bar

must resolve price direction through crowd participation. When two or more trend-lines clash, consider a quick position exit until conditions resolve. Don't confuse this event with trendlines that print within different time frames. These represent important profit opportunities. This setup predicts that price within the smaller wave will come under the influence of the larger trendline and reverse course.

PSYCHOTIC TRENDLINES

Always seek innovative methods to evaluate new setups. Many odd chart shapes have characteristics that generate original ways to look at the markets. For example, standard trading wisdom uncovers a trendline whenever three or more relative highs or lows line up. This exercise sketches a straight line under rising trends and over falling ones. But many participants fail to realize that a trendline drawn through both highs and lows contains predictive properties as well.

Psychotic trendlines (PTs) encompass all straight-line phenomena not covered by classic charting landscape rules. They recognize that some market participants will act on the extension of any two price pivots. PTs don't have the power of normal trendlines but can exert tremendous influence on price development. For example, watch their great impact when vanishing trendlines suddenly reappear after months or years. Evaluate PTs in relation to other chart elements and use them for simple cross-verification. Also determine whether they define classic S/R or swing axis events.

A straight line drawn across any two relative highs or lows should produce a random extension with no predictive power. But in *Methods of a Wall Street Master*, Vic Sperandeo illustrates how his two-point method will locate breakouts when combined with specific trading rules. Apply PTs in a similar manner. But any strategy must also address several variations since these lines represent price pivots as often as S/R levels.

First locate a PT on a chart of interest. Then see whether price gaps through it repeatedly or whether bars swivel back and forth across its boundaries. This signals a pivot bias for that line. Next categorize whether the slope trend is up or down and whether it acts more as support or resistance. Then trade primarily in the direction of the slope if the PT shows classic S/R. For example, if the trend descends and displays price resistance, sell that market at the line.

Apply simple trading rules with pivot PTs regardless of trend slope. Expect that price will hold the first two times that it strikes the line but fail the third time. This tracks the same strategy that swing traders use for the second test of a horizontal high or low. If the PT also exhibits multiple gaps through past pivots, odds increase for a gap to ultimately break the line. But don't take the trade unless cross-verification also pinpoints a breakout or reversal at this level.

PARALLEL PRICE CHANNELS

Parallel price channels (PPCs) build across the highs and lows of relative price movement. They print two sets of trendlines at an equal distance to each other and can persist for long periods of time. PPCs have greater predictive value than simple trendlines and work with many different strategies. They form on either arithmetic or log scale charts, but not both at the same time. They owe their existence to Fibonacci proportion within trend development.

PPCs can display all the psychotic tendencies of regular trendlines. They exhibit vanishing phenomena that can persist for years. They will often criss-cross into complex mosaic patterns that box price in all directions. Frequently, small chan-

F I G U R E   5.8

Lucent gaps above a psychotic trendline on the 60-minute chart. The original line shows typical support on the first test but follows with a critical violation. Price bottoms and draws a simple rising wedge several weeks later that pushes up into the line and explodes through on high volume. This chart also illustrates typical behavior for a remounted trendline as the crowd returns for another long-side opportunity.

nels embed themselves into larger ones. At times, swing traders may find three or four sublevel PPCs on a single major trend. These multiple-time-frame PPCs have a great advantage over trendlines. Complex trading systems, such as Elder's Triple Screen, can be applied with great ease when they appear.

Channels persist because the crowd sees and acts upon them. This unique formation demonstrates considerable potency, although modern PPCs print more violations than in the past. While other common patterns whipsaw participants into oblivion, channels print their classic mechanics more consistently. It may be that this stable Fibonacci structure cannot be easily altered by the insider manipulation that weakens other patterns.

How can four chart points connect so easily into parallel lines in our random walk world? They present a strong argument for technical analysis all by themselves. While logic suggests that these formations rarely occur, the opposite is true. PPCs print more often than clean trendlines on most charts. Their frequency probably generates due to self-fulfilling prophecy. Market participants naturally target a fourth strike after the chart draws the first three points. If a reversal does appear at that level, the pattern confirms and improves the odds that the next test will also succeed. The formation then strengthens with each strike and persists until a greater force overcomes it.

PPCs offer more versatility than trendlines in finding low risk entry. The two primary lines display natural reward targets and focus attention on clear violation levels. Harmonic parallel lines often form between the two extremes. These intermediate S/R levels target short-term swings, especially when they intersect with moving averages. Violation of any harmonic line raises the odds that price will continue to the next parallel support level. When the broader formation prints with embedded countertrend PPCs, swing traders access a complete pattern mosaic that guides price development.

Channels extend the reach of classic technical analysis. These unique lines reveal vital information on a trend's underlying mechanics. Channel traders maintain their edge over the competition since few books examine them in detail and the crowd remains unaware of their true power. Unfortunately, clean trendlines don't print often in modern markets. Insiders know exactly where these lines set up and repeatedly violate them to trigger volume. But those same players never see PPCs and enable low-risk positions just below the radar.

PPCs demonstrate Fibonacci behavior that allows visual traders to make accurate predictions without using a calculator. Many channel strategies closely follow trendline and S/R concepts. Choose setups based on the channel's time frame persistence. The longer a pattern endures, the more likely that it will support the trade. Always search for other S/R to cross-verify PPC extremes. When moving averages, Bollinger Bands, or Fibonacci retracements cross parallels, risk decreases and potential reward increases.

Channels may take months to form and last for years. Due to broad movement over long periods of time, locate monthly and weekly PPCs with log scale charts rather than arithmetic ones. Observe all the S/R information on these large and complex formations and then drill down to very short time periods to build detailed insight on embedded price movement.

GAPS

Gaps reveal sudden and important shifts in crowd sentiment through a single price bar. They can print anywhere within the charting landscape but tend to occur in

FIGURE   5.9

Parallel price channels build harmonic lines into Motorola's decline. Note the clear support and resistance of the two inner channels, which bounce price around like a pinball. Even down gaps within the larger pattern respond to these harmonic levels as they print. Draw new PPCs in as much detail as possible to identify these inner lines and other obvious swing pivot zones. Then use them for trade execution in combination with other charting landscape features.

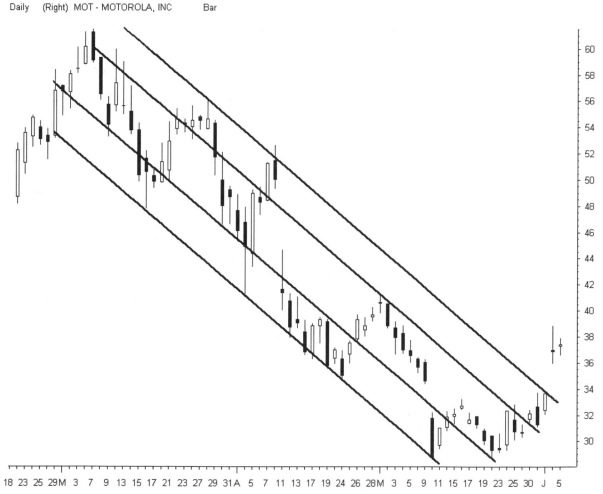

Daily   (Right) MOT - MOTOROLA, INC   Bar

several distinct patterns. Each type predicts specific characteristics in regard to persistence, response during retracements, and the impact on trend. Gaps cut through many time frames and trends, but they represent very different phenomena in each one. For example, a breakout move in one time frame may print an exhaustion event in another.

F I G U R E   5.10

Sandisk Corp. prints a five-wave rally with a well-organized gap structure on the 60-minute chart. The breakaway gap pushes through the old downtrend line into an inverse head and shoulders neckline at the (eventual) 38% level. After a short pullback, a sharp continuation gap prints right through the midpoint of the trend. Then price bases for three bars at the 62% level before a broad exhaustion gap marks the end of the rally.

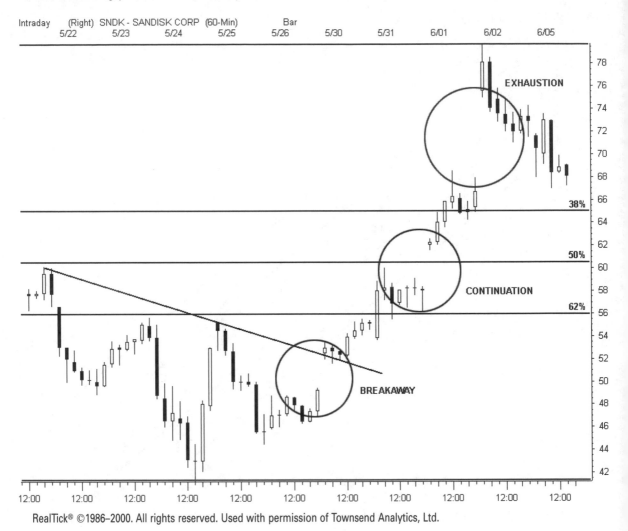

Gap importance relies upon location, extension, and volume. They can print in the major trend direction or against it. When a major gap opposes the current market momentum, it represents the only chart phenomenon that signals trend change without a common top or bottom pattern. A short or long price bar can stand at the far end of a gap move. Long bars tend to predict a quick follow-through in the direction of the gap. Short bars suggest sideways action or a pullback test into the violated space.

The gap's location reveals both the character and mechanics for subsequent price action. Sharp gaps through clear S/R signify important breakouts and breakdowns. Pressure can build so strongly at these levels that the opening tick prints far from the last close. Emotional bursts can trigger multiple gaps as active trends build momentum. Gaps that print within congestion display far less persistence and may fill with little warning or volume. And high intensity gaps that occur late in strong rallies or selloffs often signal the end of a trend.

Participation will limit or fuel gap strength. Certain S/R events only verify when strong volume accompanies them. For example, breakout gaps without adequate volume invite a strong reversal even if they print at a perfect location. This relationship between gaps and crowd participation relies upon complex interactions. For example, a high-volume gap may end price movement in that direction if it uses up the last available supply for that trend. But another gap with less volume may leave enough on the table to ensure new surges of momentum.

Old traders' wisdom advises that gaps get filled. This simple expression describes the mechanics of retracement found throughout most market trends. However, some gaps never fill. This knowledge dictates a fresh approach to these specialized patterns. Swing traders must learn the characteristics of each gap to apply the strategy that aligns best with its behavior. Start by identifying the location of the event on the trend-range axis.

Edwards and Magee popularized gaps 50 years ago in *Technical Analysis of Stock Trends*. These old masters describe three types of trend gaps found in most stock charts. Breakaway gaps appear as a market breaks out into a new trend move, up or down. Continuation gaps print about halfway through trends when enthusiasm or fear overpowers reason. Exhaustion gaps burn out trends with one last surge of emotion.

Breakaway and continuation gaps should print volume that sharply exceeds the 60-bar VMA. Both events provide excellent trades in the gap direction when the trend first pulls back to test them. They hold S/R the vast majority of the time and identify low-risk, high-reward entry. Markets retest most breakouts very quickly after they occur. If successful, price often moves sharply away from the pullback level. But many bars can pass before price retraces to a continuation gap. Crowd intensity tends to carry the trend well past the gap before it yields to any substantial test.

Exhaustion gaps print as trends and indicators reach extremes. This last burst may occur on very high volume, but a lack of participation does not negate the pattern. Exhaustion gaps fill easily and warn that the trend is over. Price fills the gap and often pulls back to the hole from the other side before a correction proceeds in the closing direction. Congestion patterns may form through wide gap ranges before yielding to substantial movement. Keep in mind that an exhaustion gap may turn out to represent a hidden continuation gap in the next-larger time frame. This

F I G U R E   5.11

Use candlestick reversals to uncover important gaps that hide in other time frames. A spinning top candle on the Texas Instruments daily chart hides an exhaustion gap within the 60-minute view. This classic gap appears at the end of five-wave trend movement just as the supply of buyers or sellers runs out. Exhaustion gaps fill more quickly than breakaway or continuation gaps. Notice how price briefly dips below 85 to fill the continuation gap overnight before springing back the next morning in a 7-point rally.

odd phenomenon requires a sharp eye and often does not reveal itself until the larger trend ends. Use the dark cloud cover or bearish engulfing candlestick patterns to uncover these dual gap candidates.

Gap creation aligns with Elliott's five-wave trend theory. The breakaway gap corresponds with the initiation of a dynamic first- or third-wave impulse. Runaway emotions emit the continuation gap at the center of the third wave. Then the trend sequence ends through the fifth-wave exhaustion gap. The continuation gap routinely marks a halfway point for the entire trend. Swing traders use this knowledge to target major reversals. Visualize the gap as soon as possible after a third wave completes. Draw an extension from the edge of the first wave to the new gap. Then double the distance and wait for a last thrust to push price into it. Consider fade entry with a tight stop loss when the target strikes, as long as substantial cross-verification supports the trade.

The first test of a continuation gap often occurs after the closure of an exhaustion gap. Markets retrace five-wave trends according to Fibonacci proportion. Pullbacks often fill the primary fifth wave completely through a first rise/first failure pattern. Without strong support, the countertrend thrust then continues until supply-demand equalizes and reawakens the underlying trend. The continuation gap marks the natural 50% retracement, providing the support needed to force a reversal.

Watch for false gap fills. Modern market action closes many continuation gaps for a bar or two before price thrusts sharply back in the direction of support. This likely reflects growing common knowledge of this fascinating S/R point. Don't let this whipsaw phenomenon negate these profitable trade setups. Entry at the far side of the gap offers very low risk as long as volume remains flat. Less aggressive traders can wait for price to remount the hole and then execute as the gap reopens.

Continuation gap trades provide high probability entry, but keep in mind that the subsequent swing will likely fail before it again tests the exhaustion gap. Deep pullbacks face an extended period of price discovery as trend volatility dissipates. Longer-term positions can survive this process, but swing trades may not. Use trend mirrors to target an acceptable reward before choosing to execute a gap trade. Exit quickly on the first reversal thrust unless patience allows an extended position.

Always distinguish between gaps in the direction of the prevailing trend and those going against it. Countertrend gaps often flag major reversals without a long series of price bars. The most important shock events occur right near major highs or lows. A sudden break in the wrong direction after a strong rally generates fear among the crowd and may ignite herd behavior that leads to considerably lower prices. This hole-in-the-wall gap has many swing trading applications, which are discussed in detail in Chapter 11.

Opening gaps fascinate participants but require solid execution skills. Market insiders know that fresh cash seeks opportunity at the start of the day and paint the tape to encourage execution. This premarket manipulation encourages supply-demand imbalance because many traders see these numbers and place ill-advised orders well above or below the market. The resulting friction sets the stage for a violent reversal just minutes into the new session.

Most morning gaps face a testing period before filling or yielding to a trend thrust. Fades can begin as early as the opening bell. But price often moves first in the direction of the gap to gather volume before it reverses by the third 5-minute bar. This classic reversal zone originates from the era when most public participants had to view the markets through a 15-minute delay. Insiders held opening price firm to give this retail crowd a chance to act before fading them.

F I G U R E   5.12

Atmel returns to test a continuation gap several weeks after filling a small exhaustion gap at 54. Price first dips sharply through 44 to take out weak hands and then snaps back strongly in a rally that quickly heads for new highs. 3× cross-verification signals a very profitable trade setup right at this bottom. In addition to the gap itself, price turns right at the 62% retracement, where it also prints a long-legged hammer reversal.

Gaps encourage execution tactics that favor or fade the open. The highest-risk tactics enter a new position at the open in the direction of the break. As with other momentum plays, price can fade sharply without a clear signal that the trade should be terminated. Execution against the gap after a two-bar thrust offers lower risk but more anxiety. This countertrend tactic requires defensive management after execution and a very quick exit or tight stop as price moves into a profit. The setup also demands cross-verification with central tendency tools. The opening bars must thrust well outside short-term Bollinger Band extremes before consideration of a fade position.

Look for a bounce at the prior closing bar if price breaks opening congestion and reverses to fill the gap. As the market pulls back, the opposite end of the hole

F I G U R E   5.13

Two ferocious morning gaps defy prediction on Lycos. On the morning that the stock opens in the low 70s, only the fourth intraday bar offers a low-risk profit. Short sellers have more luck the next day as a declining wedge telegraphs lower prices for most of the afternoon. Notice how LCOS reverses right at the third 5-minute bar after each gap. This typical morning action tests the supply-demand waters.

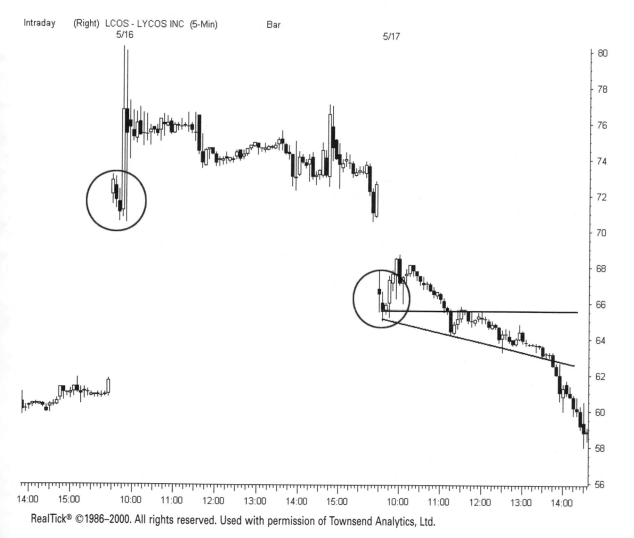

RealTick® ©1986–2000. All rights reserved. Used with permission of Townsend Analytics, Ltd.

now presents a new barrier. A reversal off this level sets the stage for price to fail and thrust well back into the prior closing range. Gaps that stay unfilled signal powerful support or resistance. Price should eventually push out of the morning range into higher or lower levels when this occurs.

Early congestion identifies signposts for safe gap entry. These range extremes provide important information on the strength or weakness of the morning move. Gaps that fill quickly should be avoided in the direction of the trend. Use classic swing strategies to prepare execution after they test and hold. In other words, buy pullbacks in up gaps and sell bear rallies in down gaps. Also consider breakout strategies at the high or low for the session. For example, look for a second test of a short-term top and enter in expectation of a breakout.

Long entry into a big market gap down terrifies many swing traders. But this profitable opportunity must be mastered to achieve consistent performance. Learn to set aside fear and stand against the crowd when the right conditions present themselves. Reprogram your natural reaction to stomach-churning down gaps by stepping in the shoes of those trapped on the other side of these shock events.

Imagine taking a questionable long position into a volatile close and spending the night wondering how the next morning will affect profit or loss. Many participants with large positions cannot sleep when they carry that much risk. Images of lottery jackpots and painful losses both creep into the irrational mind. Then the next day finally arrives and the worst-case scenario occurs. The early spread shows the position many points into the hole. The resulting pain quickly drives out rational thought, and fear-driven instinct takes over. In total shock, you sell into the open, happy to be relieved of the heavy burden.

Immediately the stock reverses and rockets above your entry price.

Market professionals use fear to generate profits. Many opening gaps allow large players to benefit their own accounts by fading the crowd. When overall conditions favor strong buying interest, these shock gaps actually represent low-risk entry for the swing trader. Learn to interpret this market sentiment correctly and capitalize on misinformed sellers.

But extreme caution is advised. Only an experienced swing trader with a solid history of risk management should execute a long position into a down gap. Poorly timed gap entry can be very deadly to an equity account. Avoid execution right at the open whenever possible. Instead, watch for cross-verification near the third-bar reversal and find a small pullback for immediate entry. Also check the news first to evaluate the severity of the shock event. The best opportunities come when no obvious reason drives the selloff.

Important news events don't always eliminate gap-down opportunities. Bad news offers insiders a chance to enter ongoing rallies at a bargain price. When everyone expects a selloff, insiders play on their fears and knock down opening bids sharply. These mechanics often produce a significant bounce after the open in strong markets. But swing traders should never expect a complete gap fill in these volatile conditions; they take whatever profits the market gives them and move on to the next setup.

Risk-averse traders can also find profitable opportunities on these fearful mornings. Watch for a first rise pattern back to the closing hour high of the prior session. This price action signifies a filled gap and the first stage of a reversal that should carry higher. Treat this simple price test as a double top and watch for a long opportunity on the next pullback or third rise into the extreme.

F I G U R E   5.14

Oracle gaps down as a volatile session begins. The opening turns out to be the low for the day as the stock heads vertical for a 6-½ point gain in under 1 hour. Focus attention on the gap itself during these events. Watch how quickly it fills and whether it offers a pullback opportunity after it closes. Notice how ORCL mounts the broken hammer from the prior afternoon, which also marks the gap's extension. After it completes a first rise, it pulls back 38% into a cup and handle pattern that ejects through the top.

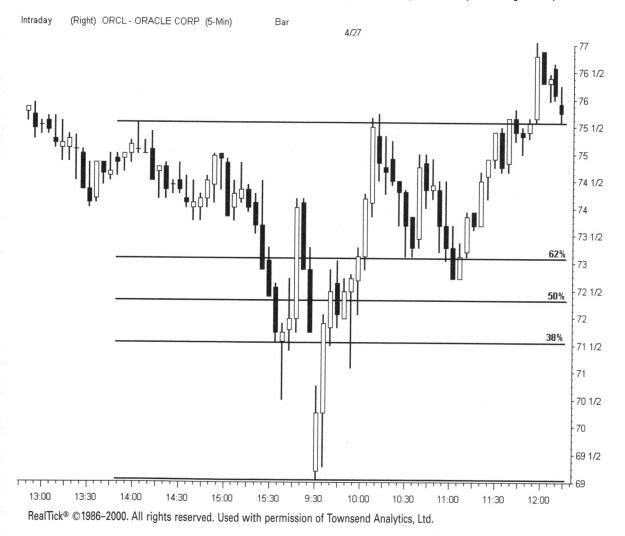

Intraday   (Right) ORCL - ORACLE CORP (5-Min)   Bar

Countertrend gap entry requires solid interpretation of the numbers, skilled reading of the emotional crowd, and excellent timing. Seasoned swing traders recognize many redundant features in these morning setups. Neither market makers nor specialists rely on original strategies most of the time. They will play the same classic price games as often as they can get away with them. Experience with their tactics over time builds confidence when warning signs of their activity start to appear.

TRIANGLES

Triangles present a major class of patterns that don't fit easily into continuation or reversal categories. Their eventual outcomes depend on their unique characteristics and positions within larger trends. Each triangle begins with a natural tendency that the swing trader must evaluate in context with the charting landscape. Ascending triangles print the most bullish patterns, while descending triangles form the most bearish ones. Symmetrical triangles display a zero bias for either outcome: the formation suggests a state of perfect balance.

Well-formed triangles gather tremendous predictive power because they point directly at negative-positive feedback interfaces. A powerful vertical thrust often develops when congested price finally exits a triangle and surges into trend. While false moves occur near these apex points, breakouts tend to print with a higher degree of reliability than many other patterns. However, the dependability of all patterns mutates with the crowd's participation. The most perfect and widely recognized triangles will cause the most grief for those trading in the direction of the common knowledge.

Angle and location define the pattern's identity. Ascending triangles rise again and again toward a ceiling resistance level. Symmetrical triangles surge rhythmi-

F I G U R E   5.15

TALE OF THREE TRIANGLES

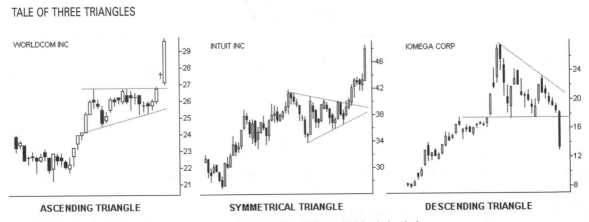

ASCENDING TRIANGLE   SYMMETRICAL TRIANGLE   DESCENDING TRIANGLE

cally across both sides of a horizontal axis that divides the formation right through the middle. The bearish descending triangle bounces weakly off bottom support. All three variations can occur at bottoms, tops, or in the middle of ongoing trends. Unfortunately, this relative location does not reveal itself until the pattern completes and price ejects out of one side or the other.

Triangles give birth in a state of high volatility. This agitation decreases sharply as they approach their termination points. This poses one of the risks inherent in trading these patterns. Volatility may flatline if no ignition sparks a breakout. This forces price to meander endlessly in sideways motion and lose its potential. Close out positions without hesitation when caught in this phenomenon.

Buying pressure builds in ascending triangles as price tests upper boundaries. The setup normally triggers on the third rise to the top. A sharp expansion through this horizontal zone signals the breakout. Watch for a failure at the third high that may print a triple-top reversal. The best patterns show precise horizontal resistance. This builds strong demand just above that level. Slowly ascending highs do not characterize these bullish triangles. They represent bearish rising wedges. The difference lies in the loss of buying power as each nominal high fails to produce a significant profit.

Ascending triangles commonly appear as continuation patterns in the middle of trend development. When they emerge near potential bottoms, upside breakouts often print parabolic rallies. Many miss this outstanding opportunity because the event tends to occur within a countertrend (bear market) environment. Regardless of location, the pattern fails if the trendline of the rising lows breaks to the downside.

Symmetrical triangles form the most common congestion patterns seen on price charts. Formations that persist for years can be found on monthly bars, while day traders note their repeated appearance on 5-minute Nasdaq stock charts. These triangles form a central pivot axis that can yield powerful moves on price ejection. The challenge is to predict which way that price will break. While popular tutorials describe a bullish tendency, the pattern really has no inherent bias and can go either way with ease. Watch for a directional signal when the pattern nears two-thirds of the distance from its inception to the apex point where the triangle lines converge.

Examine the symmetrical triangle within the context of an ongoing trend. Those that appear early in a move support that trend more consistently. General trading tactics use the lines that form the upper and lower boundaries to target breakout points. Regardless of direction, expanding price faces an additional test at the initial pattern high or low before it can thrust into a new trend leg. This last barrier often forces a final pullback to the breakout line that swing traders can use for late entry. Pay special attention to rare double symmetrical triangles in which one pattern prints right after the other. The center point between the two formations marks the halfway point of a major trend in the same manner as a continuation gap.

Study the symmetrical triangle up close to uncover its secrets. Examine price action and volume at the second and third bottoms. Look for long bullish candle reversals that suggest bargain hunting. Examine the pattern's ability to hold well above the first low on good accumulation. This stokes the breakout fires when the

FIGURE 5.16

CNET Networks prints a double symmetrical triangle during this strong 1999 rally. The twin triangles have a similar appearance and take almost the same number of bars to complete before ejecting higher. The continuation gap at the halfway point between the two patterns also marks the middle of the entire 6-month move. Right on schedule, a sharp decline to 42 carries price into a successful test of the gap after the final top prints.

Daily   (Right) CNET - CNET NETWORKS INC   Bar
                                                1999

new trend finally begins. Beware of flatline bars beyond the two-thirds point that continue for more than a few prints. Many swing traders will be watching this same dead action and go elsewhere if nothing happens.

The triangle's apex point marks important S/R for price pullbacks and future trend mirror passages. These common patterns fail when they break one way but fall back through the apex in the opposite direction. Once this type of failure prints, price should continue to fade for some time as the false breakout relieves substantial pressure in the opposite direction.

Many participants associate descending triangles with topping formations, but they can appear anywhere. These bearish patterns sap buying power through three declining highs that lead to an eventual breakdown. A horizontal bottom builds selling pressure that triggers many stops on a first violation. This triangle fails when price rises above the trendline formed by the descending highs. Price expansion through that violation will often be more dynamic than the expected breakdown move. When price pierces the horizontal bottom for a few ticks and pops back above, look for an immediate test of the declining high trendline. Any break through that point represents a buy signal.

All types of triangles turn into something else with great frequency. No guarantees exist that any pattern will act according to textbook rules. Growing knowledge of triangle formations increases the frequency of this mutation into other forms of congestion. For this reason, trade these patterns according to strict planning that encompasses both breakout and failure strategies. Demand price bar and volume cross-verification or exit the position quickly. Intraday traders must also consider time-of-day bias when patterns hit execution targets. Look for clear signals or let other participants risk their capital first.

FLAGS

Flag patterns appear as countertrend parallelograms between waves of strong trend movement. These continuation patterns exhibit characteristic behavior and provide dependable trade setups. In less dynamic markets, this common formation will often mirror the same angle as the prior trend but in the opposite direction. Flags appear equally in bull and bear markets. Bull flags decline against the rally in uptrends, and bear flags rise against the selloff in downtrends.

Vertical price movement precedes the most reliable flag patterns. Strong volume from the prior trend should drop off sharply as the range evolves. Expect price bars to narrow as volatility and interest flatline, as with other negative feedback events. Near pattern completion, volume should increase in the direction of the eventual breakout and spike just as a new trend leg begins. Flags should yield to new trends in no more than 15–20 bars. Bear flags tend to take less time to conclude than bull ones. When this pattern persists longer than expected, it may evolve into a long sideways market with little profit potential.

Flags print a minimum of four relative extensions: two highs and two lows that form parallel trendlines. S/R may also generate a price axis through the center of the formation. Expect a breakout from the pattern after a pullback from the third strike at each extreme. But watch for an early move after price touches only one line for the third time, reverses, and then drifts back toward it. The eventual breakout mimics the action of better-known parallel channels. Price bars expand sharply away from the broken line on increased volume.

Flag retracement follows classic Fibonacci proportion. The second low or high against the primary trend often strikes right at the 50% pullback, while the third hits the 62% level. If this second strike occurs closer to 38%, the third may go no further than 50% before the underlying trend reasserts itself. Fib grids provide an excellent cross-verification source for impending flag breakouts. For example, the third small rally in a descending bull flag may push upward into the bottom of a 38% retracement that also marks the location of an important moving average. This convergence of S/R increases odds that the upside price break will be dynamic.

Common trading wisdom dictates that flags fly at half-mast. This suggests that these patterns print about halfway through trends. Use this anecdotal information for general price targeting. Measure the length of the sharp price move that precedes the pattern. Add that to the flag low that initiates the new trend and look for another reversal when price approaches the target.

CANDLESTICK PATTERNS

Swing traders spend months trying to memorize the dozens of candlestick patterns found in popular books but still learn little about the subject. While technicians attempt to define many different candle sets, only a few major formations deserve attention. First, realize that each candle pattern displays an internal bias toward continuation or reversal. But so do many simple sets of price bars. Candlesticks draw their real power through an ability to highlight how the crowd will drive prices higher or lower.

Popular candlestick patterns focus on intense bull-bear conflict but rarely allow easy profit. Precise trade entry comes when swing traders drop down to the time frame below the developing bars and interpret these pockets of emotional crowd behavior. Look for more recognizable patterns, S/R, and common landscape features that place the larger action into perspective. This candle microanalysis works well with the intuitive mind to generate accurate and consistent prediction.

Examine the charting landscape in which each candlestick pattern appears. Most important formations take place within the context of ongoing trends rather than constricted ranges. Always consider timing within a trend. Some patterns will display a bullish bias near the beginning of a price move but a bearish one as it matures. Look for predictive bars that form right through other forms of S/R, such as prior highs-lows and major moving averages. Then visually compare candle length with the recent price action. The most important events will exhibit above-average volume and bar range.

Don't depend on candle reversals to last very long: most formations only offer short-term prediction. Price frequently moves back and takes out the pattern within five to seven bars. This tendency makes candles an outstanding tool for swing traders, but it also opens the door to major trend relativity errors. Long-term reversals depend strongly on precise volume, trend, and location. For example, broad dark cloud cover events may print the high price for years. But these require new highs on panic participation following a parabolic rally.

F I G U R E   5.17

Network Associates prints a bear flag that aligns with multiple Fibonacci retracements to uncover a major price decline. The flag slowly rises against the downtrend and forms three small highs. The final high reverses at the 62% pullback of the last downtrend wave where it briefly fills the gap at 50. That signpost also fits perfectly into the 38% retracement of the entire selloff. Use the 38-62 to find high profit opportunities for trends in both directions.

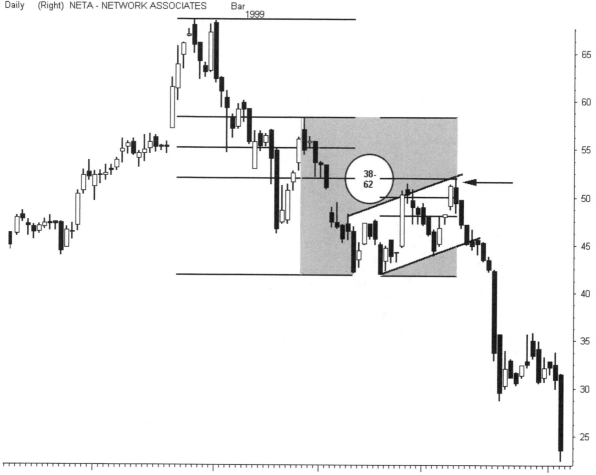

Daily   (Right) NETA - NETWORK ASSOCIATES

A tall real-body candlestick represents strong single-bar S/R. If price retraces back into its range, the subsequent action should not pierce the entire length without several small reversals. The chances of a 100% reversal on the next bar carry low odds when a long daily candle prints. For this reason, buying an immediate pullback after a tall bullish candle presents a low-risk opportunity under most circumstances. The safest trades arise when the new bar opens near the previous closing price and starts to fade immediately. This signals profit-taking by those still long from the prior candle. Price should spring back quickly through the interest of new participants when this pressure lightens up.

Candlestick patterns have great power at the edges of central tendency. Watch closely for candle shadows that shoot through the sides of Bollinger Bands, espe-

F I G U R E   5.18

The tall daily candlestick on this major PMC-Sierra reversal hides important swing trading information. This bar and the next one draw a complete five-wave rally in the next-lower time frame. This aligns retracement to classic mechanical rules. The stock pulls back and bases right at the 50% level before it ejects to higher prices. Big expansion candles rarely retrace 100% quickly and offer concealed low-risk entry.

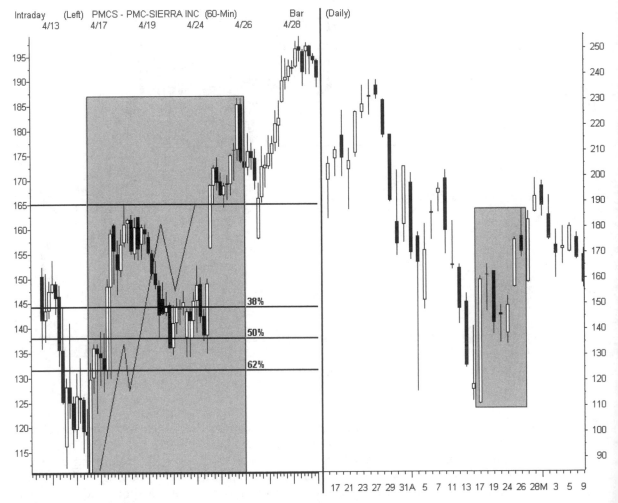

cially when they point against constricting bands. This combined pattern provides significant warning of an impending reversal. Prediction here works well through both rangebound and trending markets.

Focus on dojis and hammers more than any other candle events. These short-body, long-shadow single bars generate diverse trading strategies and offer important clues about subsequent price change. Their broad power reveals trend change in the next-lower time frame through very brief price discovery. These major candles comprise a larger collection of finger formations that includes the haramis and shooting stars. They are examined in greater detail in Chapter 10.

The harami pattern closely aligns with the classic inside day. One difference allows the candle shadow to extend outside the range of the previous bar as long as the body remains within it. This pattern represents a potential reversal when it appears within a tall expansion bar after a strong price move. Drop down one time frame and notice that the opening tick often prints a gap from the previous close. In an uptrend, this hole-in-the-wall may present a significant boundary to further price gains. In a downtrend, the gap may initiate a breakaway move to the upside.

Apply three different tactics to haramis that carry graduated risk. Each strategy executes in the same direction as the short-term break. The first enters a position when price exceeds the expansion bar high or low, the second when it exceeds the range of the inside bar, and the last when price ejects past the real body of the inside bar. Set stop loss according to the chosen entry level in each case. In other words, if the trade uses the real body to trigger execution, exit the losing position when price then violates the real body's range in the opposite direction.

The harami cross presents a specialized form of this pattern through a doji that appears inside the range of the prior expansion bar. It signals a possible 2B reversal in the time frame beneath the candlesticks. In that chart length, price dips to a new low or high but jumps back across S/R by close. Trade this formation in the direction of the reversal rather than looking for price to break through the shadow. The odds of a strong reversal increase if a long-legged doji shadow prints across S/R.

Bearish dark cloud cover and its bullish piercing pattern cousin signal sharp price reversal. They both hide significant exhaustion gaps that mark the end of extended trends. Each two-bar pattern begins with a long expansion candle in the direction of the prevailing trend. The next candle opens well beyond the last bar's close but then reverses deep into the prior range. Price typically completes this rout on the next few candles and thrusts well out of the pattern in the opposite direction.

Consider a fade entry if price returns to test the filled exhaustion gap on the chart just below the event. But when price doesn't reverse quickly off the gap, congestion may form right through it. This suggests that a continuation move will ultimately allow that market to head off into new highs or lows. If no pullback occurs, execute when the next bar or two pierces the range of the second pattern candle. Latecomers will find that the best trade often appears after the completed reversal retraces into a test that reenters the edge of the formation.

Long dark cloud cover can stop a rally for months or years when it occurs on a daily chart well into new highs. The two candles represent significant overhead supply that fresh demand must absorb before that market can go higher. A second

F I G U R E   5.19

Harami candlestick patterns signal two changes in trend on the Marsh and McLennan chart. The first inside day generates a whipsaw after a brief selloff but the second one starts a substantial decline. Note the hole-in-the-wall morning gap that initiates each pattern on the 60-minute chart. Both lead immediately to lower intraday prices with no pullbacks. Use the hole and morning gap strategy to capitalize on haramis before the closing bar prints.

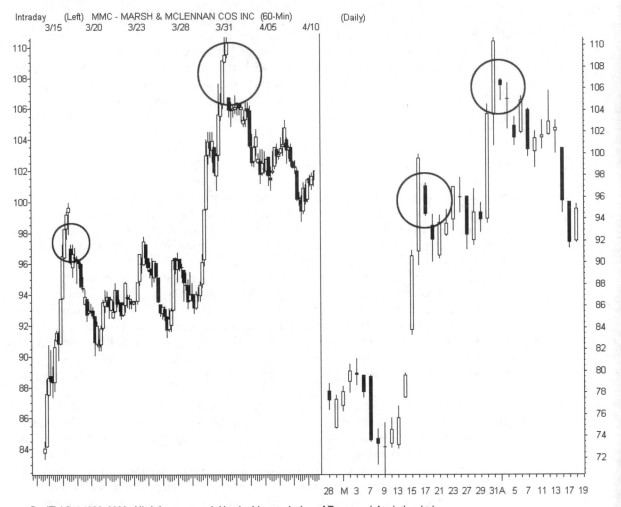

lower high often forms the rounded Eve of the classic Adam and Eve top after the sharp pattern event. Measure the ratio between this bounce and the pattern high. If it cannot rise more than 38–50% before pulling back, that market will likely move quickly to much lower levels.

F I G U R E   5.20

A cluster of dark cloud cover patterns form a major top on American Power Conversion. Five different sets of this important reversal print through a series of 22 daily bars before they finally trigger a 16-point decline. This bearish candlestick pattern will usually complete its business in a single turn.

Daily   (Right) APCC - AMER POWER CONVERSION   Bar

PATTERN FAILURE

The best trades could be in the opposite direction when patterns don't behave according to plan. Many classic formations have built-in setups that trigger contrary positions from their natural bias. Alex Elder illustrated this poorly-understood concept with his Hound of the Baskervilles signal in *Trading for a Living*. He offers the interesting example of a head and shoulders neckline that just won't break. Traders take notice of the failure and enter long positions to ride price back up to the old highs.

Patterns appear at the end of thrusting price movements. Constricted swings between key support and resistance characterize their development. Patterns complete when a new trend leg breaks through this wall and expands outward. The direction of this new thrust may be the same as or opposite to that of the previous one. A pattern between adjacent price moves in the same direction continues that trend. Alternatively, when a breakout turns and retraces the last trend, the intervening pattern reverses the prior move.

Classic tutorials categorize patterns by their tendency toward continuation or reversal. This familiar bias underlies the predictive power of these odd formations. Patterns also tend to repeat themselves through all time frames. These two characteristics generate a well-marked charting landscape that traders use to locate profitable opportunities. Most market players view patterns according to common knowledge. The majority choose the strategy that matches the formation and enter positions where directional movement will likely erupt.

But sometimes patterns don't do what the crowd expects. A powerful entry signal may flash when a setup fails to act according to its tendency. This pattern failure can trigger sharp price movement in the opposite direction from the formation's natural bias. Swing traders must prepare contrarian entry tactics to capitalize on this secondary event. But first exercise sound risk management to recognize failure in progress and wait for low-risk opportunity.

Probability underlies all prediction. Swing traders anticipate future price and enter positions to profit from it. Most times this strategy dictates execution that aligns with the highest odds. But trading plans must be flexible enough to capture setups for the less likely outcome. Start at the opposite edge from the formation's common breakout level. For example, study the declining tops of a bearish descending triangle to locate long entry if price fails and thrusts into a rally.

The classic head and shoulders pattern has been analyzed over the last century more than any other price range. In fact, one investigation concluded that this well-known pattern triggered the expected result about 74% of the time. While this intriguing measurement lies well outside the range of random outcome, it clearly illustrates just how often losses are taken when speculators sell short at the head and shoulders neckline. And consider how common knowledge further deteriorates this pattern's reliability in our modern markets.

Pattern failure now goes well beyond concepts presented in recent trading books. The contemporary market crowd recognizes most classic price patterns and takes positions according to textbook logic. This decreases the odds that price will move in the direction of the most accepted prediction. Fortunately, few tutorials teach participants about the virtues of contrary thinking. Rather than abandon their positions, the masses tend to hold on through the early stages of pattern failure in an effort to be proven right. This often leads to an eventual panic.

Swing traders must consider the opposite execution for every setup that triggers through a pattern breakout. This additional evaluation tracks the same reward: risk parameters as the original opportunity. Trade planning then visualizes what steps will be taken if the setup fades and breaks against the high-odds direction. Each failure trade must stand on its own merits. Don't consider flipping unless the new setup passes all the usual filters. Also realize that this combined workflow defines natural stop loss for both intended execution targets. Prepare for anything that the market gives and act according to a predefined plan.

Common knowledge raises the failure threat for every well-known price pattern. This unsettling fact admonishes swing traders to stand aside far more often than in the past. Lower odds for success dictate that the potential reward must be worth the additional risk. Don't jump on every neat triangle or bull flag, believing that it will provide an easy profit. Many times the failure pattern offers a far better setup and should be the only side under consideration. Train the mind to pay attention to the chart before the failure appears. These setups often signal with little warning and have a very small window of opportunity.

Pattern failure setups don't end with trendlines that refuse to crack. Whipsaws characterize modern markets and fill the pockets of insiders. Many classic patterns break out as expected, carry a few ticks, and reverse violently. If price then pulls back into congestion, swing traders can enter failure positions well before a move back through the opposite break point. The original false breakout dissipates demand in that direction and lowers risk. The whipsaw also signals that the market will likely trend sharply the other way.

Contrary entry signals arise from different S/R considerations than the original setup. An unyielding trendline does not trigger a failure trade all by itself. Congestion shows unique upper and lower boundaries. Failure patterns depend on violation as much as the opposite outcome. Learn to recognize the location of these reverse breakouts for each classic formation. For example, the head and shoulders neckline points to a classic short sale when violated. But the fade position does not execute until price mounts the descending line formed by the tops of the head and right shoulder.

The most recognizable patterns carry the greatest risk for failure. Perfection attracts attention and invites those who might stay on the sidelines in other circumstance. When setups look too good to be true, most participants enter positions on one side of the trade and attract whipsaws. Manage entry with narrow-range bars before price breaks in either direction to reduce risk and allow for a fast exit. Execution after a high-volume breakout and pullback to the trendline also improves trade success.

Pattern failures provide higher-reward opportunities than textbook breakouts because they catch the crowd leaning the wrong way. Most participants understand how patterns should work but get confused when price behavior doesn't match their expectations. They freeze like a deer in the headlights and get trapped as the failure event proceeds. This feeds on price movement until they finally capitulate. For this reason, these contrary setups exhibit highly dependable outcomes with few false moves.

F I G U R E   5.21

Ascending triangles often lead to dramatic rallies, but watch out when they fail. The rising trendline marks a breakdown level as Sigma-Aldrich suddenly rolls over and collapses. The crowd that buys into a bullish pattern provides substantial fuel in the other direction when it fails. Note how the selloff quickly cuts through strong support at 32 in response to the extreme selling pressure.

Daily   (Right) SIAL - SIGMA-ALDRICH   Bar

RealTick® ©1986–2000. All rights reserved. Used with permission of Townsend Analytics, Ltd.

INDICATOR TOOLS

Build and manage indicators to support the price pattern. Use them as truth serum to confirm or refute promising setups. Tune them properly to the intended holding period and competing crowd.

BOLLINGER BAND TACTICS

Bollinger Bands (BBs) draw their power through two important characteristics. First, they exhibit an underlying trend-range axis just like price or moving averages. Second, they constrict or expand as they move. The interaction between these two forces draws unique patterns as bars unwind through their boundaries. Candlesticks work especially well with bands. For example, a doji that strikes through a constricting band effectively signals a short-term reversal.

BBs bend and twist in response to price movement. These undulations predict how far trends should stretch before central tendency forces them back toward a central axis. Complex relationships develop between price-band direction and price-band constriction. For example, a trend tends to pause when constricting bands oppose it. It takes great skill to predict the bands' ultimate impact on price, but is well worth the effort. BBs pinpoint hidden swings better than any other tool, and telegraph whether the profit door lies open or closed.

Bands may swing through relative highs or lows and then pull back in proportional retracement to start another trend thrust. Or they may enter extended ranges that meander back and forth without direction. Movement frequently stops dead in its tracks when price rises into a falling band or drops into a rising one. Sideways bands can appear in both rangebound and trending markets. Price often fails to reach new high or low territory until bands expand to clear the path. In many ways, Bollinger Bands predict time better than they predict price.

The skilled eye watches constricted bands in real time to estimate the buying or selling force required to push them out of the way. They work extremely well during the second test of an important high or low. When markets finally break out, expanding bars often shoot into the band's edge where congestion forms a flag until the BB allows further movement. Bands constrict tightly around narrowing price in sideways markets. Apply NR7 methodology here to anticipate an impending positive feedback event.

Bollinger Bands signal early warning of trend change. Sharp price movement forces bands to expand outward. When these active markets finally turn sideways, the bands slowly tighten and roll toward price. Time passes and the BB door closes on rapid vertical movement. Experience enables the swing trader to quickly estimate the time required before bands will tighten and plan accordingly.

Strong buying or selling may push price well outside a band. A tall bar can even print completely through the barrier in extreme conditions. General tactics suggest that violent reversals often follow these major band violations. But trading against these events carries risk because markets can print a short series of these volatile bars before the reversal takes place. Also note that this price action infrequently occurs during intraday markets, except at the open.

Reduce risk by dropping down to the next-lower time frame and waiting for a reversal there before executing a countertrend position. Odds also improve if the thrusting bars run into other forms of S/R that allow cross-verification for the entry level. Stay defensive during the trade. Once price returns within the band's limits, the underlying trend can reappear quickly unless the pullback generates other re-

F I G U R E   5.22

The top Bollinger band rises toward a test of the intraday high as Worldcom drops. This sharp divergence signals the eventual breakout after price finally reverses off of the bottom band. Watch band slope closely when bars return to test important highs or lows. It often reveals the time and force needed to push price through a S/R barrier.

versal signals. Look for dark cloud cover or a similar candle pattern that fills any gap created by the bar outside the band. This complex setup can produce windfall profits if managed properly.

Thirteen-bar, 2 std dev Bollinger Bands work extremely well for intraday markets. Combine them with the 5, 8, and 13-bar simple moving averages to improve information flow. Use the averages to measure trend strength and the bands to target the length of each bar print. At new highs or lows, strong price movement will wrap tightly between the 5-bar and outside band while all three averages line up and point in the direction of the trend. As price rolls, bands tighten and signal a changing market while averages pinpoint pullbacks and new S/R. Eventually, bands shift direction, averages flip over and price breaks through toward the other extreme.

Swing traders work the quiet middle ground of Bollinger Bands for consistent profits. Build strategies that enter countertrend positions at one band and exit at the other. These swing setups face far fewer whipsaws than breakout entries at band extremes. The center band presents a natural profit obstacle that needs special consideration when calculating reward:risk. Make sure a safe exit near this center point still produces a decent profit for the trade.

Keep in mind that all bands change dynamically in response to price. This allows continuous feedback that shifts target values with each bar. Experience with this powerful indicator helps swing traders anticipate how it will move. The longer that price travels sideways, the tighter the bands become. Trend change for the bands themselves first begins with a turn by the band closest to the prior price trend. For example, when an uptrend prints along a top band, expect this side of the indicator to turn down before its twin when price moves into a range or downtrend.

Combine Bollinger Band study with momentum-based indicators. This uncovers hidden directional movement and improves trade timing. Add MA ribbons to price and display the MACD histogram across the lower pane. Price often remains well within band constriction during the early phases of new positive feedback events. As these indicators show rising momentum, shift attention to natural pattern/band breakout levels and look for entry within narrowing bars.

MACD HISTOGRAM

Gerald Appel's classic MACD (moving average convergence-divergence) tracks the interaction between two moving averages over time. Momentum increases when a shorter average turns away from a longer one and decreases when it turns toward it. The indicator smoothes these raw numbers to reduce false readings and whipsaws. It then generates a relationship between this slower average and the original calculation to trigger buy or sell signals.

The indicator yields an excellent pattern tool when drawn with vertical bars instead of two plotted lines. Alex Elder popularized this classic variation in *Trading for a Living*. The method calculates the distance between the plots at each data point and illustrates that length below price. It builds rising and falling slopes as momentum oscillates that accurately track subtle changes in a market's underlying trend.

MACD histograms locate reversals and time breakouts. Start with classic settings and customize as experience builds. Most swing traders rely on standard 12- and 26-period moving averages smoothed by 9 periods. Use this popular output through all time frames to track crowd behavior. But never apply the indicator in a vacuum. Momentum means little unless the markets offer good opportunities to capitalize upon it. Because everyone who watches the classic settings sees the same thing at the same time, successful entry requires superior trading tactics.

MACD histograms generate two types of signals. The early one rings when the histogram changes direction from an extreme level. These sharp turns often occur before price but print relatively few false readings. The later signal flashes when price crosses the central -0- line. Most whipsaws will occur right near this axis. Always cross-verify this center signal against key S/R and breakout levels on the price pattern.

Histograms often print double bottoms or tops when they shift direction from extreme levels. This natural tendency saves swing traders from unprofitable entry. While the indicator often turns ahead of a market, its double top or bottom generally forms after price reverses. One effective strategy filters setups through this lagging confirmation and then enters on the first pullback or other low-risk opportunity. Unfortunately, histograms may just draw sharp V bottoms or tops, so be prepared to miss the execution boat when this occurs.

The indicator's zero line pinpoints the center balance zone. Positive acceleration flags as columns thrust above this point. Likewise, down steps below the line point to negative acceleration. Markets may flatten as histograms approach this important signal level. Pay close attention to the angle of the indicator's rise or fall as it approaches. The sharper the inclination, the more likely that price will break through with little or no resistance.

Buy and sell signals generally track the same territory. Exit positions on -0-line violations after deciding that MACD will not whipsaw. Or use the first reversal column at an indicator extreme to exit or enter in the opposite direction. Histograms often reach the same level for two continuous price cycles before reversal. Many participants notice the first extreme and how it flagged a turnaround on the last pass. This triggers a self-fulfilling event as the histogram reapproaches that level.

Customize MACD values to speed up signals or view specific markets. Faster histograms increase false readings but allow quicker response to new trends. Try the 8-17-9 MACD for buy signals but use the traditional 12-26-9 to locate sell zones. Or place both histograms in separate panes below price and use one to filter the other. For example, when the faster calculation triggers a buy signal but the slower one does not, look to the price pattern and decide which reading offers the most reliable information.

Intraday traders can experiment with an 8-13-8 MACD histogram on 1-minute and 5-minute charts to capture very short-term momentum swings. But switch back to the traditional 12-26-9 for 60-minute and longer views. Intraday signals must trigger faster than daily or weekly ones because short-term opportunities come so quickly. With these very narrow settings, the histogram will flip more often and act more like an oscillator than directional indicator. Continue to rely upon the MACD in the time frame above the holding period for many signals but focus timing through these shorter readings.

F I G U R E   5.23

MACD histograms track shifts in market momentum but also trigger bad trades. Indicator tutorials often present the zero line crossover as an entry or exit signal. But Purchasepro.com produces sharp whipsaws when histograms pass through this important line (1, 5, and 7). Even entries at 2, 4, and 6 right after histogram extremes would have also failed. The double bottom signal at 3 and the rising slope at 8 mark the only good profit opportunities.

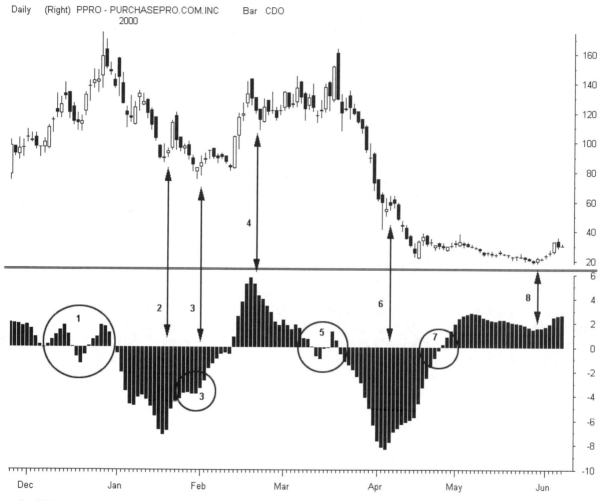

Daily   (Right) PPRO - PURCHASEPRO.COM.INC   Bar CDO
2000

RSI AND STOCHASTICS

Market conditions change quickly, and secrets often hide in very short-term price movement. The last candlestick at the chart's hard right edge may supply crucial information that will decide the success or failure of the trade setup. Strength oscillators emit continuous feedback on this last bar's contribution to recent price action. When properly tuned, they react quickly to new swings and align positions to natural market cycles.

Oscillators generate important data on relative strength and weakness. They point to overbought-oversold conditions where the prevailing crowd may lose its determination and trigger a reversal. Swing traders must always examine the hidden forces that manufacture price change. Oscillators uncover these subtle mechanics as they look forward in reaction to market input. They also respond more quickly to new information than trend-following measurements such as moving averages.

Strength tools range from simple calculations to complex pattern-based systems, but a common theme ties all of them together. Oscillators try to predict whether short-term relative strength favors or opposes the current price direction. While several tools can accomplish this task, two stand out for their durability and diverse applications. Both Stochastics and Wilder's Relative Strength Index (RSI) offer powerful methods to examine these cyclical swings.

Both oscillators assume that market strength reveals itself in the price bar's closing tick. Each applies this essential theory in an original manner. Stochastics measures the relationship of the close to the high and low extremes for that bar. RSI compares the number of up closing bars to down closing bars. These two different methodologies produce unique results. Accurate predictions come through selective use of both tools to evaluate different aspects of market behavior.

Stochastics and RSI target overbought-oversold conditions in constricted ranges. But they also have tremendous value in trending markets. Acceleration-deceleration quickly reveals itself as indicator directional movement follows price swings. These lower-pane plots draw patterns that mimic classic formations. Look for both indicators to print double bottoms or tops near important market swings. Stochastics also displays a 1-2-3 phenomenon when traversing the pane. It will often thrust, pull back in a small wave near the halfway point, and then thrust again to the other side.

Market participants spend too much time trying to adjust the exact overbought-oversold lines for each indicator. Both plots oscillate between 0% and 100%. Classic technical analysis often places extreme lines at 20–80 and advises that oscillator violations increase the odds for a reversal. Other approaches try to find this mystical turning point in different ways. For example, Elder suggests a 5% rule. Measure the overbought and oversold levels that RSI penetrates less than 5% of the time over the last 4–6 months. Draw lines at these zones and review them every 3 months.

Every market responds differently to oscillators. Most swing traders should just take the path of least resistance and choose the standard settings. For both Stochastics and RSI, 20–80 works well under most circumstances. This common level does a good job of balancing false signals against lost opportunity. Truthfully, these settings mean little to profit or performance. Success requires reading the patterns that print at oscillator reversals rather than finding exact locations for the turns themselves.

Use Stochastics for short-term feedback and RSI for longer cycle information. Simple RSI output tends to be choppier than Stochastics and requires longer smoothing averages to avoid false readings. Stochastics can be applied effectively through very short settings on intraday charts. Each indicator plots differently below price bars. Smoothed RSI shows a single line that flows slowly from overbought to oversold extremes. Stochastics flips faster and tracks a second line that rises above it or falls below it very quickly as cycles turn.

Stochastics accurately measures short-term shifts in price momentum. But useful output begins to dry up once it pierces the extremes of its wide bands. Stochastics fails completely in strongly trending markets. The plot will move to one end and wobble randomly while the market charges ahead or sells off. This again confirms the leadership of the price pattern over the indicator. But pay close attention to all oscillators once they begin to roll over. They tend to be highly accurate at these turning points.

Set a 5-3-3 Stochastics for each intraday chart at or below the main holding period. For example, plot it on both 1-minute and 5-minute charts when trading within the 5-minute view. Use Stochastics for the next-larger scale if it appears to have value. But trend becomes more important than oscillation when swing traders examine the time frame above the trade. Focus attention at these levels on a well-built MACD (or other momentum) indicator to capture the larger market swing.

Jake Bernstein examines a fascinating Stochastics phenomenon, which he calls the Stochastics pop, in *The Compleat Day Trader*. He recommends a trend-following execution just as an outer signal line crosses above a 75% or below a 25% extreme level. The trade recognizes that the last phase of a swing can offer the most dynamic price movement. The pop rings a contrarian entry just as other participants respond to exit signals. Once again, standing apart from the crowd appears to offer special rewards. He advises to exit the trade as soon as the faster line crosses back over the slower one. This suggests the start of a swing back in the opposite direction.

Daily oscillators must provide an effective reading of broad cyclical behavior. To accomplish this task, apply a longer-term RSI instead of a daily Stochastics whenever possible. Set the indicator to a 14-day period with a 7-day smoothing average for an effective view with few whipsaws. Some software applications don't have a smoothing function for RSI. Their canned 14-day RSI outputs too much noise for swing traders. Try a 14-7-3 Stochastics instead in this unfortunate situation. This will track the RSI but exhibit a plot with a bit more fluctuation and misinformation.

Long-term RSI works well through most market conditions and accurately captures major turning points. Follow the signals when RSI penetrates extreme territory after rapid price change and then rolls over. This valuable indicator also displays smooth oscillation in mildly trending markets. Plots may never reach overbought or oversold levels during these periods of frequent thrusts and pullbacks.

VOLUME TOOLS

Volume tools offer important data at major reversals. They also yield accurate signals of impending breakouts and breakdowns when their action leads the price chart.

The Stochastics pop, set to a conservative 80% level, still yields two profitable trades. This trend-following technique relies on defensive risk management. Take a quick exit as soon as the fast Stochastics line crosses under the slower one.

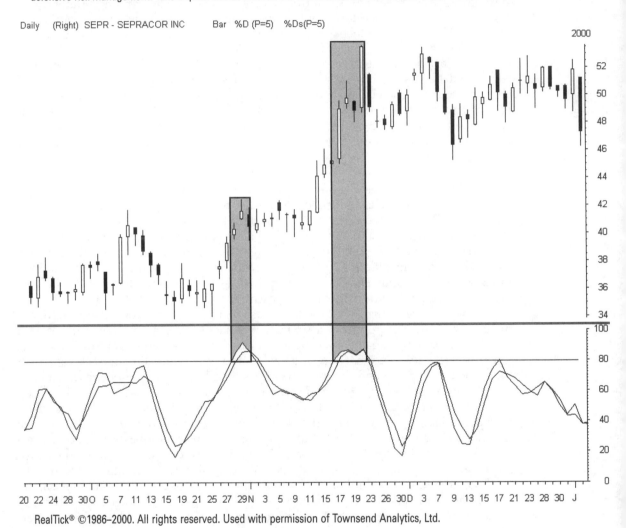

Daily   (Right) SEPR - SEPRACOR INC   Bar %D (P=5)   %Ds(P=5)

RealTick® ©1986–2000. All rights reserved. Used with permission of Townsend Analytics, Ltd.

OBV

Joseph Granville's On-Balance Volume (OBV) presents the most popular study of accumulation-distribution in the trading world. This simple indicator distributes daily volume based on each day's close. When a stock closes higher than the prior day, OBV accumulates that daily volume. Conversely, the indicator subtracts the daily volume when that stock closes down. Over time, it builds a complex picture of buying and selling behavior.

OBV displays pattern characteristics similar to price bars. This permits examination through charting landscape features such as trendlines, triangles and double bottoms. Swing traders should compare these formations to underlying price patterns and review predictive convergence-divergence. OBV will often lead price and complete an important reversal just ahead of trend movement.

Confine all accumulation-distribution study to the daily chart. Intraday time bias distorts volume measurements. Sixty percent or more of all daily trading vol-

F I G U R E   5.25

On Balance Volume draws a series of head and shoulders reversals during this Citrix Systems decline. Note how the indicator exhibits classic pullback behavior and responds to horizontal S/R from past congestion. OBV often leads the price action by several bars. Use it at new highs and lows to measure supply and demand.

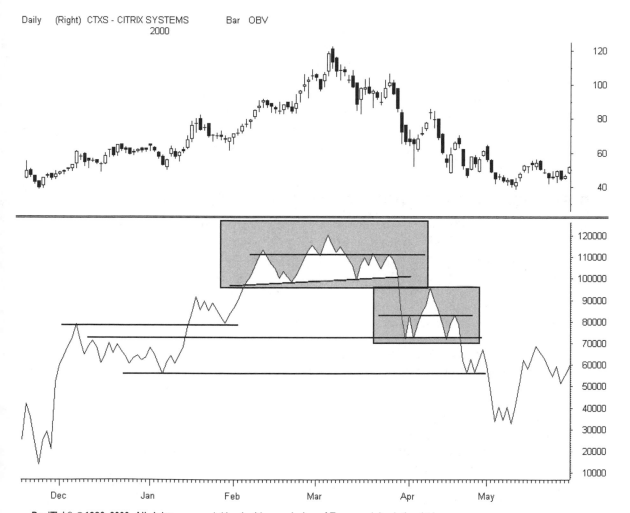

ume occurs within about 30% of the day. This defeats genuine comparisons between intraday price bars and volume. Stick with individual volume histograms rather than complex calculations during the trading session. Rely on time and sales data to interpret volume's impact on very short-term trends.

Always check OBV or another accumulation-distribution indicator at new highs and lows where they exhibit their greatest power of prediction. This study will generate two unique situations. OBV may strike new levels before price or price may break through before OBV. Follow the wisdom that price needs the crowd to move higher but can fall of its own weight. If OBV reaches a new high before price, look for bars to accelerate and catch up. If price gets there first, expect that it will pause while accumulation builds. But when price hits a new low before OBV, gravity alone will likely carry it much lower before the crowd catches up. And if OBV hits a new low before price, run for the hills—that market has lost all of its support.

Major divergences between OBV and trend point to stress between price and volume. Use that information to play swings that remain hidden from the competition. But this valuable indicator also has major limitations. It allocates the entire day to one side of the crowd and triggers very bad signals in long sideways markets. These important ranges set the stage for future price movement, but OBV routinely fails to predict important breakouts. Watch out when applying OBV to Nasdaq stocks. This exchange double-counts volume because it registers once for the purchase and again for the sale. Also avoid OBV with less liquid issues where it often triggers false volume readings right at critical price levels.

FARLEY'S ADA (ACCUMULATION-DISTRIBUTION ACCELERATOR)

Accumulation-distribution oscillates as the crowd jumps in and out of active markets. This closed system feeds on itself as constant price change encourages new participants to act and old ones to react. Within its complex boundaries, a hidden supply-demand equation forces markets to reach natural excitement levels and reverse course over and over again. While external shocks may alter this dynamic organism, they cannot change its persistent oscillation.

Farley's Accumulation-Distribution Accelerator (ADA) tracks this volume oscillation while it reduces the impact of shock events. Swing traders benefit when they locate natural levels where the crowd may turn and trigger contrary price movement. This examination of herd behavior through volume offers a classic approach to cycle discovery that often pinpoints insider activity and unexpected price change.

ADA formations print clear S/R and trendlines as well as oscillating between expected upper-lower boundaries. Use ADA to measure lag between price and volume. When price leads, expect it to pause for ADA to catch up. The most dynamic trends erupt when ADA significantly leads the price action. This valuable indicator also triggers much faster signals and cleaner pattern formations than OBV or other common accumulation-distribution measurements.

The calculation begins with the Larry Williams Accumulation-Distribution indicator. Williams formulated this handy tool in *The Secret of Selecting Stocks for Immediate and Substantial Gains* (1986). This initial mathematics represents the cumulative total of the variable X. Take this figure and add it to all preceding bars to plot his indicator.

    A. Measure LWAccDis as follows:

        1. If the current Close is greater than the prior Close, then:

$$LWAccDis = Close - TrueLow$$

        2. If the current Close is less than the prior Close, then:

$$LWAccDis = Close - TrueHigh$$

        3. If the current Close is equal to the prior Close, then:

$$LWAccDis = 0$$

    B. Calculation of TrueLow:
        1. If prior Close < current Low, then TrueLow = prior Close
        2. If prior Close ≥ current Low, then TrueLow = current Low
    C. Calculation of TrueHigh:
        1. If prior Close > current High, then TrueHigh = prior Close
        2. If prior Close ≤ current High, then TrueHigh = current High

T A B L E 5.2

Farley's Accumulation-Distribution Accelerator

(Formula uses TradeStation language)	
1. Start with LWAccDis above (and available in most charting programs).	LWAccDis
2. Calculate the difference between the LWAccDis of current bar and prior bar.	F1 = LWAccDis − LWAccDis[1]
3. Compute a 14-bar exponential moving average (EMA) of this difference.	F2 = @XAverage(F1,14)
4. Smooth this average with a 7-bar exponential moving average (EMA).	Farley's ADA = @XAverage(F2,7)
5. Plot 0 Line.	F3 = 0

Track indicator trendlines, channels, and horizontal extremes to locate natural breakout points. ADA patterns will often complete one to three bars faster than price. Watch the indicator for signs of a natural trend-range axis. Movement out of multimonth or multiyear congestion can uncover long-term price breakouts with considerable profit opportunity. Don't demand perfection with ADA trendlines. This raw tool works best when swing traders allow for small violations in both directions.

SPECIAL TOOLS

Use special tools to locate hidden S/R and gain an important market edge. These powerful resources perform custom analysis but remain poorly understood by the emotional crowd. Use their results to execute profitable trades at locations that few others will see or understand.

FIBONACCI

Fibonacci (Fib) retracement benefits all strategies that depend on price pullbacks. Swing traders examine these hidden levels when they apply Fib grids, simple calculations or physical tools to relative highs and lows on price charts. Study these important price relationships every day even if they appear arcane or mystical. Fibs have a solid basis in mathematics, although prior generations never visualized their application to the modern financial world.

Twelfth century monk-mathematician Leonardo de Pisa (better known as Fibonacci) uncovered a fascinating mathematics sequence that appears throughout nature. Begin with a simple $1 + 1$ and the sum of the last two numbers that precede it creates another Fibonacci value:

$$1 + 1 = 2, \ 1 + 2 = 3, \ 2 + 3 = 5, \ 3 + 5 = 8, \ 5 + 8 = 13, \ 8 + 13 = 21,$$

$$13 + 21 = 34, \ 21 + 34 = 55, \text{ etc.}$$

Major ratios that arise from these numbers describe a predictable interaction between trend and countertrend market movement. 38%, 50%, and 62% form the primary retracement levels. Swing traders apply these percentages through rallies and corrections to predict the extent of movement contrary to the underlying trend. Fibs also examine how far new highs or lows should travel before congestion ends the trend. These hidden points represent invisible S/R zones where prices should hesitate and/or reverse.

Fibs describe proportion within nature through a simple mathematical relationship. They work their numbers magic in both flower petals and seashell ribs. Few modern students apply Fib calculations in high school math class, although the sequence was documented over 800 years ago. This will likely change as the

F I G U R E   5.26

ADA trendline breaks signal important action well ahead of Oracle's price bars. The first arrow confirms the low in a pronged base just before a 30-point rally. The second signals an important top one bar after it occurs. ADA then flags a major mid-April low. Finally, the fourth arrow catches ORCL as it rises off a new base toward a test of its last high. Note that ADA forms ascending, descending, and horizontal trendlines that track classic S/R behavior.

number set slowly enters the mainstream of mathematical thought and application over the next century. Many decades from now, our grandchildren will likely see Fib applications revolutionize their understanding of left-right brain interaction.

The swing trader acts according to careful planning and complex logic. The emotional crowd acts according to nature. Fibs uncover the concealed interface between mathematics and emotion as they predict how the herd will respond to price development. Most participants use Fibs to examine countertrends but rarely explore their ability to generate price projections at new highs or lows. These Fib extensions require more faith because the charting landscape lacks trend mirrors to cross-verify suspected reversal levels.

F I G U R E   5.27

Use Fibonacci extensions to establish initial price targets for new highs or lows. Trend thrusts often stretch 38% beyond the distance between the last high or low and the pullback before the breakout or breakdown. Find a double bottom or top within the congestion and stretch a Fib grid from that point to the last high or low. Then set the software tool to draw a line 38% beyond that level to reveal the target.

Daily   (Right) COVD - COVAD COMMUNICATIONS GRP   Bar
1999   2000

Modern tools ease the study of Fib retracement. For many years, swing traders needed a calculator to compute each individual pullback by hand. Most charting programs now provide grid tools that do all of the math work in seconds. Locate relative highs and lows for a dynamic trend leg and stretch a grid across them. Then move outward and overlay multiple grids of different lengths (and colors if possible) that capture larger rallies and corrections. Finally, look for interactions between major retracement levels of different grids. Find these convergence zones and use their S/R for trade planning.

Set grid levels to the standard 38%, 50%, and 62%. Then forget about them. Markets tend to reverse when pulling back to these retracements in all time frames. Common wisdom dictates that if a pullback pierces the 62% level, the trend in that time frame ends and a 100% retracement should follow. This sets up the first rise/ first failure pattern discussed in prior chapters.

Fibonacci numbers consistently mark hidden S/R. Use these key pivots to enter and exit profitable positions. But Fibs work best when they cross-verify other landscape features. Key retracement levels say little about subsequent price targets all by themselves. Although a Fib bounce may offer a good setup, it may end quickly unless cross-verification supports a larger trade. Price can roll over easily to the next retracement level when it can't find strong support. But odds increase for a substantial bounce when Fibs align with important highs, lows and major averages.

Fibonacci numbers tie closely to Elliott Wave Theory. Fortunately, swing traders can apply Fibs with little knowledge of wave motion. Understand that primary trends travel in five waves (three forward and two backward), while countertrends move in three waves (two forward and one backward). Those simple mechanics allow easy Fib grid manipulation. Try to place the grid from a double top or bottom through a fifth-wave parabola. Then apply subset grids closer to the intended trade setup. Pullbacks from primary trends tend to display A-B-C countertrend motion. In an uptrend, price drops through an A wave, bounces into a B wave that usually won't reach the former high, and then falls into a C wave that violates the A bottom.

Trends in all time frames have common elements and similar proportionality. Most markets swing off Fib ratios as they move from support to resistance and back. In many respects, this proportional motion reveals the underlying nature of price movement. But Fib ratios rarely align perfectly with each other through all time frames. This generates most of the noise that prints on stock charts. Discord creates whipsaw, range, and a host of other charting features that occupy the landscape. This phasing relationship between Fib proportions illustrates the power of this mathematics. It also advises swing traders to seek price action with strong Fib convergence between trends at different levels and time frames. These well-aligned segments offer highly predictive price action with very low noise.

Include detailed reward:risk analysis in all trade decisions that rely upon Fib retracement. Other key Fib percentages will hinder progress after a price reversal. This may not hurt the trade if it depends upon a longer holding period. But should the strategy profit from a single direct price thrust, sufficient reward must justify the position. Focus on getting into the market at major Fib ratios while standing

F I G U R E   5.28

Five-wave rally stretches across the Fibonacci landscape. The first wave carries 38%, where it congests into a second wave pullback. A continuation gap then appears right on schedule through the midpoint of the trend. The fourth wave forms quickly as it whipsaws across the 62% level until a fifth wave finally ejects from the 50% line. The rally peaks and the A corrective wave carries down to the 38% retracement, where it bounces into a B wave. This small move fails and carries the C wave to a successful test at 62%.

aside as price hovers between key zones. The smartest execution will be counter to the most immediate short-term trend with most strategies.

Fibonacci defines trend movement over broad time frames as well as very short ones. This retracement science also works in bear markets as well as bull markets. Major declines frequently recover 50% or 62% of the last selloff before

F I G U R E   5.29

Strong trends frequently generate vertical third wave movement through their 38–62% Fibonacci zones. When these primary rallies and selloffs pull back into typical ABC corrections, the central B waves often tighten into congestion at the 38–62% zone of that smaller countertrend. Although multiple Fibonacci and wave levels appear confusing at first glance, they intertwine into a proportional system that helps the swing trader predict the next sharp price expansion.

Daily   (Right) INTC - INTEL CORP   Bar

rolling over to retest the lows. Keep in mind that short squeezes should not retrace 100% of the last opposing move. Use the Fib grid to locate their natural failure level for a lower risk short sale.

This proportional force tests trends while volatility and volume decrease. No guarantees exist that any particular retracement level will hold price and trigger a solid bounce. So many swing traders just wait. They adopt a defensive strategy that stands aside until the stock reaches the 62% barrier. Since this represents the deepest potential bounce, odds favor stronger S/R than other levels. Of course, many trends never pull back this deeply, and they miss opportunities. But this tactic also avoids false bottoms and tops.

Execute positions at this deep retracement as soon as it strikes if three to four forms of cross-verification support the trade. If not, stand aside and wait a little longer. While the 62% level should provide S/R, this zone can experience strong whipsaws. One excellent signal arises when 62% breaks and price expands toward 70–75% before it remounts the broken level. While this contradicts natural trend rules, modern markets demand new flexibility.

Fibonacci remains poorly understood, but this may change. Most new software packages contain grids and instructions on how to use them. As the crowd's knowledge of classic retracement grows, these levels will experience more unforeseen behavior. But don't toss aside this important tool just yet. Nature cannot be undone by manipulation. S/R at these levels should persist although violations and whipsaws will increase. Learn to step in front of, stand behind, or oppose the crowd when building swing strategies that rely on Fibs.

Intraday Fib applications keep swing traders ahead of the competition. Find an active stock and start a grid from the high or low of a session's last hour. Stretch it to the opposite end of the next morning's first-hour high or low. This grid now defines hidden S/R that may carry the stock into a new trend. This method shows great success in dynamic markets with gap opens. The gap will often stretch right across a key retracement level and allow low-risk entry. Another strategy builds a grid across the first hour's range. Use the levels to locate S/R as the stock swings back and forth. Many issues will finally base at the 38% level at either end before breaking out of the range.

Expect greater violations on intraday Fibs than longer-term charts. A single tick can distort a perfect pullback. Don't count on tight movement to the 38%, 50%, and 62% levels. Very small trends also resolve many larger mathematical forces that impact retracement. Use candlesticks instead of bar charts to filter out this intraday noise. Also keep track of larger-trend Fib levels that price might cross during that session. Larger time frames always take precedence over smaller ones in swing trading tactics.

Target new high and low extremes with Fib extensions. Look within congestion to locate the inception point for the trend that leads into the break. Price will often thrust 38% beyond the distance from this point to the prior high or low (see Figure 5.27). Then locate smaller trend impulses and lay new grids over these. They will target intermediate resistance as price breaks into uncharted territory.

Many participants can't figure out where to start and end Fib grids. In fact, the absolute lows or highs within a trend may not yield the best results. But always try them first and see whether the intermediate levels correspond with obvious S/R. Try another approach when retracements pass through zones that show little interest. High and low congestion often prints a test just before a trend impulse

Original Fibonacci analysis builds profits quickly. Pull a Fib grid from the high or low extension of the prior session's last 60–90-minutes through the first price thrust after a sharp morning gap. The boundaries now define expected pullback and breakout levels for the new trading day. Notice how Altera retraces exactly to 38% before returning to test and fail the first-hour range in a 2B reversal. The next morning ALTR completes a perfect cup and handle breakout after a final pullback.

RealTick® ©1986–2000. All rights reserved. Used with permission of Townsend Analytics, Ltd.

starts and price exits the pattern. Use this second bottom or top in place of the absolute level. In many cases, intermediate Fib levels will now fit right where they belong.

MARKET NUMBERS

Support and resistance have many faces. Trendlines, price extremes, and hidden Fibonacci levels all push markets back and forth. But the charting landscape does not end there. Trend development also responds to a common decimal system of 10 and tenths. These important market numbers spawn yet another S/R barrier with specific trading properties. And one peek at your fingers and toes will explain their simple logic.

Round numbers generate predictable trend dynamics because markets shape patterns that involve their participation. Watch a small stock pause just below $10 for months or a larger one fail to mount $100 repeatedly. Read how an index finally breaks through an "important psychological barrier" that turns out to be a big round number. This numbers logic even works in very small-scale trading. Scalpers routinely fade rallies when price mounts a whole number but then falls back after reaching 1/16 or 1/8 through the barrier. Then they flip positions as the pullback drops to 3/4 or 13/16 of the lower number.

Market participants respond to whole-number logic through self-fulfilling mechanics. The unconscious mind computes profit-loss by dropping the fractions and acting at whole numbers. Buyers plan to sell and sellers intend to buy when their favorite stocks hit prechosen ones. Analysts publish reasoned price targets at them, and even stops tend to congregate right above and below these powerful magnets.

Unique crowds tend to trade within each increment of $10 in valuation. Small retail participants favor lower-priced stocks, while institutions and professionals fill their portfolios with more expensive issues. One way to understand whole-number levels ($10, $20, $30, $40, etc.) visualizes price action as one crowd hands off to the next at these major interfaces. Demand at the new whole level must be great enough to absorb supply or price will not mount resistance.

Movement often narrows as price approaches the next level, and a range may form with one boundary limited by the market number. Even strong trends can stall into quiet profit-taking, frequent testing, and small retracements. This area of consolidation sets the stage for price to test and mount the next whole number level. Measure the reduction in price volatility and prepare for the climax of this redistribution process using classic empty zone strategy. Look for a sharp drop in rate of change and the appearance of narrow range bars. This sets the stage for price to mount the whole number. Stay alert during this quiet period—the new trend can emerge very quickly.

Whole number breakouts mimic other types of S/R. Negative feedback yields to directional momentum as the level breaks. Price may pull back and test the new barrier repeatedly in the same way as a classic breakout. When strong volume accompanies the move, small violations back across the whole number represent low-risk entry. But if congestion forms for too long on the new side of the barrier, many exit orders build and generate higher risk.

Once trend successfully tests a new market number, expect sharp movement away from that level. Price often pushes quickly to the midpoint between the last whole number and the next one. This divisor of 10 (10/2 = 5 in this case) presents a natural price magnet. Fifty, 100, and other multiples of 10 also signal major bar-riers. Price faces much sharper retracement off these points than smaller whole numbers. Look for complex patterns to form on both sides and persist longer than other interfaces.

Congestion zones below key market numbers may signal bad news for up-trends. Major trend changes occur more often near whole numbers than any other prices. These reversals first trumpet their presence after they break through the barrier. Price then falls back and turns sideways into a tight consolidation zone. The rangebound bars print a topping pattern that then fails on high volume.

Step back and study the next-longest trend when price drops sharply off whole market numbers. Significant reversals at these resistance points may not re-trace for months or years. Trend change dynamics reflect the unique crowd that holds positions through each round number series. As one group attempts to take profits, the next crowd refuses to carry their stock. The trapped longs then trigger a selloff that ends the trend.

Market numbers provide strong support in downtrends. One dependable scalping trade buys the first failure of a market number unless it gaps to get there. But exercise caution with this classic strategy. Bounce momentum back above a market number dies quickly, so profit depends upon tight stops and defensive trad-ing. Insider knowledge makes this trade very dependable. Market makers and spe-cialists know that stops concentrate just below market numbers. They manipulate price through these levels to gather the sell orders and invite new short sales. Par-adoxically, the volume surge induced by this violation quickly alleviates selling pressure and triggers a short squeeze that pushes a rebound above the round num-ber.

Knowledge of market numbers evokes interesting short sale strategies. In an uptrend, aggressive participants may sell short on the first strike when price action meets certain criteria. Look for stocks that reach the number after an extended rally. Technical indicators should show an overbought condition and suggest an impend-ing rollover. Add cross-verification whenever possible to increase safety. Then en-sure that no congestion pattern sits right below this key resistance. For example, don't short 30 when a stock pushes up out of a base at 28 or 29.

A second short sale enters at the final breakdown of the market number. De-clines below this resistance can be sharp and nasty if cross-verification confirms a break through other support, such as a moving average. In fact, market numbers routinely appear at major moving averages, Bollinger Band extremes, and key re-tracement percentages. Watch closely for those times when multiple indicators in-tersect at round numbers. Trades that initiate from these points represent high-reward opportunities.

TICK

Intraday crowd behavior generates pulses of buying and selling pressure. Although one might suspect chaos in modern markets, this constant oscillation exhibits both

FIGURE   5.31

Immunex responds to market number logic. Over this 4-month period, whole numbers reversed at least eight rallies and seven selloffs. Price first thrusts through the barrier, takes out the volume, and then quickly reverses in almost every episode. Market numbers tend to short-circuit trends because large order volume behind these barriers can quickly deplete the supply of buyers or sellers.

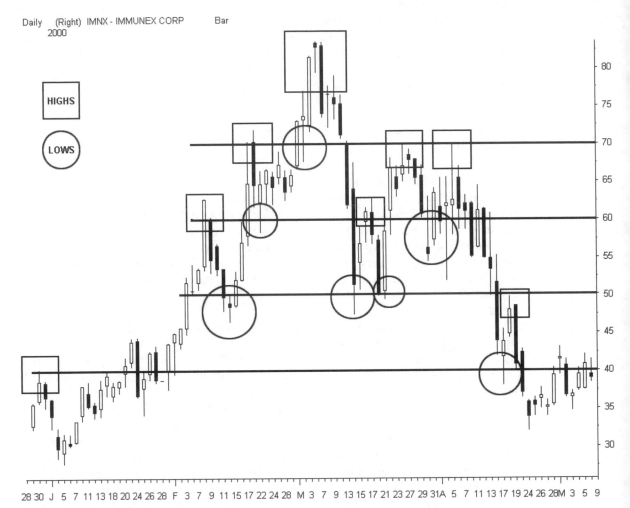

Daily   (Right) IMNX - IMMUNEX CORP   Bar

RealTick® ©1986–2000. All rights reserved. Used with permission of Townsend Analytics, Ltd.

order and dimension. These pulses track the 90-minute S&P alternation cycle but display much smaller and more detailed waves of activity. Swing traders should align intraday execution to this important phenomenon.

The TICK indicator tracks the number of stocks whose last trade represents an uptick vs. a downtick. This measurement prints for each major exchange in real time. The NYSE TICK provides a highly predictive indicator for all American stock activity. Specifically, Nasdaq traders can avoid that exchange's TICK information and use the NYSE classic for all entries and exits.

Follow the TICK through real-time quotes and build a charting landscape that illustrates recent historical activity. Avoid daily or weekly views of this powerful oscillator. The measurement moves constantly between short-term extremes of −500 and +500. Longer-term charts look like jagged mountains that reflect into clear lakes and provide little useful information to the swing trader.

The most effective TICK charts match the nature of the intraday markets. Try 5-minute or 15-minute data with 2–3 days of market action, or use 60-minute charts with 5–10 days of history. Always use candles in place of price bars. TICK charts print highly predictive doji and hammer reversals. Candles tend to print 1-2-3 waves as buying-selling behavior oscillates between extremes. Display the chart without any top-pane indicators because TICK responds to pure trendline analysis better than any other examination.

The NYSE TICK routinely forms trendlines and parallel channels that reveal complex intraday S/R. It also finds support at recent horizontal extremes that set natural limits on buying and selling behavior. Start TICK analysis by drawing lines and channels that define the recent action. Extend these lines and watch how they align to intraday reversals, breakouts, and price congestion.

Major violations shoot through the lines repeatedly. But TICK candle real bodies hold S/R and allow decent trendlines most of the time. The sharp shadow zones flash important reversal signals when they stretch out past a prior floor or ceiling. Never demand perfection when using this important indicator. Its greatest value lies in the pure oscillations that uncover small cycles of herd behavior.

TICK identifies natural entry and exit zones. When channels or trendlines break, activity surges in the direction of the violation. These bar expansions exhibit a common trait with other forms of S/R. Candles often pull back to test the break point before pushing further in the new direction. TICK movement also has a natural advantage over price movement. While price can trend for hours or days in a single direction, TICK will only carry to a short-term extreme and then reverse as supply-demand shifts. Align position entry with expected TICK behavior. Use the oscillator reversals and breakouts for cross-verification. Also prepare to terminate a trade without price verification when TICK flashes important contrary information.

TICK channel behavior organizes time into distinct units with high and low extremes appearing at predictable points. These market fractals define time resistance. In other words, swing traders can estimate the number of candles that will print before a new surge or reversal. This oscillation persists into larger market cycles. It can mimic segments of the intraday S&P cycle or even the broader 3-day swing cycle.

Watch TICK readings at important market turning points. In past years, strong reversals began when the indicator struck extreme +1000 or −1000 levels. These natural overbought-oversold boundaries persisted for years. But modern markets exhibit greater volatility than in the past. TICK prints from +1500 through −1500 now occur during severe conditions. Swing traders can still apply the older limits when estimating market turns on a relative basis. But always seek cross-verification through index chart patterns for large-scale reversals.

F I G U R E   5.32

NYSE TICK draws typical 5-minute patterns during early June. At least four distinct parallel channels and harmonics print in less than 3 days. These well-marked zones uncover hidden reversals and point to impending price breakouts during each intraday session. Note how candle shadows reach out to 400 and −400. Horizontal resistance define peaks of buying or selling that can persist for days.

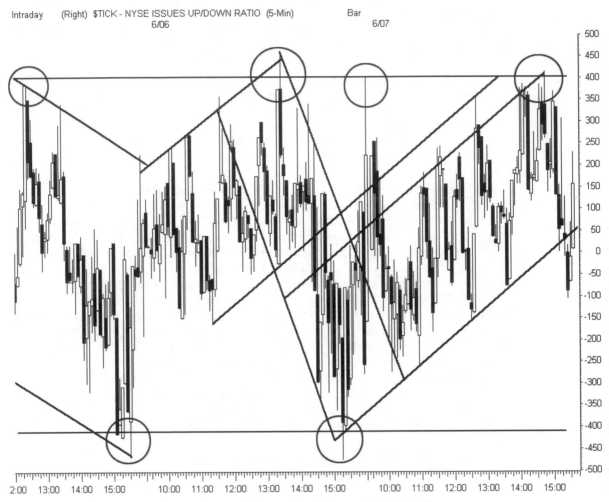

F I G U R E   5.33

TICK repeatedly strikes −1000 as the indicator signals the end of a deep correction. The third strike corresponds directly to a 6-month low that Nasdaq hits just before it ejects into a strong rally. Unfortunately, modern markets don't always respond to these classic turning points. Recent corrections have sent the indicator closer to −1500 before a significant reversal. Always look for several tests at deep TICK extremes to confirm a major shift in buying or selling pressure.

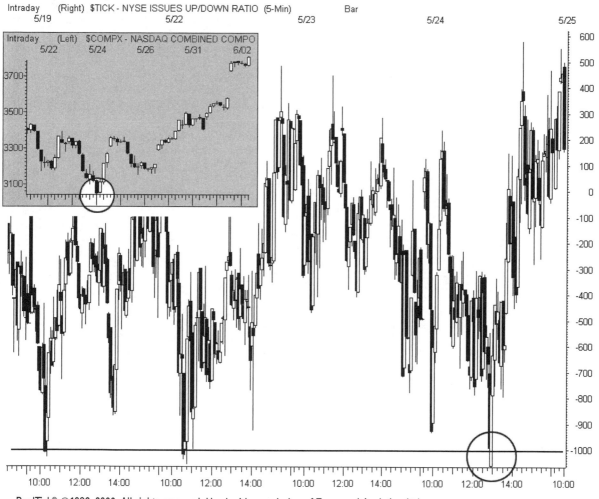

6

UNDERSTANDING TIME

THE TIME ELEMENT

Price patterns reveal opportunity. But many participants fail to comprehend how poor time management weakens tactics and empties accounts. Each promising setup has a holding period that maximizes reward:risk. This optimal phase may not match the time frame anticipated in the personal trading plan. Position and plan must synchronize time or they will lead to poor results. Unfortunately, many ignore this important consideration and jump into the market anyway.

Proper time management separates winners from losers. Lazy participants misinterpret signals and waste valuable resources when they ignore this essential strategic element. Time impacts two charting landscape features. First, it defines how execution aligns with the price swing. Second, it reveals internal market tendencies that impact trend on an intraday, daily, weekly, and monthly basis.

Match holding period to time-sensitive setups and aggressively manage the information interface. Real-time screens and databases must tune into specific time frames. It makes perfect sense to filter databases through technical screens that favor important time characteristics. Align charts, indicator settings, and focused attention to those same dimensions and synchronize tactics to a single layer of market activity.

Tune trade entry to the time frame below the setup whenever possible. This optimizes reward and visualizes short-term danger. Pay close attention to this view during active position management, but base exit decisions on the chart that produced the opportunity in the first place. Use mental time stops to manage holding period even when price avoids major violation.

Become a student of market time bias. The first and last hours as well as a variety of intraday quirks bend short-term price development. Broader time periods bring about odd phenomena such as Turnaround Tuesday, the 3-day swing, and tax loss season. Scheduled fundamental events routinely impact price and distort index charts, and options expiration ensures that unwinding positions will impact certain days of each market month.

Swing traders manipulate opportunity cost through their working capital. This important concept reveals why cutting losses efficiently is so important for long-term survival. Assumption of a stock position dictates that those funds will not be available for another trade. A critical issue then arises on account drawdowns when the wrong decision dictates failure or triggers a margin call. Mediocrity also impacts opportunity cost. Poor choices tie up capital when they lead to positions that neither benefit nor hurt the trading account.

Time ignorance triggers expensive trend relativity errors. Great trade setups in one time frame lead to terrible positions in another. All directional movement is time frame-specific. For example, a rally on a daily chart says nothing about price movement on the monthly or intraday charts. Effective planning reduces relativity errors. Calculate reward:risk, visualize the holding period, and measure S/R only for the expected duration of the trade.

Technical indicators lose their effectiveness when improperly time-tuned. Alternatively, resonant time readings produce startling accuracy with ordinary data input. Realize that canned settings offer a general crowd snapshot but rarely produce effective signals for custom time strategies. Also note that the length chosen for the chart view affects results just as much as the settings themselves.

Indicator time summation falls into three general categories:

- Moving averages such as price or volume
- Relationships between the open, close, and high and/or low of individual bars
- Repeating cycles of price or volume behavior

Indicator time frame falls into three general categories:

- Short term
- Intermediate term
- Long term

Time frame denotes relative market periods rather than absolute length. Short term to an intraday trader represents a different amount of time than the same segment for a mutual fund holder. In fact, each market strategy requires different short, intermediate, and long-term considerations. This goes back to the Triple Screen logic. Effective preparation requires time frame study just above and below the chart on which the setup appears. For example, the intraday trader may watch a triangle on the 5-minute chart but examine double-top S/R on the 60-minute chart and look for a low-risk pullback on the 1-minute chart.

Technical analysis studies a fractal market. View individual time units as periods instead of daily, weekly, or monthly lengths. Because no two participants trade exactly the same way, both patterns and indicators must serve a broad range of uses. Indicators make valid predictions whether they arise from 5-minute bars or monthly ones. But exercise caution. Prediction applies only to the time frame for the tools being used to study that market.

THE MARKET CLOCK

Very short-term cycles drive daily market momentum. Each of these small time segments contains predictable crowd, price, and volatility characteristics. The strength or absence of expected behaviors during these phases generates feedback loops that drive subsequent market activity. Intermarket relationships generate many primary cycles. The continuous battle of wills between Chicago futures and New York equities spins endless arbitrage events. The 10:00 a.m. release of government economic statistics generates volatility throughout the world markets, and 3:00 p.m. credit market settlement triggers active positioning for the last open hour of the American stock markets.

Natural rhythms guide other cycles. The composition of the trading crowd changes dramatically as the day progresses. Mornings belong to smaller retail participants who exercise impatient strategies right near the market open. As their impact winds down, professionals move in to work the balance of the day. Their influence peaks in the last hour and especially during the furious final minutes of the session.

Extended trading hours bend the market clock but rarely impact broad cycles. This may change in upcoming years as stocks move to a 24-hour worldwide exchange. Most participants now use these quieter times to complete strategies that began during the regular session. They may exit an overnight gap into an early morning crowd or dump a loser that missed the regular close. After-hour shock events occur frequently but remain the exception to the rule. Preopen trading continues to expand, but larger forces still drive most overnight action. And insider manipulation guarantees that most swing traders will still wait for the opening bell.

The little-known S&P alternation cycle drives intraday price swings. Ninety minutes of strength often follow an equal period of weakness. This cyclic tendency naturally generates five distinct phases during each trading day: three in the direction of the current trend and two countertrend reactions. While the stock market shifts time somewhat through arbitrage-driven tug and pull, dividing the day into five unique time zones presents an effective means to identify short-term market cycles.

> 9:00 a.m.–10:30 a.m.: The market OPENs with a first impulse that resolves and completes the last CLOSE phase.
>
> 10:30 a.m.–12:00 p.m.: MID-MORNING reacts to the OPEN phase but does not resolve any price action.

12:00 p.m.–1:30 p.m.: LUNCH triggers a second impulse that resolves and completes the OPEN phase.

1:30 p.m.–3:00 p.m.: MID-AFTERNOON reacts to the LUNCH phase but does not resolve any price action.

3:00 p.m.–4:30 p.m.: The market CLOSEs with a third impulse that resolves and completes both the OPEN and LUNCH phases.

Each 90-minute phase triggers a new action or a reaction to the last impulse. Each impulse digests the prior market action but raises new conflict that affects price development. This triggers a reaction phase that tests the themes and boundaries of the prior impulse. Finally, this action-reaction axis ignites a subsequent impulse that resolves the conflict of the last one. Also note that the reaction phase for the CLOSE impulse occurs through the overnight markets rather than equities themselves.

Markets oscillate through intraday sessions within this complex structure. Swing traders try to uncover these sentiment shifts and align positions with them. Keep in mind that short-term cycles can generate considerable noise or not appear at all. Watch for these general time tendencies with the 5-minute TICK and intraday stochastics. Follow them when they generate strong signal and directional response but avoid them when cross currents build negative feedback. Cycle interfaces may not show up on schedule. Negative feedback periods tend to overshoot their time allotment, while sharp trends often complete more quickly than 90 minutes. Avoid narrow rules and try to recognize this important time swing wherever it occurs.

The market clock prints three distinct thrust phases and two counterreactions. Each thrust completes and resolves market activity initiated during the prior impulse. For example, the first 90 minutes align with preopen positioning, the actual market open, and the first hour of trading. This important period resolves imbalances that originate during the closing hour of the prior market day as well as the overnight session.

A testing and reaction phase follows each impulse. This counterforce measures the thrust's strength and durability. Major reversals are less likely to occur during these reactions but can show tremendous power when they appear. This phenomenon results from testing that dramatically fails and traps one side of the market that had been in control during the prior phase.

The CLOSE impulse offers no simple reaction phase. The overnight and world markets handle this chore as they digest the U.S. exchange results as well as new impulses that their own participation creates. The Globex-based 24-hour S&P futures markets supply the primary outlet for this off-hour reaction. Post-CLOSE mechanics may change substantially in upcoming years as extended trading hours expand liquidity.

Reaction phases (MID-MORNING and MID-AFTERNOON) do not resolve prior market impulses. Price action must pass through a complete action-reaction cycle before it can successfully digest the new imbalance. The reaction phase often determines the strength or weakness of the underlying impulse and how price change can resolve it. The completion of this testing phase allows participants to initiate appropriate decisions and fuel the next impulse.

Separate impulses generate positive feedback when well aligned and negative feedback when in conflict. For example, a strong OPEN impulse followed by a supportive LUNCH impulse (with weak countermovement through their reactions) sets up a high probability for a strong CLOSE impulse. Alternatively, a weak second move that follows a strong opening tends to resolve itself into a directionless or reversal CLOSE.

POSITION TIMING

Profitable intraday trading requires execution in harmony with daily time cycles. Momentum strategies generally correspond with impulse phases, while swing tactics characterize reaction periods. Time these positions to large-scale trend-range conditions whenever possible. For example, enter momentum positions in active markets during the impulses rather than reactions, but trade pullbacks during reactions rather than impulses.

Avoid execution during noisy cycle periods. Markets trend only 10–20% of the time even at the intraday level. Impulse phases can display little directional movement or conviction by the crowd. Reaction zones may exhibit few themes or boundaries. This restless market action induces many discordant phases without clear signals or opportunity. Never force a position when the TICK chart doesn't identify the current phase clearly.

Specific tactics avoid entry during certain times of day. Many experienced participants stand aside during the OPEN period. They use this phase to exit overnight positions and gather feedback to make informed decisions later in the day. Others aggressively trade the morning but take off at lunch hour and never come back. Some prefer to scalp the quiet middle of the day, when lower volume equals less risk. And at the last hour many morning players return to feed on late-day volatility.

Intraday chart-based tactics favor certain execution times. Overnight gap strategies encourage positions during the opening minutes of the market session. A first-hour breakout system must wait 60 minutes or longer for the new range to develop. Simple charts that rely on 5-minute bars may not print enough data to predict price change until the late morning or early afternoon. And many complex intraday patterns wait until the last hour to complete breakouts or breakdowns.

Specific holding periods focus awareness on different aspects of this short-term tug and pull. Intraday traders seek profit through single momentum thrusts. Positions that align to cyclical interfaces enhance reward and minimize risk. Swing traders find particular value in the cycle's similarity to classic wave motion, that is, thrust-reaction followed by thrust-reaction. This promotes a natural rhythm that allows them to buy weakness and sell strength. Position traders watch these cycles to improve portfolio results as they avoid market-at-open orders with a few simple observations.

The market clock offers a powerful method to improve timing regardless of individual holding period. However, intraday cycles don't always evolve neatly from one phase to the next in real life. Time zones often demand a skilled eye to see when one cycle ends and another begins, even in the best of conditions. So how can less-experienced vision develop this important talent?

Each zone displays unique characteristics that set it apart from all other time phases. Start with their tendency to correspond with specific phases of the trend-range axis. Then examine common observations associated with certain times of day. For example, what occurs at the open and close that make those periods so volatile? How does the lunch hour affect the natural trading flow? How long do dull midday conditions tend to last once they begin?

Experienced participants sense intraday swing cycles with very little objective confirmation. But everyone else should ask important questions that identify the market's location in this endless action-reaction cycle:

What is the current time zone?

Don't rely on the real clock to identify the current market phase. Look instead at the price action and see what it represents to the trading day. Classic first-hour volatility may last only 30 minutes or take the whole morning to wind down. New highs and lows signal an impulse phase in progress. Sharp testing of recent levels or dull, sideways movement points to a reaction phase.

What themes will the current action complete?

Markets unwind short-term imbalance through price movement. In turn, each subsequent impulse generates new imbalance that must face testing and resolution. Examine both price and short-term sentiment to capture the current theme. Communicate its message through a single sentence and then predict the price action that will likely resolve it.

Does the impulse converge with or diverge from a specific trend?

Convergence predicts synergistic price change through subsequent impulses. Divergence predicts choppy range movement and volatility. Consider the broad market activity level. Convergence won't matter without a strong trend and dynamic market environment. Watch for those times when all the ducks line up in a row. This can induce the CLOSE impulse to run quickly higher or lower.

Should the position execute on the next impulse or the next reaction or stay on the sidelines?

The market clock optimizes entry and exit decisions after all the other questions have been answered. Use intraday time cycles in conjunction with cross-verification to locate an appropriate execution target. The best positions arise when price thrusts cleanly through an impulse, pulls back through the reaction, and thrusts again on the next impulse.

FIRST HOUR

The first and last market hours favor strong directional price movement. This positive feedback often dries up through the middle of the day as negative feedback takes over. These two pivotal hours capture the majority of significant price movement over many sessions. The shares traded during this time may exceed 60% of the total volume for the entire 6½-hour session.

Price extremes that print during these hours may represent the high and/or low bars for the entire day. The 4½ hours between 10:30 a.m. and 3:00 p.m. New York time frequently reflect narrow range movement bound by first hour price action. Spreads and volume contract through this middle phase as market movers position themselves into the expected closing impulse.

Look backward to understand the first hour's message. Market players naturally study preopen sentiment, spreads, and the latest news for clues to the new session's supply-demand. Important themes really begin during the prior session's final hour. The last impulse often triggers unexpected price development that builds instability into the close. This late action provides insight into the next day's first impulse. But remember that supply-demand must first pass through the filter of overnight world markets before reaching the new day.

OPENING IMBALANCE

Participants watch the opening action to identify key short-term price levels for the new session. Early swings define the first-hour range, while gaps provide immediate signposts for reversals and breakouts. Penetration through either end of the first hour's range may signal sharp bar expansion. Gaps that hold through this testing period also favor expansion through their initial highs or lows. Alternatively, failure to exceed these levels invites fading strategies as orders build against the short-term extremes.

Closing momentum influences the next morning's opening trades. Simple physics describes this common price mechanism: an object in motion will tend to remain in motion unless met by an intervening force. While inertia slowly pulls market movement toward center, a major trend that persists into the close should try to reassert itself the following morning.

Many forces can modify the CLOSE impulse before the next session. Late news and extended hours allow trading well into the evening. The Globex world session takes over for index futures and smaller contracts. The Nikkei and Hang Seng respond to American market action and contribute their own issues. Europe awakens and its bourses add new twists to the changing environment. Finally, western markets reassume dominance as market makers post early spreads and ECNs open for business.

Overnight world market influence illustrates how sharply sentiment can swing between one session close and the beginning of the next one. But overnight shocks move markets less frequently than most swing traders realize. Because trends persist only 10–20% of the time, American exchanges often generate price action that doesn't impact world sentiment. Only new activity on those local exchanges can finally resolve their internal imbalance.

Intraday traders avoid overnight risk by going flat into the close. Many use the open to determine which trend direction should prevail as they prepare strategies for the day. These short-term tactics force them to miss overnight price movement. Unfortunately, stocks can gap in the direction of a rally or selloff for days in a row during strongly trending markets. This is no coincidence. Insiders use these price shocks to take short-term traders out of the profit game for as long as they can.

Swing traders use intersession volatility to execute two types of strategies. The first tactic expects flat conditions as positions are held overnight. A quiet close favors a quiet open. Stocks in well-defined trends should resume price movement through adjacent sessions unless other forces intervene. While risk increases overnight, positions play the odds and seek greater rewards. But this strategy backfires if overnight shocks or insider manipulation twist the opening.

The other method relies on overnight volatility as swing traders hold positions in expectation of a morning gap. This highly popular strategy carries great risk through most market conditions. Although odds favor a continuation of the prior day's trend, an immediate reversal may trigger if the shock does not materialize. And morning gaps now print frequently in the opposite direction of the close as insiders fade the crowd's well-known intentions.

Overnight strategies rely on an estimated 80–90% continuation bias. A trending stock that moves to a new high or low near closing should surge in that direction the next morning. The first hour provides an excellent opportunity to unload short-term positions that capitalize on the closing trend. But this strategy always presents greater risks than intraday or broader position-based trades. Use it in runaway markets, but avoid it the rest of the time.

THE GAUNTLET

The close marks a standoff between supply and demand that reflects equilibrium or imbalance. Overnight activities may release tension on this spring or pull it to the breaking point. Western markets seek stability through price discovery as the sun rises in New York. On listed exchanges, specialists estimate retail demand through their order book. Nasdaq market makers communicate with ECNs before the open and represent prices that test boundaries until the most aggressive participants win the inside bid-ask spread.

The S&P futures contract impacts the preopen through fair value arbitrage. But rather than offer leadership, this frantic market often paints the opening tape to invite trade execution and then fades immediately. These whipsaws have grown in lockstep with the introduction of small-sized mini contracts and electronic execution. The Nasdaq 100 futures present a popular new indicator for opening demand. But equities traders should realize that the stock markets themselves provide the best leading information about the eventual opening tick.

Changing spreads seek the moving target of opening momentum. But no one really knows how the public or institutions will impact price when the broad markets open. The opening surge may or may not ignite a subsequent trend. The first hour searches for direction as it forces action through a testing gauntlet in order to gauge demand. This price discovery builds a road map to guide both the trading floor and retail public in setting balanced prices for securities.

Look for a third-bar reversal about 11 or 12 minutes into the new day. This frequent test refers to the third bar or candle of the 5-minute S&P futures contract or equity indices, as measured from the 9:30 a.m. opening of the U.S. stock markets. This time zone corresponds with the 15-minute market quote delay built into most retail access until recent years. In past times, painting the tape for this crowd ensured some additional volume for the market makers and specialists. Because retail traders were often the last paper in the door, other market forces could then take over and trigger a reversal or sideways action. Although real-time access to the markets has grown substantially, the third-bar reversal still shows its face in many morning sessions.

A second time zone right after 10:00 a.m. tries to reverse any trend established at the open. The origin of this fade could be the frequent release of government economic data at this time. But even on days with no news, a strong expectation for this 35-minute test often turns into a self-fulfilling event. This specific time zone has tremendous importance for swing traders. Many professionals will not enter positions until the gauntlet ensures that the trend they want to trade will remain intact. They rely upon the outcome of this 35-minute test more than any other for making their early decisions.

Trends that survive first-hour testing may continue throughout the day. These early mechanics trigger another unique behavior of the market open. The last 15 minutes or so of the first hour often reflect capitulation by the gauntlet's losing side. Price movement shifts to the winning trend for the day and can escalate as many swing traders fill their first executions.

Watch for this 10:20 a.m. impulse very closely. An opening trend should resume right at this time if the gauntlet shows little countertrend strength. But if the expected move does not appear, an immediate reaction can trigger a major reversal. Examine the 10 minutes that lead into this time zone to determine the likely outcome. For example, weak countertrend rallies that fade into 10:20 a.m. will often ignite strong selling right at this interval.

This 50-minute move originates through several internal forces. First, many swing traders rely on first-hour breakout systems. Although this method requires that they wait through a full 60 minutes for the daily trend to exert itself, many jump the gun and enter positions early. Second, other participants wait for opening volatility to dissipate, and this time promotes their first daily executions.

The first hour sets themes that repeat themselves throughout the trading day. Market participants reveal their strengths and weaknesses during this testing gauntlet. Volume then drops sharply, constricting price movement and setting range re-

F I G U R E   6.1

The third-bar reversal prints right on schedule during two consecutive Nasdaq sessions. The NYSE TICK and S&P futures often signal this early morning shift better than indices that suffer from reporting delays due to opening volume bursts. The third-bar reversal may shift forward or backward in time, depending on market conditions. If it fails to appear at all, the void signals a strong bias in the opening direction.

Intraday   (Right) $COMPX - NASDAQ COMBINED COMPOSITE INDX (5-Min)   Bar
             5/31   6/01

sistance difficult to penetrate until one side gathers new momentum. This often provides clear boundaries for the action that follows.

Intraday traders use first-hour breakout systems to beat the market. This early strategy sets up support and resistance at short-term price extremes, especially in choppy markets. Breaks through these important levels should induce profitable bar expansion in the direction of the penetration. These known tendencies support classic setups such as buying momentum, fading resistance, and buying pullback dips.

MIDDAY MARKETS

A new crowd emerges as the action of the first hour fades. While public participation dominates the open, the balance of the day belongs to institutions and professional traders. The resolution of opening orders, driven by overnight supply-demand imbalance, creates an upward, downward, or sideways bias that will likely persist for the entire day. This initial market character fuels trade strategies for those making their livelihood in the daily price swings.

Trend days appear less frequently than rangebound ones. Swing traders take their cues from whatever the markets offer and choose long, short, or stand-aside strategies. This often requires waiting for countertrend weakness after the first hour before they enter long positions or countertrend strength to sell short.

TIME FOR THE PROS

Many low-risk opportunities appear throughout the middle of the day. Price swings tend to exhibit more dependable movement so entries can be held through small pullbacks with less risk. Scalping tactics also work very well within these very short-term cycles. But intraday participants understand that market character changes sharply in the last hour. They must choose to terminate positions if their active strategy cannot capitalize on that volatile environment. Fortunately, the last hour also provides convenient opportunities for profitable exits.

Execute longer-term positions in the middle of the day to improve reward: risk significantly. Trade fills during this quieter time benefit from compressed spreads, and speculators make better decisions after observation of the bull-bear struggle that guides the opening gauntlet. But remember that market timing cannot turn a bad trade into a good one. It can only make a good one better.

First-hour range, total volume, and the current bar's relationship to short-term highs or lows offer important feedback to determine reward:risk for potential trade entries. Break of the first hour range or other significant high-low extremes sets up profitable bar expansion. Swing traders also initiate fades at intraday S/R in anticipation of reversals. For example, when a stock thrusts through a first-hour high, pauses, and breaks back into the morning range, the odds for a successful short sale near this high increase greatly.

The midday trader must face continued testing of the short-term trend. As the day progresses, reversal of first-hour sentiment becomes more and more unlikely. While this early trend remains dominant on most days, strong midday shocks can generate contrary forces that trigger powerful reversals. Two classic zones for this

F I G U R E   6.2

JDS Uniphase sets up a well-marked first-hour range that finally yields to a strong mid-afternoon breakout. Price then responds to the range with classic S/R behavior on pullbacks. Place a Fib grid across this early trend to estimate swing levels and predict which way the market will finally break. Keep in mind that first-hour range strategy only works well about 3 out of 5 market days.

Intraday   (Right) JDSU - JDS UNIPHASE CORP (5-Min)   Bar
            6/06   6/07

unexpected shift lie near 11 a.m. and 1 p.m. These important times correspond with trading that surrounds lunchtime on Wall Street.

Sharp, short countertrend activity often characterizes the late morning test. Tape readers will notice that market movers and institutions press one final attempt here to gauge strength or weakness of the primary trend. Directional price movement can quickly resume once they complete these games. The period from shortly after 11:00 a.m. into the lunch hour can ignite very strong trend development. Alternatively, if an expected price move does not materialize by 11:30 a.m., the market often fades into undependable swing movement.

Countertrend movement may not emerge during early afternoon activity if the day exhibits strong directional bias. A rally or selloff can begin right after lunch in these trending conditions. But erratic activity becomes much more likely if direction is not clear. At times like these, one can almost hear insiders plotting their manipulation over lunch and drinks at New York corner bars.

Trust nothing you see or hear during the lunch hour. As primary market players head out to fill their stomachs, the second team arrives to play a variety of fake-out games that generate volume and test the supply-demand waters. False breakouts and breakdowns occur with great frequency as clever stop-gunning exercises push through well-established S/R. This negative feedback can work to the swing trader's advantage. The lunch hour provides a very attractive exit point if the push and pull of false price movement benefits an existing position.

The midday quiet carries one final danger to the bottom line. Every short-term trade must show sufficient price movement to generate gain or loss. Positions that don't exhibit sufficient volatility generate substantial risk as range narrows after the first hour. Trading is never a zero-sum game, and these small losses can lead to significant transaction costs. Make sure that executions anticipate an active market or leave them for the next participant.

FINDING MIDDAY WINNERS

The midday swing trader must locate issues that will generate predictable range movement. Expect no more than 20% (10 or 12) of the stocks within a real-time quote screen of 50–60 issues to display positive characteristics of trend and volatility on any given day. The setups for these trading vehicles must reveal their intentions through prior analysis of momentum, key S/R, and prevailing Pattern Cycles.

Supplement overnight study with classic intraday price analysis. Exercise strong discipline and keep the Level II screen at some distance while an unbiased evaluation of all technical factors decides the next execution. Always ask the right questions before making the trade:

Has the stock broken out of its first hour range?

First-hour breakouts signify trending markets. A breakout can lead to a series of strong price thrusts in the direction of the break. Alternatively, when price remains stuck between early trading extremes, it lacks sufficient crowd enthusiasm or fear to push it through these barriers. The longer that markets sit in this early price range, the less likely that any significant movement will occur until (at least) the end of the day.

Is it close to its high or low for the day?

Many eyes watch markets that trade close to their highs or lows. Important tests at these levels invite the crowd to jump in or head for the exits. Don't be fooled by one- or two-tick penetrations of these extremes, especially on the first test. Professionals know that stops build right at these points and will take them out, regardless of their other intentions. Momentum players should concentrate on the third rise to a high or the third descent to a low. This wave will more likely trigger a sharp price break than the first test.

Are profitable entry points easy to recognize?

The best entries always jump out to experienced eyes. Their location in the maze of 1-minute or 5-minute price bars makes them obvious. No two patterns are alike, but all promising setups share a common feature: they speak for themselves and require little interpretation. If you have to think about it, move on to the next opportunity.

Is the market displaying positive feedback or negative feedback?

Dead markets rob profits as easily as losing positions. Study volume to decide whether anyone really cares. How wide is the price range compared to recent days? Narrow-range days make profitable intraday entries very difficult. Does enthusiasm build on the time and sales screen, or is dull money controlling the action? When the markets just sit there, change the channel.

Execute the appropriate trade once an opportunity appears. Midday markets favor constricted action, so the most effective tactics apply classic swing strategy. Experience suggests that the best results will come from buying weakness on up-trend issues and selling strength on downtrend ones. Expected holding period and price momentum determine which intraday trends provide the best reward:risk. Even 1-minute and 5-minute trends offer profitable swing trades as long as midday volatility induces wide range movement. Align entries with market clock impulses or reactions, and always keep one eye on the TICK.

Odds favor an increase in selling right at 2:30 p.m. This time bias originates in the bond market. On volatile days, their 3:00 p.m. closing forces many equity participants to the sidelines to avoid reversals and shakeouts. Over time, this sell zone has established itself as a natural exit point and now appears even during quiet credit markets. Insiders also use 2:30 p.m. to measure selling pressure in anticipation of the last hour, and locals turn quick profits by reversing rallies into this point. As with the 10:20 a.m. move, strong buying can ignite when selling doesn't appear right at 2:30 p.m. But this late event always carries a negative bias regardless of the intraday trend.

LAST HOUR

Midday participants need well-defined strategies to deal with the closing hour. The last phase of the market day displays unique characteristics that will enhance or undermine profits. Intraday traders seek to exit all positions prior to the closing bell. Professionals know this and will do everything in their power to pick those traders' pockets. Longer-term swing traders can go flat into the close or maintain

FIGURE   6.3

The 2:30 p.m. sell reverses small rallies and generates painful whipsaws. Remain very defensive when strong TICK and futures movement signal a new uptrend just 15–20 minutes before this critical period. Insiders often paint the tape here so they can fade price through the reversal. Alternatively, this time zone allows low-risk entry in strongly trending markets as a positive bias kicks in near 3:00 p.m.

Intraday   (Right) $COMPX - NASDAQ COMBINED COMPOSITE INDX (5-Min)   Bar
6/01

positions as part of their broader strategy. When time permits, they should apply a quick reward:risk analysis for open positions and evaluate the likely impact of an overnight hold on the trading account.

U.S. stocks undergo a rapid change in character as trading in the credit markets closes. Market participants realize that 4:00 p.m. concludes most financial transactions for the day. This simple fact ignites a new market impulse that responds to the major intraday themes. Both retail and institutions contribute to this last hour's volatility through active trading. Classic buy-sell programs strike throughout the last 60 minutes, while mutual fund activity surges during the last 20 minutes of the day. This dramatic increase in institutional participation heightens price movement and stirs up an emotional brew that leads into the close.

CHANGE OF CHARACTER

Swing traders plan final executions during this hour and remain sharply focused on the powerful forces at work. This compressed period tries to discount all of the day's news and emotions. Much of the action depends on what precedes it. This daily event can pass with little excitement after quiet or rangebound sessions. But if conflicting market forces need final resolution or a very strong trend persists, wide bar expansion and whipsaws will develop.

The last hour frees stocks from the influence of credit-related arbitrage and allows index futures arbitrage to drive price movement. This third market clock impulse also marks decision time for a multitude of active strategies that began during the prior hours. Participants must use their time wisely. Trends that develop through the first 20 minutes of the final hour tend to fade sharply at 3:30 p.m. and price action loses predictability as closing strategies take over the last 20 minutes of the session.

Participants closely watch the 15 minutes that lead into 3:00 p.m., looking for evidence of strong momentum that may predict the direction of a last-hour surge. Although this short period carries a buy-side bias, it can also lead to major selloffs. Gauge demand through review of the TICK and market breadth (advance/decline) data. Examine Level II as well as time and sales to identify bursts of enthusiasm or fear. If the measurements flatline during this important phase, they signify a market without immediate direction. This can offer a very useful signal that most of the crowd will miss.

Swing traders who buy weakness and sell rallies all day must shift gears during the final hour and become trend followers. Odds favor continuation of the intraday trend during the last hour and into the next day's open. Shorting stocks that sit at new highs or catching falling knives in selloffs both trigger very bad outcomes. Alternatively, momentum strategies allow profitable trade exits as positions follow this final impulse and break beyond their intraday ranges.

Major trends rarely reverse in the closing hour, but contrary price movement can escalate very rapidly when they do. Late reversals trap the crowd that controlled most of the action up to that point. Powerful moves erupt as they unwind large commitments with little time to trade. Don't wait for too much confirmation when the warning signs appear for this event. The lack of available time speeds up the action and often fails to offer pullbacks or other low-risk execution.

Knowledge of daily range and key S/R levels improves results during last-hour trades. Congestion sets up well in advance of closing near key highs and lows.

Stops build just above or below these extremes while the crowd watches very closely. Price pushes into these levels during the last hour as invisible forces guide its movement. Insiders want to gauge whether demand is great enough to support an expansion move. At the least, they benefit from stop volume and ensure that orders don't disappear overnight without execution. And with a little luck, they generate enough momentum to keep things active well beyond the current session.

QUITTING TIME

The session's last 15–20 minutes close the books for most traders, institutions, and market movers. This generates unique but unpredictable price behavior. Spreads often set up to penalize one or both sides of the market. These can rapidly shift in the final minutes to take advantage of MOC (market on close) orders, intraday traders going flat and covering shorts. Avoid new positions during these last minutes unless a specific overnight strategy manages them. Use this time instead to exit existing plays at the best possible price. Also watch to see how institutions view the closing. Their willingness to commit capital can predict how the next morning will open.

Insiders paint the price chart at closing so they can access demand from the fresh surge of retail market orders the next morning. Overnight strategies must trust the daily trend here, although whipsaws can occur just minutes before 4 p.m. Even thin issues get a paint job at this time to try to fool technical indicators that rely on range closing information. Stocks with spreads that average more than ½ point can produce a host of inaccurate signals if they just close on the ask or bid day after day.

Multiday trends develop when a single session fails to discount the common pool of information. The finality of the approaching close intensifies greed and fear. Many actions reflect ill-advised decision making as loss and frustration creep into rational strategies. These emotions generate additional supply-demand imbalance that can carry into the close. This peaking volatility makes the last few minutes dangerous and unpredictable. The master swing trader has already concluded the day's transactions by this time and stands aside to the final bell.

TIME OF WEEK AND MONTH

Time bias does not end with daily cycles. Clearly defined time quirks appear through weekly and monthly periods as well. Swing traders study these events to avoid being on the wrong side of the market when they strike. Start with individual days of the week and look at their special characteristics. These five trading sessions open new themes, test them, and work to resolve price imbalance before Friday's closing tick.

F I G U R E   6.4

eBay breaks support just after 3:00 p.m. and descends into a major selloff. A restless crowd waits as congestion and a rising trendline develop during the market day. Longs grow impatient and decide to exit if the line breaks. Potential shorts set stops to enter new positions at the same time. Insiders and self-fulfilling mechanics keep the line intact until the last hour draws substantial volume from the sidelines. A last push breaks the barrier and the host of trading strategies strike at the same time.

Monday morning greets market participants the same way that offices around the world receive tired worker bees. The weekend break disorients the crowd and forces reevaluation of major assumptions. The session often opens to confusion as players try to find their rhythm and the next market direction. Light volume characterizes many Mondays, especially in the summertime. This lack of commitment may continue well into midweek. The morning can trigger selling pressure that lasts for many hours. Mild rallies often begin late in the day as this finally dissipates and the market floats upward.

Turnaround Tuesday describes a well-known time bias. Trends that begin on Friday and persist through Monday frequently reverse during the first hour of this session. New trends that start at this time may trigger sharp price expansion for the next two days. But choppy action can persist throughout the week when a clear trend does not appear. Volume often spikes on Tuesday as large players execute their first strategies of the week. Watch Instinet closely to see how the institutions position themselves.

Wednesday and Thursday tend to reinforce themes initiated earlier in the week. Strong trends should continue through these days unless external shock events intervene. Trading action starts to hesitate on Thursday afternoon as aware-ness of the upcoming weekend enters the market psyche. This wall grows stronger if the crowd fears government statistics that will be released the next morning.

The government issues economic reports through a regular publication cycle. The major ones can impact markets on any day of the week. But the monthly unemployment report, which always appears on the first Friday of the month, wields the greatest hammer. The credit and futures markets can respond violently to these important numbers. This ensures that arbitrage and crowd response trigger broad equities movement. But placing bets in advance of fundamental reports can be very dangerous. Earn consistent profits by reading the charting landscape rather than speculating on external influences.

Fridays have other major forces to contend with. Options expire the middle Friday of each month. That week often generates unusual volatility that peaks on expiration day. Market action during this period can be highly unpredictable. Swing traders should consider an early weekend before the climax and think twice about all executions during that week. Most participants also use the week's end to digest themes and imbalance from the prior 4 days. Many institutional strategies focus on weekly price bars. As the week draws to a close, professional technicians determine the need for portfolio adjustments and take appropriate action to protect large po-sitions. Many players act recklessly near the weekend if positions stand at a large profit or loss. The losers jump into volatile stocks as they try to get even, while the winners dump profit vehicles that still have many points to run.

Markets seek equilibrium as they head for the weekend. This can trigger strong trends in either direction to accommodate current themes. But Fridays tend to end with a whimper rather than a bang. Many players wind down and disappear by the afternoon, especially in the summertime. This frequently leads to a choppy close on light volume. But when strong conflict or imbalance carries into the final session of the week, everyone will stay at their desks until the last minutes.

SEASONS AND SEASONALITY

Well-defined seasonal variations can signal false opportunity. For example, options expiration reflects high levels of manipulation. Classic breakout and breakdown rules must be closely managed during these volatile times to avoid the risk of serious loss. Other times of month and year generate special bias that can affect trade alignment. Learn these cyclical quirks before taking a position that falls under their influence.

Holiday and preholiday trading sessions elicit a positive bias but carry increased risk. Martin Zweig catalogued the mechanics of this interesting phenomenon in his classic *Winning on Wall Street*. He noted that U.S. holiday markets finished up 83% of the time during the period from 1952 to 1985. Holiday trading has grown choppier since he published his findings but this bullish tendency continues. Unfortunately, participants can still lose substantial money on these rally days.

Light volume characterizes holiday sessions. This gives professionals a great opportunity to manipulate the tape and induce wide price swings. Christmas week and the day after Thanksgiving provide the perfect environment for this type of false volatility. Swing traders can get on the right side of this action and turn excellent profits. But classic technical analysis often fails as S/R, patterns, and price extremes violate without pullbacks or crowd participation. The best advice during these holiday periods is to turn off the computer and go to the beach.

The end of each quarter triggers window dressing by mutual funds and other large institutions. Intense fund buying tends to appear after a very strong market rally. Funds must report their profit or loss on a quarterly basis. They have great motivation to publish excellent results—their managers would like to keep their jobs. Even when they miss the original rally, funds buy certain issues near the end of the quarter's last month to boast that they own the stock in their public reports.

The January Effect provides a liquidity-driven seasonal event. Fresh cash pours into the stock markets through 401(k) contributions at the start of each year. At the same time, tax selling pressure eases and invites new value investors. These two forces combine to generate a very strong bullish bias that often leads to powerful rallies. Most investors associate the January Effect with small cap stocks. But the popularity of large cap funds has broadened the impact into more sectors in recent years.

Market character changes through the summer months. But June no longer denotes the start of Wall Street's prolonged vacation. Heavy retail participation now keeps trading volume high until late July. Although the summer months traditionally display a bullish bias, recent years have seen substantial volatility and less-dependable action in the period between mid-June and late July. After the fireworks, August's dog days take center stage as market professionals disappear and light, choppy action becomes more likely until Labor Day. As with holiday periods, these thin sessions exhibit wider price swings and many technical violations. Choose more active stocks and event-driven issues to capture cleaner moves until the crowd returns for the fall season.

September presents market players with the most dangerous period of the entire year. It represents the only month that has generated an average decline in portfolio value over a 45-year history. Although October has witnessed the Black October events of 1929 and 1987, the harvest month offers relatively good historical returns. On the other hand, September rarely rewards investors. Year-end anxiety

FIGURE   6.5

Special trading conditions fill the seasonal landscape. Take the time to understand these important market influences and align individual positions to their broad power. Keep a copy of the annual **Stock Trader's Almanac** by Yale Hirsch close at hand. It provides an excellent desktop reference on seasonality and market performance.

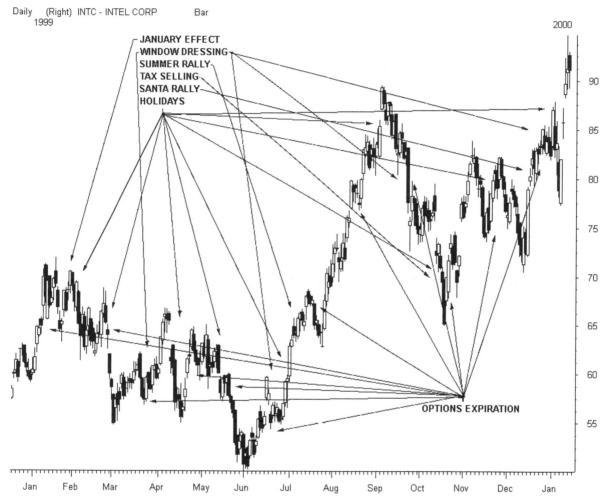

drives part of this negativity, but a more fundamental process underlies the poor results. Autumn initiates the start of tax selling season for retail and institutional participants.

Tax loss selling infects fall market activity for several months. Investors reduce their year-end tax burden by taking capital losses on nonperforming positions. This selling often limits broad rallies until close to Christmas. This event's intensity de-

T A B L E   6.1

Average Monthly Gain in the S&P 500 1950–95 and the Percentage of Time the Market Rose

Month	Average Gain	% of Time Market Rose
January	1.55%	62%
February	.38%	58%
March	.78%	62%
April	1.23%	68%
May	.18%	58%
June	.09%	50%
July	1.29%	59%
August	.39%	53%
September	−.60%	39%
October	.45%	58%
November	1.42%	62%
December	1.78%	77%
All	.75%	58%

SOURCE: Technical Analysis of Stocks and Commodities V14: 6, 241–243.

pends on the months that precede it. Long periods of market decline increase tax loss pressure, while stable rallies relieve it. Mutual funds face their own major reallocation near the end of October as they prepare for end-of-year reporting. This can trigger ferocious volatility with broad strategies that dump old losers and chase new winners.

The Santa Rally marks a psychological end to tax loss selling as investors jump the gun on next year's bargains. The last few weeks before the Christmas holiday carry a positive bias that often triggers a substantial rally. Although investors can sell losing positions through December 31, most of their negative impact eases by mid-month. Market players then concentrate on rebuilding portfolios with cash directed toward broad sectors. This combines with natural holiday bullishness to favor a pleasant end to the trading year.

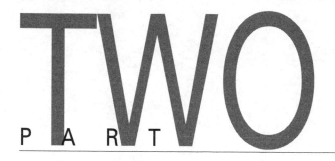

PART TWO

THE 7-BELLS: TOOLS TO LOCATE OUTSTANDING OPPORTUNITIES

7

C H A P T E R

MASTERING THE SETUP

CLASSIC VS. ORIGINAL PATTERNS

Swing traders study the charting landscape to measure the active environment and identify promising setups. They pick opportunities that match the current Pattern Cycles, implement thoughtful positions, and respond quickly to changing conditions. They take small losses when proven wrong, without hesitation or second-guessing. Defensive trade management guides their tactics, emotions, and logic from initial planning through final profit-taking.

The seeds of change reveal themselves through repeating price patterns. These signposts define characteristic crowd behavior at major Pattern Cycle intersections. They uncover classic market mechanisms that should resolve in a predictable manner and have consistent reward:risk profiles. They work through the force of herd behavior but lose their effectiveness when the crowd finally responds and catches up to the prevailing market direction.

Opportunity has many faces. A few classic setups have captured the imagination of both traders and the media over the last century. But charts exhibit dozens of lesser-known, highly predictive formations. Since these patterns avoid the crowd's common knowledge, they yield better results over longer periods than popular setups. They also require greater attention than a classic double top or esoteric Holy Grail. Swing traders must review endless charts, apply complex filters to lower noise, and play only those formations that have the highest odds for success at any time.

A very simple mechanism underlies all setup opportunity: patterns predict outcomes as they reveal the will of the crowd. Patterns point to direction and time because emotional herd behavior drives a common will at market turning points. Choose the right direction at the right moment and book a profit. Diverse crowds respond to different time frames and conditions. This allows predictable setups to print through the different layers of the 3D charting landscape.

Skilled eyes will uncover both classic and original setups. Market evolution works through a variety of complex, directional forces. These induce broad Pattern Cycle variations within all time frames. Some draw perfectly according to the blueprint, but others have never been catalogued even though they carry great predictive power. So how can the swing trader recognize these special patterns and apply effective strategies that capitalize upon their behavior? The answer lies in the left-right brain interaction.

Patterns represent archetypes of market inefficiency. The artistic mind instinctively perceives this order through a purely visual process. In other words, the new pattern looks bullish or bearish but the brain doesn't understand why. The scientific mind then joins the process and studies the formation. Objective analysis uncovers many pieces of classic patterns buried within the original setup. This familiarity permits the swing trader to quickly review reward:risk, study the numbers, and formulate a promising strategy.

These logical tactics capitalize on the original setup because they respond to the vision of the artistic mind. The best opportunities come when many classic patterns combine to create signposts that emit strong tension and release points. This complex application of Pattern Cycle behavior rewards original vision with many dependable methods to take profits from the markets, although the formations have never been named, categorized, or compared to a book illustration.

PATTERN RECOGNITION

Learn the classic setups first to recognize them instantly in any time frame chart. Then move on to more original predictive patterns. The 7-Bells setups present the next generation of dependable market mechanics. These classic archetypes describe predictable market forces that print through all time frames and offer outstanding trades. They fill in the missing tactics between well-known setups and broad market movement.

Swing traders master original setups that don't appear in print. Watch closely when Pattern Cycles shift toward a new environment. Markets will draw many variations of better-known patterns at these logical intersections. Even simple reversals may morph into a variety of complex mutations that can offer substantial profits. First see if the pattern looks like a classic one. If so, list the potential differences in terms of underlying tendency and S/R mechanics. Then examine the broad formation to locate any natural ejection points. Consider execution when it organizes well in time, direction, and breakout level.

Many trading signals appear within the daily noise. But so do whipsaws and fakeouts. Filter all potential setups through their misinformation. Look for stop gun

F I G U R E   7.1

Three well-placed lines and a triangle draw a 12-point Xilinx profit. This complex pattern uses important elements of the Big W, five-wave decline, first rise, and 3rd watch. Yet the setup depends only on basic trendline interpretation and good timing. Original patterns that generate the most visual tension offer the greatest profit opportunities.

violations at key S/R barriers. Each one can desensitize enthusiasm or fear when price returns to that level. Evaluate the sequence of highs and lows within the pattern. Do they carry a common message through a series of ascending or declining prices? Or does conflict pull the action into unexpected places? Check external forces for alignment with the setup bias. Avoid positions when they lack support from the broader market.

Swing traders fail when they lose vision. The scientific mind assumes so much control that all charts start to look alike and excellent setups fade from view. Perfect patterns and indicators rarely print in the modern market environment. Learn to execute comfortably in a debris-filled landscape. Alternatively, don't chase every crossover as a major signal or see meaningless price bars as textbook setups. When the eyes start to play unfortunate tricks, get away from the execution terminal and head for the beach until they can be trusted again.

Pattern recognition does not work for everyone. Many Western participants have great difficulty dealing with intuition and visualization. They will find far greater success if they build trading systems that rely on heavy math input and frequent back testing. Systems and discretionary trading do not mix well. If headed down the scientific path, abandon classic setups and rely on pure numerical output.

MANAGING OPPORTUNITY

Good patterns never signal exactly when to trade or when to stand aside. They point to directional and time interfaces that will trigger predictable movement under the right circumstances. Swing traders must then formulate tactics that capitalize upon price change if it proceeds and protect them from loss if it fails. There is no single method to trade any pattern, and no setup will evolve the same way twice. So the chosen strategy must capture expected opportunity while managing unexpected risk.

Categorize each setup as original or classic. This predicts the level of public participation and whipsaw. For example, the odds for a pattern failure greatly increase when the herd sells the same head and shoulders setup. But a carefully chosen dip trip that combines several diverse patterns responds very well to basic tactics because the setup does not encourage a popular response. Shift strategy when a large crowd trades the pattern. Always consider going the other way if it fails or standing aside through a first whipsaw until the true direction emerges.

Enter an opportunity before its breaks whenever possible. Risk remains low until price finally expands. Swing traders can efficiently enter and terminate several low-cost positions while they wait for a bigger move. But always keep one eye on the clock. Time eventually moves against a promising setup if it just sits there. Technical indicators start to roll over and the pattern suddenly telegraphs an unfavorable message. Choose entry levels wisely and exit immediately if conditions deteriorate.

Exercise patience when a setup ejects without trade entry. Risk rises dramatically and volatility expands as a crowd joins the action. Shift execution tactics to pullback entry, but be willing to stand aside if the market starts to run. A promising setup must stand on its own merits after a pattern break. The price expansion alters the reward:risk calculation and forces a real-time reevaluation. Execute on a pullback if this new analysis supports the opportunity. But consider that many good patterns only predict a single price swing and profit potential evaporates as soon as the move begins.

FIGURE 7.2

One good Adobe triangle deserves another. An overnight gap completes one triangle breakout, and price action immediately draws an identical pattern. This invites many new longs who missed the first move and now hope for an easy profit. Unfortunately the market has other plans. Professionals use this common formation to shake out weak hands with a sharp decline. True direction reappears the next morning when price jumps back above the broken triangle and heads higher.

Intraday   (Right) ADBE - ADOBE SYSTEMS (5-Min)   Bar

Predefined strategies work well when setups print on daily bars and allow detailed evening analysis. But many excellent patterns suddenly appear in real-time during the intraday session. The swing trader must internalize these archetypes so that their midday appearance permits spontaneous action. Very short-term setups produce excellent short-term profits. But intraday charts exhibit much higher noise levels than daily charts. Don't wait for perfect pattern alignment or good opportunities will be lost. Expect more stop gun extremes, trendline violations, and dirty candle prints during the trading day.

Align intraday setups to natural time-of-day tendencies. For example, the middle of the day exhibits fewer pattern failures than the first or last hour. But 2- or 3-day setups that point to a first- or last-hour ejection can offer highly profitable opportunities. Some patterns work better in the intraday environment than others. Avoid those that depend on specific volume characteristics. Intraday bias ensures that false volume readings will confuse signals.

Excellent setups never reduce the need for cross-verification. Broad elements of the charting landscape combine to define that pattern's reward:risk. Breakout and swing levels should always correspond to other well-established support or resistance. Use multiple time frames to confirm that larger market forces align with the opportunity. Check major moving averages and indicator settings to uncover any divergences that could undermine the position.

Combine original and classic setups into a trading style that produces continuous profit opportunities. Look for these important patterns through all markets and time frames. Choose an appropriate strategy for each trade that defines low-risk entry, profit targets, and stop loss. Always consider the impact of pattern failure. When these setups eject in the wrong direction, they may offer a better reward: risk profile than the expected outcome.

TWO CLASSIC APPLICATIONS

The following patterns represent classic applications of trading science. Their persistence over the years has established them as profit-makers for many generations. Although the 2B top executes from the short side, it also flips over to trigger an effective bottom trade. Note that these applications seek to defensively manage risk at natural entry levels due to their popularity. Keep in mind that every good trade has more than one successful strategy. This presentation illustrates just a few ways to pick the market's pocket.

2B TOP

This setup presents a double top variation that allows much earlier entry than other classic topping formations. Low-risk short sales can execute as early as the first bar after price falls below a prior high.

FIGURE 7.3

Multiday setups improve results when they execute during specific intraday periods. This 3-day Qualcomm channel points to an impending breakout right near the session's close. Last-hour entry could exit the next morning with a healthy profit as opening volatility favors an expanding market. Use time-of-day bias whenever possible to fine-tune setup decisions.

RealTick® ©1986–2000. All rights reserved. Used with permission of Townsend Analytics, Ltd.

Description

- The 2B top pattern capitalizes on a failed test of the last high.
- Subsequent rallies to this price level do not reactivate the setup because the odds then favor a breakout to substantial new highs.

- Price must exceed the first high for at least one bar before it falls back below that level.
- The rally into the second high should take more bars than the rally into the first high.
- Look for the test to print a candlestick shadow above the last high but a real body below it. This may draw shooting star or doji pattern.
- Keep an oscillator active in the lower pane as price rises into the test. The indicator should roll over from an overbought state before the second high prints.
- Flip over and apply identical setup rules to 2B bottom reversals that appear at new lows.

Swing trade entry after initial failure depends on the topping pattern. Never expect an immediate decline to much lower levels, since the 2B reversal falls back into congestion that must still be broken. Odds increase that the second high will fail when the first high rises into a parabolic rally. Watch for heavy volume at the first high and much lower participation as price rises into the test of that level.

Setup Tactics (FIGURE 7.4)

- Novell doubles in price in less than 3 weeks and prints a major high at 43. Note the deep pullback and small descending triangle failure before price pushes back into a test of the first high.
- Stretch a Fib grid across the original rally (1) to locate S/R for the topping formation. The triangle pattern sits right on the 38% retracement.
- Use the congestion low (2) to signal the eventual top breakdown.
- Track the rally into the second high with a Stochastics or RSI oscillator. Watch for a rollover pattern right near the test. NOVL Stochastics prints a small double top (4) right at the reversal after falling from an overbought level.
- The stock breaks to a new high and closes with a bullish bar (3), but it gaps down next morning in a hole-in-the-wall.
- Visualize the next-lower time frame. That pattern also exhibits a hole-in-the-wall reversal. The first sell signal generates when the gap remains unfilled after the first hour of trading.
- Next support level sets up just below 40 (5). A second sell signal triggers when that trendline, horizontal line, and market number all break together.
- Realign the Fib grid to the second high (6) and use that setting to study the topping pattern. Note how the shift moves the congestion low right to the 50% retracement.
- The longer trendline (7) breaks and pushes the selloff into the center Fibonacci retracements, where it tests the congestion low several times.

FIGURE   7.4

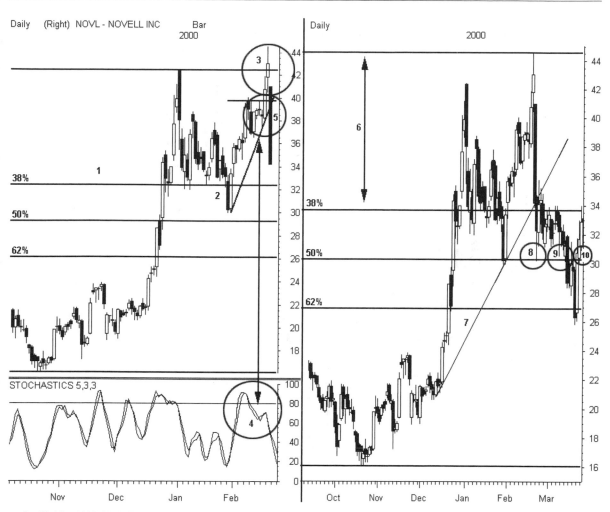

RealTick® ©1986–2000. All rights reserved. Used with permission of Townsend Analytics, Ltd.

- Look for simple swing opportunities within the congestion (8) or stand aside until the breakdown completes.
- The pattern finally breaks at 50% (9) but progress slows at 62% support. A sharp bounce develops (10) as Fibonacci works its magic.

Execution and Position Management (FIGURE 7.5)

- Many swing opportunities appear within the double top congestion. Most of these depend on real-time market access and a short holding period.

F I G U R E   7.5

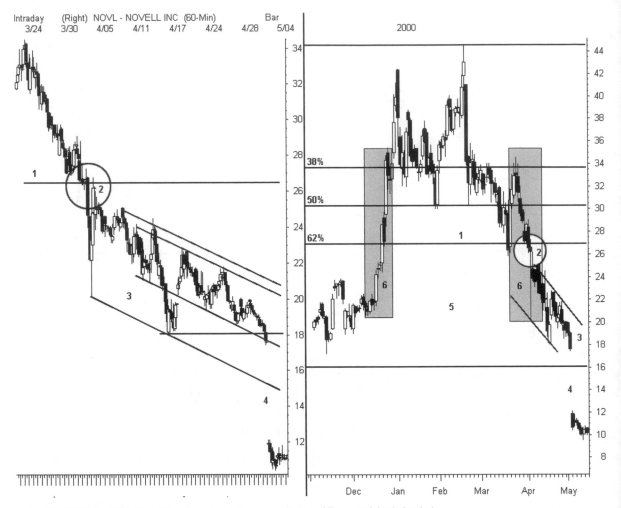

As the pattern evolves, price approaches a final breakdown that allows broader position trades.

- Violation of the 62% retracement (1) finally signals the start of the new downtrend. Price takes out the old low and expands sharply. Sell the break with a tight stop on the other side of the 62% level. Execute close to the break point or pass up the trade. Remember that a 2B bottom can reverse price quickly here.
- The sharp initial drop from the second high predicts a possible mesa top reversal with a decline that prints at a trend mirror image to the prior

rally. The collapse between 34 and 20 (6) perfectly matches the December parabola (6) through this level.

- The initial break pulls back to the 62% retracement (2) and generates a high-profit, low-risk short sale entry.
- The downtrend evolves into a descending parallel price channel (3) that drops NOVL through a large first failure (5) pattern that marks a 100% retracement of the major rally.
- The channel finally breaks and expands into a huge down gap (4), but the small violation on the last bar offers few clues to the overnight shock event.

Reward:Risk

Swing traders risk frequent trend relativity errors with this evolving reversal pattern. Some believe they can short the entire decline by selling into the second high. Others cheat themselves by taking a small profit when a little patience yields a much bigger one. This setup illustrates the importance of the charting landscape and the need to find all of the hidden obstacles before trade execution.

CHANNEL BREAK

Parallel trendlines set up sharp price expansion when they break in either direction. These parallel price channel breakouts tend to be highly dependable and free from whipsaws.

Description

- Price channels generate from two sets of parallel trendlines, but each trendline may form through only two points instead of three.
- Harmonic parallel lines often mark S/R within major channel boundaries.
- Bars should expand sharply when price breaks out of either side, regardless of the channel's angle.
- Impending breakouts may signal in advance when price congests along a boundary and bars narrow.
- The intensity of bar expansion often reflects how often price struck that side of the channel before the breakout.
- Price should return to test the channel break before moving higher or lower.

Channel strategy fades trendline boundaries or bets on expansion momentum. Well-defined harmonics allow precise swing trade entry with low risk. Try to execute within the channel itself just before the expansion event begins. The pattern should signal its intentions one or two bars before the move.

Setup Tactics (FIGURE 7.6)

- This rising Ciena channel feeds off a prior high to trigger an outstanding short sale pattern. Watch what happens when the continuation gap (1) at 145 turns out to be an exhaustion gap for the 2-week rally.

F I G U R E   7.6

- Parallel price channels build complex harmonics (2) within their wider boundaries.
- Uncover channels early in their creation and use them until they break. Start to test parallel lines as soon as three relative highs and lows print.
- Treat breakouts to new highs (4) with caution when they occur on the first test of a prior high. The scenario sets up a possible 2B top reversal.
- Price strikes the top trendline (3) and appears ready to break out after it pulls back to test the harmonic. Prepare to buy quickly if rising bars congest against the top trendline.
- CIEN suddenly breaks down through the harmonic and builds congestion on top of the continuation gap (1). The false breakout alarm rings and invites a closer look at the pattern.

Execution and Position Management (FIGURE 7.7)

- Shift down to the next-lower time frame and analyze that pattern in detail. This focuses timing and identifies hidden forces that drive the potential price decline.
- The smaller chart uncovers a descending triangle (4) with a whipsaw (3) that generates a 2B top reversal. The combination of these two patterns looks more bearish than either by itself.
- The continuation and exhaustion gap (2) completes one successful test on 5/16 (7) but finally fills as the triangle pattern breaks and marks new resistance.
- A small rally to 147 (5) after the breakdown signals a perfect CV×4 short sale opportunity for the impending channel break. It represents the pullback to triangle resistance, the top of the filled gap, and the 38% Fibonacci retracement. It also prints a bearish reversal candlestick.
- The channel line (1) holds through the test of the triangle breakdown. This complex resistance traps longs and sets up an explosive situation. A 30-minute time window permits low-risk entry in the two small bars that sit right on the channel line beneath 144.
- The line breaks at 143 but rapid movement makes further short sales difficult to execute. The combined patterns draw so much selling power that price never pulls back to retest the line.
- Tight congestion forms under the 62% retracement (6) and could indicate an imminent rally back above S/R. But examine the three failed tests before the market closes that day. An observant swing trader with a very strong stomach might consider an overnight hold with correct interpretation of that bearish action.

RealTick® ©1986–2000. All rights reserved. Used with permission of Townsend Analytics, Ltd.

Reward:Risk

Risk decreases sharply as different patterns and time frames all point to the same outcome. This setup combines the 2B top, descending triangle, continuation gap, and Fibonacci into a single profitable channel break trade. These overlapping patterns occur very often in modern markets, but they require a skilled eye to see and an experienced hand to guide through profitable execution.

INTRODUCING THE 7-BELLS

The world of market noise buries many profitable opportunities. Swing traders apply a variety of search tools to uncover these hidden signals and prepare active positions. Self-reliant participants build powerful charting databases to find dependable setups. Many other players rely on someone else's knowledge to find the best patterns. Stock picks work well as long as they first pass internal trading filters that limit execution to specific qualifications. They fail miserably when used as a substitute for personal effort and discipline.

Effective strategy must guide each setup from identification to exit, regardless of origin. Robust scans can sift through all the market garbage in minutes and find excellent plays that wait for execution. But at some point the swing trader must set aside the processor and rely on gray matter to guide critical decision-making. Market survival lies near this center of human and machine interaction.

ORIGINAL SETUPS AND EXECUTION

Mathematics and vision must work together to accurately predict short-term price movement. The 7-Bells capitalize on highly predictable crowd behavior through the application of classic Pattern Cycle techniques. They also define numerical scans for original setup criteria that represent outstanding profit opportunities. Market knowledge misses many lesser-known price patterns. 7-Bells returns these forgotten trades into the arsenal of modern tactics. These highly original setups reveal powerful mechanisms that feed directional price movement. They expose key elements of crowd psychology, multiple time frame events, and complex breakout triggers. And they represent advanced trading strategies to step in front of, stand behind, or fade the emotional crowd.

Consider both probability and time frame before using the 7-Bells candidates. Although these setups uncover outstanding prospects for short-term profit, many fail to trigger promising trades within a specific holding period. Swing traders should review the limitations of each pattern as well as their powerful predictive characteristics before they execute positions. Not surprisingly, this is also true of all successful market strategies. The greatest value of 7-Bells has little to do with the daily output. Stock charts repeat these familiar patterns over and over again in all time frames. Internalize their mechanics and understand their powerful message. Then watch market vision grow and new opportunities come quickly.

Remember that 7-Bells represent setups that may never happen. Lazy participants will lose money if they just take candidates and enter blind positions without completing their own analysis. These patterns display characteristics associated with predictable and profitable outcomes. But a specific stock may never act according to expectations, and only personal skill and excellent timing will book a profit, even if everything lines up perfectly.

Each bell setup focuses on a different aspect of market behavior. Some define breakout conditions while others signal the start of swing movement. Several of the patterns may break either way and require strategies that choose direction based on subsequent price movement. Extend focus and planning beyond the first bar that follows the original bell signal. Price action often lags the pattern by several bars and rewards patience.

Review the patterns and decide which ones fit into the current personal trading plan. Experiment with a few ideas that consistently produce the best results and master them before moving on to others. Participants should not try to execute all of the setups at the same time. Choose only the strongest candidates from each type of opportunity and cross-verify the patterns with other landscape features. Marginal setups will fail unless overall conditions strongly support the play.

Short-term market conditions always favor some setups over others. Dip trips and coiled springs respond well to strong bull markets. 3rd watch candidates may dry up during corrections. Finger finders and power spikes continue to print through all environments. Identify the broad Pattern Cycles before choosing a bell strategy, and align tactics to current sentiment. Then move to other opportunities if an original setup fails to do its job.

7-BELLS CHARACTERISTICS

Dip Trip—Price That Moves against a Strong Trend Will Rebound Sharply

This bell recognizes that buyers wait for pullbacks from strong rallies. It seeks to locate the natural level where a primary trend will reassert itself and force a reversal. Some dip trips head naturally to new highs after they bounce. Others eventually fail and roll over into new declines. The swing trader must execute dip trips defensively and take whatever profit the market offers.

Coiled Spring—Constricted Price Gives Way to Directional Movement

This classic trade recognizes the importance of NR7 narrow range events. It points to potential empty zone interfaces between directionless negative feedback and the eruption of positive feedback momentum. The setup looks for stocks with very high relative strength that favors upward price expansion to new highs. But the best trading results build a bilateral strategy that enters a position in whatever direction that price eventually breaks. Coiled spring expansion often occurs two to three bars after the 7-Bells signal appears.

Finger Finder—Candles Flag Reversals in the Next-Smaller Time Frame

Hammers, dojis, and haramis represent one-bar predictive candlesticks when they print at certain levels. Finger finders locate these important reversals and advise the swing trader to study the chart under the event. This setup provides early warning for several profitable opportunities that capitalize on subsequent price behavior. In favorable conditions, movement in the next-smaller time frame allows specific strategies to beat the crowd in the door.

Hole-in-the-Wall—Gap Downs after Strong Rallies Signal a Trend Change

Classic gap theory rarely discusses countertrend gaps that occur at the end of dynamic uptrends. Tops should take time to dampen buying pressure and roll over. But the hole-in-the-wall points to a single bar that signals a major trend change. The gap may look like a breakaway gap that appears without a major topping formation. The hole prints suddenly and invites swing traders to look for low-risk short sales while the crowd still believes the uptrend is in progress.

Power Spike—High-Volume Events Print the Future Direction of Price

Volume events reveal the will of the crowd. Power spikes uncover several different scenarios where participation peaks and establishes an important market direction. The swing trader must identify which type of spike prints before choosing an appropriate strategy. Some power spikes point to breakouts or breakdowns, while others evolve into pivoting ranges, with price that swings across the level attained during the event.

Bear Hug—Weak Markets Drop Quickly after Rallying into Resistance

The bear hug combines two specific patterns that flag impending low-risk short sales. The first searches the markets for stocks in major bear markets that rally into resistance and reach overbought levels. The second finds declining stocks with low relative strength and other criteria that favor downward price expansion out of an NR7 congestion. Each pattern requires a different strategy to maintain risk management and capitalize on the breakdown.

3rd Watch—Breakouts through Triple Tops Signal Major Uptrends

The markets rarely break out on the first test of a prior high. 3rd Watch recognizes this double top failure and looks for strong stocks that exceed the old highs after another pullback. This classic setup flags major breakouts after well-defined bases as well as cup and handle events. 3rd watch also works through all time frames and identifies intermediate opportunities in smaller congestion patterns or short-term ranges.

TRADING STRATEGIES

The next seven chapters discuss each bell pattern in detail. Most swing traders can access these promising setups through review of their favorite charts. Daily 7-Bells candidates are also available free online at the Hard Right Edge (http://www.hardrightedge.com). This financial portal publishes top scan output daily within 90 minutes of the traditional U.S. market close at 4:00 p.m. ET (U.S.). Technically-oriented traders who wish to recreate these scans for their own personal databases can find this information through Hard Right Edge as well. But keep in mind that simple pattern recognition will find these original opportunities in all markets and time frames.

A detailed narrative follows the description of each pattern. This describes the environment that creates the opportunity, the crowd that drives it, and various methods to capitalize upon its behavior. It provides a background on the chart structure that generates the price movement and presents illustrations of character-istic moves. Also use this narrative to investigate the bell's mechanics in different time frames.

The materials offer tips and suggestions to master specific strategies associated with each original setup. These may include timing, risk management, charting landscape features, and time frame hierarchy. Look here to examine expected Fibonacci retracements and central tendency outcome as well as crowd behavior observations.

The applications sections offer detailed case studies that present trading guide-lines for many bell strategies. They review reward:risk considerations and stop loss for a variety of pattern scenarios. Specific trading rules within each presentation broaden tactical considerations and build effective position management. These seg-ments also provide detailed illustrations to assist with pattern recognition and trade planning.

8

CHAPTER

DIP TRIP

CHARACTERISTICS

Strong rallies generate sudden corrective movement to shake out weak hands. Swing traders can buy these pullbacks within a tick or two of a major reversal under the right conditions. The dip trip setup recognizes that many of these selloffs represent low-risk buying opportunities. But countertrends often last longer than expected, and no one wants to be stabbed by a falling knife. So effective risk management requires careful stock selection, the right decline, and precise timing.

Markets tend to pull back at the same angle that they rise. This tendency supports quick visual analysis for different types of trading candidates. Steep selloffs bounce sharply, but only experienced swing traders can manage their increased risk. Healthy bull flags offer lower volatility and well-defined entry points but require a longer holding period to book profits. The most successful positions execute with very strong stocks that decline on low volume into solid support. These profit vehicles also display one other common trait: the pullbacks don't violate any important S/R levels.

Dip trip prints within a momentum market but invokes classic swing tactics. It offers interesting variations that appeal to speculators in all time frames. Raschke and Connors discuss one related strategy with their Holy Grail setup in *Street Smarts*. The bell also tracks the classic investor behavior of "buying on the dips," although the swing trader must exercise better timing due to the very short holding period.

F I G U R E   8.1

Exodus Communications pulls back to a well-established Fibonacci retracement after each trend wave of this powerful 300% rally. Hammers mark the major reversals as they reach across the barrier but then pull back by the bar's close. Note how each congestion zone tests the retracement low with a second candle that completes a small double bottom pattern.

Daily   (Right) EXDS - EXODUS COMMUNICATIONS   Bar
2000

TRADE MECHANICS

Greed-based bull psychology controls the physics of rally movement. This hidden crowd support reduces the risk that a sharp dip will trigger an important trend change. Carefully evaluate volume on the decline to confirm that no concealed factors drive the selloff. Natural profit-taking should print less participation than the last few rally bars. High-volume pullbacks may bounce sharply but generate instability as the last downdraft draws in new sellers. Stay away from these undependable conditions.

Dip trip favors candidates in earlier trend phases and avoids overbought markets. This reduces risk and promotes a higher reward. But promising setups may still appear after moderate climax events. These selloffs tend to carry further but bounce more strongly than simple pullbacks. However, cautiously avoid major blowoffs where candle reversals suggest that significant supply now overhangs that market. These may appear as high-volume dark cloud cover or shooting star formations.

The setup carries a high %WIN with careful execution in favorable conditions. The disciplined swing trader may profit on 60–75% of all positions. The key to success lies in defensive management and an appropriate exit strategy. Some dips carry to new highs immediately, but others just bounce weakly and roll over to new lows. Pattern analysis often suggests which outcome has the higher probability for the specific setup, but both reversals can still lead to profitable trades. Use a trailing stop loss or an expansion exit to take whatever the market decides to give after the bounce.

Dip wave mechanics often depend on a B wave correction rather than a primary first-wave impulse. This suggests that the bounce will eventually dry up and fail. The most defensive strategy requires that swing traders take their profits as soon as momentum from the bounce starts to fade. More aggressive participants can place a stop under any short-term congestion near this high and hope that the market shoots higher. In either case, don't wait around for a test of the initial entry level. The odds favor price violating support if a subsequent decline reaches that far.

Corrections may retrace 38–50% of a strong rally before a significant bounce. Countertrends often deny a profitable entry when they occur in small increments. Trends pull back through both price and time. When price takes too long to reach a specific target, declining volatility dampens the trade mechanics and bounces lose elasticity. Alternatively, when corrections strike the target within a few bars of the prior high, the subsequent reversal can exhibit great range and profit potential.

Time absorbs price. Always compare the time proportionality of each selloff to the prior rally before taking a position. In other words, the time that a market takes to reach a countertrend bottom affects its ability to generate a profitable bounce within the holding period. Time also absorbs volatility. Low volatility induces flat markets that empty trading accounts as efficiently as losing positions. Count the number of bars within the last rally wave to measure time's impact on the expected bounce. Compare that number to the bar count since the dip began. Corrective moves should complete in less time than the prior trend in all cases.

Active markets shorten the window of opportunity. A setup signal may trigger a strong reversal as early as the next open under the right conditions. Risk increases when the pattern requires buying the target price without confirmation and holding through a possible shakeout. But reward also increases in this volatile environment

F I G U R E   8.2

The dip trip may bounce to a new high or quickly reverse and roll over. Rallies typically correct through simple ABC patterns before they gather enough strength to move higher. Profitable dips signal at the end of A and C waves. The B wave eventually fails but can produce a profit if the swing trader exits at the first sign of danger. The impulse (1) that follows the C wave may eject to a new high after overcoming resistance.

Daily   (Right) AAPL - APPLE COMPUTER INC   Bar

because price can respond with a sharp rally. Decide quickly to enter or stand aside before the opportunity disappears.

Slower markets offer greater entry precision. Build a strategy that relies on a longer holding period to capture larger profits. Sit back and watch the price action very closely in anticipation of a bounce. Once price reaches a buying target, shift attention to the next-lower time frame to confirm a substantial reversal before considering a position. Less active conditions also offer cleaner escape opportunities when trades go sour.

DIP STRATEGIES

Target low-risk entry through Fibonacci and other charting landscape features. Locate natural pattern S/R that converges with key retracement percentages. For example, look for a reversal at a prior high that also marks the 62% correction of the last rally. Always read the unique pattern of the moment. Pullbacks should bounce at 38%, 50%, and 62% but often overshoot the mark before they turn. One classic strategy aligns retracements through several time frames before execution at a classic percentage (see the 38-62 in Applications). This 3D analysis seeks lower-risk entry with fewer whipsaws.

Place a Fib grid across the rally to uncover natural pullback S/R. The second bottom of a double bottom pattern often presents a better starting point than the actual low. Place more grids within smaller time frames to examine detailed price behavior. These lines slowly enclose the ascending major lows and final high. Look for primary retracement levels across different grid lengths to converge. This results from the internal mathematics within trend movement.

A dip trip series can occur in sequence in a strongly trending market. These require remeasurement and fresh analysis after each surge. Every trade must stand on its own merits, and some trend thrusts will offer better reward:risk than others. Favor earlier trends before the market reaches an overbought level, and keep the rule of alternation in mind. Congestion tends to alternate between simple and complex patterns in dynamic trends.

Dip trips print in all time frames and trigger profitable intraday trades. A simple 5-minute bar chart provides an effective framework to locate profitable dips. Broaden intraday setup analysis with original methods. Common retracements of the first-hour range or 2-day range can signal excellent dip trades. Try to align reversals through several time frames, but a single view will suffice if the trade lasts only a few minutes. Remember that profitability increases when positions synchronize with broader retracements and classic indicator settings.

Fibonacci works well on intraday dips, but expect more noise as holding periods shorten. A single tick will throw off key retracement levels on short-term charts. Stick with liquid markets and more powerful trends before looking at intraday Fibonacci. Then accept small violations at all levels and use the tool for secondary reinforcement only after other pattern features point out promising opportunities.

Watch the next morning closely after an active market reveals an encouraging signal. Major bottoms often print within 45 minutes of the open. Follow-through selling tends to climax around this time and lead to a short-term bottom pattern.

F I G U R E   8.3

Sapient bounces off a 38%, 50%, and 62% retracement at the same time. Multiple trend legs coexist through individual rallies. Use Fibonacci grids to isolate each separate wave and then look for converging retracement percentages to predict major reversals that remain hidden from the crowd.

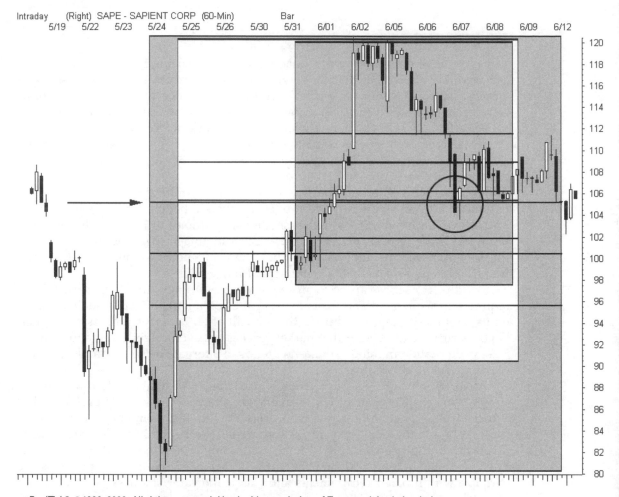

This will flag a low-risk entry if external conditions support the trade. Avoid buying a dip trip during the final hour, especially if the stock sits near its low for the day. Wait until the next morning, even if that means missing the opportunity.

The first test of a continuation gap marks an excellent bounce point. The market retraces from a fifth-wave top all the way back to the middle of the third wave to reach the gap. Continuation gaps rarely fill on the first try, and they raise the odds for a profitable dip trip. Consider execution even when the gap fills as long as volume remains low through the selloff to the other side of the hole. But less

FIGURE   8.4

Ciena follows natural Fibonacci proportion during this five-wave rally on the 60-minute chart. Note the reversals right at the eventual 38% and 62% levels. Dip trips provide excellent intraday opportunities but try to focus on the 60-minute rather than 1-minute or 5-minute chart. Noise increases dramatically in very short time frames, and dip trades at these intervals rely more on skilled tape reading than chart interpretation.

aggressive traders should reduce risk and stand aside until price remounts the gap. Real broken gaps should telegraph their shock through high volume or a bearish Island reversal formation (see Figure 11.8).

Price action uncovers an unusual phenomenon when these gaps remount support. It often reveals a continuation gap in one time frame that overlays an exhaustion gap in the next shorter trend. The swing trader can pick out this odd event with candlesticks and informal wave analysis. Two classic candle patterns that reveal these powerful 3D gaps are dark cloud cover and counterattack sequences.

Buy the first test of a prior consolidation pattern when it lines up with Fibonacci support. Look for reversals to climax at the horizontal top of an ascending triangle or the apex of a symmetrical one. Each congestion zone has unique architecture that supports descending price and encourages an equilibrium point that will reverse the trend. Look at price violations at range extremes to evaluate how deeply bars may penetrate the pattern before they emerge. Pullbacks easily enter thin violation levels but should not pass through more solid support.

Dip trips risk major trend relativity errors. An active bounce within a small trend will disappear quickly as large-scale corrective movement begins. Fortunately, these poor entries often permit several safe exit opportunities. When in doubt, get out first and ask questions later. Risk-averse participants can wait for extreme retracement numbers to print before any dip entry. They will miss many good trades, but those that execute may book dramatic profits. Odds shift dramatically in the swing trader's favor, and few poor entries exist at extended prices.

APPLICATIONS

The best dip trips combine Fibonacci, the charting landscape and common sense to locate natural reversal levels. Always consider lesser-known S/R in preliminary trade analysis. Whole numbers and Elliott Wave make great companions when searching for fresh profit. Remember that the perfect setup rarely prints and many great patterns require execution with limited information.

THE 38-62

Fib grids that overlay two or more adjacent trends often reveal hidden reversals. Look for the 62% retracement of a shorter trend to align with the 38% pullback of a longer one (that includes the shorter leg within its boundaries). Dynamic trends should not retrace more than 62% of their primary rally before they bounce strongly at least once. The convergence between these waves signals a strong multi-time frame event.

Description

- The setup begins with a completed major rally.
- The last rally leg starts from the eventual 62% retracement level.
- Draw 2 Fib grids: the first across the entire rally and the second from the last rally leg inception point to the extreme high.
- Look for multiple types of support at the 38–62% intersection through prior highs, moving averages, and other classic S/R.

- The bounce faces resistance as it approaches the smaller 38% retracement.

This setup occurs in all time frames. The swing trader first sees the natural proportion between two trends and then places Fib grids to confirm how well they align. Scans fail when they try to uncover this exact scenario and yield poor results. Instead, rely on the skilled eye to find it when it occurs. Similar setups work at the 50–62% intersection but do not trigger the same powerful results. Watch for three or more trend lengths to align and produce excellent profit opportunities.

Setup Tactics (FIGURE 8.5)

- A selloff begins at (1) and marks the eventual 50% level for the subsequent rally. The pattern also draws a Big W reversal that completes first rise at the same level.
- A small 2B bottom marks the end of the selloff and natural inception for the new uptrend. The W center prints between (2) and (3) but offers few simple entry points.
- Congestion at the center of the rally builds a small triangle pattern between 38% and 62%. The pattern low (4) starts the final trend wave at the eventual 62% level.
- The double bottom test (7) aligns the new trendline (3).
- The trendline break (6) signals the completed rally and allows Fib grids over the price action.
- The 38-62 lines up at (5). This level also cross-verifies with the whole number 20 and top of the center triangle.

Execution and Position Management (FIGURE 8.6)

- Line from (1) to (2) marks the trendline. The hammer at (1) shows a stop gun low that represents the 38% resistance. Any bounce will need to mount this resistance after a successful reversal.
- Bull flag (4) builds from the descending lows. The lower channel adds another support zone on the drop.
- A small doji at 20 (3) and a tall candle signal the reversal. With 4× cross-verification, aggressive traders can execute a blind entry right at 20. Place a stop loss just under 19¾, below the real bodies on the two-candle reversal.
- The bounce reverses off the 38% resistance (8). Less aggressive traders can execute the small pullback on the black reversal bar (7). Drop down to a lower time frame and use whatever support is available just below 21.
- The flag top and hammer resistance (5) align at 22¾. The high odds play takes an exit close to 23.

Daily   (Right) ANDW - ANDREW CORP   Bar

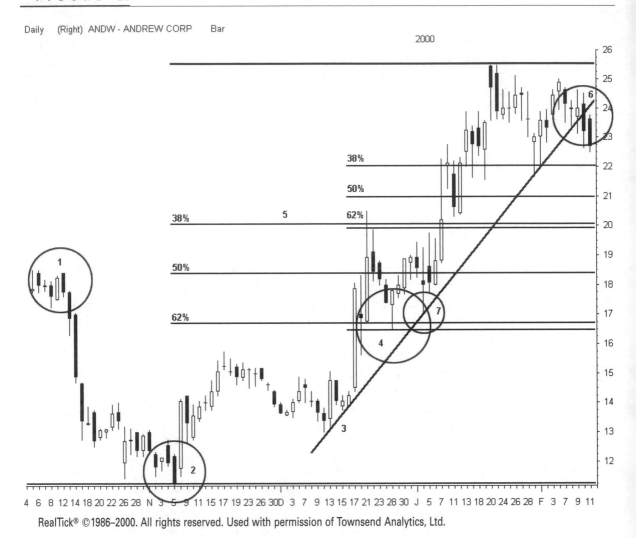

- The trade rewards longer holding periods because the bounce quickly mounts resistance and moves higher (6).

Reward:Risk

The setup could collapse and force the smaller trend into a first failure down to 16½. But the stop should prevent a major loss from this outcome. Consider that an

F I G U R E   8.6

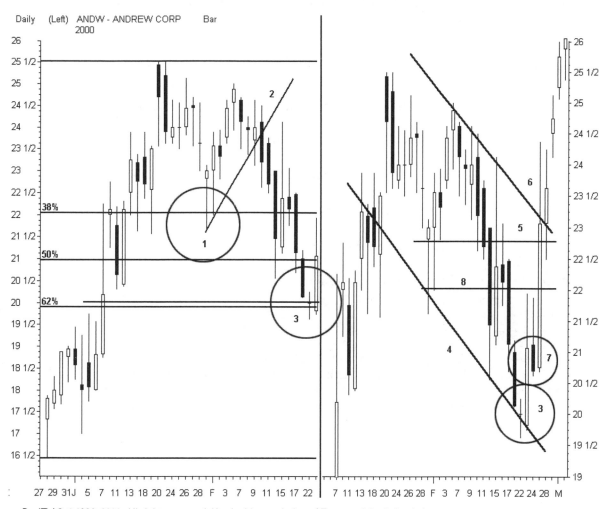

entry at 20 carries a 3:1 reward:risk on an issue with limited volatility. Combine that with 4× cross-verification and the result offers an excellent short-term setup.

CONTINUATION DIP

The first test of a continuation gap marks a high-odds dip trip play. The test comes in many varieties. The trade always appears within the context of a strong rally just like the 38-62. It may follow completion of a third wave but more often appears after the entire rally completes. A continuation gap should not fill and reverse on the first test.

Description

- Visualize the continuation gap by its appearance at the midpoint of a strong trend.
- The setup usually begins with a complete five-wave rally but works with any test of the gap.
- Draw a Fib grid across the rally structure. Start with the double bottom test rather than the first low.
- The gap should appear right at 50% but can also print anywhere within the 38% to 62% boundaries.
- Look for gaps hidden in reversal candles at the middle levels when no obvious gap appears.
- Locate other types of support at the same level as the continuation gap.
- Trade potency increases substantially when the setup occurs on the first pullback after a new high rather than the C wave of an extended ABC correction.

Retracement levels can't be drawn until a rally completes. This requires that a reversal signal tell the swing trader that the change has occurred. Topping patterns, broken trendlines and reversal candles all meet this requirement. Levels can always be redrawn if they don't line up when more information becomes available. Many gap trades work well without Fib cross-verification. When one appears within a limited time window, apply defensive strategy on the pullback and save the calculations for another setup.

Setup Tactics (FIGURE 8.7)

- A selloff begins at (1) and marks the eventual 50% level for the subsequent rally. The pattern also draws a modified Big W reversal that completes first rise at the same level.
- A long hammer (2) marks a 2B bottom that rises into a double bottom test at (3). This second low provides a better terminus for the Fib grid because the retracement often measures a five-wave rally that embeds itself within the third wave of a larger dimension.
- Vertical five-wave rally (5) prints a continuation gap (6) right at the 50% level.

F I G U R E   8.7

Daily   (Right) BBY - BEST BUY CO INC   Bar

- Hole-in-the-wall (7) signals the end of the rally. This allows the Fib (4) grid to be drawn across the five-wave trend.

Execution and Position Management (FIGURE 8.8)

- Level (1) identifies the last intermediate high before the selloff. This cross-verifies with the gap (2) and improves odds for the trade.

F I G U R E   8.8

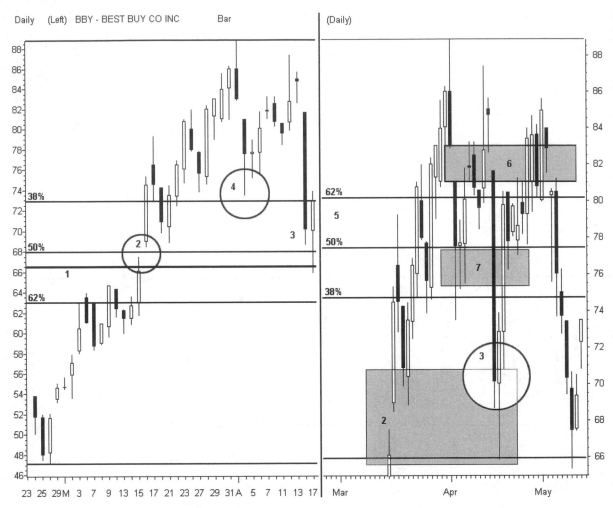

Daily   (Left)   BBY - BEST BUY CO INC   Bar   (Daily)

- A barrier forms when price action violates the double top (4) near the 38% retracement.
- Strong reversal follows the long black expansion candle (3). Note how the gap fills briefly during the intraday price action. Drop down to a smaller time frame if possible to lower execution risk.
- Take first aggressive entry just as the gap fills. Use congestion at 63-64 for stop loss.

- Take second aggressive entry as price recovers above the low of the prior bar. This signals a 2B reversal in the smaller time frame. Place stop loss under this prior low.
- Draw a new Fib grid (5) across the ABC correction. This adds guidance on resistance for the bounce.
- Price pierces double top resistance (4) (7) quickly but stalls at the 62% bounce retracement. Exit trades here due to stronger resistance at (6). Many participants fall into a trap because the tight congestion below 80 marks the first pullback after the dip trip reversal, so they enter new long positions.
- Resistance (6) obstructs a move to new highs. The hole-in-the-wall gap and double top failure gap both reduce odds of further gains.

Reward:Risk

This setup works best with execution within or close to the continuation gap. The vertical rise after the reversal offers few pullbacks until the high 70s. The resistance overhang from the broken double top increases risk substantially through the rise. The setup occurs as a C wave of an A-B-C correction. This improves reward but requires that price first remount the A low before it can go higher.

FIRST PULLBACK

The first countertrend after a breakout to an intermediate high offers a low-risk entry as long as the original move fulfills certain characteristics. Price should thrust away from prior resistance on good participation. The pullback should meet fresh buying at each step down. New gaps or expansion candles should hold together and support price as it falls.

Description

- Locate a 3rd watch, channel break, or other high-tension breakout event.
- Find multiple types of support at the breakout level.
- Watch for reversal bars and place a Fib grid from the last intermediate low to the intermediate high. Major retracement should align with the breakout level.
- The first pullback has greater odds of moving quickly to new highs than any other dip trip setup.
- The pattern offers an excellent intraday trade after a tall expansion bar. Buy the first-hour selloff as long as price opens near the high of the prior candle and does not gap down into the open.

Setup Tactics (FIGURE 8.9)

- Checkpoint Software draws a 2-month rising parallel price channel (1) on the 60-minute chart.
- Whole number resistance sets up at 200 (2).
- Price gaps strongly (3) through the upper channel-whole number interface.
- A hole-in-the-wall prints after a tall expansion bar (4) and signals the end of the rally.

F I G U R E   8.9

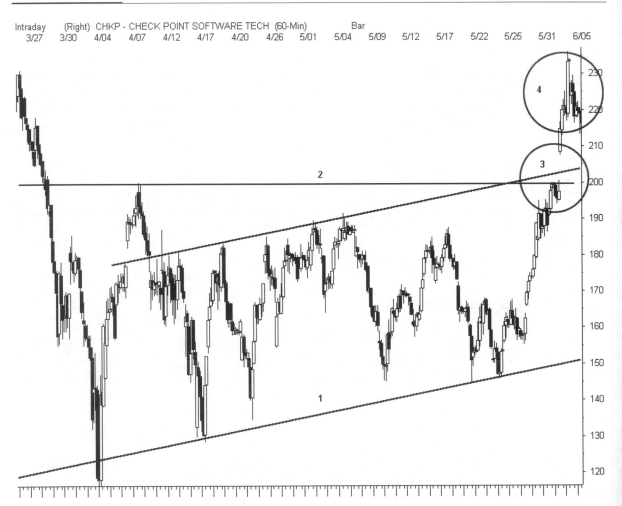

Execution and Position Management (FIGURE 8.10)

- Hole-in-the-wall (3) marks strong resistance for rising price at 230.
- Place a Fib grid over the rally extension. Note that the 38% level lines up with the gap (2), upper channel line (1) and whole number support.
- 4× cross-verification sets up a high-odds entry at 200, but price never reaches it. The upper channel violates but the market reverses at about 201.

F I G U R E   8.10

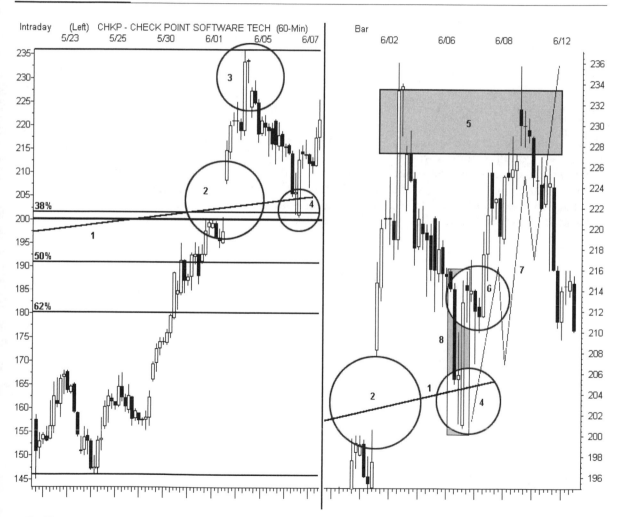

- The two 60-minute candles (4) point to a double bottom test with a small 2B reversal within the 5-minute time frame. Aggressive traders can enter this formation if possible, but stop loss must be well under 200 and perhaps as low as 198.
- The next entry signals as price mounts the channel line and recrosses the gap. This also completes a five-bar first rise pattern (8). This forces execution around 205 with a stop loss under the old low at 201.
- Pullback forms near 210 (6) and permits several good entries. Reward:risk deteriorates, but the tall candle out of the 201 low and first rise (8) offer new support.
- The rally off the bounce forms an embedded five-wave structure (7).
- Tall candles between 201–215 and 211–222 offer profitable exits. They also provide new pullback entry.
- Price prints a gap echo (5) right over the hole-in-the-wall. The breakthrough also extinguishes the rally with an exhaustion gap that quickly fills.

Reward:Risk

Many swing traders have difficulty measuring reward:risk in high-priced issues. Stop loss 5 points or more away from an entry makes perfect sense for a volatile $200+ stock. Control risk by reducing position size to a manageable level. Avoid deep pullbacks that rob profits and consider reentry as long as momentum stays intact. Drop down and study the 60-minute patterns in detail. Major congestion at 212 and 224 both offer low-risk execution on the 5-minute chart.

9

C H A P T E R

COILED SPRING

CHARACTERISTICS

Markets cycle continuously between bursts of intense activity and periods of relative calm. This natural pulse of inhalation and exhalation allows price to step to a new level, thoroughly test its boundaries, and thrust forward (or reverse) after it marks territory. As this cycle evolves toward a fresh impulse, telltale signs appear on the charting landscape. Swing traders read this unique signature and capitalize on the awakening trend while the crowd waits for later signals.

TRADE MECHANICS

Markets change character as participants lose confidence about price direction. Negative feedback awakens and builds the constricted ranges found in many popular chart patterns. Triangles, flags, and wedges all exhibit this directionless swing between known boundaries. The declining volatility also initiates the crowd psychology and price mechanics that trigger the coiled spring signal.

Many predictive ranges never fit into the narrow definition of a classic pattern, so swing traders must look elsewhere to decide if a profit opportunity exists. One of the best methods examines bar congestion rather than the range itself. This empty zone interface should flag new trends and mark low-risk entry. The coiled spring setup seeks this elusive interface through NR7 analysis.

F I G U R E   9.1

Adept Technology prints a series of coiled spring signals over a 5-month period. Narrow-range days trigger setups that offer quiet prediction of impending price movement. Some bars quickly lead to major rallies, while others precede single-day events against the prevailing trend. Always place narrow-range events in context with the ongoing trend-range axis and evolving price pattern before taking a position.

Daily   (Right) ADTK - ADEPT TECHNOLOGY   Bar
        2000

This tiny signal represents the narrowest range bar of the last seven bars. The bar that immediately follows a NR7 often triggers a major price expansion. When price fails to eject immediately, the breakout may still appear one to three bars later. Sometimes the appearance of another NR7 on the next bar (NR7-2) rings a louder bell as odds increase for an immediate breakout event.

New trends begin after congestion absorbs the prior trend's instability. This fresh impulse continues or reverses the last one. A single expansion bar may flag the start of these active conditions. The coiled spring setup attempts to execute a position just as a market begins this active phase. The opportunity depends on the lower volatility and narrow bar range that characterize the end of congestion. But trade success also requires accurate prediction of price direction and very good timing.

Recognize range conditions early and wait for volatility to dissipate. Constricted price bounces back and forth between extremes while gathering force for the next move. Most participants miss the transition to a more active state because the event gathers no crowd until it passes. Volatility, bar width, and volume all decline as a rangebound market nears this cyclical change. Skilled eyes can recognize this empty zone as it approaches, but detailed analysis must filter marginal events to permit a sharp focus on the best candidates.

The most profitable coiled spring signals arise from continuation of the prior trend. The relative power of the last rally predicts the force of the subsequent price thrust. Sharp vertical movement out of congestion signals a powerful new leg. Past rallies assist profit targets and trade planning. Odds for a strong trend improve when the chart shows two prior waves at the same angle but decrease after three or more.

SPRING STRATEGIES

Pure NR7 bars have a reputation for sharp expansion in either direction without much preference. The coiled spring requires high relative strength to filter opportunities toward long side breakouts. Alternatively, the bear hug (see Chapter 13) filters NR7 bars through low relative strength to locate those candidates that should elicit profitable short sales. Keep in mind that pattern failure occurs frequently on strong candidates and represents a good opportunity in the opposite direction. The most effective strategy invokes bilateral tactics that enter setups in whatever direction price moves out of the NR7 range. This takes advantage of whatever the market offers.

Swing trading requires a high degree of directional certainty before execution, so choose only the strongest relative strength stocks as coiled spring candidates. Look for price action near intermediate highs or the top of congestive patterns. Find stocks in bull markets through their 20-bar, 50-bar, and 200-bar moving averages. Examine congestion in detail to confirm that the bulls remain in control. And keep in mind that this pattern rarely registers on technical indicators, so don't rely on them for signals.

Trade preparation requires close visual inspection of the congestion. Look for overall narrowing range over time rather than an isolated NR7 print. Check proportionality of the current range to the preceding trend. As the old wisdom states, the bigger the move, the broader the base. If RSI or Stochastics just begins to roll off the overbought state, the congestion likely has a long way to go before it can absorb the last rally. Remember that the most promising patterns slowly narrow toward a natural apex or ejection point before a major breakout.

Volume must trend downward as congestion progresses. The lower-pane histogram should show declining interest with few jagged upticks. Intervening volume spikes that do not trigger immediate expansion reduce the odds of a clean breakout. General price direction should counter the prevailing trend but not accelerate to the

FIGURE   9.2

Congestion builds visual tension that predicts its ultimate outcome. The most dynamic price action erupts when a range moves sharply against the prevailing trend or flatlines right through the middle of a pattern. Note how Ross Stores alternates rapid price change with countertrend movement that pulls the coiled spring tightly before it releases.

downside. The most powerful trends will erupt after a correction that does not violate any significant S/R. Use Fibonacci and moving averages to cross-verify the terminus of this countertrend extreme.

Patterns within the next-lower time frame reveal effective trade entry points. Congestion between powerful rallies frequently prints an ABC wave against the trend. Cautious participants also review the next time frame above the one that flags the setup. Broad S/R may limit or defeat momentum if the large-scale trend counters the current trade. Alternatively, coordination through several time frames improves odds and suggests a very dynamic result.

Utilize narrow-range bars on intraday charts as conditions permit. Trading volume must show good liquidity within each tick to consider this setup. This rules out all but the highest volume stocks on any given day. Since short-term action requires real-time analysis, watch congestion closely for the coiled spring event rather than run complex scans. Valid setups will appear on both the 5-minute and 60-minute charts, but avoid them on 1-minute views. Insist that their appearance coincide with TICK, index swing, or meaningful price levels. Then shift to a longer view before entry to confirm favorable trading conditions.

False signals increase as holding period decreases. The best short-term coiled spring strategy avoids 5-minute bars completely and trades NR7s off the 60-minute chart or longer. But if other factors converge, NR7s will provide valuable cross-verification for very short-term intraday setups. Trade coiled springs wherever they appear in massive liquidity events. Major Nasdaq 100 stocks occasionally print over 50 million shares per day. Individual issues take on index characteristics in which each tick offers opportunity at this participation level.

MORE ON RANGE BAR ANALYSIS

The futures markets apply range bar analysis to numerous trading strategies. Toby Crabel popularized these short-term tactics in his classic *Day Trading with Short Term Price Patterns and Opening Range Breakouts.* Using extensive research, he investigated how expanding candle and bar patterns predict price change through many commodities and indices. Bar range typically stretches in the direction of a prevailing trend as price breaks out. Through the fuel of the emotional crowd, price surges forward in a series of leaps until climax bars print a high-volume reversal.

Stochastics and other relative strength tools measure bar range indirectly, but simple visual examination of the bars themselves yields an excellent leading indicator. Range analysis cannot accurately examine all markets. For example, low-volume stocks carry high spreads that will distort signals. Limit bar analysis to highly liquid markets with low spreads and high average daily movement. Avoid range signals that appear early in new congestion when volatility remains high and price movement becomes erratic.

Movement out of a NR7 should continue in the direction of the original violation. Place an entry stop just outside both range extremes at the same time and cancel one after the other order executes. This directional tendency permits a tight

exit stop just beyond the opposite range extreme. Place this order at the level of
the cancelled stop. This strategy takes advantage of price bar expansion regardless
of market direction. Risk remains low because the NR7 range allows a very small
loss when the trade fails.

Target a coiled spring exit through examination of expansion-contraction tendencies. When the breakout hits first S/R, odds increase that price movement will

F I G U R E   9.3

Applied Micro Circuits registers seven NR7 bars over a 3-½ month period. Six of these coiled springs lead to profit with a simple
range strategy to guide trade execution. Enter a position in whatever direction price moves out of the narrow bar's range and place
a stop at the other side of the bar. Then use trailing stops to lock in profit. Only the second entry would have triggered a loss
through all of the AMCC action with these classic tactics.

Daily   (Right) AMCC - APPLIED MICRO CIRCUITS   Bar

pause as the next few bars contract. For this reason, wide-range bars themselves signal caution as well as profit. Make sure to identify all obstacles before taking the trade. The initial breakout often needs to mount intervening levels before momentum will escalate. Decide before entry whether or not to hold the position through this testing. The odds favor pullbacks that will draw down profit considerably before breaking into another primary wave. Take a quick exit on the first expansion bar if time does not permit price to pass through these obstacles.

Exit the coiled spring as price expands into S/R. This strategy follows the advice to "enter in mild times but exit in wild times." Keep in mind that expansion out of NR7 congestion may not signal a breakout. If a large barrier blocks the profit door, get out quickly and move on to the next opportunity. The expansion bar may represent a short covering rally or a stop gun exercise that will quickly reverse.

Book consistent profits through direct price thrusts unless multiple cross-verification opens greater rewards. When coiled springs align in several time frames, hold the position through a series of expansion bars and place trailing stops to lock in profits. But remember that markets trend only 15–20% of the time and odds favor the trade that grabs a few quick bars. Use skill and reasoned judgment to recognize when conditions strongly support longer positions.

APPLICATIONS

The coiled spring trade arises through a wide variety of circumstances. It can signal many other types of setups through perfect location and time. The most common patterns appear near the apex of triangles and the tops of declining bull flags. Look for the NR7 bar wherever S/R suggests an impending breakout. These tension zones may materialize at 3rd watch tops, simple trendlines, or even Bollinger Band extremes. Always use the coiled spring for low-risk entry while the crowd waits for perfect hindsight.

TRIANGLE COIL

Triangle breakouts exhibit classic coiled spring behavior. Volatility peaks at the start of the pattern and ebbs just before a major breakout occurs. The upper and lower pattern boundaries define time as well as price. Extend them to see where they meet and what other important S/R they will cross to get there. Keep in mind that the NR7-2 signal in this trade offers one of the best in all of technical analysis.

Description

- High and low boundaries for the congestion pattern should form very early in the range.

- Look for price swings to shorten and volume to drop as the pattern evolves toward the breakout.
- The pattern should not extend beyond a 50% retracement of the prior trend.
- Look for three hits of the top and bottom trendlines before final breakout.
- Breakout should occur about two-thirds of the way from the start of the pattern to the projected apex.
- The NR7 will likely print either at the middle of the triangle or right against one of the trendlines.

Triangles can complete with or without NR7 bars. Well-placed narrow bars allow low-risk entry within the formation just before price ejection. Watch out when the signal appears too early within the developing pattern. Chances are that nothing of interest will occur until later, when most traders turn away to find other opportunities.

Setup Tactics (FIGURE 9.4)

- Long-legged hammer reaches through test of prior low and 50% retracement (1). Price then closes above the 50-day SMA (2).
- Trendlines form from upper and lower boundaries (3) at similar but opposing angles.
- Trendlines create a midline (4) at equal distance between the top and bottom. Price action pivots across this horizontal axis.

Execution and Position Management (FIGURE 9.5)

- Midline (1) shows natural price swing.
- NR7 prints at midline exactly between 20-day SMA and 50-day SMA. Then a second NR7 in a row (NR7-2) appears right next to it.
- Buy immediately or as soon as price rises above the 5-day congestion range (6). Place a stop loss below the first NR7 range near 36.
- Stock breaks on the next bar and closes near the high. An exit at 43 before closing captures a nice profit. But triangle breakouts favor price to exceed the pattern high (5). Consider taking some money off the table and riding the rest.
- Next bar carries price outside Bollinger Band top (7). Consider exit before closing if possible. Profit on the following bar adds 10 points, but the entire bar prints outside the band. A trailing stop strategy for runaway trends would capture part of this movement.

F I G U R E   9.4

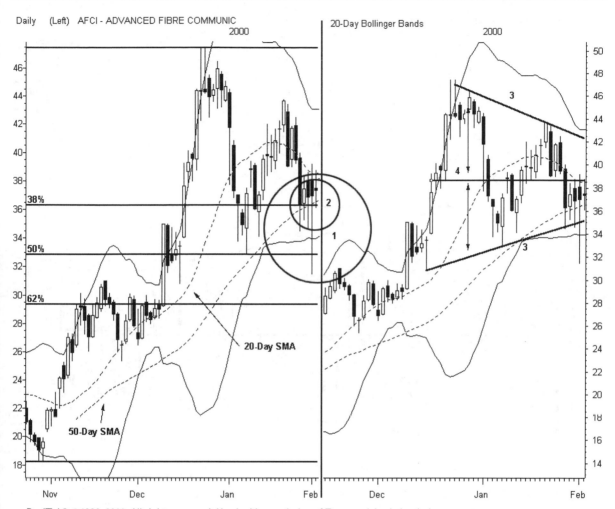

Daily   (Left)   AFCI - ADVANCED FIBRE COMMUNIC

20-Day Bollinger Bands

Reward:Risk

Risk remains low, as with other coiled spring strategies. A 2-point loss compares with a potential 20-point gain. Clearly marked resistance at 44 and 48 offer easy targets and planning. Failure at the descending trendline within the pattern might still yield a 2-point profit for an early position. Risk rises after the breakout because runaway gaps hide simple entry points. Once again, trading ahead of the crowd shows many advantages.

F I G U R E   9.5

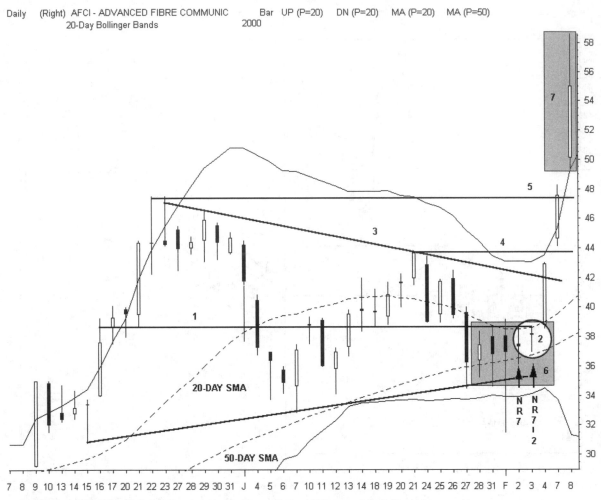

Daily   (Right) AFCI - ADVANCED FIBRE COMMUNIC   Bar   UP (P=20)   DN (P=20)   MA (P=20)   MA (P=50)
                 20-Day Bollinger Bands   2000

FAILURE COIL I

The coiled spring often signals pattern failure just before it occurs. These entries
tend to produce dramatic results because the breakout fools the crowd that waits
for the alternate outcome. Watch market action closely as price approaches a failure
point. It may print the NR7 one to two bars ahead of the actual breakout event.

Description

- The setup often appears while the opposite strategy draws the trader's
  attention.

- Locate the trendline or price level on the alternate setup that signals a pattern failure on violation.
- Any pattern failure that prints a NR7 before it breaks constitutes a failure coil.
- Any coiled spring that moves in the unexpected direction also constitutes a failure coil.
- The most common failures appear in simple triangles, flags, and trendline breaks.

The failure coil setup works powerfully because it occurs when the crowd least expects it. Remember that failure trades go vertical because they trap so many speculators who have little choice but to incur large losses to escape their pain.

Setup Tactics (FIGURE 9.6)

- Gemstar draws an apparent head and shoulders pattern that begins with a first failure (1) retracement.
- The decline ends at a horizontal neckline (2) and prints a small double bottom (4).
- The neckline captures the crowd's attention. The herd follows the next rally and looks for the formation of a right shoulder. The right shoulder (3) appears on schedule and price starts to drop.
- Price returns twice to test the 50-day SMA successfully (4), (5). Note within (5) how the 20-day SMA drops to the 50-day SMA and bounces off in support.
- A rising trendline (8) forms from the moving average tests.
- Another reversal at (6) reinforces a descending trendline. The pattern now looks like a symmetrical triangle as well as head and shoulders.
- The Stochastics oscillator (9) starts to flatline and move toward 50.

Execution and Position Management (FIGURE 9.7)

- Rising trendline (1) supports price through nine bars as a small rally pushes toward the triangle apex.
- A NR7 coiled spring (2) signals at the triangle's dead center.
- Price bar (5) strikes the falling trendline (3) on the next bar while the top Bollinger Band (4) rises to support price.
- Enter on (5) with a stop loss below the rising trendline. This also marks a violation of the bottom of the NR7 range.
- Price ejects strongly in a pattern failure that makes further entry difficult. First resistance at (6) marks a good profit for those in a position from the mid 70s. But both pattern failure and triangle breakouts favor price to

F I G U R E   9.6

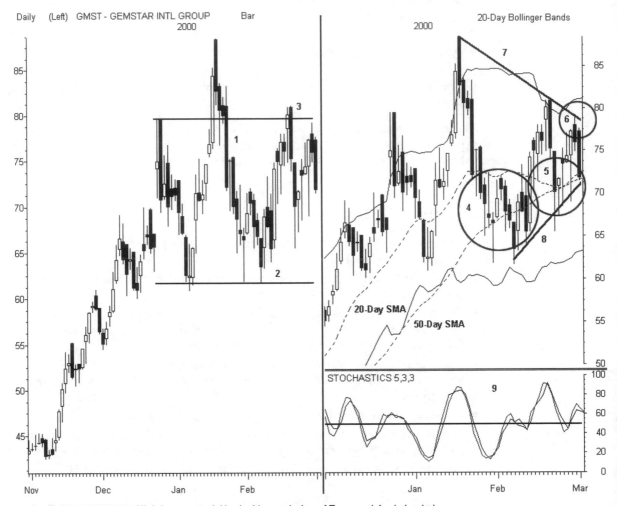

exceed the pattern high (7). Consider taking some money off the table and riding the rest.

- The rally shoots out the top Bollinger Band (8) and demands a quick exit. Those who stick around with a trailing stop strike gold because price rises another 15 points before it finally reverses.

Reward:Risk

This setup displays an excellent reward:risk profile if the trade executes on the bar after the coiled spring signal. The minimum target would yield an approximate

FIGURE   9.7

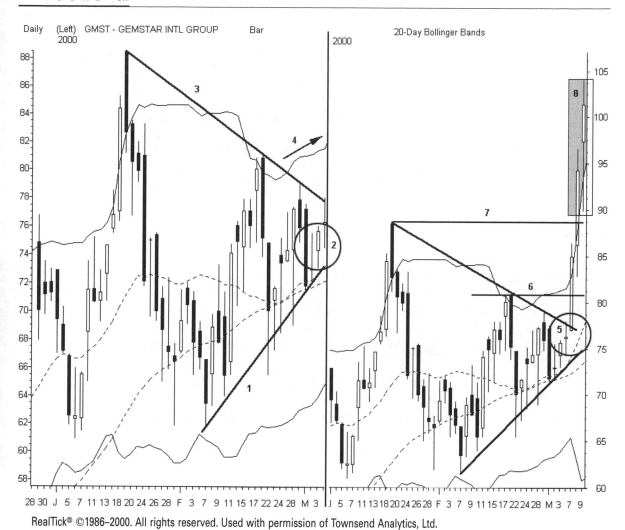

Daily   (Left)   GMST - GEMSTAR INTL GROUP   Bar   20-Day Bollinger Bands
2000   2000

2:1 reward:risk, while a managed 3-day holding period would book an amazing
9:1. Realistically, few swing traders would maintain their positions through the
series of expansion bars and price resistance. And entry after the breakout faces
increased risk because the pattern exhibits few pullbacks.

FAILURE COIL II

This setup reminds swing traders that long-term success relies on probability and
risk management, not pattern reading. The most perfect coiled spring setup can go
sour at any time or any place. When all else fails, follow the written trading plan

or face the fires of hell. Fortunately, even the hottest inferno can turn a nice profit from time to time.

Description

- See Failure Coil I.

Failure coils arise from complex patterns or standard coiled spring setups. When they suddenly appear in an unexpected location, swing traders reverse gears quickly to capitalize on the trapped crowd. But effective strategy recalls that classic NR7 signals have an equal chance of going in either direction. This requires that trading plans include a bilateral response to most standard coiled spring signals.

Setup Tactics (FIGURE 9.8)

- Sandisk prints a standard dip trip or coiled spring setup. A sharp rally reverses and pulls back in a classic ABC correction (2). A Fib grid (1) drawn over the price action reveals a very bullish scenario.
- The C wave ends in a sharp double-bottom pattern (3) right at the 62% retracement.
- The two bottoms trigger wide swing pivots (7) across the whole number 100.
- The retracement turns into a large bull flag (4) with the double bottom right at the far extreme of the pattern.
- Price action draws a rising trendline (6) out of the bottom and pushes toward the upper flag channel.
- A tiny NR7 appears (5) right at the interface between the declining channel and rising trendline.
- Price sits below both the 20-day SMA and 50-day SMA.

Execution and Position Management (FIGURE 9.9)

- Place a sell short stop under the low of the narrow bar and a buy stop above it (2). This captures bar expansion, regardless of which way it goes.
- Manage the sell stop with a limit order that avoids entry if few upticks appear near the breakdown.
- Once filled, lift the other order and replace it with a stop loss at the same price.
- The next bar opens within the range of the NR7 but below the trendline. This offers a little whipsaw room in case of a false breakdown.
- Price quickly violates the NR7 to the downside and triggers the sell stop as long as it can fill near the broken range.

F I G U R E   9.8

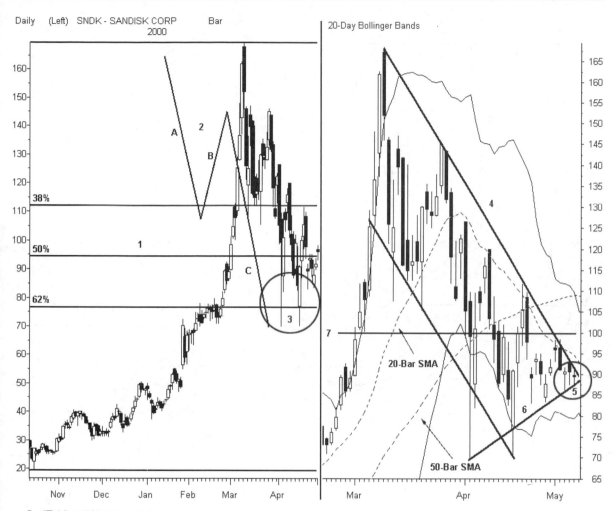

- The next price bar approaches the double bottom and 62% retracement
  (3). It then pushes through the bottom Bollinger Band.
- Both support levels tell the swing trader to exit with a 10–15-point profit,
  but there is a problem. The scenario sets up an inverse 3rd watch. As
  with uptrends, downtrends favor that price break through the second test
  of a significant S/R level. This presents a tough choice after building a
  nice profit. The best strategy takes some money off the table and leaves
  the rest.
- The next bar gaps through the low (4), expands out of the Bollinger Band,
  and leads to a pullback short sale opportunity.

FIGURE 9.9

Daily   (Right) SNDK - SANDISK CORP   Bar UP (P=20)   DN (P=20)   MA (P=20)   MA (P=50)   20-Day Bollinger Bands

- The small doji (5) signals another entry as price drops below 60.

Reward:Risk

A long position carries the greatest risk for the setup. The classic retracement and flag pattern suggest an upside breakout and rally back to the old high. But the moving averages and failure of price to mount 100 both telegraph the ensuing selloff better than the pattern. The NR7 bar right at the interface between the two trendlines offers an excellent low-risk opportunity. Price movement out of that small range in either direction triggers a breakout.

10 CHAPTER

FINGER FINDER

CHARACTERISTICS

Swing traders throughout the world apply Japanese candlestick charting techniques. This venerable practice presents a method to look at individual price action and a means to uncover short-term market signals. Most equity software now offers the option of displaying charts with this powerful application. In fact, many seasoned participants have abandoned Western bars entirely and trade only with candles.

Their change in tactics comes at an opportune time. Modern market noise cripples the ability of classic bars to locate reliable signals as violations rip through important charting landscape features. Candles reduce this whipsaw with their unique shadow and real body structure. Where the bar enthusiast sees broken support and moves on to the next setup, the candle trader may find that same level still intact. This additional layer of information protects pocketbooks and opens opportunities that others will miss.

The finger finder studies single-bar candlestick patterns to identify markets that print important directional signals. This outstanding tool flags hidden price action that takes place in the time frame beneath the bar that triggers the setup. Look for fingers to reach across well-marked S/R, clear out the stops, and then jump back across violation points. These underlying mechanics set the stage for price swings in the opposite direction.

F I G U R E   10.1

Hammer and doji candlesticks repeatedly signal short-term reversals on the Crown Castle charting landscape. The finger finder opens a window to hidden price action within a single bar. Consider both the length of the candle and its location when predicting how this setup will impact the next price swing.

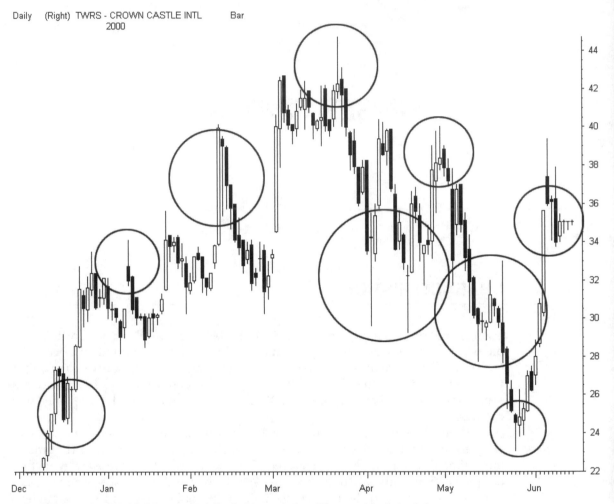

Daily   (Right) TWRS - CROWN CASTLE INTL   Bar
                 2000

Candles generate complex visual data from short-term price movement. They define natural extremes and open a window to the next-lower time frame without the need for a separate chart. Shadow zones may mark hidden pullbacks and reversals within this shorter view. They can also signal broad changes in direction when they print at major price intersections.

Trade Mechanics

Single-bar hammers and dojis provide the most powerful immediate feedback of all candlestick patterns. Western technical analysis rarely offers such dependable short-term signals. These formations print when a significant battle between bulls and bears ends in a draw. Two specific requirements generate their predictive power. First, the high-low range must be greater than average. Second, the closing tick must equal or stand close to the opening tick.

The candlestick's real body must print near one extreme of that bar's range to complete the hammer or doji pattern. The longer the high-low range compared to the recent average, the more powerful the signal. Reversal candidates should also oppose the direction of the last few price bars. For example, the real body on a hammer after a downtrend that lasts several sessions should print at the top end of the range. This suggests that opposition has mounted against that trend in the lower time frame.

These powerful candles also predict strong continuation movement when they appear in the right place. Ongoing trends often gap forward and print a finger with the real body pointed in the primary direction. This fish hammer swims strongly and predicts the ramping move will continue. Also watch for a new trend to generate an apparent reversal finger early in price development. This actually signals increased momentum in the shadow's direction and should get taken out immediately.

The spinning top has little predictive power and confuses trade planning. This conflicting pattern occurs when the real body prints a standoff between participants near the middle of a high-low range. But the spinning top can signal the much more useful harami under certain circumstances. The entire real body must fit within the open-close range of the prior bar to generate this useful pattern. And the prior candle must exceed the high or low range of the bar that precedes it.

Finger finder sets open-to-close height at one-third or less of the total high–low range. This captures both doji and hammer events. It also outputs both spinning tops and haramis. Subsequent filters attempt to remove spinning tops from consideration and highlight the other three formations. But finger finder candidates rely on visual analysis more than any other bell. The skilled eye does a better job picking out promising candle opportunities than any mathematics.

Dojis represent perfect opening-closing balance because price finishes exactly where it started. Hammers demand less perfection. They must close so that the central body of the candlestick is less than one-third the length of the bar's total range. Swing traders will often find a dramatic V-bottom or top when reviewing the chart beneath the action of the candle. This embedded price action provides the basis for many of the trading strategies associated with the two patterns.

The harami draws the candle equivalent of the Western inside day. Different rules extend the reach of this powerful pattern beyond its classic applications. The candle's high-low range can violate the prior bar's range as long as the real body remains within it. The Harami signals a likely reversal when it prints within a tall

F I G U R E   10.2

Long candle shadows can yield big price gains. Rallies often print a false reversal candle early in a new trend. Price quickly exceeds the shadow high and thrusts forward in a sharp expansion move. Short covering fuels this dependable phenomenon as amateur candlestick technicians misinterpret their pattern signals.

Daily   (Right) RATL - RATIONAL SOFTWARE   Bar

expansion bar after a strong rally or selloff. Close examination will reveal that the opening tick actually prints a gap in the next-lower time frame. This often signals a hole-in-the-wall in the opposite direction that should hold through a first test (see Figure 5.19).

These gaps should present a significant boundary to short-term price gains. Watch the action after the signal to pick the appropriate strategy to execute. For example, aggressive traders can sell short when price violates the real body low. Defensive traders can wait until a violation of the shadow low of the pattern bar. Consider a long-side execution if price rises above the signal bar shadow and continues the prior trend. This represents a pattern failure because the bearish candle should start a reversal. Use range breakouts of the tall bar that precedes the harami for long entry as well. Set harami stop loss according to the chosen entry point, regardless of direction. In other words, exit the position when price reenters the real body's range if the setup uses a real body breakout to trigger execution.

FINGER STRATEGIES

Finger finder often predicts a reversal within the signal time frame as well as the trend below the candle. The long shadow foretells larger-scale price direction when other conditions support the event. The significance of these one-bar patterns relates directly to their location within the overall charting landscape. Fingers represent major swing levels when they appear on high volume or near significant S/R. But they lose significance when buried within congestion or the impact of larger candles.

Candle patterns work well at the intraday level when sufficient liquidity makes bar range meaningful. As with the coiled spring, limit these techniques to stocks that trade high volume within each bar. Then apply all three primary candlestick signals with confidence. But take time to cross-verify their relationship to major S/R swing levels. Also estimate average bar range for that chart on that day. Then look for dojis or hammers that print well above average and haramis that print well below average.

Professionals trigger finger signals when they clean out stops at the edge of congestion. This activity occurs for two reasons. A slow market may bore participants and the quick price expansion captures their attention. Or the professionals may want to relieve demand on one side of the market so that trend can break out in the other direction. For example, a pool of sell stops below congestion may be hard to resist just before a stock prepares for a new rally.

These congestion dojis and hammers give away insider secrets. Price should not jump back into congestion if buying or selling pressure is great enough to initiate a true breakout. The activity impacts market chemistry because it relieves stress in one direction by filling the standing orders. Determine the point in range development that these candles print. Finger reversals represent significant price discovery in the restless period at the start of new congestion, but those that appear after volatility dissipates signal a market ready to cycle into positive feedback.

Odds favor a strong move against the direction of a significant stop gun event. Estimate the strength of this spring action by the length and volume of the candle. Small violations with little participation will quickly evolve into more rangebound action. But long-legged dojis that print on high volume may signal an immediate vertical break in the opposite direction. These can end the congestion phase with no empty zone or other quiet interface.

The harami cross combines the inside day pattern with doji power. This special formation prints when the harami real body has identical opening and closing prices. When one appears inside the range of a prior tall bar, it can represent a significant turning point for that market. Look for a long-legged doji shadow to increase the odds of a strong reversal. Drill down to a lower time frame and study the charting landscape below this pattern. It often reveals an embedded 2B reversal. Price pushes into a new low or high but springs back through S/R by that bar's close. This predictive formation works best as a reversal, but consider pattern failure setups as well.

Ignore candle signals in all thin or flat markets. Filter volume closely when building watch lists to keep these stocks out of consideration. Single bars become meaningless in these environments because wide spreads, noise, and manipulation draw many false patterns. Expand to a weekly or longer chart view, but only for general investment decisions. Move on to other timing tools if considering this type of stock as a short-term trading vehicle.

OTHER CONSIDERATIONS

Aggressive traders can sell short at doji tops and go long at doji bottoms in recognition of this candlestick's hidden power. Place a stop loss just outside the bar's range because any violation negates the reversal signal. More profitable setups often appear a few bars later. Most new reversals face at least one test before they yield to substantial price change. After a finger event, look for a double top or bottom to form in the next-lower time frame. This will complete the reversal pattern and point to a low-risk execution level.

Pullback tests to finger highs or lows often take place within three to five bars. Expect price to expand sharply when the finger breaks, especially if overbought-oversold indicators show no divergence. Specifically look for the new trend to surge as it passes the extreme of the wave generated by the initial candle reversal. Shift down one time frame when the finger holds and trade the setup according to classic double-bottom or top strategy.

Examine any gap created by the bar after a candle event. If price action printed a gap just before the candle, this gap echo completes an island reversal in the lower time frame and an abandoned baby pattern on the signal chart. In either case, those gaps should offer solid support or resistance on the pullback. Therefore they represent a potential low-risk entry level.

Combine candlestick analysis with technical indicators to reduce whipsaws and improve profitability. Use short-term Stochastics to verify that a stock sits at an extreme overbought-oversold level when an apparent reversal prints. Look for the MACD Histogram to change direction at the same time. Find support through MA ribbons that confirm the changing patterns. But above all else, combine candles with Bollinger Bands to confirm or refute trading signals.

F I G U R E   10.3

Finger finders trigger powerful signals when combined with Bollinger Bands. Long candle shadows throughout this 60-minute Mercury chart point to pullbacks and reversals when they push outside of the band extremes. Notice how the 4/24 action reveals the start of a major rally through two long shadows at the lower band's edge within a well-defined island reversal pattern.

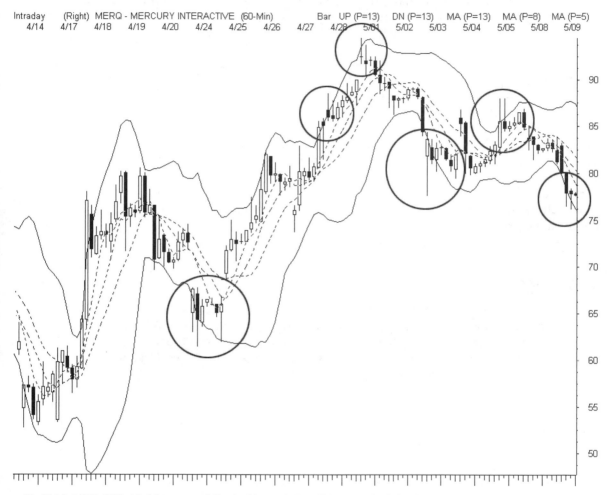

Major finger reversals should strike through Bollinger Band extremes or the center band itself. Price action at the outer bands often rings a louder signal than the center plot. Shadows should pierce the band sharply while the real body stays within the boundary. Look for the band to remain perpendicular to the candle after the immediate crossover. This reveals strong resistance to further movement in that direction. Sometimes candles will align on band edges through several time frames. This predicts an immediate and significant reversal opportunity.

Watch the first wave out of a candle bottom or top. Its extension reveals which trend the finger event is trying to reverse. The move after a doji or hammer often completes a first rise/first failure pattern within the smaller time frame. If it succeeds, it greatly reduces the odds that a return test will fail. Also examine the angle of the initial thrust. The stock may print a V-bottom or top and offer no pullback opportunity before the new wave continues.

APPLICATIONS

Trade the finger finder with one eye on the time frame below the chart of interest. Judge the extent of the reversal through other charting landscape features and use the signal wisely. Finger events often play out within two to three bars. Consider whether a test of the finger extreme is likely from its location and the price action on the subsequent bar. Always keep Bollinger Bands in view when examining finger finder setups. Action at the extremes offers more opportunity than swings through less dynamic price zones.

HIDDEN 100

Finger finder signals may uncover impending first rise/first failure events in the time frame below the chart. These allow low-risk entry after price violates the 62% retracement on its thrust towards 100%. The reward for this last 38% must be high enough to justify a position. The setup also generates profits when other dynamics allow entry before price passes the 62% retracement.

Description

- Signal candle range will be well above normal for that market.
- Signal candle shadow will reach through Bollinger Band extremes and reverse.
- The length of the shadow will not exceed 62% of the price swing that terminates at the candle extreme.
- Look for vertical V-bottom or V-top price movement with few retracements in the smaller time frame chart.

The setup works because of V-bottom and V-top trend dynamics. Pass on the trade if the retracement already exceeds 62% in the smaller time frame. This dissipates the potential reward because the signal comes on closing price and entry must wait for an open market. Manage the setup defensively—many reversals will fail right at 62% rather than complete the FR/FF pattern.

Setup Tactics (FIGURE 10.4)

- Newport prints a bearish head and shoulders pattern.
- Price breaks the neckline (1) and the selloff carries into a test of the psychotic trendline (2), where it bounces strongly.
- The rally (3) ejects in vertical movement and returns to a test of the head and shoulders neckline (1) from below.

Execution and Position Management (FIGURE 10.5)

- A tight symmetrical triangle (2) starts to form as the market closes on the signal day.
- The triangle sits right below the neckline (5) and the 62% retracement.
- The prior short-term lows print horizontal resistance (1) at whole number 40.
- Aggressive traders can enter the triangle breakout as it pierces the neckline. The small move sets up a pattern failure event for those still short the head and shoulders formation and generates substantial buying power. Place a tight stop loss just under the apex of the triangle at 35.
- Price bases for 4 hours above 62% (3) but below horizontal resistance (1). Top Bollinger Band opens to higher prices.
- Enter long on the morning gap above 40 with a stop several ticks below (1). Exit at market as close to the 100% retracement (6) as possible.
- Market shows a complete V-bottom pattern (4).

Reward:Risk

The setup goes against classic head and shoulders rules, which view the first pull-back to the neckline as a low risk short-sale opportunity. The triangle tells the swing trader to make other plans and watch for pattern failure. The four bars above the 62% retracement strongly suggest that a further decline is unlikely and the next morning's gap presents low-risk long entry.

2B FINGER

Finger finder shadows may point to small 2B bottoms or tops that mark important reversals through several time frames. View this pattern in different chart lengths to focus setup timing. The smaller price action often points to a major profit opportunity one or two bars ahead of the crowd.

F I G U R E   10.4

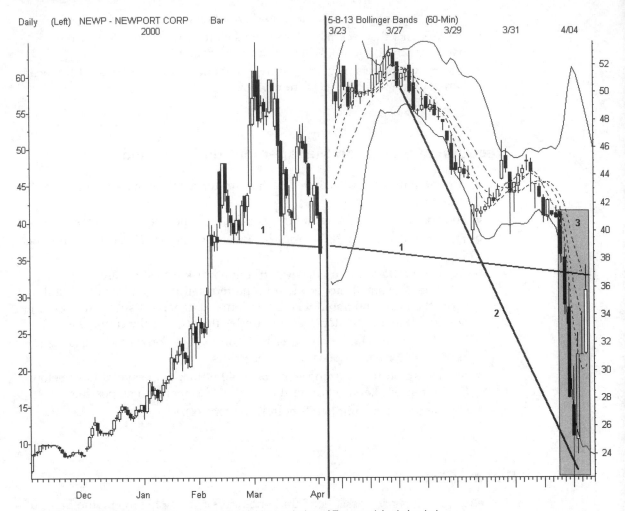

Description

- Signal candle range will be well above normal for that market.
- Signal candle shadow will reach through Bollinger Band extremes and reverse.
- Shadow reaches past an intermediate high or low but the candle real body closes within S/R.
- Chart pattern within the same time frame as the signal shows a potential reversal within the next two to four bars.

FIGURE   10.5

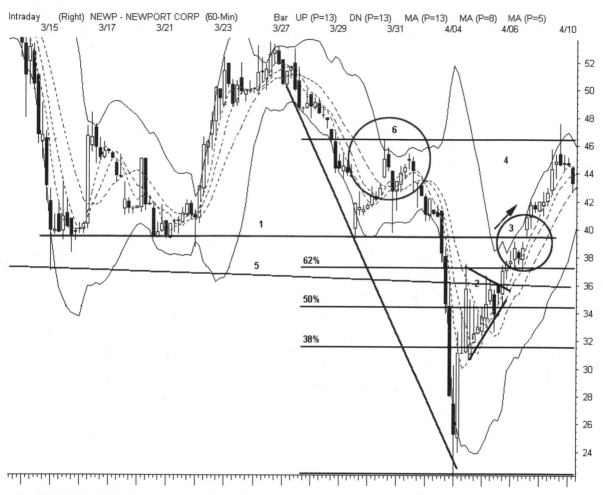

This setup illustrates the importance of location and timing in the interpretation of finger finder signals. While the candle focuses on events in the next-lower time frame, the proximity to larger breakout and reversal levels aligns the setup into a 3D event that carries greater profit potential.

Setup Tactics (FIGURE 10.6)

- Antec completes a first failure pattern (1) on the signal bar.
- A declining trendline (2) marks progress on the 6-week selloff.

F I G U R E   10.6

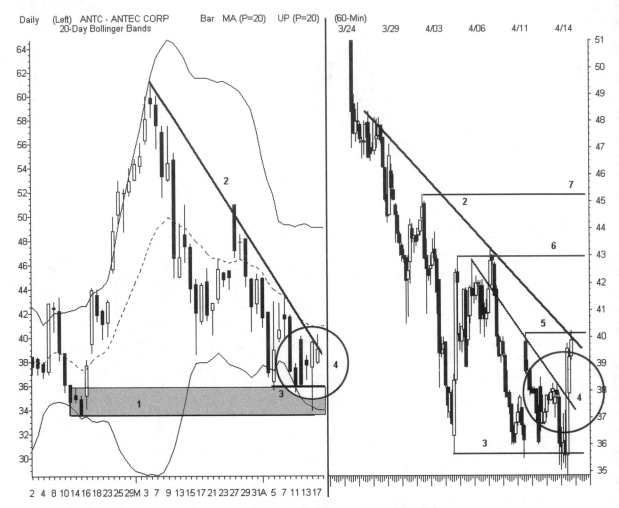

RealTick® ©1986–2000. All rights reserved. Used with permission of Townsend Analytics, Ltd.

- The finger pierces an 8-day triple bottom (3) but closes well above the violated low in a 2B reversal that also signals a pattern failure on a small descending triangle (4).
- The signal bar rises to the declining trendline that now converges with the last high (5) and whole number 40.
- Highs at (6) and (7) mark resistance and price targets if price breaks out of the downtrend.

Execution and Position Management (FIGURE 10.7)

- Place a Fib grid over the correction to track the new uptrend.
- First bar after the finger signal sits below the trendline and offers little evidence of the imminent breakout.
- The next bar breaks the down trendline (3) and price carries to the center Bollinger Band, where it forms a small harami (1) on the daily chart.

F I G U R E   10.7

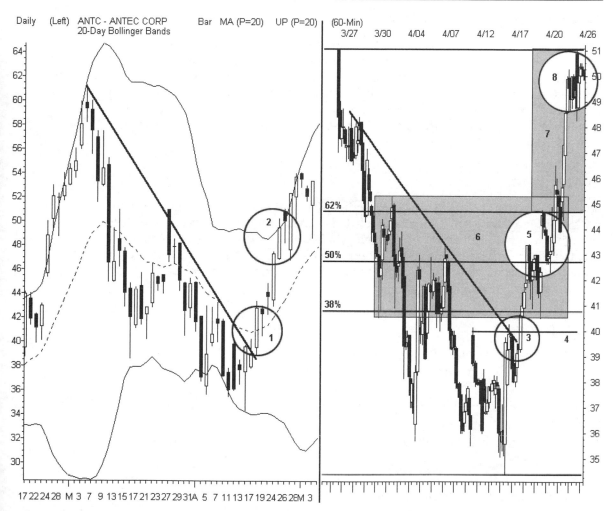

RealTick® ©1986–2000. All rights reserved. Used with permission of Townsend Analytics, Ltd.

- Initial breakout entry requires fast reflexes as the market carries much higher in the next few hours. The best opportunity comes at the top of the small 3rd watch pattern (4) that forms whole number resistance at 40.
- The harami triggers a buy signal when the next bar gaps up (5). The gap prints right at 50% and raises the possibility that it represents a continuation gap which will carry the market through a first rise retracement.
- Trend mirrors (6) generate strong whipsaws between the 38% and 62% barriers that make low-risk entry difficult to locate.
- Price reaches 100% retracement at the Bollinger Band top (2) (8).

Reward:Risk

The market offers no narrow-bar entry prior to the trendline break. This forces momentum tactics that buy morning strength or stand aside to wait for a good pullback. The 3rd watch may present a small window of opportunity on the 5-minute or 60-minute chart. Many whipsaws shake out weak hands between 41 and 46. Overall the setup favors position traders that hold about 1 week and protect profits with a loose trailing stop. But shorter-term traders never face a loss greater than 2-½ points.

DEATH STAR

Bollinger Bands and the shooting star candle often combine forces to signal a major reversal after a strong rally. Together they flag an overbought market and high odds short sale that requires a very strong stomach. Death stars uncover volatile markets that trap the momentum crowd and offer no escape. Keep in mind that this setup should trigger a quick selloff. Get out without hesitation when price just sits there or starts to whipsaw.

Description

- Vertical expansion bars precede the finger signal.
- Price pierces the upper Bollinger Band on two or more candles before the signal.
- The signal prints a long-legged shooting star with a tall upper shadow and small real body close to the candle's low.
- The signal prints a candle close to 100% outside the upper band.
- The bar after the signal goes no higher than one-half the range of the shooting star.
- The bar after the signal closes within the upper Bollinger Band limits.

Always review new death stars through examination of the lower time frame to identify natural short sale entry levels. Look for a double top test before price

F I G U R E   10.8

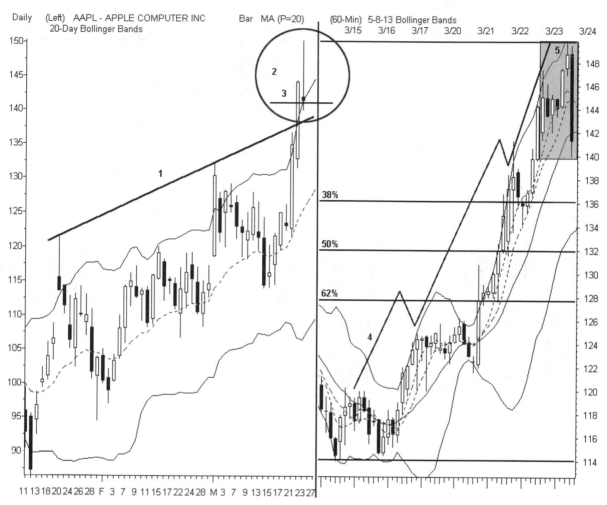

RealTick® ©1986–2000. All rights reserved. Used with permission of Townsend Analytics, Ltd.

moves substantially lower. Profitable execution can be quite difficult because this pattern occurs in very volatile market conditions. Maintain a tight stop loss and consider a longer or shorter holding period to escape the whipsaws.

Setup Tactics (FIGURE 10.8)

- Apple Computer starts a 3-day vertical rally in the low 120s.
- Price carries to the top of a rising trendline (1) and breaks out strongly for two bars.

F I G U R E   10.9

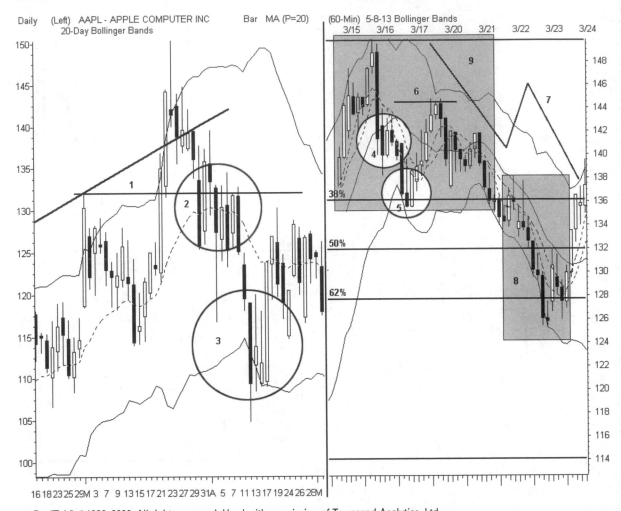

- The last two bars before the finger signal expand out of the upper Bollinger Band.
- The signal bar (2) opens outside the band (3) and closes right at its edge with the candle range almost 100% outside the band.
- The rally forms a complete five-wave structure (4).
- The intraday price action (5) shows a small triangle breakout and major selloff during the last hour.

Execution and Position Management (FIGURE 10.9)

- The reversal breaks through the center Bollinger Band (4) on the 60-minute chart before the daily close. This sets up an aggressive short scalp as it carries below 138.
- Better opportunity comes after the bounce at 38% (5). A weak rally rises to the 62% retracement of the initial selloff (6). Note how the top Bollinger Band narrows toward the high at 145.
- Cross-verification signals an excellent short sale entry. Place a stop loss just above the apex of the small triangle that prints before the 150 top. This also marks the upper Bollinger Band level.
- A bounce starts at 138 after a morning down gap but can't reach the original entry. Use a gap exit strategy to depart on the open or before the gap fills. Longer holds can consider an exit near the double bottom test under 136.
- An Adam and Eve reversal (9) breaks at 136. Short entry here faces several whipsaws but pays off with an 11-point decline (8).
- Price reverses off the 62% retracement and bounces strongly.
- Review of the 60-minute price action reveals a possible ABC correction (7).
- The daily chart focuses attention on horizontal S/R at 132 (1). Congestion forms under this line (2) at the center Bollinger Band but shakes out short-term traders with violent whipsaws for 8 days.
- The congestion finally breaks and the selloff pierces the bottom Bollinger Band (3) after a 20-point drop and reverses.

Reward:Risk

This volatile setup presents greater risk for 1–3-day swing strategies than intraday or position trades. Major whipsaws tend to shift through different time frames as a trend progresses. Swing traders may need to respond quickly and shift holding period if their strategy becomes the current shakeout target. This requires advanced trading skills and a well-developed sense of market timing.

11
C H A P T E R

HOLE-IN-THE-WALL

CHARACTERISTICS

Active trends rarely flip over quickly. Crowds feed dying rallies and selloffs long after the real move ends. As volatility slowly winds down, cash finally dries up and a new primary impulse erupts in the opposite direction. So it goes with most market cycles. But under rare circumstances, shock events can sharply quicken this evolutionary process so that a new trend begins in a single bar.

TRADE MECHANICS

The greedy crowd drives rallies higher and higher. But when the herd runs for the hills, markets will fall from their own weight. The hole-in-the-wall setup recognizes this dynamic process in action. After reaching a new intermediate high in an uptrend, the stock gaps sharply out of a rally as external force shocks the bull psyche and damages it. Volume on the decline exceeds the last rally impulse and flags a sudden new downtrend.

The hole-in-the-wall ends the preceding trend and may trigger profitable trading conditions. Measure opportunity through the width of the gap, the participation intensity, and the relative strength just before the event. Study the intense conflict from one side of the trend to the other. This reveals whether that market might rally back into gap resistance or just roll over and head lower. This bell offers several

F I G U R E   11.1

A hole-in-the-wall gap ends Breakaway's 50-point rally. These sudden breaks allow swing traders to quickly shift strategy and prepare for a downtrend well ahead of the crowd. Note how the hole violates a major trendline and 20-day EMA support as it sets up a classic head and shoulders reversal pattern.

Daily   (Right) BWAY - BREAKAWAY SOLUTIONS

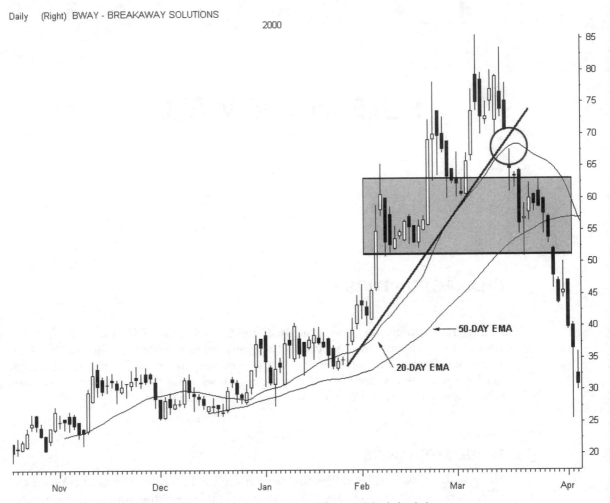

natural short sale entry points. It also presents long-side swings for more aggressive traders.

Not all holes ignite significant downtrends. The subsequent action may signal the start of a dynamic trend in the opposite direction. Or it may represent an intermediate move that flags sideways conditions until price fills the gap and carries higher. These different outcomes reflect the intensity of the shock and subsequent price tests. Even in minor events, the first pullback into the gap should not fill. This offers a consistent short sale opportunity regardless of the eventual trend. Every hole has different strength characteristics. Take the time to measure the potential outcomes before committing long-term positions.

Mindless hole selling may end on the first bar in an exhaustion move or continue for some time. The short-term direction after the gap determines the nature of the opportunity. The best hole setup generally occurs on a pullback to test the break, but a tight sell stop placed just above the open may produce fast and substantial profits. In either case, swing traders must understand the mechanics at work to pick the best spots for execution. Most strategies should stand aside as the gap occurs and follow price bars to the first bottom. Then draw a Fibonacci grid from this low to the last high and see how the gap fits in the retracement scheme.

Edwards and Magee indirectly point out the hole-in-the-wall in *Technical Analysis of Stock Trends*. They highlight the important second gap that completes an island reversal pattern in their discussion on trend theory. This presents one variation of the hole. Although they refer to this violation as a countertrend breakaway gap, it doesn't meet the rules they list for that event. In fact, the hole doesn't match characteristics for any of the three classic trend gaps.

Edwards and Magee categorize gaps by their physical momentum properties and forecasting value. Breakaway, continuation, and exhaustion gaps define clear focal points for price action that appear over and over again through dynamic trends. But beyond these few formations, the authors dismiss other gap phenomena as having little value. This is simply not true. While these classic definitions were once adequate, the swing trader now requires fresh gap tactics.

Hole-in-the-wall adds a new gap into the trader's toolbox. The pattern looks like an exhaustion gap that sits on the wrong side of a high. This raises the possibility that the event may actually print a breakaway gap in the opposite direction. But those shocks generally require a basing period before the big break, so the hole fits into its own niche within pattern analysis. But rather than being a new phenomenon, this classic gap has been hiding in stock charts for years.

Hole-in-the-wall triggers intense conflict as sudden price action counters the prevailing crowd sentiment. This shock event then spirals trend according to well-defined herd mechanics until volatility eventually dissipates the movement. Through the early stages, hole strategy enters short positions after bear rallies carry price into strong resistance. Tony Plummer documents how these sudden conflicts induce predictable Fibonacci-based crowd movement in his complex book *The Psychology of Technical Analysis*.

This price shock occurs in all time frames. Swing traders can apply its tactics to both intraday and longer-term positions. In fact, the hole has better applications for intraday trading than any other bell. Because most gaps occur as the new market session opens, signals appear immediately on multiday 5-minute and 60-minute charts. The intraday trader can quickly apply hole tactics to take advantage of the active first hour. These same formations may or may not print on the daily chart because some gaps fill before the closing bell. But fast confirmation within the shorter time frame allows many active strategies regardless of the closing price.

F I G U R E   11.2

Breakaway prints a June hole on the 60-minute chart. Intraday strategies short first-hour gaps to take advantage of new breakdowns before position traders see the closing bar. Apply momentum tactics that follow the intraday decline with a tight trailing stop. Then draw a Fib grid and sell the first test into the hole when resistance cross-verifies at a major retracement level.

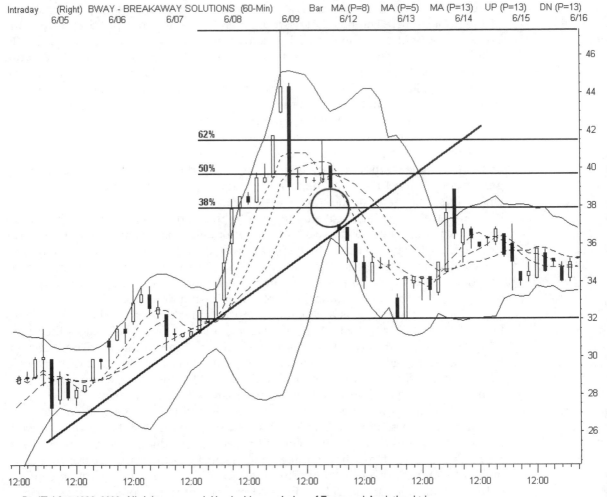

HOLE STRATEGIES

Intraday traders can lay a Fib grid across the last intermediate uptrend and locate the retracement level of the morning hole. This will determine the prospects for a successful short sale on a pullback test. Extend the grid over longer trends and see whether price action corresponds with those levels. Very wide gaps can suggest trading strategies through three or more different trend lengths. Identify converging retracements and match these to obvious pattern S/R on the intraday charts.

A morning down gap can lead to lower prices immediately. These short sales may be difficult to execute during the volatile market open. But intraday traders have an excellent time tool if price rises into a hole pullback test. Market wisdom suggests that gaps will not fill during the session if they remain open after the first hour. So if price takes too long to bounce and return into the intraday hole, subsequent short sales should have very high odds for success.

The best hole setups in all time frames come after waiting for the first short-term bottom. Intense volume on the down gap often dissipates selling pressure immediately. Short sales on the signal bar face high risk unless tightly managed. A damaged stock can bounce quickly after this shock event because it carries a strong supply of hopeful buyers from the previous uptrend. When this occurs, the next short sale opportunity may come quickly, so stay prepared. Look for a penetration into the gap on weak volume that hits natural Fibonacci retracements and other broken pattern support.

Holes that immediately carry lower suggest very weak demand. Execute a trend-following strategy with a tight stop loss. Place the stop over the top of the high for the shock bar and drop it down immediately when the position moves into a profit. Stay defensive and take what the market offers, as a short covering rally can ignite at any time. Note the level where the decline finally ends. It often marks a clear first failure event with major support on the other side of the trend mirror. If so, look for a subsequent bounce to the 62% level where the gap sits. This sets up an excellent reversal pattern. In the meantime, the retracement may offer a long-side scalp if Stochastics flips over from an oversold level.

Gap echos can fill holes immediately. These gaps in the other direction occur infrequently but can induce large losses. Measure demand through volume analysis to confirm that the initial break did substantial damage. Then watch the pullback for declining interest into the rise. On daily setups, try to enter the short sale early in the day to avoid overnight turnarounds. Major gaps rarely occur midday, so this allows the position to move into a profit before the close. Keep in mind that gap echos will trigger price change similar to the original event, so avoid getting caught in the trap.

Each holding period will demand different exit rules, but execution will be similar regardless of the time frame strategy. The lowest-risk entry takes place during the rally back into the hole. The simplest exit follows the subsequent downdraft. Defensive measures must be exercised with this formation because the stock still carries high relative strength and finds many willing buyers. Use cross-verification techniques to locate multiple confirmations for timing and measure reward:risk carefully.

The best initial break violates both the 20-bar and 50-bar EMAs, but good holes still appear above these levels. Markets that hold above their intermediate moving averages retain more relative strength than those that violate them. Watch how price interacts with the 50-bar average after a hole to measure the technical damage. Use more defensive exit strategies until this average violates.

Longer trends and their pullbacks take precedence over shorter ones. Look for a bounce at 38% of the longest trend applicable to the gap. This may be below the first failure level of several smaller uptrend legs. Try to locate this key level in

F I G U R E   11.3

Gap echos trap short sellers and rob profits. But they rarely occur after a hole breaks through solid support on high volume. Consider where the price bar drops after a hole event. If it sits on a trendline or important average, stand aside and allow the market to work out the conflicting conditions. Note how the Keynote hole drops price into a trendline rather than breaking through it. After a bar or two the stock jumps back through the gap and continues the rally.

Daily   (Right) KEYN - KEYNOTE SYSTEMS INC   Bar

advance by taking a step back and looking at the chart from a distance. The skilled eye may see proportionality in this longer view that uncovers many natural reversal levels.

APPLICATIONS

Study each signal to see if it generates crowd conflict. First determine whether or not the hole breaks obvious support. That violation marks a natural short sale level on a subsequent bounce. When a gap drops into the top of support, it often triggers a sideways condition rather than an immediate selloff. The bar that follows the signal provides input on the market's strength or weakness. For example, narrow price action near the bottom of the prior bar's range should lead to a rapid decline. And always look closely at volume on the breakdown. Some holes flag tired markets, while others point to major trend changes.

1-2 DECLINE

Rally support often presents two well-marked lines of defense. A reversal into a new downtrend requires that both levels break before downside momentum can accelerate. Pullbacks may pierce the first level but print a solid bottom at the second. Or both can violate in a single shock event. This hole setup breaks first support on the signal bar. Traders then short the subsequent test and decline through second support.

Description

- Hole-in-the-wall breaks support but a second major level remains intact.
- Price tests and fails the broken first support.
- The selloff carries price into a test of the second support.
- Price breaks the second support.

This hole prints in a lower time frame than the second violation. The gap signals that the larger breakdown may soon take place. Price action mimics a typical ABC pullback but violates natural Fibonacci support. It offers yet another strategy for low-risk entry ahead of the crowd.

Setup Tactics (FIGURE 11.4)

- Flextronics rally draws a rising 2-month parallel price channel (1).
- Breakout pierces upper channel as price expands out of the top Bollinger Band into a death star (2) reversal.
- The selloff breaks through support at 72 in a hole-in-the-wall (3) that fills a prior gap at 71 (6).
- Expanding bars fill a second gap at 68 (4) before finding support at the channel bottom (5).

F I G U R E   11.4

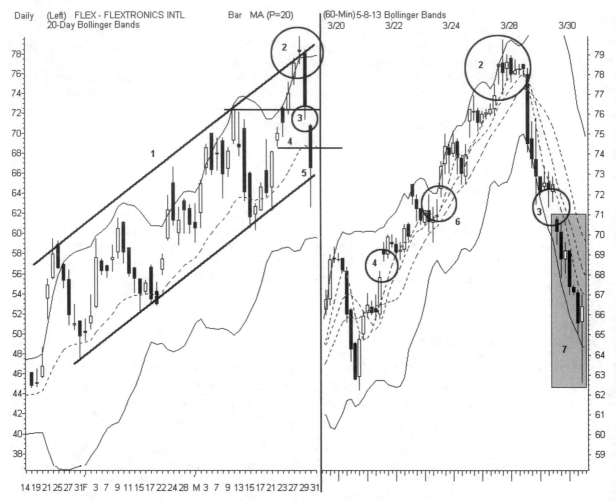

RealTick® ©1986–2000. All rights reserved. Used with permission of Townsend Analytics, Ltd.

- A long shadow (7) violates the bottom Bollinger Band, completes a first failure pattern, and reverses the market.

Execution and Position Management (FIGURE 11.5)

- Place a Fib grid over the prior rally.
- The grid reveals a hidden continuation gap (1) at 71 that sits right at the 50% retracement.

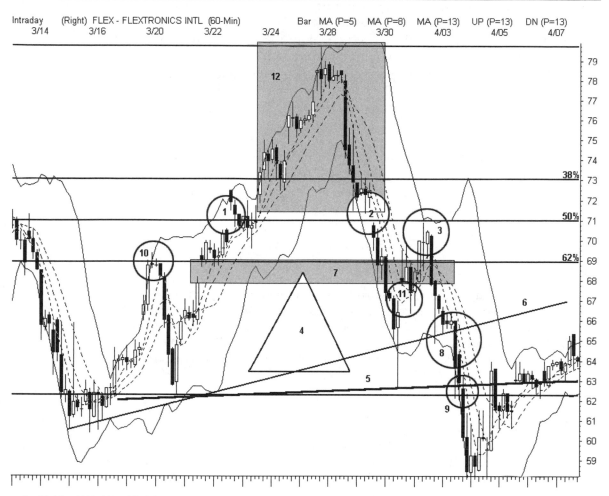

- Hole-in-the-wall (2) breaks through the same price in a gap echo that completes an island reversal (12).
- First failure (4) generates two trendlines (5) (6) that suggest a possible head and shoulders reversal.
- Small breakout gap (11) ends the short-term downtrend but long entry represents a high-risk countertrend play within the larger price action.
- Short entry at the same level anticipates a right shoulder to match the height of the left shoulder (10) but the first gap (7) and 62% resistance generate whipsaws.

- The test of the hole (3) marks a good short sale opportunity as a small doji prints at the top Bollinger Band right at the 50% retracement and bottom of the gap. Place stop loss at the top of the hole around 72.
- Two gaps (7) (11) limit the reward target for the decline. Consider a defensive exit under 69 or a tight trailing stop loss.
- The last gap (11) fills and price congests (8) on the bottom of the major parallel price channel (6). The NR7 bar just before the drop invites a new short sale. Place stop loss in the middle of the filled gap (11) at 67-½ or 68.
- The neckline (5) limits the reward target. Consider a defensive exit near 63 or a tight trailing stop loss to capitalize on the channel break.
- The neckline breaks at (9) but the action shows few upticks. Stand aside and let the crowd play the head and shoulders or place a very defensive short sale near the break and get out on any whipsaw.

Reward:Risk

The charting landscape pinpoints low-risk entry and natural danger zones throughout the setup. One major whipsaw level increases risk, while several good short sales produce measured rewards between support levels. Risk rarely exceeds 2 points on opportunities with 3-point reward potential. This mediocre ratio contrasts with good cross-verification for the major channel break on the daily chart.

SUPPORT HOLE

Note the similarities between this setup and the prior one. Both print rising channels before the hole-in-the-wall. But this pattern breaks the channel on the signal rather than dropping price into support. This invokes a more bearish scenario and faster decline.

Description

- A market rallies strongly on increasing momentum.
- The rally reverses sharply and a hole-in-the-wall breaks major support.

This setup occurs frequently with rising channels because support prints very high in the rally's development. Look for a break of a major moving average on the signal. The 20-day or 50-day MA on a daily chart marks a violation level that cross-verifies a channel break or similar pattern outcome.

Setup Tactics (FIGURE 11.6)

- Genome Therapeutics draws a 1-month rising parallel price channel (1).
- Price expands out of the upper channel but reverses in a tall dark cloud cover (7) pattern.
- The selloff bounces off the bottom channel and forms horizontal support (4).

F I G U R E   11.6

- The support and channel break (2) in a hole-in-the-wall.
- Price pulls back to test the gap during intraday trading (5).
- Price again gaps down on the bar after the hole (3).
- Price pulls back to test the second gap during intraday trading (6).

Execution and Position Management (FIGURE 11.7)

- The first two pullbacks (4) (5) occur before or on the signal bar (1) so they don't offer entry unless the swing trader had the stock under observation in the first place.
- The second gap (2) offers a midday short sale opportunity as it pulls back to test resistance (6). Place stop loss 1–2 ticks within the real body of the prior candle.
- Price drops 5 points and whipsaws in a short squeeze back to 45. Defensive management would exit the position with a profit before it returns to the original entry level.
- Another short sale appears as price takes out the 2-day low (9). A defensive position requires entry near the violation with a stop loss just above the prior low.
- The daily chart signals caution (3) when the price bar strikes the bottom Bollinger Band and 50-day EMA.
- The next range slows the action until the bottom Bollinger Band turns down.
- Price returns to test resistance (7), finally breaks to a lower level (8), and allows a last short sale entry.

Reward:Risk

Simple pullback and breakdown strategies work well throughout this setup. Only one whipsaw endangers profits, while risk remains very low with clearly defined stop loss. Reward could average between 5 and 8 points with a 1–2-point risk. The setup also illustrates the advantage of early warning systems that flag the hole event before the signal bar closes. At the least, regular Genome traders could see the developing pattern before the rest of the crowd.

ISLAND REVERSAL

Every island reversal off an intermediate high prints a hole-in-the-wall variation on the down gap. Trading considerations for this classic pattern must include the crowd's inevitable participation. This invites more uncertainty than other hole set-ups. But the double gaps still strongly resist bounces and invite low-risk short sales.

F I G U R E   11.7

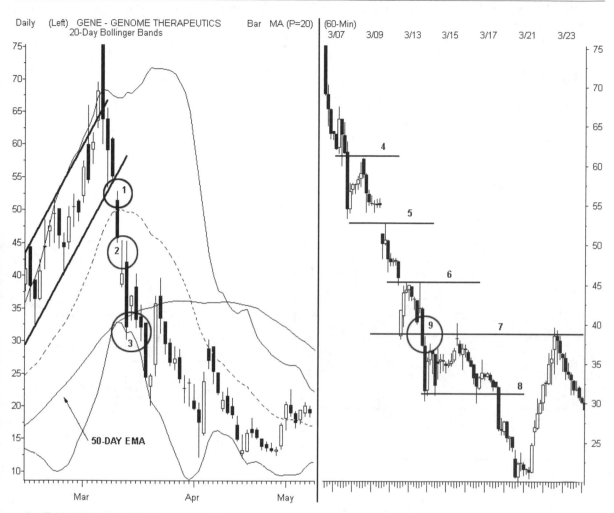

RealTick® ©1986–2000. All rights reserved. Used with permission of Townsend Analytics, Ltd.

Description

- A vertical rally gaps up in a final exhaustion event.
- Price prints a series of topping bars and gaps down in a hole-in-the-wall.
- The hole occurs at the same level as the prior exhaustion gap.

The topping pattern can break at any time. Fully developed congestion may use 30 bars or more. Single-bar events print the very bearish abandoned baby pattern. The longer that congestion takes to roll over, the weaker that market becomes.

This offers both advantages and disadvantages. The hole relies on high relative strength to force a sharp pullback into the gap. But weak markets drop faster with fewer whipsaws.

Setup Tactics (FIGURE 11.8)

- Itxc Corp prints an exhaustion gap (2) that signals the end of its 90-point rally.
- A nine-bar topping pattern (1) draws a 2B reversal.

F I G U R E   11.8

F I G U R E   11.9

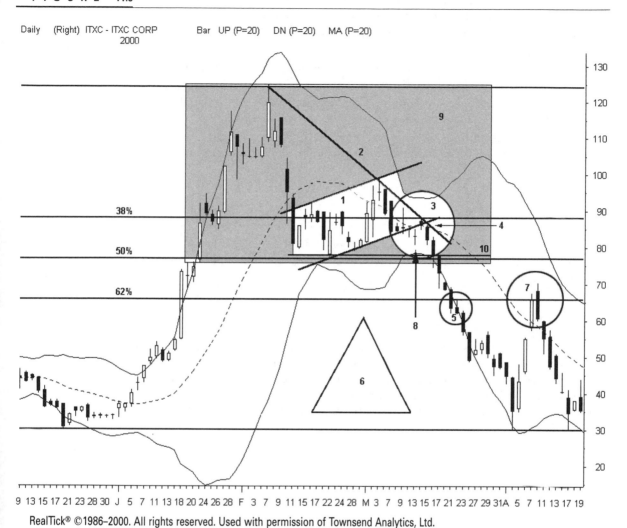

Daily   (Right) ITXC - ITXC CORP   Bar UP (P=20)   DN (P=20)   MA (P=20)
2000

- The stock gaps down in a hole-in-the-wall (3) that completes an island reversal pattern.
- The selloff finds support at the 50% retracement (5).
- Price action pulls back into resistance below the gap (4) and reverses in a doji top.

Execution and Position Management (FIGURE 11.9)

- The weak bounce forms a bear flag (1).
- The declining highs draw a potential descending trendline (2).

- Bollinger Bands tighten as a narrow candle prints right at the intersection between the trendline and bear flag bottom channel (3).
- Short entry here carries increased risk with the false breakdown just one bar ago (8).
- The next bar expands downward and confirms the trendline. Price also fails the center Bollinger Band (4).
- Risk remains high at this point. The best short sale strategy enters when (8) violates. Use a stop loss several ticks above the (8) low.
- Price pushes into an inverse 3rd watch (10). Although entry on the prior bar places the trade in a 3–5-point profit, odds still favor a breakdown through the lows.
- An Adam and Eve top (9) completes and price breaks lower.
- The selloff gathers momentum. The next support stands at the 62% retracement. Price action breaks it and pulls back to test it from below (5).
- The decline carries into a large first failure (6).
- Dark cloud cover at the 62% retracement (7) offers a final short sale opportunity.

Reward:Risk

The setup manages risk with a tight stop loss over the potential short sales. Small classic patterns and candlesticks provide early warning of impending price movement. Very small landscape features offer good advice on entry and exit. Pullbacks proceed on schedule and with few surprises. Longer-term position traders benefit from this profit pattern more than short-term players.

12 CHAPTER

POWER SPIKE

CHARACTERISTICS

Each market establishes average participation that fluctuates through shifts in out-standing float, volatility, and external events. Price development speeds up sharply when intense volume suddenly shocks this median flow of buying and selling be-havior. This emotional interaction can trigger at new price levels or as trend ap-proaches past battle zones. Regardless of location, the final impact may affect the charting landscape for months to come.

TRADE MECHANICS

Power spikes signal when volume jumps above natural levels for that market. These trend hot spots identify emotional crowd events that may induce excellent short-term opportunities. A candidate may signal an immediate trade or future oppor-tunity or just emit frustrating noise. Study the price action that prints with the volume event to filter out low-yield patterns. First determine whether the chart shows a possible reversal, breakout, breakdown, or swing pivot. Eliminate all stocks that don't represent one of these outcomes. The power spike uses only these chart-ing landscape features. Also rule out mergers and acquisitions. These events will print dramatic price change and volume, but their future may depend on funda-mentals such as arbitrage or predetermined value.

F I G U R E   12.1

A two-bar power spike signals the end of a long Jmar Technologies rally. Climax volume uses up available buying power and short circuits further price gains. Power spikes induce a variety of price mechanics that support or terminate ongoing trends. To predict the impact and persistence of this emotional event, look to its placement within the pattern.

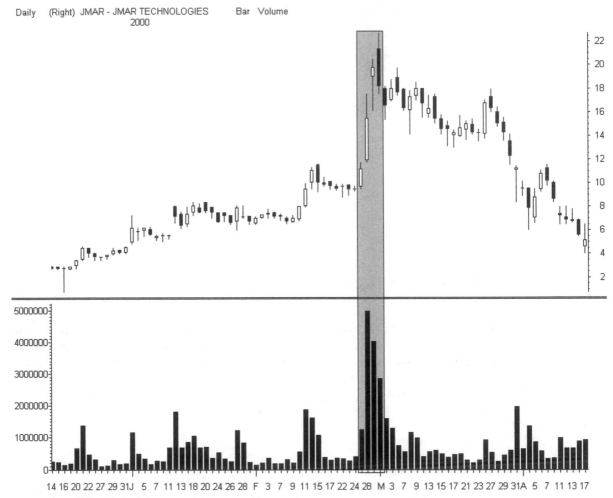

Daily   (Right)   JMAR - JMAR TECHNOLOGIES   Bar   Volume
2000

Breakouts from bases into new uptrends or downtrends provide an immediate short-term opportunity. Breakouts to new highs or lows require patience until a pullback offers safe entry. Reversals can trigger either outcome. Swing pivots print psychotic trendlines and S/R in which price cycles repeatedly across the spike boundary for many bars after the event. Trading strategies with these odd setups can become quite complex.

Heavy volume allows markets to move past established barriers. Swing traders examine this telltale emission to find evidence of the crowd's next intentions. False breakouts become more difficult to engineer when high volume appears right at new highs or lows. But keep in mind that a price surge may already be over by the time the spike signal arises. Exercise discipline and wait for a pullback to enter many of these candidates.

Power spikes near old highs and lows signal long-term market direction. These past battlegrounds mark the profit or loss in many portfolios. Urgent shareholders start to unload positions as the market returns to these critical levels. New players see opportunity at the same time and take the other side of the trade. Conflict builds until bar expansion confirms price direction. When this battle prints on high volume, it captures great attention and ensures further momentum on subsequent bars.

Short-term price action generates many questionable volume signals, so always stay defensive. Routine buying and selling frequently mask the true nature of insider interest. The best path stands aside and avoids signals from most natural volume fluctuations. But at certain times crowd participation rings a very loud bell and demands an immediate response. Swing traders find these opportunities by looking for volume events that print well outside the normal routine.

Use the power spike signal only on daily charts. Time bias within the intraday markets distorts short-term volume output and triggers false signals. First- and last-hour volume can comprise 60% or more of the total intraday action. This induces setups to trigger on the opening ticks rather than natural crowd emotion. Intraday volume also displays a high noise-to-signal ratio for all but the most liquid stocks. And block trades that scroll well after actual execution greatly distort 5-minute and 60-minute chart data.

But volume histograms may still provide valuable intraday signals under certain circumstances. Noise decreases as liquidity increases. The massive crowds that trade highly liquid stocks create virtual index markets. These issues display such high participation within each tick that volume analysis can yield fluid data measurement and accurate price forecasting. But limit their use to trending histograms rather than single spikes. This avoids late block reports and other false signals.

Study short-term participation at intermediate tops or bottoms on a liquid intraday chart. Volume will rise into the event and peak as a reversal or breakout occurs. Combine this analysis with candlesticks and look for hammers or dojis. They will often generate important signals to within a single tick of price expansion. Also pay close attention to potential intraday 2B reversals. Stops trigger sharp histogram spikes when a prior high or low breaks. Then watch for price to jump back across the broken boundary and signal a fade entry.

Use peak relativity to determine short-term crowd interest. The first hour sets a natural participation level. Compare the subsequent action against this burst of activity and other small spikes throughout the day. This establishes volume levels to check for convergence or divergence during short-term price breakouts. Also draw a trend line across the tops of the peaks to identify when volume may lead price to new highs or lows.

F I G U R E   12.2

Volume surges during the first and last hours of each market session. It also reaches a nadir shortly after lunch, as this Microsoft chart illustrates. Important signals hide within the tall volume walls that mark high participation. Look for relative spikes that stand out against other histograms in that time zone. These point to intermediate price swings and important intraday reversals.

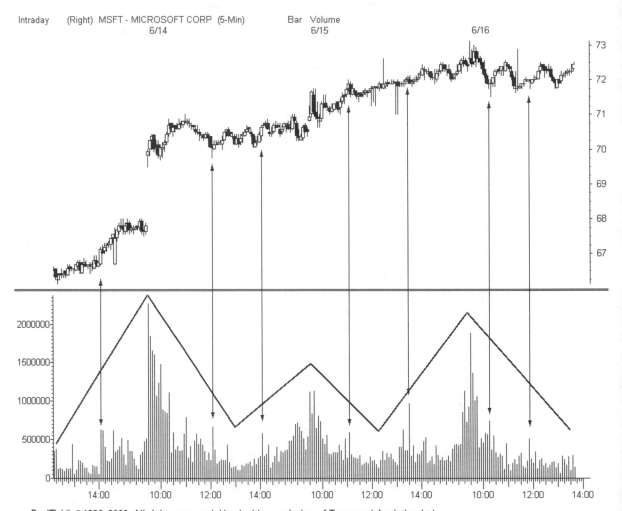

SPIKE STRATEGIES

Power spikes print as volume escalates dramatically. But sometimes one price bar cannot resolve the entire imbalance that the setup triggers. These spikes evolve over a number of intervals but have the same impact as single session events. In either case, the phenomenon represents an influential event that should leave a footprint on the underlying trend for months to come.

Identify power spikes through their divergence from intermediate moving averages of volume (VMAs). A single day signals a spike event when volume equals or exceeds three times the 50-day VMA. If significant activity stretches across a series of trading days, ratchet down the individual daily requirement. In these cases, volume must equal or exceed two times the 50-day VMA for two days in a row. Adjust these levels according to personal interest. One highly effective modification tightens up requirements so that only the most dramatic market action makes the cut. For this narrow output, move up to five times the VMA for a single bar and three times for multiday events.

Apply the right spike strategy to each setup. First identify whether the opportunity relies on a breakout, breakdown, reversal, or swing. Then apply classic Pattern Cycle tactics. Breakouts and breakdowns rely on pullback entry or tight arbitrary stop loss if the stock moves vertically. Shift down to the next-lower time frame for reversals and enter by relying on that pattern for support. Use a 1-2 pierce strategy for swing spikes. Let it pierce the axis and test it once. On the next test, enter in the direction of price swinging back through the center pivot.

The power spike may draw so much energy that it short circuits subsequent price movement. The active trend quickly flatlines after these spikes as crowd interest dissipates. This phenomenon will often induce a series of inside days and narrow range bars. Stand aside when these conditions appear because they generate few good trading opportunities. Look for this exhaustion move after extreme volume prints five to six times the 50-day VMA.

Signals that follow a long uptrend or downtrend generally flag a significant reversal. These find confirmation through relative strength indicators that turn sharply from overbought or oversold territory. Spike volume provides breakout cross-verification when price surges through significant support or resistance. Pivot spikes exhibit more subtle properties. These events often arise in the middle of well-defined trading ranges. They predict markets that will swing (pivot) back and forth across affected prices until time absorbs instability.

Watch out for preplanned stock activity that negates a spike's technical value. High volume days may not arise from an emotional crowd. The underlying company could be issuing a secondary stock offering of many million shares. Or a significant investment by a single holder could execute on that date. And always adjust for stock splits as soon as they happen so that the eyes have legitimate data to crunch.

APPLICATIONS

Since high volume can signify many different events, power spikes present a wide variety of possible setups and patterns. Place most of the trading effort on potential

F I G U R E   12.3

A March Level 3 power spike induces 8 months of pivot price action. High-volume events can signal a major redistribution from one set of investment hands to another. This process may take months to unwind after the initial shock. This forces price to swivel back and forth across the boundary that induces the change. Look for this type of action after a fundamental shift such as a stock's addition to the S&P 500 Index.

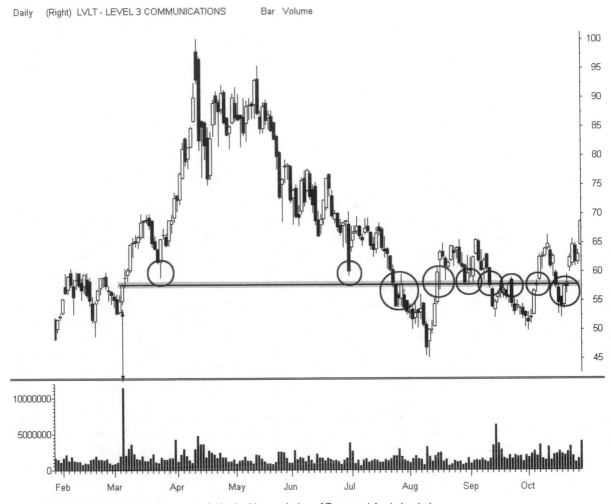

Daily   (Right) LVLT - LEVEL 3 COMMUNICATIONS   Bar   Volume

RealTick® ©1986–2000. All rights reserved. Used with permission of Townsend Analytics, Ltd.

tops, bottoms, and breakouts. Then combine power spikes with other classic patterns and charting landscape features to identify promising opportunities. Keep in mind that pivoting spikes generate complicated strategies that most market players should avoid.

BREAKDOWN SPIKE

Breaks of major support should trigger high volume. This signifies that the event shocks the crowd and incurs enough damage to keep price below that violation level for some time. The most damaging breaks come when price action raises false hope and then crushes the hopeful.

Description

- The stock sets up an obvious support level that persists for months.
- The level breaks down in a high-volume event.
- The price decline then continues at a milder angle than before the event.

Power spikes rarely signal the first breakdown within a downtrend. They set up with such great force because volume remains low on prior selloffs. The wounded survivors draw a common price where pain will become too great to carry their positions. Action strikes this level and forces everyone through the exit door at the same time. This raises an exhaustion issue for the subsequent trend. How can that market head lower if everyone has already sold? The answer comes from basic physics: it just continues to fall from its own weight.

Setup Tactics (FIGURE 12.4)

- Marimba marks an August low near 20 (1).
- The next 6 months draw a slowly rising trendline (6).
- A decline (7) starts in March and carries the stock down 40 points on low volume.
- The rising trendline breaks (2).
- Price tests the August low (3), holds, and bounces into a pullback (4) of the broken trendline.
- The low penetrates an inverse 3rd watch (5) and triggers a power spike.

Execution and Position Management (FIGURE 12.5)

- Price pulls back to the broken horizontal support (4) and signals an ideal short sale entry (1).
- Price action on the mid-April low before the breakdown shows a hidden gap between 21 and 22 (5). Place a stop loss at the top of this gap near 22.
- Additional short entries appear at (6), (7), and (8).
- Consider exit as price approaches each test of a prior low or prints an expansion bar.

F I G U R E   12.4

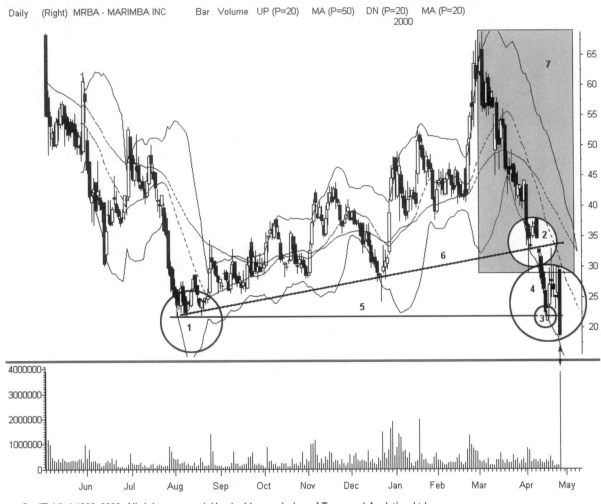

Daily   (Right) MRBA - MARIMBA INC   Bar Volume UP (P=20)   MA (P=50)   DN (P=20)   MA (P=20)
2000

- Price returns to test the spike at the 50% retracement of the major decline (2), (4). Bollinger Bands move to horizontal (3) and telegraph the reversal.

Reward:Risk

The setup presents many small opportunities with limited reward and risk. Lower volatility follows the power spike event. This reduces whipsaws but also limits

F I G U R E   12.5

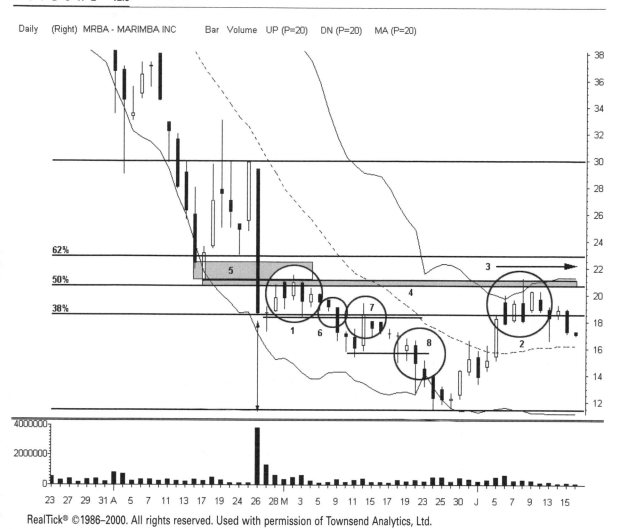

Daily   (Right) MRBA - MARIMBA INC   Bar Volume   UP (P=20)   DN (P=20)   MA (P=20)

profits. Short-term holds could book 2–3-point rewards with risk of 1 point or less. A single short sale right after the signal would yield a 50% profit in just over 3 weeks, with only one test of a trailing stop loss.

PULLBACK SPIKE

High-volume breakouts should generate further price gains after the initial power spike absorbs the crowd. The most dynamic events occur when the rally jumps out of a long base. Look for classic elements to support spike prediction. Fibonacci and S/R should both align to identify low-risk entry before the follow-through event begins.

Description

- Price movement establishes a long and stable base.
- A wide-range bar gaps above the base on very high volume and triggers a power spike.
- The bar closes above the midpoint of its high-low range.
- The next bar does not exceed the high of the spike bar.

Focus analysis on the first two bars that follow the event. The setup negates if price drives higher immediately. Look for a pullback that retains some volatility while volume declines. A harami often appears on the first bar after the event. Drop down to the next-lower time frame and measure the hole-in-the-wall resistance produced by that candle pattern.

Setup Tactics (FIGURE 12.6)

- Meade Instruments breaks out of a long base with a power spike (1) that prints a 23-point-wide range bar.
- The next bar marks an inside day that completes a tight symmetrical triangle on the 60-minute chart (5).
- Meade gaps down out of the triangle (4) the next morning and declines to a 62% retracement (2) of the entire rally.
- The Fib grid (3) shows an extension reward target 38% above the high of the spike bar.

Execution and Position Management (FIGURE 12.7)

- Enter a high-risk position as price jumps back above the 62% retracement (7). Place a stop loss under the low near 35.
- Plan an exit as price approaches a test of the gap (4) from below.
- Enter a lower-risk position as price fills the gap and jumps to the other side of the triangle apex.
- Plan an exit as price expands into a test of the spike high (1) (5).
- Momentum above the spike high builds quickly and offers few safe entries. It also comes without the expected double top failure.
- Price reaches Fibonacci extension target (2) and reverses.

F I G U R E   12.6

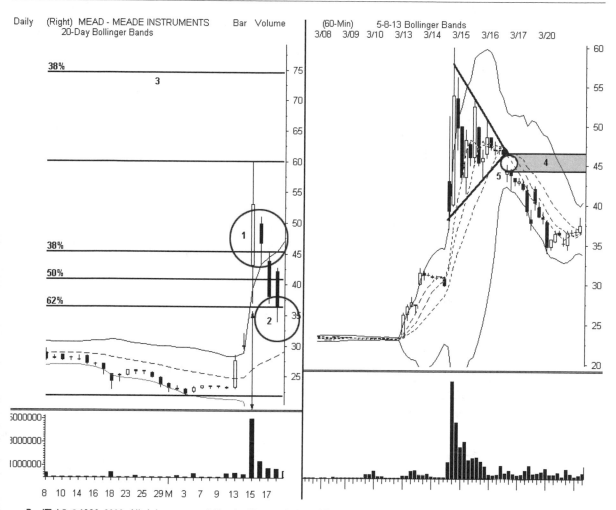

Daily   (Right) MEAD - MEADE INSTRUMENTS   Bar   Volume   (60-Min)   5-8-13 Bollinger Bands
        20-Day Bollinger Bands

- Two pullbacks to the spike high (3) and whole number 60 offer good entry. The first prints a hammer reversal (6) on the 60-minute chart.

Reward:Risk

The setup presents limited risk for a 23-point power spike. Features on the 60-minute chart establish well-defined S/R and target high-odds execution. The trade through the triangle apex offers a 2–3-point risk and 10–15-point reward. The stock

FIGURE   12.7

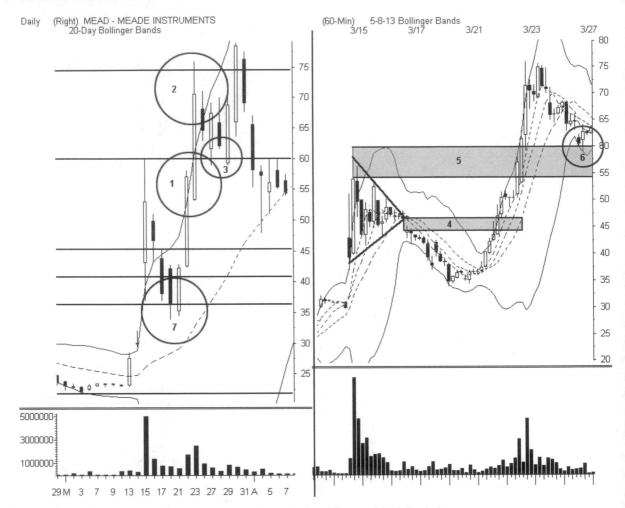

Daily   (Right) MEAD - MEADE INSTRUMENTS
          20-Day Bollinger Bands

(60-Min)   5-8-13 Bollinger Bands

then goes right through the old high without drawing a 3rd watch pattern. The vertical movement makes safe entry difficult to locate.

CLIMAX SPIKE

This setup should look familiar by now. It focuses on a major reversal at the end of an extended rally. Price shoots out the top Bollinger Band in a power spike and reverses violently back within its boundaries. The event prints a notable candlestick pattern, such as a long-legged doji or dark cloud cover. The swing trader then enters short sales that use supporting features of the charting landscape to minimize risk.

Description

- Stochastics or RSI indicator climbs to overbought levels and stays there.
- An extended rally precedes the signal.
- A sharp increase in short-term momentum precedes the signal.
- Price pushes out of the top Bollinger Band close to 100% of its range.
- The stock triggers a power spike when it reverses violently on high volume.
- Price action on the reversal displays wide range.

The preceding trend often prints a rising parallel price channel just before the climax event. The bars that lead into the signal feature an upside channel break. This flags a momentum surge, which draws in heavy participation for the subsequent reversal. Remember that the signal does not produce opportunity by itself. Setups arise from price interaction with key landscape features after the shock event.

Setup Tactics (FIGURE 12.8)

- Ramtron International draws a 6-week rising parallel price channel (2).
- A two-bar power spike (1) begins as price shoots through the top Bollinger Band in a 14-point bar.
- Dark cloud cover reverses momentum and pulls price back under the top Bollinger Band.
- The daily chart and 60-minute chart both record similar Bollinger Band violations.

Execution and Position Management (FIGURE 12.9)

- A hidden exhaustion gap (7) marks strong resistance on the first pullback (4).
- This pullback rally between 30 and 32 (4) identifies a good short sale but the position must execute in a very active market.
- Place a Fib grid over the decline to focus short sale entry points. The rally into the gap stops right at the 62% retracement and offers a perfect entry into gap resistance (1). The position whipsaws for 1 day but never tests the entry point.
- Consider an exit as soon as price breaks below the whipsaw and toward a test of the intermediate low at 25.
- Price completes an Adam and Eve top (5) that breaks down at (2). Sell the break and place a stop loss above 25.
- A down trendline (6) sets up from the declining tops.
- Price bounces sharply off 20 (3) at the 20-day Bollinger Band center.

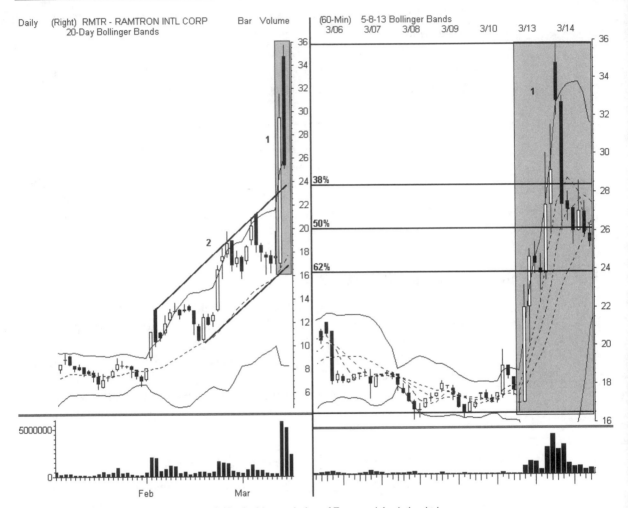

RealTick® ©1986–2000. All rights reserved. Used with permission of Townsend Analytics, Ltd.

- A rally breaks the down trendline (6), pulls back to resistance at 25 (2), and offers another low-risk short sale.
- The major trendline (8) and center Bollinger Band break on the next selloff.
- The violation triggers an 8-point, 3-day decline. Sell the trendline break or bar expansion below 20.

FIGURE   12.9

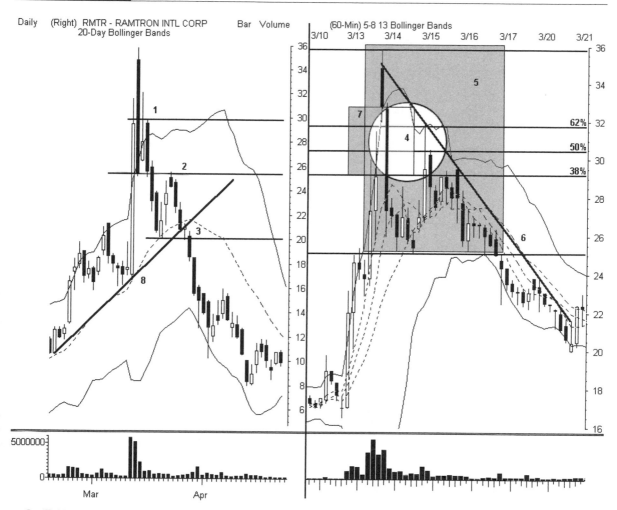

Daily   (Right) RMTR - RAMTRON INTL CORP   Bar   Volume   (60-Min) 5-8 13 Bollinger Bands
20-Day Bollinger Bands

Reward:Risk

Take the time to study volatile conditions after a spike event to identify the pattern's unique message. Short entry at the second double top high offers tremendous profit potential for a longer-term position. The setup also presents many short-term opportunities as the decline gathers momentum. Notice how volatility slowly drops through the course of the bear market. Later entries face fewer short squeezes and turn south right at broken support.

13

BEAR HUG

CHARACTERISTICS

Short sales require greater precision than long entries. Swing traders who just flip over successful long-side strategies often get burned. Different mechanics push rallies and selloffs. It takes demand and strong volume to lift stocks, but they can fall for long periods on low volume under the right circumstances. Violent market selloffs can end quickly and with little warning. And stocks that should fall when they break support just sit there or rally as broad bullishness infects the most hopeless issues.

Market professionals know exactly where uninformed participants will try to short stocks. They lie in wait and trigger short squeezes to take advantage of the buying pressure that these orders build into the market. Short sale strategy must deal with short covering rallies. Try to stay flat into a squeeze and sell the top of the rally just as other participants give up. As with many swing strategies, this uncomfortable trade requires patience and a skilled eye.

TRADE MECHANICS

The markets carry an underlying bullish bias. Many participants simply buy momentum and practice few other tactics. These speculators never learn the true trading art, in which profits come from both sides of the market. Take the time to

F I G U R E   13.1

Verio offers excellent short sales above and below the 200-day moving average. Markets undergo an important change in character when they cross this important psychological barrier. Buyers rule above the average and sellers rule below. But bear markets tend to exhibit much lower participation and volatility than bull markets. This can limit or enhance short-term trading conditions.

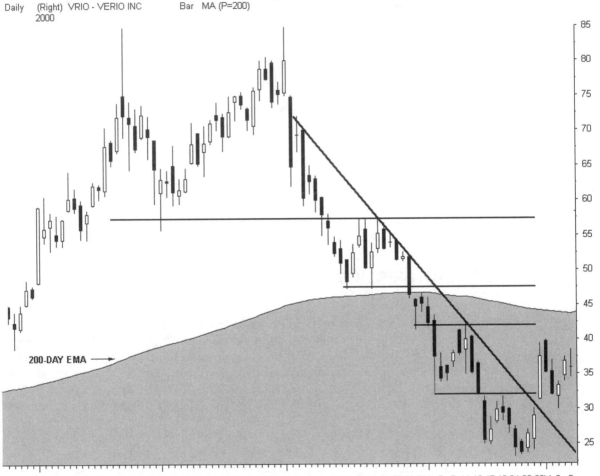

RealTick® ©1986–2000. All rights reserved. Used with permission of Townsend Analytics, Ltd.

practice this important skill. Start with small short positions even if long-side tactics require larger lots. Avoid common momentum mistakes such as chasing entry in major selloffs. Be defensive and watch the ticker closely. Squeezes begin at the same levels at which participants expect fast declines. When price suddenly finds support for no reason, get out first and ask questions later.

Align short sales to low-risk market conditions. Avoid selling during the first and last hours until experience recognizes the many dangers of these active periods.

High-float, lower-volatility stocks make great trading vehicles with limited risk. Learn to hit many singles before swinging for the short sale home run. Favor sideways-to-flat up markets over falling ones. These dull conditions keep the crowd away while still generating excellent profit potential.

Bear hug uses two different setups to identify short sale opportunities. Each relies on a different profile that favors further price decline. The first searches for bear market stocks that complete countertrend rallies into resistance. The second follows the coiled spring setup, but candidates must exhibit low relative strength. In both cases the hug finds many weak stocks on the verge of further breakdown.

Downtrend stocks can only fall for so long. A relief rally can erupt at any time to squeeze out shorts and build hope until resistance invites new selling. Or these beaten-up issues may base for long periods and make several unsuccessful attempts to return to bull status. The first bear hug pattern seeks these types of market conditions rather than trying to find uptrends about to break. Short interest tends to be lower in this environment, and setups produce more dependable signals with fewer surprises.

Look for failed efforts on the verge of rolling over into new downtrends. These bear rallies often rise into intermediate resistance such as the 50-day EMA. They can retrace 62% of the prior breakdown or bounce sharply off a horizontal ceiling. The pattern should display strong resistance and several obvious reversals. These testing levels point to new bear impulses about to emerge.

Careful timing builds profits after finding good candidates. Selling short into an oversold market can have undesirable results. Look for a RSI plot that rises to an overbought level and then turns down. Or find a Stochastics plot that drops off the top into a series of lower lows. In either case, the setup must suggest that the last bulls have used up the available demand for that stock.

Read the pattern closely before taking a position. The bear rally should print a clear topping formation such as a double top or descending triangle. When the chart looks bearish but doesn't fit all the definitions, drop down and study the short-term bars. They should confirm or refute the rollover and identify potential entry points. But don't be in a hurry. Breakdowns take time to build momentum. Avoid positions that may evolve into sideways markets by waiting as long as possible for the pattern to give up its secrets.

The second scan follows the narrow range logic of the coiled spring. Because the generic NR7 lacks directional bias for price expansion (i.e., it has an equal chance of going either way), visual filters attempt to tilt the odds in the bear's favor. In this setup, price constricts into a very tight range after a selloff and volatility declines. This dissipates bull power through a different mechanism than a relief rally. Gravity eventually takes hold and the stock rolls over.

Enter a short sale after the NR7 or place a sell stop to catch the breakdown as it triggers. Price will quickly expand in a series of stepping moves when the trade works. Keep a tight stop loss on the other side of congestion to recognize a bad position. This trade has an excellent reward:risk profile when other factors support a decline. Even without confirming indicators, swing traders will know quickly when a position fails and can cut their losses economically.

F I G U R E   13.2

Excellent short sales appear early in a decline after a stock breaks the 50-day moving average. This intermediate measurement offers strong resistance on a pullback when other landscape features cross-verify that price level. Note how Viant breaks below the 50-day EMA and fills an old gap before bouncing up to test the average. A buzzsaw of other resistance in the low 40s supports an immediate short sale position.

Measure reward for both hug strategies by finding the next major low. Bear rallies can rise off an unstable floor or a sharp climax reversal. Old support may fail as soon as price approaches or hold firm in a significant bottom formation. So look for adequate reward between entry and this low to justify the position. One strategy retains a piece of the trade as price reaches a low test in anticipation of a break. But if tactics limit holding period, exit completely on expansion toward this support.

The best short sale profits come from the quick drop. This requires excellent timing or a well-defined pattern. Mesa tops (see Figure 15.3) offer a little-known short sale with unique reward characteristics. This setup presents a specialized double top failure. Its power lies in the price mechanics that trigger on the breakdown. Mesas fall at exactly the same angle as they rise. Their decline often prints only a single bounce before reaching the 100% retracement.

Recognize the pattern by its squared top or sharp twin peaks after a parabolic climax. Look for the initial decline from the second high to draw a mirror image of the preceding rally. This signals that the selloff will likely continue at the same intensity after violation of double top support. The most profitable short sales come after price breaks the 62% retracement of the last uptrend.

BEAR STRATEGIES

Choose short sale entry that manages risk. Always try to sell at resistance where a small move against the position will confirm that the trade has failed. These well-defined execution points require a strong stomach. They print just as a rally suggests that a new uptrend has begun. Less aggressive traders can sit back and wait for a price rollover rather than trying to catch a rocket ship. Alternatively, watch for whipsaw violations of key resistance with price that falls quickly back below the barrier. These will form shooting stars or doji candles that signal a top within the lower time frame.

Learn to see less obvious resistance that allows safer entry due to the crowd's absence. Execution at these quieter levels greatly reduces short squeeze risk. While the crowd concentrates on horizontal ceilings or moving averages, focus attention on secondary barriers. Declining parallel price channels or Bollinger Band extremes offer high-reward short sales with fewer whipsaws. Or apply Fib grids but overlay several trend lengths to reveal small turning points that few others will notice.

Short squeeze completion generates excellent conditions for new short sales. The covering rally cleans out buying pressure and restores balance. Upside momentum ebbs and the environment that generated selling in the first place suddenly returns. Market players sense this and quickly reverse the short-term trend. Swing traders can anticipate the end of a squeeze better than their competition. Apply a Fib grid over the selloff that the rising market retraces. The rally should not exceed 62% of the prior fall unless strong buyers enter the action. Squeezes rarely break above major resistance, so the technicals should not trigger their participation. More likely, only weak longs with very bad timing place their bets as they watch the market rise.

Avoid selling into strongly negative momentum. Risk escalates dramatically chasing a decline just as it does during a sharp rally. Wait for a bounce or short squeeze before considering a new execution. Ironically, flat-to-minor up markets

F I G U R E   13.3

Short squeezes ignite repeatedly and without warning during an extended decline on Talk.com. Overnight gaps trap shorts, but sellers quickly reappear after the squeeze ends. The squeeze leaps as high as a 100% retracement early in Talk's bear market. But as conditions deteriorate, so do the rallies. The last two can only reach the 38% retracement of the last decline leg.

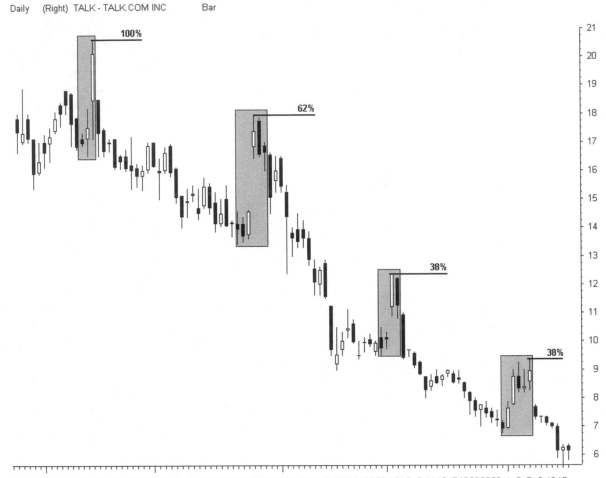

Daily   (Right) TALK - TALK.COM INC   Bar

offer better shorting conditions with less risk and fewer squeezes. Never place a market order into a rapid decline. The squeeze can occur at any time and without warning. The order will catch the upticks of a sudden rally and force the trade into a major loss before an exit appears.

Down gaps make excellent short entry vehicles. Watch for the first rally after the break and consider execution if price pierces the space. A down gap initiates strong selling pressure from shareholders trapped in positions when the shock event occurs. The first bounce gives them a chance to limit damage and get out. If the gap also breaks a topping pattern, look for dojis or hammers that mark the lower boundary of that congestion. Their shadows tell the swing trader where selling should reverse the market. But always keep an eye out for a gap echo reversal. Exit trades immediately if price jumps back across the barrier in a new up gap.

Intraday short sales follow the same strategies as longer-term positions. But the reduced holding period offers fewer exits, so the short squeeze generates greater risk. The first hour often establishes trends that persist throughout the session. Try to sell stocks that open weak and stay under pressure after the first 60 minutes. Many of these issues will attempt one strong rally as the day progresses. This bounce often provides the most rewarding short sale if the swing trader can locate a natural failure point. That price level should be well below the intraday high as long as the issue did not gap down to start the day. Use Fibonacci retracement to predict the top and time entry to a short-term Stochastics rollover.

APPLICATIONS

Bear hug concentrates on weak markets rather than attempting countertrend entry into strong ones. It finds stocks in bear declines that look ready to start another leg down. Remember that this setup actually relies on two different scenarios. The NR7 hug produces fast results as price expands out of a narrow range. The bear rally hug may need to push below congestion after the signal before decline momentum accelerates. Many short sale strategies work best in small bites. In other words, consider brief entries that depart at the first sign of danger and reenter as soon as the swing shifts back in your favor.

50–200 PINBALL

The zone between the 50-day and 200-day moving averages may induce sharp swing movement when price gets caught within its boundaries. Under the right conditions, the range ends with a breakdown through the 200-day MA in a major bear decline. Initiate short sales at failed tests of the 50-day near the end of this odd congestion. These allow profit even if price cannot pierce the lower barrier.

Description

- The stock pierces the 50-day moving average in a selloff after a solid bull run.
- Price tests but remains above the 200-day moving average.

- Relative strength rises but the subsequent bounce fails at the 50-day moving average.
- The congestion pattern completes and the market moves lower.

Look for a familiar topping pattern within the congestion even though it prints at an intermediate low. A head and shoulders or Adam and Eve formation at this location portends good news for short sales. The frequent appearance of this profitable setup ensures that swing traders will see it often during routine chart examination.

Setup Tactics (FIGURE 13.4)

- Vical rallies along a solid 3-month trendline (1).
- The trendline breaks in a hole-in-the-wall gap (2).
- Price pierces the 50-day EMA (3).
- Congestion forms below the 50-day EMA and 62% retracement (4) but above the 200-day EMA.
- Price fails at the 50-day EMA (5) and forms a possible double top pattern.
- The stock falls to the 200-day EMA, where a small NR7 (6) prints.

Execution and Position Management (FIGURE 13.5)

- Price gaps through the 200-day EMA (1) on the next bar and enters a major 2-day decline. This rewards short sales from the 50-day EMA or NR7.
- The congestion pattern holds together for another hour at the two lower trendlines (2), (3) before it breaks. Short entry between 28 and 26 requires a narrow limit order to control risk.
- The expansion bars on the daily and 60-minute charts encourage an exit before the close. A momentum-based, trailing stop loss produces better results and manages growing profits as the decline accelerates.
- The selloff ends (5) at a first failure retracement to the starting point of the prior rally.
- The next opportunity comes at the 38% retracement of the selloff (6). A doji signals a short-term reversal that eventually carries back into a double bottom test.

Reward:Risk

The only danger between the failed test at the 50-day EMA and the final low stands at congestion support near 30. A simple trend-following strategy would book an outstanding profit within the 50–200 zone and through the ensuing decline. This

F I G U R E   13.4

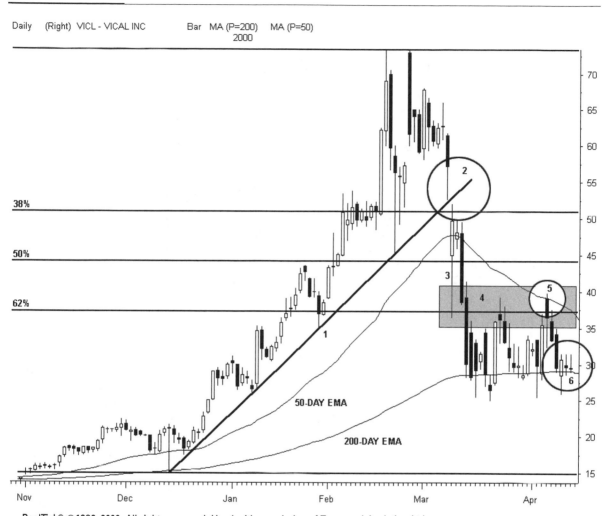

Daily   (Right) VICL - VICAL INC   Bar MA (P=200)   MA (P=50)
                                              2000

setup has great potential due to the crowd that builds within the congestion. They all abandon ship quickly once the 200-day violates.

CHANNEL SHORT

This setup executes short sales within a parallel price channel rather than trading the channel break that ends the formation. PPCs and their related harmonics define clear S/R for low-risk entry. Always bet on a channel to stay intact unless price

F I G U R E   13.5

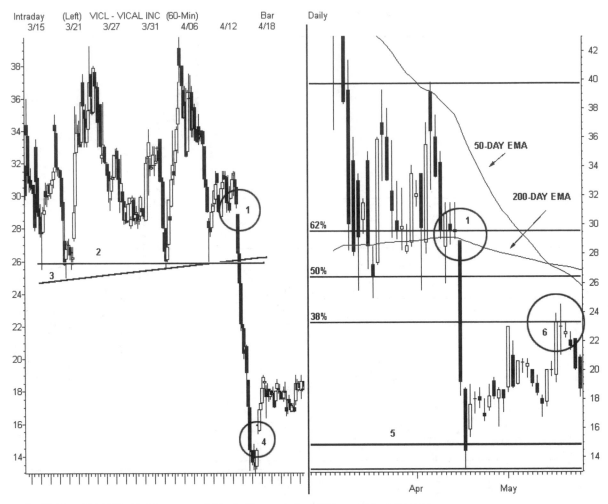

action congests and narrows along one of the trendlines after a recent strike. Draw smaller lines and channels within the larger pattern to locate converging points where price expansion should erupt. Two or three sets of embedded PPCs often hide within the boundaries.

Description

- Parallel price channel forms with at least two points at each extreme.
- Channel harmonics develop within the larger pattern.

- Falling channels offer more bearish opportunities than rising ones.
- Locate trendlines and channels within the PPC.
- Trade breakdowns of the smaller landscape features.

Execute the first trade right at the channel extreme, if possible. A series of entries then follows as smaller patterns identify reward:risk targets. When price action finally reaches the other extreme, continue the same strategy if a channel break sets up.

Setup Tactics (FIGURE 13.6)

- Wit Soundview draws a 6-month parallel price channel (1).
- A channel harmonic (2) forms near the lower trendline.
- A small uptrend (3) rises from the last lower channel strike (5).
- Price gaps into the top channel and reverses (4).
- The 50-day EMA remains below the 200-day EMA.

Execution and Position Management (FIGURE 13.7)

- Sell short the reversal at the upper channel (1). The best entry sets up on the gap that fills at 21-¾. A second opportunity signals on the breakdown of the small double top at 20.
- Price declines toward 15 in a series of small waves. The action may require a fast exit to avoid whipsaws.
- Price approaches the small rising trendline (2) and violates it (5). Enter on the break if the trade fills close to 15-½.
- Exit on price expansion into the harmonic (3).
- Price retests the broken trendline (6) and builds another small one (4). Short entry at (6) works as a 2B top reversal. A better short sale comes as the second trendline breaks (7).
- The tests at the trendline (2) form the right shoulder of a head and shoulders pattern (9) with the channel harmonic (3) as the neckline.
- Trade the harmonic breakdown (8) as a head and shoulder reversal. Enter close to the break point or stand aside.
- Exit on the expansion candle as it strikes the lower channel (10).

Reward:Risk

A series of low-risk opportunities appears on the swing from the upper to lower price channel. Reward potential of 2–3 points matches well with the one-half-point risk of a bad trade. Each price twist and turn seems to draw another classic pattern in this example. This phenomenon is quite common and can be used to find many profitable channel trades.

F I G U R E   13.6

Daily   (Right) WITC - WIT SOUNDVIEW GRP INC   Bar   MA (P=200)   MA (P=50)
2000

INTRADAY SHORT

Highly liquid stocks offer excellent intraday short sale opportunities. While an up-trend may continue in the larger time frame, short-term strategy shifts downward to trade 5-minute charts that display strong bear market declines. Because these selloffs only persist for hours instead of days, find an impending 60-minute break-down and use that chart to locate the first position. This allows the strategy to capture a larger proportion of the smaller decline.

F I G U R E   13.7

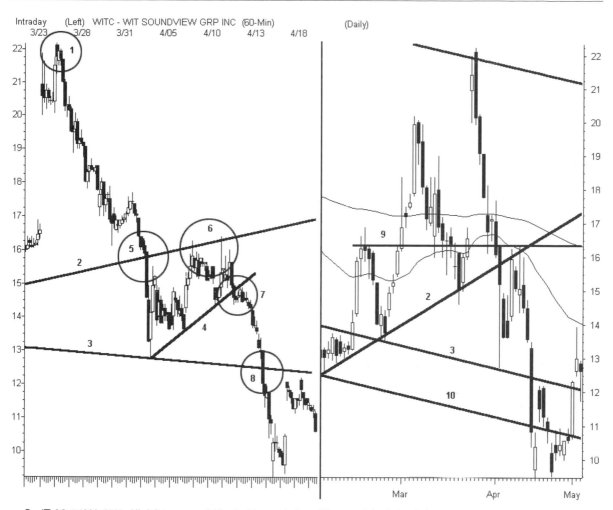

Description

- Consider only highly liquid stocks and active markets.
- Locate a 5–10-day uptrend that starts to pull back on a 60-minute chart.
- Draw a Fib grid over the trend.
- Look for a failure near the 38% or 62% retracement.
- Drop down to the 5-minute chart and trade a 38% failure down to the 62% level.

- Drop down to the 5-minute chart and trade a 62% failure down to the 100% level.

Enough reward must exist within the trading zone to make entry worthwhile. The setup relies on finding low-risk short sales within the 5-minute chart. Stand aside if the right patterns don't appear. The nature of breakdown on the 60-minute chart determines profitability and odds. Failure at the 38% often constitutes a C wave that will be very dynamic. Failure at the 62% may initiate a primary fifth wave that triggers a vertical decline.

Setup Tactics (FIGURE 13.8)

- Amazon prints a 7-day uptrend on the 60-minute chart.
- The rally breaks to new highs (1) in a continuation gap (2).
- It climaxes in a tall expansion bar (3) that quickly reverses.
- The pullback (5) successfully tests the old high and continuation gap as it strikes the rally trendline (4).
- Narrow price action draws a small descending trendline (6).
- The two trendlines form a symmetrical triangle at the 38% retracement.

Execution and Position Management (FIGURE 13.9)

- The triangle breaks down (1) and invites a short sale at 52. Place a stop loss on the other side of the rising trendline.
- Watch whole number 50 (4) or exit as soon as Level II starts to build rising tick.
- The stock sells off without a bounce until 50-½ (3). The quick reversal above 51 reduces profits and demands a fast exit.
- The stock pulls back to the 38% retracement of the small selloff (2) and the 8-bar moving average. The first pullback after a major breakdown should not bounce sharply, and aggressive traders can consider short entry while others wait for safer opportunity.
- The low breaks and offers a scalp down to 50 (4). The one-half-point reward target should force most traders to the sidelines.
- The pullback to 50-½ (3) strikes the 13-bar moving average and top of last resistance. It also marks an excellent short sale entry. The next violation should take price below whole number support at 50. This offers good reward and gets the trade in motion before the crowd joins in.
- Price breaks 50 (4). Exit as the bar expands out of the bottom Bollinger Band to 49-¼ or as soon as the small hammer (8) forms.
- The pullback to 50 (4) marks another good short sale entry level.

F I G U R E   13.8

- Hold the position as price tests the hammer and fails (5). The weak action signals little danger and the short position may carry through past 48-½.
- Break of the down trendline (6) flags a potential bottom and approach of the larger 62% retracement.
- A 3:30 p.m. selloff (7) carries the stock to the lows for the day, but profit requires very fast fingers.

F I G U R E　13.9

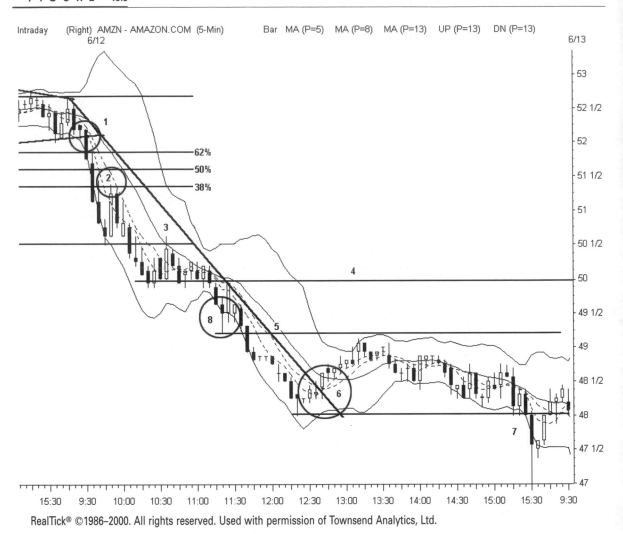

Reward:Risk

The triangle break signals a major bear market within the 5-minute charting land-scape. The setup works with a simple pullback strategy that enters at resistance. Whipsaws are manageable, and active short entry that day leads to consistent prof-its. Pay attention to changing conditions. The afternoon ends the active selloff, and the last hour traps short sellers in a quick squeeze.

14
C H A P T E R

3rd WATCH

CHARACTERISTICS

William J. O'Neil defined the cup and handle (C&H) pattern in his classic *How to Make Money in Stocks*. Since that time, popular market culture has adopted the C&H through a series of articles in *Investors Business Daily* and other journals. But few swing traders recognize this formation's versatility or its appearance through all time frames and markets.

The classic pattern looks like a rounded cup and small handle. It represents a breakout through a triple top. Price first rallies into a high and fails as it forms the left side of the cup. The issue finds support and builds a sideways base. A new rally erupts and rises toward the old high. This forms the cup's right side. Sellers appear at the double top and the stock pulls back. The next decline draws the smaller handle until price again stabilizes. It rises into a third rally and breaks out sharply to new highs.

TRADE MECHANICS

Look at the market mechanics behind this pattern. After the first high, price pulls back sharply before it bounces. This forces oscillators to roll over and encourages longs to exit positions. Swing traders then enter new short sales as price approaches the double top test. This contributes to selling pressure and forces the market to

F I G U R E   14.1

Keithley Instruments prints a well-proportioned cup and handle breakout that completes a 3-month congestion pattern. The small, rounded handle follows a deep, wide cup that takes much longer to form. Note how the hammer at the handle's bottom telegraphs the subsequent rally. The 3rd watch setup digests price action after a failed double top to locate many variations of this classic pattern.

Daily   (Right) KEI - KEITHLEY INSTRUMENTS   Bar Volume

pull back again. It eventually reaches support while indicators recover from oversold levels. Longs then sense a new opportunity and build volume back toward the old highs. This forms a handle base that discourages further selling and builds accumulation. Price reaches the high for the third time and breaks out.

Volume must support price action for the new rally to succeed. The original O'Neil approach demands that breakout volume rise at least 50% above the 50-day volume moving average before the new high. It searches for candidates that have more participation on up days leading into the breakout than down days. The classic definition also filters volume action within the cup itself. The rising days on the cup's right side should print higher volume than both the falling days and the 50-day VMA.

These strict requirements lead swing traders to misunderstand this pattern's power. Many predictive C&H formations never meet these standard definitions. Handles can retrace deeply or actually build a base at new highs above the cup. Volume can break all the rules as the pattern forms but still show excellent accumulation by the time the breakout erupts. And a deep handle may even push toward the low of the cup's bottom before the final rally begins.

The 3rd watch scan seeks the classic pattern but cuts the dimensions in half. It locates breakouts that occur within 6-month highs rather than 52-week highs. The handle language captures many variations of this complex formation. It requires only that the market print no new high within 4 weeks of the signal. This allows a short base and pullback before the stock erupts through the barrier. The scan also looks for volume to spike at least 150% of average on the breakout bar.

Use 3rd watch strategy to trade triple-top breakouts. While mathematics outputs a specific type of C&H, the markets draw this pattern in many unique ways. Both ascending triangles and rectangle formations rely on the same price mechanics. Channel resistance often breaks on the third high as momentum triggers bar expansion. Sometimes relative highs will print at an equal distance to each other rather than in a proportional cup and handle. This powerful setup offers swing traders valuable insight and profitable tactics for all of these breakout incarnations.

The handle's location provides accumulation feedback. A previous chapter noted that volume tends to lead or lag price, especially at new highs and lows. When the handle forms below the cup, it suggests that accumulation needs to build before a breakout can proceed. Alternatively congestion right above two old highs denotes a very strong stock that should trend sharply once it completes the new platform. Keep an eye out for a double handle formation. This odd pattern forms bases on both sides of the two old highs. If this cup and two handles (C&2H) appears, measure the last trend just below the first handle. Add that length to the bottom of the second handle to estimate a price target for the next rally.

The pattern works well through most intermediate highs. This gives swing traders another valuable tool to execute breakouts from narrow congestion. Look for any horizontal resistance and count the highs. Follow the action back to the third high and watch for price to pause at the barrier. Measure the potential reward on a price break. Many short-term watch candidates will not generate enough profit potential to trigger an entry. When a setup shows promise, enter on a narrow range bar near the high or wait for the breakout and execute on the first pullback.

3rd watch offers excellent intraday trades. The setup carries few of the restrictions that limit most other bells in the short-term environment. This dependable pattern appears frequently on short-term charts and encourages many quick profits. In addition to simple highs, look for first-hour range to break on the third try. Even

F I G U R E   14.2

Clarent's cup and two handles prepare the way for a vertical rally. A breakout to new highs must attract enough interest to move that market higher. When it lacks good sponsorship, the developing trend may pause to build new congestion until accumulation generates enough horsepower for higher prices. The C&2H provides an efficient pattern to accomplish this important task.

Daily   (Right) CLRN - CLARENT CORP   Bar

scalpers can apply effective watch strategy. Locate intermediate highs on a 1-minute chart and trade quick thrusts or tick breakouts above that level.

Major intraday setups tend to peak in the last hour. A strong trend often reaches a first climax early in the day and spends several hours testing its new range. Positive bias then carries it back towards the intraday high late in the day if the market stays strong. This encourages new speculators who hope for another trend leg or want to buy in anticipation of a continuation move the next morning. Sometimes the markets will close just as the stock reaches the peak but doesn't eject. Odds then favor a breakout gap when trading resumes the next morning.

WATCH STRATEGIES

Always look for a breakout from congestion rather than a trend that begins well below the old highs and ejects without a base. These issues can retrace deeply, not find any base support, and break even lower. Insist on horizontal resistance rather than a series of ascending highs. The setup mechanics require strong tension at the breakout level so that price can expand sharply into a new trend. Ascending highs relieve demand a little bit at a time (similar to a rising wedge) and often run out of stream before price can break through an upper trendline.

The 3rd watch scan on daily charts provides an excellent indicator for market corrections. Candidates dry up more quickly than any other bell as broad conditions deteriorate. They may even disappear for long periods as most stocks fail to make new highs. Move on to other bell strategies during these phases or shift down to shorter-term charts. Strong rallies will continue to print on 5-minute and 60-minute views through the most severe market corrections.

Consider entry within congestion prior to the actual signal. Watch as price builds into the third high and look for narrow-range bars. Then enter quietly after locating an acceptable stop loss just below the tight pattern. This method works very well for short-term charts where breakouts trigger strong Level II demand and induce slippage. Congestion entry also limits risk because a small failure proves that the trade was in error and any breakout pushes it into a profit.

Use closing price for daily 3rd watch signals to avoid false breakouts. Try to execute as near to the old highs as possible to reduce risk. After a sharp breakout, this will only occur on a deep pullback. If a strong move doesn't retrace to this level, look for high, tight congestion near the top of one or two expansion bars after the breakout. Another sharp move may erupt shortly if price narrows toward the top of the range on the fourth or fifth bar. When all else fails, drop down to the next-lower time frame and enter the trade on any small pullback that appears. Then use a flat stop loss to catch momentum without incurring excessive risk.

Avoid chasing runaway moves through new highs. The prospects for a violent reversal increase dramatically after stocks go into parabolic rallies. As price extends vertically through new highs, it moves above natural support levels and finds no trend mirrors to offer guidance. When a reversal finally begins, nothing holds up the stock until supply dissipates or it reaches a support level. Flat stop loss controls some of this risk, but slippage will increase dramatically if the selloff becomes violent.

3rd watch encourages many profitable exit strategies. Swing traders should consider longer holding periods on new high breakouts than other types of setups. Place a trailing stop below price as soon as the position moves into a profit. These

F I G U R E   14.3

Tight congestion at the third high offers a low-risk opportunity just before a market ejects to higher prices. Most of the crowd waits for a breakout before committing to a new position. This increases risk and limits reward. Narrow-range entry uses the crowd's enthusiasm to ride a position into a fast profit and escape before whipsaws damage the trade.

trends can move sharply higher, and this simple strategy lets profits run. Or consider immediate sell limit orders after entry that reflect both a profit target and a stop loss. Shorter holding tactics benefit when they sell into the first sharp expansion after the entry. This reliable strategy also books quick profits and moves on to the next trade just as the crowd piles in.

    Exit strategies depend on whether entry lies within a trend mirror or at an all-time high. Breaks through intermediate highs still face overhead resistance that limits profit. Measure the distance to the next obvious barrier to establish a profit target. If the trade makes sense, exit just below this resistance unless the personal plan controls risk on the expected retracement. One excellent tactic buys a deep pullback from a double top failure after it reaches support. Then hold the position through the rally into the 3rd high, take some money off the table, and let the rest ride into the breakout.

F I G U R E   14.4

Always keep one eye on overhead supply when considering a 3rd watch setup. This Emisphere pattern shows a perfect retracement and breakout but the intermediate high just above the entry level may limit reward. The most powerful 3rd watch events push price into uncharted territory. But excellent setups still execute through breakouts within larger congestion. Take the entry as long as the pattern shows an adequate profit target before the required exit.

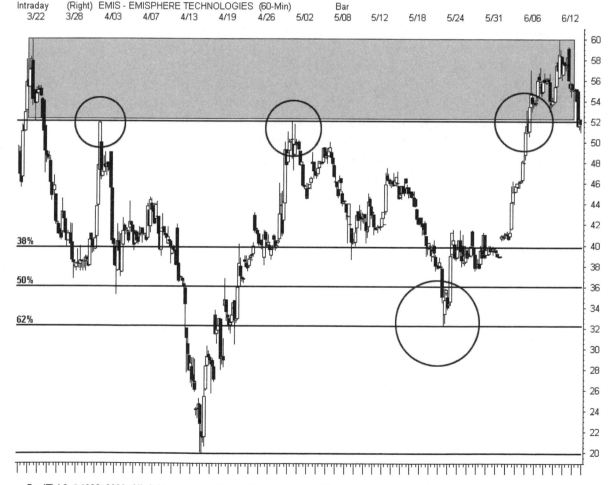

APPLICATIONS

3rd watch breakouts occur through all time frames. The daily setup offers a small subset of the trading possibilities with this versatile pattern. Learn to recognize the many forms and variations that this opportunity takes. The pattern wields more power when tight congestion builds below the second high and generates a smaller breakout before the major resistance gets taken out. Congestion above the high may trigger frustration. The formation can induce a trendline of rising highs that limits momentum acceleration.

WATCH ECHO

One good pattern deserves another. This fascinating setup illustrates the importance of fractals in trend development. The price chart draws one complex 3rd watch breakout and immediately moves to a new high, where it draws another similar pattern. Close examination also reveals that both handles form complete 3rd watch patterns by themselves.

Description

- Market draws a new high and failed second top.
- Price retests the failed top in a smaller time frame and pulls back.
- Price rises into a new test that synchronizes through both time frames.
- The market breaks out through resistance in both time frames.
- The chart starts the same process again at a higher price level.
- The vertical distance from the base low to high resistance measures a price target for the breakout.

Don't plan for a watch echo, but evaluate this complex pattern when it appears. The repeating nature predicts retracement levels and multi-time frame breakout points.

Setup Tactics (FIGURE 14.5)

- Global Industries prints a major high at 11-½ (1).
- Price sells off into a small double bottom and retraces 62%, where it fails in a doji reversal (9).
- A test of the lows at (4) sets up a Big W bottom.
- Price completes first rise (2) and fails in a double top test (3).
- The next low pulls back to the 62% retracement (6), forms a double bottom, and starts to rally.

F I G U R E   **14.5**

Daily   (Right) GLBL - GLOBAL INDUSTRIES   Bar
1999   2000

- Congestion (7) builds under the second high. This completes a 3rd watch variation (5) with a breakout point just below 10-½.
- Price breaks out (8) of the small 3rd watch and larger pattern in 3 bars.

Execution and Position Management (FIGURE 14.6)

- Enter long when the smaller pattern breaks near 10-½. Hold through a test of the horizontal high at 11-¼ because odds favor a breakout through

Daily   (Right) GLBL - GLOBAL INDUSTRIES   Bar

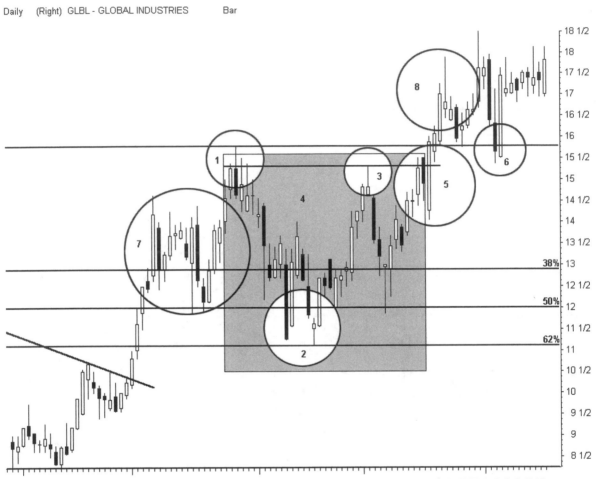

that level on the third try. This offers a 30% profit before whipsaws start a
shakeout under 14 (7).

- A new 3rd watch pattern (4) starts to form at (1). The lows (2) print at the
  62% retracement of the rally leg.

- The lows (2) also mark the first pullback to the prior 3rd watch and offer
  an excellent entry point. Place a tight stop loss just below 11.

- The new high fails a test over 15 (3).

- The next pullback ends in a long hammer. Price rises to 15-½, retreats for
  one bar, and releases to higher prices (5). Enter on the breakout with a
  stop loss just below 15.

- A quick shakeout tests the position (8).
- The first pullback to the 3rd watch top (6) offers another low-risk entry.

Reward:Risk

This less-volatile stock reduces risk while allowing nice profits. Risk remains under 1-point through most opportunities while reward stands at 2–3 points. The smaller movement rules out very short-term strategies and favors longer position trades. Note how well the pullbacks respond to the support of the 3rd watch highs. These natural barriers offer low-risk dip trip plays.

3rd WATCH CLASSIC

This setup presents the classic cup and handle breakout that appears through daily chart examination. These represent position trade opportunities unless the short-term action offers quick profits. The fun starts after the initial breakout, when momentum strategies produce the best rewards. Buy pullbacks as long as the underlying market stays strong.

Description

- The stock prints a long-term high and strong reversal.
- A base forms that persists for at least 1–3 months.
- Price rises into a test of the old high and fails.
- The next pullback remains on top of support that forms during the basing period.
- The stock rallies back into the old highs and breaks out strongly.
- The vertical distance from the base low to high resistance measures a price target for the breakout.

The setup signals after the new high breakout. This increases initial risk because the crowd has joined the action. Try to wait for a pullback or get promising candidates into the watch list a few sessions before price reaches the new high test. These breakouts tend to show great strength. This limits early pullbacks and may force a simple trend-following strategy with an arbitrary stop loss.

Setup Tactics (FIGURE 14.7)

- Idec Pharmaceuticals ends a long rally with a double top (5) that breaks down in a hole-in-the-wall (1) gap.
- Strong resistance (4) sets up in the long shadow at the top of the pattern.
- Price pulls back to a 50% retracement of the rally and finds support through a 2B bottom (2) test.

F I G U R E   14.7

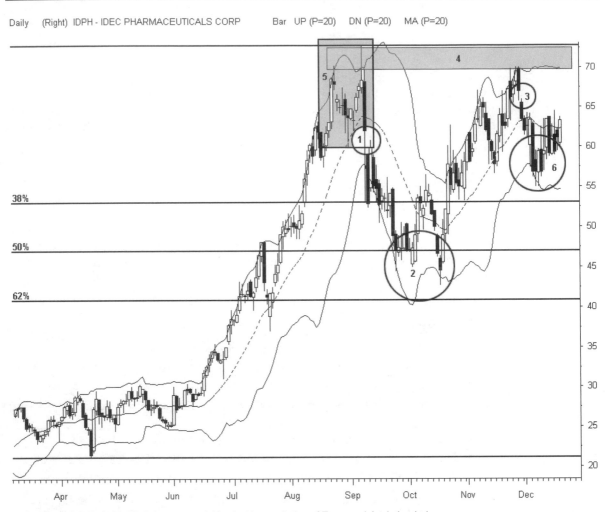

Daily   (Right) IDPH - IDEC PHARMACEUTICALS CORP   Bar   UP (P=20)   DN (P=20)   MA (P=20)

- The stock rallies back into the first high and fails in a new hole-in-the-wall (3) gap.
- The pullback finds support above the base low (6) and starts to rally for the third time.

Execution and Position Management (FIGURE 14.8)

- A long expansion bar (2) thrusts into the September high (1) and signals the 3rd watch breakout.

F I G U R E   14.8

Daily   (Right) IDPH - IDEC PHARMACEUTICALS CORP   Bar UP (P=20)   DN (P=20)   MA (P=20)

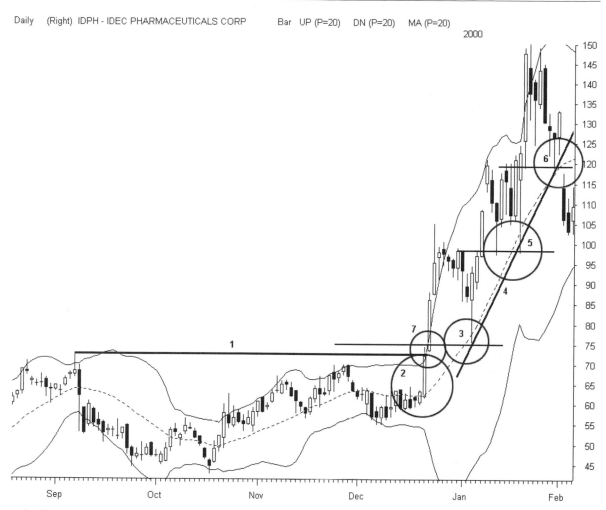

- The next morning opens with a small gap (7). This marks an excellent intraday entry if the swing trader can watch first-hour action to confirm that the gap will hold.
- Place a stop loss just below the September shadow for a longer-term position trade. Place a stop loss just behind the gap for an intraday or short-term swing trade.
- The next two bars shoot out the top Bollinger Band and demand a quick exit.

- First pullback (3) to the 3rd watch high requires great skill to enter because it doesn't reach support. The shorter-term chart may reveal a low-risk intraday opportunity.
- The two pullbacks to 100 (5) both offer good entry but require fast hands.
- Trendline (4) forms from the pullbacks.
- A final pullback (6) bounces and breaks through the trendline into a hole-in-the-wall that ends the rally.

Reward:Risk

The setup requires wide stop loss and great risk tolerance. High volatility makes this a dangerous environment for short-term entry but a rewarding one for position trades. The market offers one excellent opportunity for all traders at the small gap that breaks the 3rd watch into new highs. Many classic setups feature a single point in price and time that marks a perfect execution.

SWING WATCH

Short-term markets set up many 3rd watch variations. These often appear within congestion and require defensive management. The 60-minute chart provides the logical starting point to identify these swing opportunities. Don't demand perfect horizontal S/R for the intraday watch breakout. This volatile arena prints many small violations, and swing traders need to apply skilled vision to measure setup reward and risk.

Description

- The intraday market prints a failed double top across 5–10 daily sessions.
- Price pulls back no further than 62% and rallies into the testing zone.
- The market breaks out to new highs.
- The vertical distance from the base low to high resistance measures a price target for the breakout.

The pullback can violate deep Fibonacci levels by a few ticks, but stand aside when it drops toward a 100% retracement. That signals a possible trend change or a different congestion pattern. Try to find the logical breakout point when chart noise makes interpretation difficult. Remember that time of day impacts short-term setups. Small 3rd watch breakouts often align better with time than with price.

Setup Tactics (FIGURE 14.9)

- Texas Instruments prints a doji (4) at 75 that signals the end of a swing.
- Related price bars set up a resistance line (1) at 74-¼.

F I G U R E   14.9

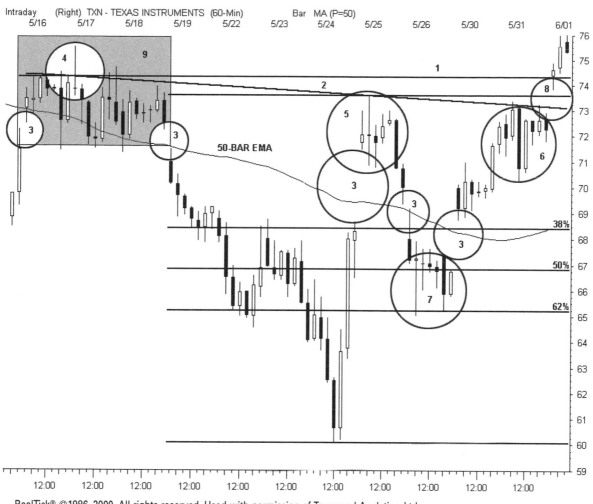

RealTick® ©1986–2000. All rights reserved. Used with permission of Townsend Analytics, Ltd.

- The first high breaks down in an island reversal (9).
- Price gaps repeatedly (3) through the 50-bar EMA.
- The double top test (5) generates a down trendline (2).
- Price pulls back to the 62% retracement and prints a small double bottom (7).
- The next rally pushes back into the trendline (2) and congests (6) for 1 day.
- A morning gap (8) breaks though both the trendline (2) and resistance line (1).

Execution and Position Management (FIGURE 14.10)

- Enter on the gap (1) after first-hour testing. The narrow range of the breakout bar reduces risk.
- Price rises throughout the day with few whipsaws, prints a NR7, and breaks to a new high in the last hour (2). The stock sits at the daily high near close and encourages an overnight hold.
- The next morning prints a strong gap (3) and wide-range bar. The 5-point gap encourages a fast exit. The expansion bar also signals the need to take profits.

F I G U R E   14.10

- The 3rd watch breakout stands at the midpoint (5) for the entire rally.
- Over the next six sessions, price action draws a tight symmetrical triangle (4) that finally breaks down, fills the gap, and reverses the market.

Reward:Risk

A 2-day swing trade could easily yield a 10-point profit with very limited risk. The breakout over the 3rd watch high faces few whipsaws. The price action encourages an overnight position. A fast exit without an overnight hold still books a 1–3-point profit. The greatest risk comes from buying the wide gap. But this type of risky strategy never shows up in the swing trader's playbook.

PART THREE

MAKING THE TRADE

15

C H A P T E R

PRECISE TRADE EXECUTION

TIMING AND METHODS

Bad execution ruins a perfect setup. Seek highly favorable conditions for trade entry or stay out of the market until they appear. Apply the right strategy when pulling the trigger and manage the position into a profitable exit.

EXECUTION TARGET

The execution target (ET) defines where to buy or sell short. A promising setup points to this narrow price level through detailed S/R analysis, pattern recognition, and evaluation of reward:risk considerations. Swing traders also review all external elements that might affect the opportunity before picking this important number. Keep in mind that the ET changes dynamically as new data supplement the prior analysis. A single tick may impact the calculated reward:risk and remove the position from consideration for execution.

The execution zone (EZ) stands between short-term price movement and the prechosen ET. It marks an attention boundary for impending entry. Swing traders shift their focus toward the ET when price penetrates the EZ. Draw this interface at a distance that allows sufficient time to examine whether or not to execute the setup when price hits the target. Use common sense to identify useful EZs. One simple method just looks at recent volatility and measures an adequate fixed distance from the ET. Another finds the last intermediate S/R that the stock must pass before reaching the ET and places it there.

Watch short-term chart and tape action closely as price moves through the EZ. Substantial evidence should appear to confirm the setup analysis and anticipated execution. Time, crowd, and trend movement must all validate that the pre-

F I G U R E   15.1

Nextel pulls back after a morning gap. The big hole survives the opening hour and raises the odds of a successful test. A trendline sets up at whole number 60 and the 38% retracement. Logic places the execution target around 59-¾ since the pattern promises a low-risk entry under 60. The execution zone fits well right under the small bounce at 61. The swing trader then places a limit order that can be lifted quickly if price action turns sour through the EZ.

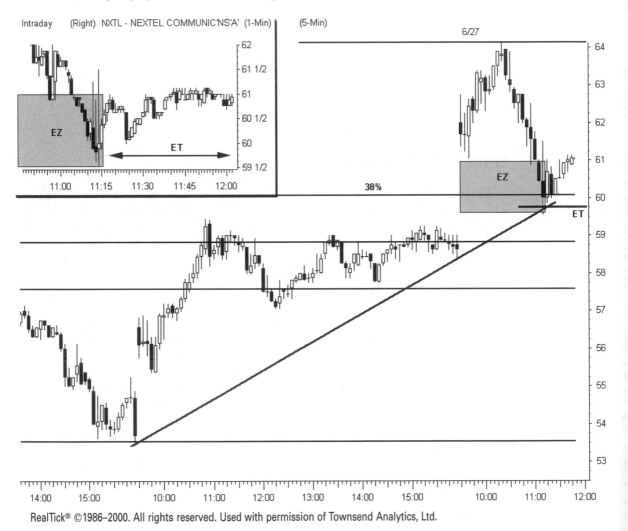

dicted reversal, breakout, or fade will print as expected. Often a burst of activity on the time and sales ticker will supply all the required confirmation. But remember that some excellent signals require a lack of participation. For example, entry into a contracting empty zone interface offers a very narrow EZ and low-risk ET.

The swing trader must choose to execute or stand aside as price strikes the ET. This important decision requires both skill and experience. The markets never provide enough information to make fully confident choices. All opportunities carry risk and limited odds for success. Even perfect trade setups will yield very bad positions under certain circumstances. So learn to think and act logically in this uncomfortable environment and realize that pulling the trigger will never be easy.

The required EZ feedback changes with every new setup. But this attention process yields successful trades quickly. It promotes low-risk and high-opportunity because it relies upon the best execution price for a particular pattern. In addition to building profits, a well-managed EZ strategy enables swing traders to avoid losers as they uncover the secrets of time and tape before risking capital.

Longer-term positions require less active time management. Execute setups as soon as price strikes predefined targets and avoid small details on the real-time screen. Rely on well-placed physical stops to enter the market rather than elusive EZs. But time and timing gain importance as holding period shortens and undivided attention becomes a vital element in every trade decision. The intraday chart takes precedence over the daily view for most swing traders. Rely on it to confirm or refute short-term setup analysis and execution planning. When the real-time chart and tape action don't support the intended trade, pass it up and move on to the next opportunity.

Always filter timing considerations through the personal trading plan. This additional analysis forces the swing trader to stand aside on many good setups. For example, an ET that strikes during the first hour will not trigger a position if chosen tactics avoid that time period. Opportunity must also match execution. A low-risk ET may not signal a good trade within the predefined holding period, or a lack of liquidity may prevent a complete fill at the expected price.

THE TRADING DAY

Decide how actively to manage trade executions and open positions during each session. Professionals watch every tick and respond to very short-term market turns. Investor hobbyists just read the morning paper and gather enough information to follow their favorite stocks. Most active swing traders fall somewhere in between these two extremes. They often have full-time jobs in other professions but can access real-time markets periodically through a network or dial-up connection.

Overnight positions benefit greatly from real-time market access. One–three-day and 3–7-day strategies require solid execution skills to maximize profits. Daily bars lack the important details that swing traders need to manage short-term tactics. Both of these multiday holding periods respond well to the 60-minute charting landscape. This broad intraday view reacts slowly so participants can carry on their

F I G U R E   15.2

Broadvision gets ready to break out of a downtrend. A Fib grid over the first hour range shows rising congestion right at the trendline and 62% retracement shortly after 11 a.m. The stock mounts the trendline and starts a first pullback. Place an EZ under the breakout bar and buy at support if conditions stay favorable. But the 1-minute chart quickly draws a small head and shoulders pattern while price drops below the 62% retracement on the 5-minute chart. These two strong warnings should be enough to stand aside or exit the new trade quickly.

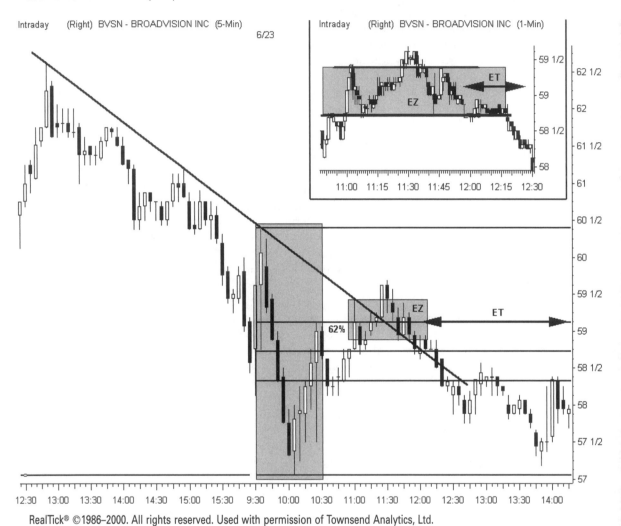

other responsibilities. It also allows them to check real-time market development at regular intervals and make informed decisions.

This important time zone responds to a variety of execution strategies that take advantage of opportunity and control risk. But a standard direct-access interface may not provide the limit order options needed to manage these longer holding periods. While the classic discount broker offers one alternative, first investigate broker-dealer hybrids that permit execution through market makers and specialists as well as a variety of ECNs. These versatile order screens allow greater flexibility for the part-time participant who steps in and out of the market.

Each trading day signals unexpected opportunities. Trending markets may generate fresh patterns or economic reports may push price into new territory. In either case, the swing trader must quickly separate the ETs that represent good profit setups from those that carry danger. Liquid stocks under intensive examination prior to the new session offer the most dependable prospects. Intraday price action invokes confident strategies when major swing levels have already imprinted deeply into short-term memory.

Overall sentiment, shock events, and volatility all affect the success of swing trade execution. Always try to take positions that converge with current market conditions. Watch for the major indices and NYSE TICK to line up just as the ET strikes. Good profits can come from hot picks that swim against the stream. But both %WIN and AvgWIN improve when short-term market cycles support positions. This natural alignment provides a powerful filter for consistent risk management and builds trader longevity.

Use time of day knowledge to track the 90-minute cycles that drive short-term markets. Look for the hidden buy-and-sell swing within the restless intraday crowd. This classic oscillation follows a larger 3-day cycle that alternates buy, sell, and sell short days. With a little practice, swing traders can find their place within all of this quirky market behavior and employ strategies to take advantage of those that execute against the clock.

Watch for first- and last-hour action to disrupt important cycles as larger influences unwind through the markets. Shock events will shift emotional behavior and establish new timing considerations as they strike a hidden reset button that changes the flow of buying and selling. This sudden imbalance offers opportunity when swing traders shift gears quickly to take advantage of new conditions.

Pay close attention to intraday signposts for evidence of unusual price behavior. A third-bar reversal often tests and fades the opening trend. One side may capitulate near the first hour's end and trigger a sharp trend move. Whipsaws and false moves may characterize the session as it treads into the lunch hour. Look for the early afternoon to bring new bursts of volume and interest. Observe 2:30 p.m. closely for a selloff as the bond market enters the final half hour. Check for a last fade at 3:30 p.m. just before the market day draws to a conclusion. And always remember that markets can reverse quickly into contrary movement if signpost events fail to show up on time.

Stand apart from the crowd and avoid its irrational behavior. Emotional bursts of buying and selling often signal opportunity in the opposite direction. This contrary mechanism reveals a frustrating characteristic of modern markets: profit rarely follows the direction of the herd. Consider that price may move opposite to the current popular wisdom through all time frames and opportunities. Choose the reaction and avoid the emotion whenever possible. Successful careers can be built

F I G U R E   15.3

Time execution to broader market forces and improve results. Altera spends a full day building a significant mesa top. Price then approaches the breakdown level at 104 just as Nasdaq starts the last leg of a small descending triangle. Support breaks and begins a midday decline after it pulls back to pick up well-timed short sales.

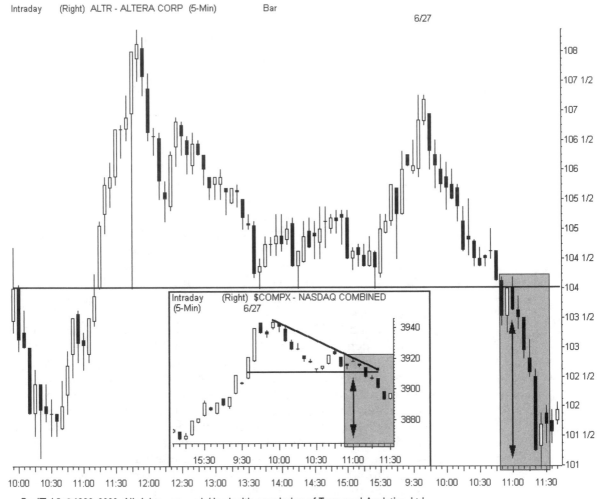

on divergent opinion. And the most profitable trades come in the most uncomfortable situations.

BUILDING EXECUTION SKILLS

Successful execution requires logic and simplicity. The 7-Bells and watch lists locate classic setups on the verge of sharp price expansion. Pattern Cycles measure op-

F I G U R E   15.4

Chiron swings repeatedly through short-term reversals on the 60-minute chart. Note how often price bars reach toward a new high or low but immediately jump back in the opposite direction. Only the trend from 34 to 43 rewards momentum players, while noisy violations and painful whipsaws mark the balance of chart activity.

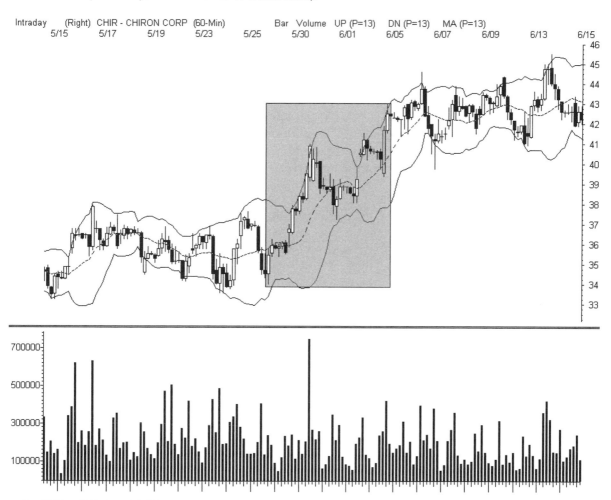

portunity through many time frames in a single glance. Time of day places the setup into a favorable or unfavorable cycle while the charting landscape focuses attention toward the lowest risk entry. Advancing price pierces the execution zone, and the swing trader pulls the trigger just as it strikes the execution target.

Consistent performance requires original thinking and seeing. Maintain an open mind and allow intuition to point out new trade prospects. Then apply execution tools to filter bias and confirm the obvious. Swing traders miss many opportunities when tactics depend on rigid definitions or narrow systems. Each setup looks different than the last one. Never trade anything the same way twice.

Avoid head games and just enter at the ET when a setup presents major convergence. The CV×4 represents one such profitable opportunity. When an ET cross-verifies in four or more ways, consider the trade on price alone. Setups produce a very high signal-to-noise ratio when they point repeatedly to a single number. This sharply raises the odds of a successful position. However, this strategy can also trigger major discomfort. It often requires buying a down gap or breaking a personal strategy rule. So take care to require narrow precision through each verifying element and pinpoint entry to within a few ticks. Then exercise defensive loss management should the trade go badly.

Experiment with many execution methods until they embed themselves firmly into your subconscious mind. Effortless entry comes when the skilled intellect can quickly digest complex information in original ways. Fortunately, the trading puzzle contains only a limited number of important pieces. Focus on those key concepts that exert influence over and over again. The trend-range axis, S/R, and cross-verification all define repeating tactics through each market session.

Indices point to key changes in market momentum. Individual stock trends will lead or lag major index movement. This important spread provides a quick reading of that stock's relative strength (as compared to the index) that signals convergence or divergence with the intended execution strategy. In turn, this relationship follows or opposes the current buying or selling bias. Together they align entry according to major market cycles.

Look for stocks that move more sharply than their related indices. This tendency gains importance when the index breaks into expansion. During general market rallies and selloffs, swing traders may have several promising stocks to choose from at the same time. Always trade the one that provides the highest reward potential at the lowest measurable risk. This favors stocks that lead the market at the time of execution. But first make sure that equity and index relate to each other in a logical way. For example, a large technology stock may compare well to the Nasdaq 100 but a small cap may not.

Price movement reacts to round market numbers. These whole numbers can trigger hours or days of swing activity when they strike during key cycles. One excellent way to find opportunity scans market action for stocks with above-average volume that trade at or near market numbers. Take the scan output, pull up the price chart and see how that number played out through past retracements. Extensive conflict at the barrier will spike volume and volatility upon its return. Note whether it previously acted as support, resistance, or a pivot. It will likely show the same characteristics on the next pass.

Intraday charts respond to whole numbers as well. In addition to multiples of 10, single digits act as swing levels for smaller-value and less volatile stocks. Stops congregate just beyond these numbers and trigger volatility spikes when hit. Look for a small penetration through each new number, followed by a short pullback. Tiny congestion patterns will appear on the 1-minute chart that use one side

F I G U R E   15.5

CMGI prints a high-odds CV×4 short sale pattern on this morning gap down. Note the converging elements: (1) Price breaks through the 62% retracement. (2) Price breaks the descending trendline. (3). Price gaps through major support. (4) The gap fills an opposing gap and completes an island reversal. Also note how the action on the first bar violates the whole number 50. This setup demands immediate execution as close to the opening price as possible.

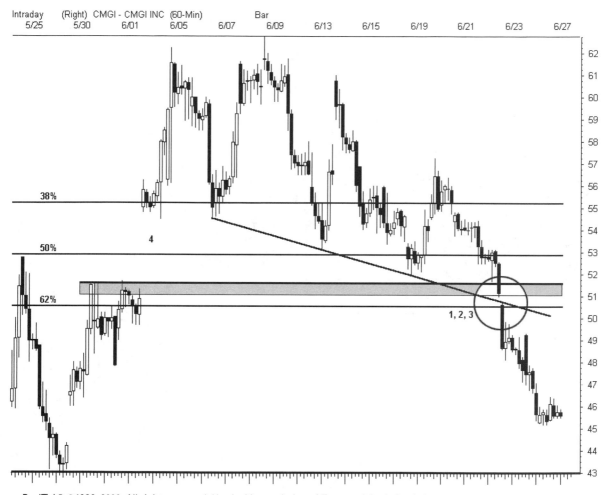

of the digit to draw S/R. Keep in mind that single numbers represent minor barriers that will get taken out easily when larger forces are at work.

First-hour range breakouts carry over an effective strategy from the futures markets. The high and low set from 9:30 a.m. to 10:30 a.m. often reflect key S/R for that day's action. Swing traders enter positions on breakouts above and below

Rambus swings continuously off whole numbers during these 2 days of violent price movement. Note the numerous candle shadows that reach across round levels but then jump back before the 5-minute close. This price action quickly cleans out mental and physical stops while it signals strong movement in the opposite direction. Focus trade execution on whole number S/R to improve timing.

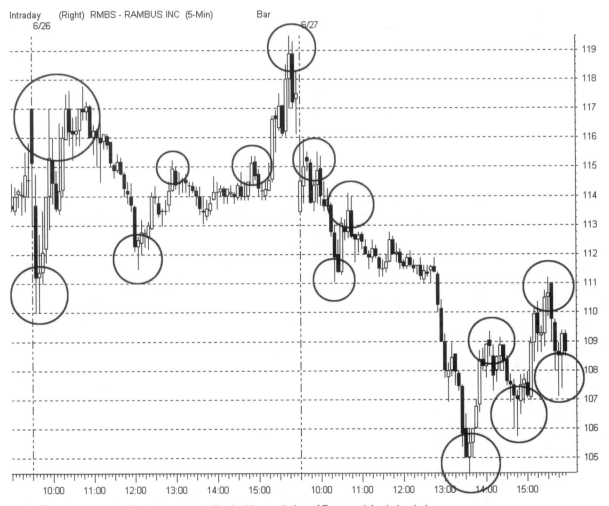

these levels or fade midday attempts to break through them. Classic pullbacks often follow first-hour breakouts and provide low-risk entry that relies on the same tactics as other types of S/R. Early range extremes may set up well past the first hour, so don't watch the clock too closely. These highs-lows as well as 2- and 3-day extremes all respond to the same execution tactics.

Keep intraday Fibonacci study simple. Even a single tick will print violations of classic retracement levels. Apply Fib grids to larger intraday trends and avoid using them for very short-term swings. Don't bother with any minor retracement levels. Apply only the 38%, 50%, and 62%. Stay aware of broader retracement levels on the daily chart and stay out of their way unless they are part of a larger strategy. Fibonacci exerts influence in many different ways, but don't go crazy looking for all of them. The best positions come to the swing trader, not the other way around.

Overlap Fib grids across several days of trading to locate hidden swing levels. The extremes between the last hour of one session and the first hour of the next offer clues to how far price will pull back before breaking through a first-hour range. Or lay a grid across the first-hour range to assist different breakout strategies. These fascinating trend measurements also define the charting landscape after sharp opening gaps. Fill areas frequently appear right at the 62% retracement and confirm a trend reversal if price action closes the hole.

Recognize and categorize each gap before planning a strategy to trade it. Consider that most gaps represent multiple-time frame events. The same price bar may signal a continuation move in one time frame and an exhaustion reversal in another. When a gap conflicts through different trends, it invokes major whipsaws and should be avoided. The price action shortly after a gap suggests how it will handle a first test. If bars thrust away from a new up gap immediately, it signifies demand that should produce a solid bounce on the first retracement. Price should not fill the gap unless that bounce fails and rolls over. When price immediately reverses after a new gap, it may fill quickly and keep going through a new expansion move in the opposite direction.

Learn to position trade profitably before considering intraday execution. Longer holding periods reduce risk and let newer participants apply tools in a less demanding environment. Build knowledge through lower-volatility stocks that move in slow motion. Regional phone carriers, utilities, and retail sectors offer clean trends that respond to classic technical analysis. But they react sluggishly and permit many trading errors with little penalty. Decrease position size, sit back, and work methodically through each analysis and execution without hurry. Then seek more aggressive positions after confidence grows and trade management becomes instinctive.

Day trading demands the skilled application of complex tools in a very noisy environment. Intraday profits require quick thinking, fast fingers, and advanced market knowledge. Many unqualified applicants fall into this difficult execution practice and fail miserably. The bright colors and flashing numbers of a real-time quote screen look just like a video game. But nothing could be further from the truth. Behind the numbers, a master game of trickery seeks to rob novice trading accounts. And the neophytes never realize that their survival depends on joining the insiders rather than fighting them.

Scalping and intraday swing trading constitute two different strategies. Some Nasdaq traders scalp tiny movement on the Level II bid-ask and 1-minute charts. This contrary practice works through the smallest oscillation available within the

FIGURE   15.7

Lay a Fib grid across the first hour range to identify natural intraday swing levels. ADC Telecommunications prints a 4-point morning range that persists through most of the session. Price draws a first rise pattern after the opening selloff and then pulls back to test the 62% retracement. A last-hour rally finally lifts price through the earlier highs and sets up a gap for the next morning.

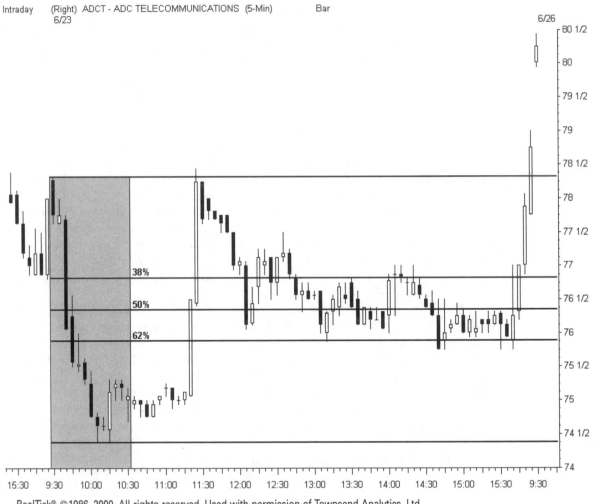

market day. But dozens of other intraday trends respond to classic swing tactics. Holding periods from 5 minutes to 6 hours capture many different opportunities. Even 15-minute to 30-minute positions offer better rewards than the teenies that occupy the scalping game. And swing traders can apply the same Pattern Cycle techniques on the 30-minute setup and the 3-week pattern.

F I G U R E   15.8

The head and shoulders pattern signals a profitable short sale on this low-volatility electric utility chart. Also note the pullbacks that reward precise entry with small gains during the 10-point rally. Neophytes build account size and gain needed experience when they trade stocks not favored by active or professional speculators.

Daily   (Right) TXU - TXU CORPORATION   Bar   UP (P=20)   DN (P=20)   MA (P=20)   MA (P=50)

PULLBACK EXECUTION

A promising stock takes off and rises sharply, but the swing trader misses the entry and watches in frustration as it clears one hurdle after another. Finally, the trend slowly stops and reverses. As the 5-minute chart shows a decline and selling pressure builds on the Level II screen, an important entry decision looms. Should the trader buy the pullback after missing the first opportunity or stand aside to avoid the risk of a false breakout?

Intraday trend pullbacks require both skill and patience to trade profitably. Some corrections or bear rallies persist, while others reverse quickly toward new highs or lows. So what signals determine which outcome is more likely? And what short-term tools predict how far a trend will retrace before the primary direction reassumes control?

The first pullback after a breakout or breakdown has high odds of rapidly ejecting in the direction of the new trend. But watch the countertrend depth closely for hidden obstacles. For example, if a correction breaks through several minor support levels before a bounce, the new rally will likely fail when price first tests the short-term high. This common scenario may still produce a good trade. With enough reward between the entry and short-term high, place a sell order 1/16 or 1/8 below the double top and ride the bounce into a quick fill.

Try a 6-out rule to measure and trade the first pullback. Start a count with the first bar lower than the parabolic extension of a new uptrend. The next leg should begin no later than the sixth congestion bar. Why does this work? Many intraday traders set their short-term chart indicators to periods that measure five to eight price bars. Six-bar corrections display short-term support at these common settings and induce participants to enter new positions. If price does not eject quickly, the next bar may signal a short-term trend change on many of these charts and trigger waves of reflex selling. This induces a larger-scale pullback that prints a more complex pattern before testing the price extension.

Odds increase that a breakout or breakdown will resume when the chart draws a pullback at a mirror angle to the new trend. For example, price often pulls back at a 45° slant after an uptrend prints at the same inclination. This angle reflection suggests a bull flag formation that will eject into a continuation move under most circumstances. If the pattern does not print clearly on the pullback but the angle is right, shift down to the next-lower time frame and see how it looks in that view. Flags often hide in this lower dimension.

Look for a small sideways pattern after sharp expansion through a breakout level. In an uptrend, this congestion prints near the upper price boundary and clings to it. These high, tight flags mark classic continuation patterns that can be used for low-risk trade execution. They also work well in bear markets after breakdowns. Apply the 6-out rule to manage this simple range. The next surge should not begin until signals flash across many chart screens. So execute on the fourth or fifth bar with a limit order deep within the small pattern. This order placement allows a cheap exit if the 6-out rule triggers a failure.

Intraday markets often correct in the classic ABC wave pattern. Countertrends to rallies follow a natural tendency to pull back, bounce, and then pull back again before finding support. Swing traders often fool themselves and jump on the first bounce rather than wait for a correction to completely unwind. This strategy may produce a profitable trade but it also incurs many trend relativity errors. The deeper a trend corrects, the less likely it will take out the old high or low quickly and break into another wave. For this reason, only tight and small ABC patterns provide dependable signals for new primary impulses.

F I G U R E   15.9

Two pullbacks offer fast profits on Phone.com. Price falls to a new low near the end of the lunch hour and then pulls back for trade execution before dropping 3 more points. It slowly climbs back to the old trendline, broken low, and 38% retracement. Price then pierces the top Bollinger Band and prints dark cloud cover on the 1-minute bars. Use the Adam and Eve pattern on the 1-minute chart to execute a quick short sale that yields another 2–3-point gain.

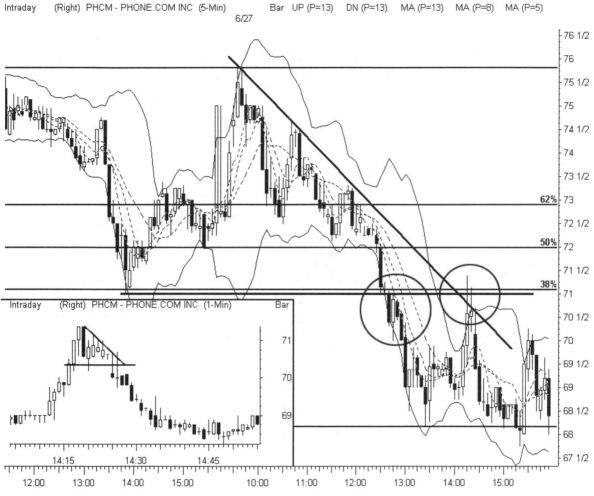

Measure the ABC pattern with a Fib grid. Because corrections tend to reverse at 38%, 50%, or 62%, well-formed waves may signal which level is most likely. As the pullback breaks into a C wave, target the extension by adding the length of the A wave to the starting point for the C wave. They often match size and project right into a major Fibonacci level. Or just wait until this pullback completes and prints a short-term reversal pattern, such as a double top or bottom. Then trade a

breakout in the opposite direction. Overlay grids of different trend lengths to improve accuracy. A 38-62 pattern targets major bounce zones and important reversals.
Expect whipsaws and a high level of market noise when different lengths don't
match up.

Apply swing strategy through ranges and momentum tactics through trends.
But don't get confused when buying a pullback. Dip buying in an uptrend actually

FIGURE   15.10

Ciena breaks to a new low and pulls back to test resistance. The small opening gap drops price below solid congestion between 155
and 160. It finds support at 150 and rises through an ABC bear rally. Note how the A and C waves print almost the same length. The
38% retracement marks an obvious short sale target with cross-verification from the gap and overhead supply. But several
whipsaws shake out early shorts until price action finally violates the intraday low.

signifies a swing trade. Execution takes place in the pullback's shorter time frame as price action moves in the opposite direction to the underlying rally. This time alignment provides safer entry than chasing price gains at new highs.

TRADE MANAGEMENT

Successful swing traders master both time and information. Their short-term speculation mines an attractive time/cash profile that allows greater profit than simple investment. But it also incurs heavier losses without highly-skilled execution and management.

PERFECT ENTRY

Short-term participants exploit individual quirks of market behavior that reveal themselves through Pattern Cycles. They measure reward:risk carefully, stay defensive at all times, and book high-probability profits. As holding period lengthens, they stand firm when small violations and whipsaws shake out weaker hands. They realize that the trend-range axis works through all time frames and all market conditions.

Success requires flexibility but not too many tactics at any given time. Experienced swing traders execute a few well-defined setups for weeks or months before the crowd catches up and forces a change in planning. Consistent profits don't require chasing the hottest stock or latest news. Lower beta issues make excellent trading vehicles with managed risk. Focus on taking a little money out of the market each day. Over time, it can lead to a sizable fortune.

Well-timed execution produces a very high percentage of profitable trades. Focus on optimizing entry and exit over all other considerations. Examine the time character of each part of the market day and align positions in accordance with its major cycles. For example, never buy weakness in the last hour if price is near the bottom of its daily range. Keep one eye on external events that can turn rallies into selloffs in a few seconds. Then believe the numbers and forget the news.

Remember this golden rule of swing trading: excellent entries on mediocre positions will make more money over time than bad entries on good positions. Consider execution of a single direct move rather than holding a stock through a nerve-wracking pullback. Increase share size to book a substantial profit but walk away quickly to manage risk. Or only scale in with part of a position and then wait for the next big price move. In either case, remember to enter in mild times and exit in wild times.

Learn to step in front of the crowd on pullbacks and behind it on breakouts. Always be ready to move against it when conditions favor a reversal. Stand aside when confusion reigns and the crowd lacks direction. Recognize herd emotions through the tape and become a student of their psychology. Every pattern has a natural breaking point where the crowd will lose control, give up, or show irrational exuberance. Find it and execute just before the curtain rises.

Use market orders to get in fast when positions can be managed closely in real-time. Place limit orders when active participation is not an option or when trading systems require them. These conditional orders also satisfy the need to bind decisions to specific numbers. They offer an excellent vehicle for strategy and risk-management. For example, place a limit order near the far side of an ET and walk away. It will trigger only if a low-risk opportunity appears. Pull the order and go on to the next trade if price doesn't reach that level.

Stay away from external information that does not advance trading performance. Avoid stock boards, financial TV, and the news ticker through most market sessions. Never mix fundamental and technical numbers: one lies while the other tells the truth. Watch out for personal bias that can affect short-term decisions. The end of the financial world may come soon, but probably not in the next 30 minutes or 3 days.

Focus on execution numbers and learn technology later. Swing trading requires broad skills and a solid understanding of the charting landscape. Modern technology makes a good trader better but will not bring success to a loser. As market software evolves, execution systems will become more transparent and less urgent to the active participant. This will never happen with swing tactics or strategies. Master the technology as your trading experience grows. But remember that long-term success requires highly original methods to beat the competition.

THE FILL MACHINE

Choose the swing trade broker-dealer wisely. Modern markets offer many routes for execution, and this selection will strongly impact results. Discount brokers charge lower commission rates in exchange for access to standard and wholesale order routing. The direct order interface costs more for each transaction but executes through ECNs and faster exchange systems. A new generation of broker-dealers features execution hybrids as well as fees based on single shares rather than fixed commissions.

Consider the impact of slippage and commission in your personal trading plan. This will rule out specific strategies and narrow broker choices. Invariably, newer traders underestimate these costs and miscalculate their performance. High transaction fees undermine profitable trading. The greatest impact comes from tactics that require high trade frequency or small share size. Alternatively, when swing traders execute small positions and hold them for longer periods, transaction costs take a smaller piece of the total profit.

Discount brokers work orders through a variety of market interfaces but favor the payment for order flow system. Large wholesale market makers contract with brokers to handle segments of their trading volume and receive a small fee for each transaction. Limit orders will appear on Level II screens through the wholesaler system. But trade execution depends on the quality of the contract between the broker-dealer and market maker. Many wholesalers provide guaranteed fills in ordinary markets. But participants rarely see price improvement through these executions, and they are plagued by late fill reports, broken trades, and missing stop orders.

Late fill reports adversely affect trade strategy. Avoid new intraday positions when fill reports don't return immediately after a marketable order. Extend holding period when using any discount broker interface. Minutes may pass in a volatile position before receiving trade confirmation. This builds risk because no exit can be taken until the position shows as active. Longer holds reduce the odds that mental stops will strike before receiving the fill report. In any case, change trading accounts or consider a direct-access interface if the broker consistently reports late fills.

Direct-access brokers combine ECN participation with advanced exchange order routing. Public posting through Level II takes place within 1–2 seconds after entering an inside order. An execution will be almost instantaneous when it crosses with another customer who trades in the opposite direction. Direct-access traders can buy on the bid and sell at the ask with ease in flat markets. But this practice becomes almost impossible during strong trends.

Modern advanced systems suffer from a lack of liquidity. ECNs depend on strong customer participation to enable cross-orders through all market tiers. Even with competing ECNs, only high-volume stocks exhibit enough interest to avoid major slippage. Swing traders who use these brokers must avoid stock setups that don't permit easy execution or they must choose longer holding periods where slippage will take a smaller bite. Direct access permits order broadcast directly to market makers and Instinet. This solves some liquidity problems, but these systems grind down in fast markets as participants quickly pull existing orders.

Neophytes gravitate toward expensive direct-access systems regardless of their needs. These colorful real-time screens mesmerize the unskilled brain as they blink market information. Developers purposely build this software to resemble a video game rather than a serious tool. Everyone wants to be a player and hopes that technology will compensate for lack of trading experience. And the forces behind these systems do little to discourage that fantasy. They present these terminals as ultimate power machines to their predominantly white male audience.

Many brokerage accounts cannot support full-blown software systems. They chew up capital quickly and encourage overtrading by those who can least afford it. They also build the illusion that Level II has major secrets to reveal. Many insiders present this valuable screen as a trading tool rather than execution tool. This has little basis in reality. The high noise-to-signal ratio masks longer-term buying and selling pressure while professionals cloak true demand so that no one can accurately predict the future beyond a few ticks.

Level II still offers a powerful execution system. ECNs shine when positions execute against the short-term trend. As markets turn, high liquidity allows instantaneous fills without slippage. Swing traders use these times to initiate strategies that fade the current emotions. Neophytes that don't require a full-blown execution system should still consider Level II access even if they use a discount broker.

Direct-access systems require a tactical shift by those who emigrate from discount brokers. The lack of guaranteed fills opens up new slippage danger and requires learning several new skills. Take the time to investigate the available routing methods and their limitations. New users should avoid the software's smart entry options that shop through various methods until the order executes. While this artificial intelligence saves brainpower and supports advanced trading strategies, it also works more slowly than direct ECN placement and can lead to trouble if a position moves away from the limit price. Apply basic routing first, and add smart routing after learning how these tools work in different market conditions.

Very small accounts should focus on transaction costs more than trade execution. Low capital may build fortunes, but the odds do not favor long-term success. Choose inexpensive Web-based quotes to control costs and rule out all forms of day trading. Take only small positions after extensive analysis and extend holding period to manage risk. Avoid multiple positions and don't be in a hurry. Seek one decent profit at a time before moving on to the next trade.

WATCHING ACTIVE POSITIONS

The moment of truth arrives. Price pierces the EZ and favorable conditions signal a possible ET entry. At that moment, swing traders must already know their position size and intended exit price if proven wrong. The ET strikes and they pull the trigger through a phone call, limit order, Web entry, or direct input. The fill report comes back and immediately forces a recalculation of setup assumptions. If execution occurs more than a tick away from the ET, reconfirm risk tolerance and recalculate the intended exit. Now the hard part begins.

Review the tape and chart to confirm that trade entry was the right choice. Set a physical stop if the personal trading plan lists that as part of the execution strategy. If not, mentally target the price and conditions under which the trade will be terminated. Update this instant analysis as each price bar prints and modifies the charting landscape.

Get out immediately if price hits the level where the trade proves to be wrong. The failure could turn out to be a whipsaw, but don't delay the exit in an effort to learn the truth. If a later performance review shows too many shakeout exits, revise the trading plan to give positions more room or locate better-risk targets. Remember that a setup can always be reentered. But make sure that each new entry stands on its own merits. This requires a fresh reward:risk calculation as well as a new ET. Keep in mind that trade reentry tends to fail because an initial shakeout often signals a pattern failure and change in trend.

Take losses manually whenever possible. This builds excellent discipline because the affirmative action accepts responsibility for the trade. It also recognizes that stop loss represents an evolving condition and not a fixed number. Each price

F I G U R E   15.11

Things can go wrong even when a trading opportunity fires on all cylinders. A breakout on good volume carries @Home above a 4-month down trendline. It then pulls back and surges above the 50-day EMA on even stronger volume. Unfortunately, that ends the rally. Swing traders should exit as soon as the gap fills and price falls back below the moving average. Waiting for further confirmation could lead to disaster. The trendline itself doesn't fail until the selloff carries down another 9 points.

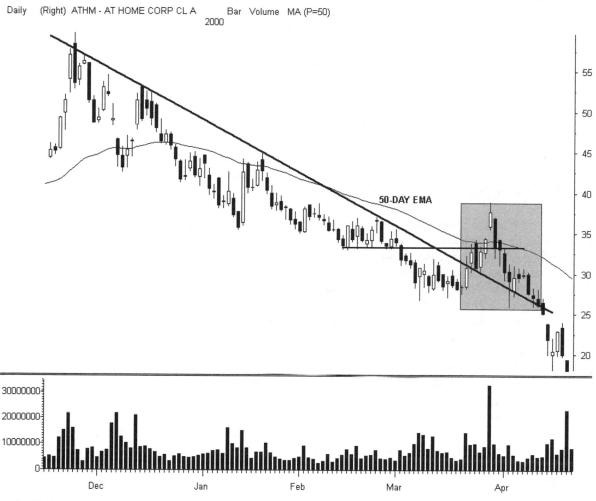

Daily   (Right) ATHM - AT HOME CORP CL A   Bar Volume MA (P=50)
2000

50-DAY EMA

bar, TICK reading, and time cycle affects the potential profit or loss for the trade. Physical stop loss can rarely hit this moving target accurately.

Always consider mental time stops. The longer that it takes for a position to move into a profit, the more likely that it never will. Target a predetermined holding period and dispose quickly of nonperforming trades. Watch out for positions that just move sideways into low volatility and die. Use the weak swing to get back transaction costs through a limit exit order if conditions permit. And keep one eye on the closing bell if strategy requires going flat regardless of profit or loss.

Intraday charts sketch feedback in real time. Watch the action and try to anticipate how individual candles will close. See how the buy and sell ticks affect the curvature of the surrounding Bollinger Bands. Watch out for thrusting candles that break through the center of the bands and signal shifting momentum. Look for small but significant gaps between candles at key price levels. Follow price movement to key S/R or MA levels and visualize an appropriate response if it violates them. Pick the point where the pattern says that the stock should eject into a profit. Anticipate the proper reaction if time passes quietly with no expansion.

Swing traders lose control when they overanalyze positions. Each entry must speak clearly for itself. If it has little to say, get out and move on quickly. As trades evolve, different indicators, tools, or times may assume leadership. Skill and experience pinpoint which one to follow for any given position. This process eases when both sides of the brain contribute to active trade management. An ominous feeling or a confident buzz represents a subconscious connection to the emotional crowd. Combine this gut feeling with solid numbers knowledge and then take what the market gives.

Follow the tape closely after entry. If you are trading momentum, price should keep trending as quickly as it did just prior to execution. Look for confirmation that selling pressure has eased after buying a pullback. Measure pulse and volume through the time and sales ticker. Then compare that to the associated price change. When a surge of participation does not move price, it can signal hidden supply that will trigger a reversal. Tape reading also means interpreting the spread. Watch how it expands and contracts as price searches for short-term boundaries.

Level II provides a comprehensive view of the major Nasdaq participants. But this information screen may be inappropriate for some trading styles. For example, the NYSE offers no similar information through its centralized specialist system. Many swing traders benefit when they can interpret the much simpler Level I tape. This summary display prints the outcome for all of the conflicting forces at work during the market day. Use Level I to measure narrowing spreads that follow rallies or selloffs and signal that the move has ended. Or find a quiet tape with tightening spreads and dull transaction levels. These can provide excellent scalps or low-risk entry in anticipation of a breakout.

The 5-8-13 Bollinger Bands encase intraday candles in a continuous feedback mechanism. Throughout the day, these settings measure the strength and direction of a stock's short-term trend with little effort. Dynamic moves hug the 5-bar, healthy pullbacks move to the 8-bar, and violation of the 13-bar center band signals a possible change in trend. Keep in mind that this central axis defines the interface between very short-term bull and bear markets. Use BBs, first-hour range, and other charting landscape features to quickly locate danger points after entry. Always consider exit as soon as price pushes into a new S/R barrier, such as a band extreme or major high.

Position size must reflect several strategies. First, it must match the odds that a particular setup will succeed. More points of cross-verification naturally lead to

F I G U R E   15.12

The 5-8-13 Bollinger Bands and a few well-placed lines build intraday trading profits. Technical themes focus price action on specific ejection points. Locate these in advance with simple trendlines and time of day analysis. Then manage open positions with a sharp focus on price movement through the bands and averages. Notice how the 5- and 8-bar MAs support active trends while pullbacks to the 13-bar signal rangebound conditions.

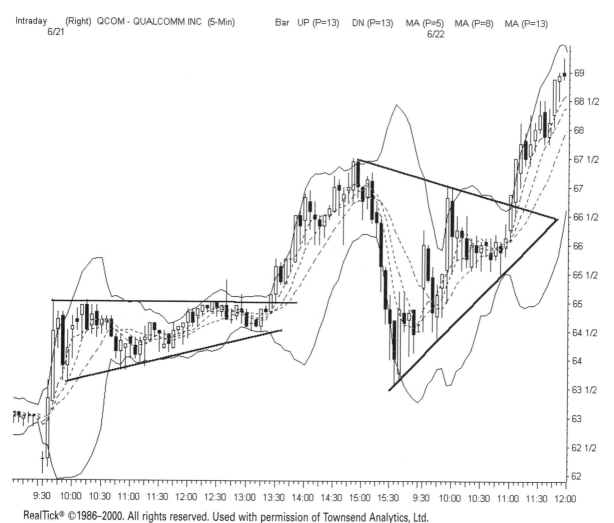

larger positions while a lack of clear signals encourages smaller bets. Second, size reflects the swing trader's experience level and choice of tactics. While seasoned participants tend to take larger positions, they may go the other way. Drawdowns, longer holds, and higher-volatility markets all suggest smaller positions to manage risk. Experienced participants respond to these environmental changes faster than most novices.

Neophytes should take small positions to avoid trouble. Many inexperienced traders ignore sound risk management and trade size well above their ability. Because they open margin accounts, they believe that the total buying power must be committed for every trade. This is dangerous and inaccurate. Strategy dictates that each position have a right share size, regardless of trading account capital. During winning streaks, increase position size as performance suggests reduced risk. When experiencing major drawdowns, lighten up significantly until the clouds pass. Newer participants should concentrate on learning to trade well and not worry too much about making money.

EXIT

Swing traders exit positions to book profits, take losses, or terminate poor opportunities. How well they accomplish these important tasks affects trading capital significantly. Graceful exits require discipline just as peaking emotions cloud judgment. So take a deep breath and clear your mind before attempting to close out a trade. A good exit is far more valuable than a great entry.

Get out immediately when proven wrong. Identify this trigger price before position entry. The failure target (FT) signals that a setup has collapsed and the trade must be broken. S/R violations point to natural FTs. Intraday traders see them when price crosses primary moving averages or prints a pattern rollover. Position traders find them in first rise/first failure events and false breakouts. Good reasons arise to alter FT values after execution, but many traders risk deceiving themselves when they do so. Rely on the written plan and leave FTs intact until experience allows greater flexibility.

Take profits when the market allows them. Try to exit as advancing price approaches a strong barrier. Choose a profit target (PT) during the initial reward: risk evaluation, but reconsider that location as each price bar offers new information. Pullbacks can begin at any time. Waiting through a retracement will draw down good gains unless the strategy includes holding through several price waves. The best exits come when the crowd leans the other way.

Good exit doors open and close throughout the trading day. After missing one, immediately determine the next available course of action. Sometimes swing traders must take their medicine and get out no matter where they are. This may hurt the bottom line but still present the best strategy under the circumstances. Perhaps a long position pushes into a nice gain but then suddenly catches a deep pullback. As it breaks back to even, end the trade right there, or risk a small loss and wait for the new swing back up. The right choice often comes only with experience. Some pullbacks will surely bounce while others drop into the pit of hell.

Become the deer and it's bye-bye Bambi. Our antlered friends freeze in the headlights of oncoming vehicles and pay a gruesome price. Swing traders face the same result when they don't respond quickly to danger. For example, a hot stock gaps up and a neophyte buys the opening rally. External shock hits and the market

Two Ariba setups highlight the importance of well-chosen profit and failure targets. Enter the small 3rd watch on the congestion bar before the breakout or as close to the trendline as possible. Use the low of the prior candle for the FT. The initial PT targets a first surge over the top Bollinger Band because no other resistance appears on the landscape. A dip trip follows a month later with execution right on the pullback test at 105. The FT stands just under the June 12 high in the 3rd watch, and the PT reflects the increased risk as soon as price pulls back within the bottom Bollinger Band.

Daily   (Right)   ARBA - ARIBA INC   Bar   UP (P=20)   DN (P=20)   MA (P=20)
2000

starts to sell off. A few bad decisions during the next 15 minutes can easily force the end of that new career.

The first natural reaction to shock is disbelief and denial. Unfortunately, this inhibits quick defensive action. Prior visualization pays strong dividends at times like these. Swing traders that mentally practice their fire drill over and over will act automatically when the right time comes. Simply put, they get out first and ask questions later when their positions go into freefall. They don't wait for a bounce, a reason, or Mommy to come hold their hands. They grab the nearest exit door they can find and run. Someone inside just screamed FIRE!

Big losses rarely come without warning. Technical analysis tools provide early clues to reversal activity if the swing trader is willing to listen. Most well-defined patterns offer clean S/R lines that signal trend change when broken. Gaps provide instant one-bar feedback on momentum shifts. Overbought-oversold oscillators point to divergence between price and buying power. And a clearly defined personal plan identifies risk tolerance and specific exit filters well in advance of trouble.

Locate, evaluate, enter, analyze, and exit. Within the 5-minute or daily charting landscape, opportunities rise to the surface and trigger positions that will book profits or incur losses. Swing traders don't hold positions through adversity unless strategy targets two or more price waves and uses at least 2 hours of the market day. The 90-minute alternation cycle encourages the single direct move for positions under this time frame. Longer-term tactics benefit from position-oriented exit styles, such as holding through minor retracements and whipsaws. Scalpers and short-term opportunists don't have this luxury. They must escape on the bar that expands into resistance or one that violates a key moving average.

Swing traders throw away gains when they change their holding periods midstream or forget the important numbers. When a position moves into a profit, greed exerts a strong emotional force that can trigger violation of important personal rules. This makes no sense, since they were created to manage situations just like this. The odds favor thoughtful rules. Don't dwell on those times when breaking them would have increased profits for an individual position. They are filters to build longevity in the trading game.

BEATING THE GAME

The odds stand firmly against long-term trading success. Many novices set out on the path to market knowledge each year. Most soon realize that swing trading presents the most difficult challenge of their lives. This simple fact sends the majority to the locker room with their tails between their legs. But a handful of serious aspirants stays in the game long enough to learn successful execution skills. Will you be one of the winners or one of the losers?

Trading styles change flavor according to the latest software or media spin. For example, Nasdaq Level II took center stage when Net technology boomed in the late 1990s. But classic swing trading techniques precede direct-entry systems by many decades. Over the years, technical analysis and chart reading have spun off

F I G U R E   15.14

Mortal danger can come at any time and with little warning. Intermedia Communications starts the day on a positive note after a very strong rally during the prior session. It builds a bullish triangle through the lunch hour as many speculators prepare for the rocket ship to take off again. But ICIX has other plans. It begins a slow afternoon decline that suddenly accelerates into a total freefall. Those who stick around to find an explanation have no choice but to take an exit in the mid 30s.

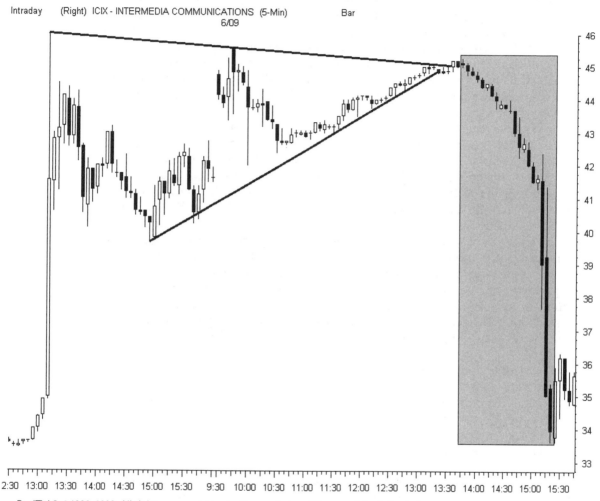

Intraday   (Right) ICIX - INTERMEDIA COMMUNICATIONS (5-Min)   Bar
6/09

the vast majority of profitable market strategies. Technical trading dominates the futures markets to this day. Of course, they don't have much choice, as there are no market makers to follow or Axes to grind in that volatile arena.

Consistent profits require standing against the restless crowd. This requires a level of courage that most aspirants cannot achieve. Start to build this skill early and practice it at every opportunity. Most market professionals quietly use the stock chart to locate and execute outstanding trade setups. They learn the secrets of this classic art and set themselves apart from the uninformed herd. After all, that's the pocket they try to pick each day.

The markets offer a bipolar experience. Swing traders experience winning and losing on a regular basis regardless of ultimate success. This emotional rollercoaster drives many hopeful participants out of the game quickly. The testosterone culture instills an overwhelming desire to win throughout the Western world. No matter how effectively participants take their losses, negative emotions will always follow an unfruitful exit. Perhaps this is why the feminine principle (regardless of one's actual persuasion) offers valuable lessons for any trading style. Accept gain and loss equally. Nurture and grow profits and skills. Bear the weight of bad positions with maturity and good humor.

Build trader wisdom into your personal plan and internalize it. Old market clichés work because truth rarely changes over time. Read classic technical books such as John Murphy's *Technical Analysis of the Financial Markets*, Edwards and Magee's *Technical Analysis of Stock Trends*, and Alexander Elder's *Trading for a Living*. They permit far more focus on specific issues and strategies than any website or weekend seminar. Broaden market knowledge every day and hone that solid edge over your competition.

Cut losses quickly and learn from mental mistakes, bad decisions, and lousy executions. Don't trade when personal problems use up time and physical energy. Remember that a lack of discipline ends trading careers far more efficiently than a lack of knowledge. Avoid overtrading. The slow bleed will destroy capital and dull the mind to real opportunity. Find an experienced mentor or sit at a guru's feet, and ask about bad habits and losing strategies. But make sure your mentor really knows how to play the game before the questions begin. Bad teachers yield very bad results.

Most new traders don't want others to share in their errors. They avoid mentoring programs that will contribute to success, just to avoid embarrassment. They'd rather commit their errors in private and hope they learn their lessons anyway. This mistake costs many novices their trading careers. Find that mentor before taking the very first execution. Confess all sins in detail and don't lie about gains or losses. The guidance you receive will save you a fortune in money and months of frustration.

The current trading strategy won't work in 6 months or a year from now. Write it down and make it a living document of professional growth. Put it into a word processor, revise it often, and save the old copies. Compare the current style to previous tactics frequently. This helpful exercise shocks most traders. True market knowledge takes years to build, and most aspirants venture into many dark corners before finding their natural bias.

The personal plan goes far beyond simple charts and setups. Successful trading exhibits grace in action. This venerable practice closely aligns with the Eastern concepts of meditation and yoga. Like a skilled musician, learn to play each note perfectly rather than considering the whole piece. Remember the joke about the tourist who asks how to get to Carnegie Hall: the answer is practice, practice, practice.

Don't fall into the complexity trap. Some participants buy expensive chart systems to test, back-test, smooth, and optimize complex trading systems. While this process works well with specific tactics, it often reflects an inability to take personal responsibility for one's results. The best opportunities always sit right under the trader's nose. They set up now the same way they did 50 years ago and will likely book profits for our grandchildren in another 50 years. Just throw away the software and trade when the perfect setup appears.

The market chase arises from the desire to free oneself from the rat race of the business world. The media reinforce this noble pursuit when they characterize modern traders as rogues and renegades. Who would turn down living the bandit's life after spending 20 years at the company water cooler? But the doors to wealth open only for those traders who play the game with great skill. Most will eventually fail and be forced to search elsewhere for the golden goose.

A little Zen: Before enlightenment, chopping wood and carrying water. After enlightenment, chopping wood and carrying water. Intelligent people learn many skills during their lives, and trading mastery is like any other discipline, only far more difficult. Those who succeed find an unexpected world. Their excitement fades and trading becomes like any other profession. This is natural. The true masters of the game enjoy their market power but find new ways to explore life's goals.

MASTERING THE TAPE

Swing traders learn to read the ticker tape as effectively as the price chart. While this education may take years, it requires little complexity. Just pick some favorite stocks and memorize key S/R levels. Then watch the ticker until odd behavior catches your eye. Notice how participation often spikes sharply as price approaches natural swing levels. Marvel at how the tape both hides and reveals the next move all at the same time. Pay extra attention when price enters an execution zone. Observe how the tape reacts and see whether key reversals can be predicted in advance.

ECNs AND DIRECT ACCESS

The direct-access environment forces swing traders to learn new skills. This high-tech interface allows orders to cross directly between retail participants or be broadcast in real time to a variety of commercial players. But it offers few guarantees and carries considerable risk in the wrong hands. Complex order routing can induce substantial losses, while careless entries can produce repeated partial fills. But direct-access benefits far outweigh the risks because it bypasses the expensive market middleman. So most serious participants should eventually face the music and learn this machine language for order execution.

Direct access is the playground of the ECN (electronic communications network). But many participants who come from e-brokers have a poor understanding of how these systems work. They become so dependent on the market middleman that they automatically expect ECNs to execute their orders when placed at the inside market. Unfortunately no ECN order fills without a matching customer order. Swing traders who play in markets with little ECN depth risk getting caught in major downdrafts without any means to escape their positions.

Direct-access brokers charge higher average commissions than e-brokers. Swing traders must overcome this disadvantage through execution technique. Work on placing orders that go slightly against the short-term flow so that fills cross the spread a large percentage of the time. While some discounters permit clients to buy at the bid or sell at the ask through limit orders, direct access provides real-time fill reports and incredible speed. Participants can place orders or lift them in seconds as conditions change. They can cross a newly placed ECN order instantly or execute in pieces to obtain a better average price. Lethargic software and a series of middlemen make this rapid response impossible through the typical discount broker.

The direct access trader must understand the Island book to manage liquidity issues. Island currently has the greatest depth of any retail ECN and publishes its order book in real-time free of charge. Always check there first for crowd participation before entering a new position. Look for many order tiers and watch how they change as the stock moves. This simple exercise predicts execution liquidity. Remember that the crowd has more discretion when it enters a position than when it exits. Make sure the Island book shows plenty of warm bodies to hand over a stock when it's time to say goodbye.

Learn to execute efficiently against the Island book. Confirm liquidity and follow the ISLD ticker on the Level II display. Retail traffic drives this ECN and orders that stack up on either side of the market provide great feedback on current supply-demand imbalance. Realize that once the stack appears, efficient fills in that direction become unlikely until the swing completes and shifts back in the other direction. Try to wait for a pullback rather than chasing an execution. The Island crowd includes many scalpers who run for the hills as soon as very short-term momentum fades.

Island tends to issue many partial fills. Avoid these by checking the book for very small orders embedded between more active entries. Those stuck with these tiny positions often place limit orders well away from the inside market to dump them at the first opportunity. This may take days. So this game of hot potato goes on endlessly from one participant to the next. Fortunately, the book displays most of these infuriating shares so that smart traders can stand aside or apply alternate routing methods when they see them.

Trade through the oldest and largest ECN when strategy permits. Instinet offers commercial customers anonymity and great depth. Retail traders will find Instinet expensive to access but a necessary evil. INCA often stands at the inside

F I G U R E   15.15

Large Nasdaq stocks exhibit great ECN depth and liquidity. This will spread to more issues and other exchanges as these popular execution systems gain acceptance and find their way into discount order interfaces. But beware of partial fills that chew up commissions and waste attention. Note how order size as low as four shares waits to trap unsuspecting participants.

AMAT - APPLIED MATERIALS

740441	36 7/16	600	11:10:25	746341	36 9/16	200	11:10:26
743241	36 7/16	100	11:09:35	E 725182	36 9/16	200	11:09:24
738295	36 7/16	90	11:08:14	743249	36 5/8	100	11:09:35
738369	36 7/16	30	11:08:15	712233	36 15/16	2,000	11:01:35
E 725831	36 3/8	30	11:05:12	729524	37	425	11:05:48
730413	36 1/4	500	11:06:02	696603	37	200	10:58:09
736988	36 1/4	300	11:07:53	705886	37	36	11:00:11
103403	36 1/16	600	09:18:19	723279	37	20	11:04:10
121566	36 1/16	200	09:25:46	641008	37 1/16	500	10:44:34
384788	36	500	10:03:01	547224	37 1/8	100	10:26:59
105203	36	500	09:20:28	568648	37 1/4	200	10:30:51
109102	36	200	09:21:21	547626	37 1/4	200	10:27:04
108693	36	150	09:21:16	617400	37 1/4	50	10:39:37
566024	36	100	10:30:21	546826	37 5/16	240	10:26:55
534132	36	100	10:24:38	519118	37 7/16	1,200	10:22:22
508667	36	100	10:20:44	510772	37 7/16	100	10:21:04
445092	36	100	10:11:18	E 141769	37 7/16	100	09:32:17
109067	36	100	09:21:21	319809	37 7/16	60	09:54:12
108291	36	100	09:21:14	483740	37 1/2	3,000	10:17:02
107782	36	100	09:21:11	534581	37 1/2	900	10:24:42
69631	36	90	08:53:08	719298	37 1/2	100	11:03:09
40730	36	75	07:58:21	579418	37 1/2	50	10:32:35
319862	36	50	09:54:13	395107	37 5/8	200	10:04:29
108352	36	10	09:21:14	733156	37 5/8	100	11:06:47
66098	35 15/16	1,000	08:45:29	197069	37 5/8	15	09:38:57
729938	35 3/4	350	11:05:55	485107	37 3/4	2,000	10:17:13
104530	35 3/4	300	09:19:39	65572	37 3/4	1,000	08:44:00
224959	35 3/4	200	09:42:04	518052	37 3/4	230	10:22:13
108261	35 9/16	600	09:21:14	105753	37 3/4	145	09:21:01
669366	35 17/32	25	10:50:57	692803	38	250	10:57:11
47801	35 1/2	5,000	07:59:12	495896	38	200	10:18:47
463923	35 1/2	150	10:14:06	268429	38	200	09:47:16
109078	35 5/16	300	09:21:21	43200	38	175	07:58:34
53387	35 1/4	250	08:07:09	449393	38	100	10:11:56
549922	35 1/4	200	10:27:28	296080	38	100	09:51:15
109316	35 1/16	600	09:21:28	108163	38	100	09:21:13
109315	35 1/16	300	09:21:28	100912	38	100	09:15:30
719358	35	200	11:03:10	108941	38	80	09:21:19
104289	35	200	09:19:19	570165	38	60	10:31:07
37654	35	200	07:58:05	108280	38	60	09:21:14
269939	35	171	09:47:28	108127	38	50	09:21:13
50898	35	150	08:00:04	107711	38	4	09:21:11
248191	35	100	09:44:53	294386	38 3/16	500	09:51:00
210173	35	100	09:40:24	46664	38 1/4	100	07:59:00
108563	35	100	09:21:15	624758	38 1/4	50	10:41:10
108287	35	100	09:21:14	33738	38 3/8	250	07:57:47

market when no other player steps forward. Their solo participation can represent institutions that buy or sell according to their own logic or market makers that hide behind the ECN to mask their real intentions. In either case, INCA's massive liquidity lets swing traders in and out of positions when no other parties will touch the orders.

Consider standing aside when direct access offers no favorable execution price. The personal trading plan needs to manage the additional risk of using this environment. New positions require liquidity to enter and assume liquidity to exit. Fast-paced markets force instant analysis of these changing conditions. Recalculate reward:risk quickly when a position will not fill according to original planning. For obvious reasons, choose to enter the most promising setups at less advantageous prices but require precision for all borderline opportunities.

Direct-access exits face more danger than entries. This interface requires that participants take an available exit door before it disappears. Many selloffs and short-covering rallies erupt with little warning. The sudden volatility dries up liquidity in one direction as the retail crowd quickly lifts orders. The ensuing vacuum forces price up or down to the next S/R where the swing completes. This induces major slippage unless the swing trader takes immediate action. Place an order slightly above or below the current inside market to encourage a quick fill. If it doesn't execute immediately, pull the order and resubmit it further away from the current quote until it does. Also, consider smart routing methods that may improve the odds for a quick exit in these volatile conditions.

Try to exit winners while the move is still in progress. ECNs offer dramatic price improvement during these fast conditions. For example, use sharp rallies to place sell orders one-quarter to one-half of a point above the inside ask. The excitement generates greed, which encourages dumb orders from those in a hurry to get into the stock. Smart players willingly exit into these anxious hands to increase profit. But act quickly. Other participants will use the same tactics and start to undercut orders to get out. This will eventually short circuit the rally and could trigger a deep pullback.

Trade slower stocks and build comfort with complex direct-access tools before attempting more volatile positions. The Nasdaq 100 components offer many issues with stable characteristics and consistent price movement. These provide a great learning ground for rapid execution methods. Gain experience and then look for other markets that show good depth and allow conservative risk management. At all times, develop a sense of where to find the escape hatch and when to run for it.

THE TAPE

Swing traders now access three levels of ticker tape information. At one time market professionals relied solely on the scrolling ticker. This early version of what now flashes across the bottom of financial TV screens followed transactions rather than individual stock activity. This simple solution worked very well when there were only a limited number of issues to track each day. This scroll survives in modern software but has little use in its generic form. However, it can effectively capture important institutional and block trading bias when data first pass through narrow size barriers.

Level I introduced real-time data that display the inside bid-ask and individual trades for each issue. All major exchanges currently provide this real-time information for capture by quote vendors. Many successful traders still rely on Level

I alone for reading the tape. Rather than deal with market complexity, this summary information digests the ongoing battle between bulls and bears. It resolves winners and losers at each turn while trading rhythm pulses through the unit transaction display. Level I has grown substantially since its release. Increased processing power and lower data costs triggered the addition of historical time and sales grids as well as other sophisticated features that enhance the original product.

Nasdaq Level II revolutionized trade data with a central display that tracks all of the key players in a single market. Vendors and other wise men insist that LII will reveal great market secrets through correct interpretation. Unfortunately, most of this hype lacks truth. This valuable tool usually tracks only very short-term buying and selling behavior. But it does permit highly effective tape reading when combined with swing levels on the intraday chart. It also allows direct-access traders to determine available execution levels through tier depth and order flow.

More detailed information does not necessarily improve trading results. Level II emits substantial data on market makers and the size of their markets. Unfortunately, this may focus the swing trader on the process rather than the result. The final resolution of short-term price competition presents more valuable signals than many of the indecisive battles to get there. Pay greater attention to the inside market than the outside order flow. Watch price development on the time and sales ticker more closely than the Axe or INCA.

Always look outside the tape flow before execution. Time of day, market sentiment, characteristics of a particular stock, and chart swing levels all affect the reliability of transaction data. Keep in mind that skilled tape reading depends on one key observation to locate profitable signals: insiders consistently move their markets in whatever direction yields the greatest volume. The most basic tape mechanics manipulate crowd emotions against the order flow coming in the door.

Understand the many ways that professionals manipulate the markets. They always keep one eye on their stock and the other on external conditions that affect price. They apply knowledge of the order book to bend the tape towards the highest potential volume in an effort to trigger execution. The lunch hour, holidays, and other quiet times offer prime conditions to gun key support and trigger common stop locations. During long rangebound phases, they can push price toward important levels with very little volume and test the breakout waters to see how much new interest they can generate.

Filter the ticker tape's message through TICK, market breadth, and index charts. Measure convergence-divergence between these indicators and the tape's order flow. For example, stocks often track related index movement. The tape on an individual issue should reflect agitation and excitement as it responds to an index breakout. Also, a very strong tape can ring a very loud bell in a weak market. The activity may uncover impending news or major insider knowledge.

Profit or loss results from four basic activities: picking a promising market, choosing to go long or short, finding a point of entry, and exiting the position. Swing trading depends on skilled tape reading to accomplish each of these important tasks successfully. Numbers provide fuel for the markets. Core values and their rate of change over time characterize all stock trends. Observation of price pulses

on the time and sales log or Level II screen offers highly accurate short-term prediction, when used in conjunction with other tools. Just as the chart uncovers hidden patterns of herd behavior, greed and fear reveal themselves quickly through
the rapid bursts seen on the ticker tape.

The bid-ask spread tracks underlying supply and demand within the ticker
tape. For years, it also represented a market middleman who was certain to get a
substantial cut before allowing an investor the right of passage into their chosen
stock. This unfortunate and inequitable system has evolved substantially over the
past few years. Class action suits, ECNs, and alternative markets combined to
shorten the distance between a security's buy and sell prices. This positive trend
will surely continue, and a single unified price or spread as low as one penny may
guide market transactions in the future.

The spread engine compresses and expands constantly as it responds to shifting market conditions. But most bid-ask movement emits only noise and won't
predict future price movement. While a scalper can execute an inefficient spread to
grab a quick profit, the swing trader must stand aside and wait for clearer opportunity. The spread will issue directional signals at times and generate rewarding
entries.

Bid-ask distributes market transactions and helps establish fair value for equities. This complex mechanism frustrates participants because all executions require hitting a moving target. Nasdaq spreads arise from competition between all
participants. NYSE specialists and their order book control that exchange's bid-ask
display, although third markets impact their unique auction. The spread emanates
both price and volume components that shift according to demand, manipulation,
and legal necessity.

Learn to read the spread through each component's relative strength. Bid and
ask present strong, neutral, or weak states at any given time. For example, strong
bid reflects intense buying interest through many participants stacked up for execution or a very high number of displayed shares. Weak bid shows little support
through few participants and low displayed shares. Neutral bid prints a mixed
picture with little conviction one way or the other.

Compare the strength of one side of the spread against the other to predict
very short-term movement. When strength meets weakness, look for price to break
through the weak direction. When both sides show similar demand, it represents a
standoff. Neutral interest on one side of the market offers few directional clues
when it combines with strong or weak conditions on the other side. Keep in mind
that this short-term information will only predict the next tick or two in most cases.
But this micro-momentum can fine-tune trade execution and offer important clues
near major S/R extremes.

Price may test a major S/R level repeatedly before the barrier breaks. Watch
the spread as it strikes these important levels to see how supply-demand plays out.
Consider any defense that shows up to maintain the boundary and whether
counter-force looks ready to oppose it. Which side seems more determined in the
conflict? These battles can play out for hours at major price points before one side
yields.

Take time to learn the spread profile for each trading vehicle. When conditions generate volatility or imbalance, the bid-ask range widens and price tends to surge farther on fewer shares. While this movement can be nerve-wracking, the mechanism provides a good part of the price swing that setups depend upon each day. Wide spreads make great partners when positions sit on the right side of the action, but they induce misery when the market heads the wrong way.

The electronic markets operate differently than the listed exchanges. Nasdaq Level I shows only the best bid-ask that underlies their competitive market maker system, while Level II lists all the players chasing the inside price. A single specialist and several third party exchanges direct the price action on the NYSE. The size of available shares shown on the tape tends to be accurate on the listed exchanges. But Nasdaq size remains highly deceptive. While the drab 10×10 mystery lots of previous years have disappeared, exchange rules distort spreads to profit insiders but hurt both investors and traders.

Although the marketplace ultimately decides price direction, market professionals constantly use inside knowledge to trigger volume and profit their own accounts. Specialists have the little black book that shows the location and size of all stop orders. Market makers have a similar advantage through Level III and advanced Instinet terminals. In the absence of more pressing market conditions, insiders will always push price in the direction that yields the most volume or the one that sets up their own accounts for the most gain.

A neutral to neutral-negative bid-ask or high volume, strongly negative bid-ask provides the most supportive environment to catch falling knives and go long. In neutral markets, cash waits for opportunity and price can jump quickly when it strikes. And very active markets with wide, highly negative spreads often signal short-term bottoms that offer quick bounce profits. But never execute on spread alone. Enter these high-risk trades only after cross-verification confirms a major reversal opportunity.

LEVEL II

Use the Level II screen to fine-tune the execution target. As price pierces the execution zone, shift focus to very short-term action in anticipation of the new entry. Observe the intraday chart and pay close attention to the outer LII tiers where the ET resides. This allows preliminary S/R analysis before price reaches the target. At times these levels will offer few clues. But they may show other participants ready to trade the same opportunity.

One final look at Level II can confirm or refute the trade when price strikes the ET. Strong demand in the intended direction may not offer the best entry, since the new order must sit in a queue. Very often the best conditions show price with only moderate support that refuses to get taken out by opposing force. This suggests hidden interest in the expected direction that still allows precise execution at the target. Every situation requires a different approach. It makes little sense to miss an excellent opportunity just because other participants see it. But stepping in front of the crowd before it acts offers less risk and better odds for the position.

Level II presents the complex interface between knowledge of a stock chart and execution of a specific trading strategy. Consistent profits require skill and insight into both market disciplines. Excellent chart technicians will lose money through tape reading incompetence. Expert screen readers can make the small play but miss out on the big opportunity. Successful swing traders master the charting landscape but manage execution through Level II.

No two markets trade alike. After uncovering a new opportunity, take the next step and learn that stock's action profile. Observe price movement through Level II and check out important risk characteristics. Look at the depth of ECN participation and which market makers actively spend time at the inside bid-ask. Measure volatility through the natural width of a price swing in a quiet market. For example, if a $50 stock moves back and forth 2 points in a few minutes, it displays much higher risk than one that swings three-eights of a point in an hour.

Then watch the same stock in a fast market. Observe how quickly bids disappear during a selloff. See how many points the stock can rise or fall in 2–3 minutes. Does posted size appear to reflect reality, or do participants constantly refresh with new offerings? Does price appear to swing at natural chart levels, or does Level II have its own internal S/R logic? Look at participation a few tiers to the outside. An active market here suggests good depth and interest.

A promising setup may generate great excitement but have undesirable tape action. Opportunities need to fire on all cylinders to produce profits. If Level II does not support the pattern, wait for better confirmation or move on to the next setup. When the tape presents a mixed message, don't hesitate to enter the trade, but first recalculate reward:risk based on this new challenge. Often the tape will lag the pattern itself. In other words, the setup first moves in the intended direction and then builds excitement that pulses on the LII screen.

Interpret the Level II screen with answers to these important questions:

- How do the spreads move and who is moving them?
- How do they widen and contract?
- At what times of day does the stock tend to act or react?
- When does it reach intermediate highs or lows?
- How easily does it violate the first hour range?
- What happens during the first and last 15 minutes of the market day?
- What happens during lunch hour?
- How easily does it gap from close to open?

Level II will cross-verify stock chart observations, improve reward:risk profile significantly, and add to profits. Prepare a classic swing trade at S/R when tape momentum moves counter to the intended entry direction but volume starts to fade. Confirm a breakout when Level II shows strong evidence of synchronization in the direction of the setup. Bulls must observe underlying strength through small pullbacks, while bears see distribution interrupted only by feeble rallies or short squeezes.

Many swing traders ignore the time and sales log to concentrate on a chart's more attractive graphics. But the rapid flow of individual sales transactions offers vital information on breakouts, reversals, and other market swings. Bar charts also lack data on changing spreads and how that underlying tension may resolve into price change. Use Level II in conjunction with time and sales to look for clues to the market markers' intentions, how they interact with each other, and their trading bias.

MARKET LIES

The markets lie in many ways. Price can shoot above resistance, draw intense buying interest that exhibits all the signs of a breakout, and then suddenly drop back into a range. Patterns can show perfection but never leads to trends. Level II sellers can stack up high on each other and watch the market head straight up. Deception shadows every legitimate move, and fakeout follows every real observation.

FAKEOUTS

Insiders deceive because deception works. Instructional books and the media tutor neophytes on the financial world's many rules and regulations. But they do a poor job communicating the shades of truth that move modern markets. For every action there is an equal and opposite reaction. Insiders have little motivation to carry price directly toward the current fair value. They grab better profits along the way by taking two steps forward followed by one step back. Eventually they reach the goal, but not before leaving a scarred landscape of short-term losers.

The markets evolve through perverse logic. If the crowd sees up, then it must be down. When the time says breakout, the danger of breakdown increases. Understand this frustrating concept with this simple truth: whatever the market says should happen right now probably won't happen right now. For example, don't expect a breakout to occur on schedule when popular forces fit into perfect alignment. Odds still favor the market eventually breaking out since supply and demand prevail over time. But internal mechanics will turn that anticipation against the crowd until the majority gets thrown off guard. Then the trend will likely proceed as originally anticipated.

Adapt timing to this discordant rhythm and stand behind, step in front of, or fade the crowd. Consider when to pause and wait although the signals say buy or sell. This strategy misses excellent trades, but it also avoids major fakeouts. Refocus execution toward the natural shakeout point that should terminate a false move. Jump in the shoes of those who act prematurely and visualize where they will likely

F I G U R E   15.16

Hewlett-Packard sets up a perfect 3rd watch that traps buyers and triggers a sharp selloff. The market then heads back through the breakout level after the NYSE specialist takes out the losers and short-term traders. Recognize the fakeout when a pattern does what it was supposed to do as soon as the crowd loses confidence.

RealTick® ©1986–2000. All rights reserved. Used with permission of Townsend Analytics, Ltd.

give up. That level probably represents the market turn and best opportunity to get on board for a trip through the breakout.

Many participants find this timing shift very difficult. The competitive market atmosphere ingrains a natural bias toward being early into new positions. Of course, those who yield to this temptation face the greatest fakeout danger. Learn to hesitate at the moment of execution and consider past experience. What are the odds that this moment represents a trap rather than an opportunity? Be willing to miss a profit if a trade takes off without entry, but prepare to act when others run for the hills.

WHIPSAWS

Breakouts occur where an irresistible force meets an immovable object. This odd description illustrates the underlying physics of the bull-bear conflict. No one really knows how much pressure or volume will push price into a profitable trend. Every position carries considerable risk, no matter how perfect the setup or underlying news. And every market action triggers a strong reaction.

Painful whipsaws arise naturally or through conscious manipulation. Because markets move constantly in and out of balance, sudden reversals can occur when conditions trap one side of the action. While everyone knows where key breakout numbers reside, no one can be sure what will happen when price gets there. S/R demands greater volume for breakouts as it builds over time. Each test triggers more recognition among the crowd and raises the stakes. When price returns for a new test, everyone watches to see what happens.

Successful breakouts generally occur in two phases. First, price thrusts through S/R on increased volume. It expands a few ticks and then pulls back while interest ebbs. A second surge then carries price well past the initial thrust as the trend strengthens into a ramping event. Success requires that both crowd impulses appear and contribute to awakening momentum.

Whipsaws push price backward when breakouts don't generate this second surge efficiently. This failure swing may or may not elicit a false breakout. The pullback forces weak hands to dump positions quickly and can generate a self-fulfilling event with price spiraling into a major reversal. But another breakout surge can appear if exit pressure ebbs quickly. Of course, this produces great frustration for those who just cut their losses.

Markets overshoot natural targets all the time. They crash through S/R, Bollinger Bands, and moving averages with ease. Then, just as participants look elsewhere, the trend reverses and carries price back within expected boundaries. These frustrating whipsaws have become far more common in recent years. The crowd's love of technical analysis ensures that they will be part of the charting landscape for many years to come.

Overshoots capitalize on S/R knowledge. Insiders know that trading strategies shift on key price violations, so action pushes through these levels to force volatility and volume. The apparent signal increases momentum in the broken direction and carries price further into the hole. As it reaches the next major barrier, a reversal finally begins that returns price back across the original violation. So how can the swing trader tell if an overshoot signals a real trend change? Unfortunately, there is no simple answer. An apparent overshoot may reflect a real violation or just a routine shakeout. Use candlestick shadows after the event to interpret overshoots whenever possible and always exercise defensive risk management.

F I G U R E   15.17

Burr-Brown takes the first step but fails to follow through. Lack of volume on the 3rd watch breakout offers a clue to the ensuing whipsaw. Price pulls back right on schedule and encourages a low-risk entry. But it reverses near the intermediate high and rolls over in an Adam and Eve top that prints a high-volume failure.

Daily   (Right) BBRC - BURR-BROWN CORP   Bar Volume

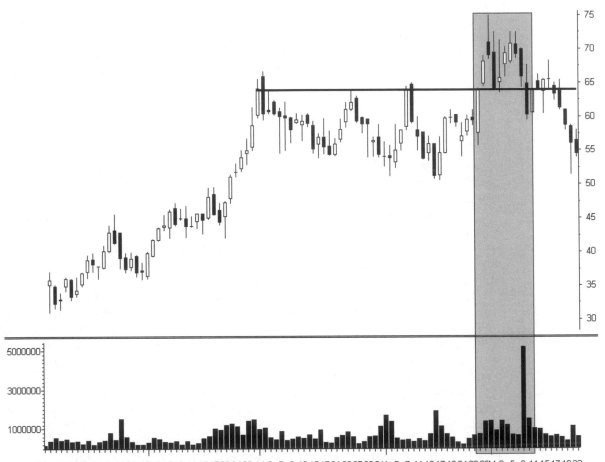

RealTick® ©1986–2000. All rights reserved. Used with permission of Townsend Analytics, Ltd.

Fibonacci retracements should hold 62% to remain intact. But pullbacks often overshoot all the way to 75% before they reverse. When a market reaches the 62% barrier, stand aside and watch for overshoots. Price may violate the level several times while shaking out the expectant crowd. Consider a trade after the overshoot ends and momentum starts to build in the opposite direction. Use candlestick shadows to watch Fibonacci support levels. These allow deep violations as long as the bar closes within retracement boundaries.

Markets try to fool swing traders at every turn, but the ability to see past the violation game grows with every successful execution. Insiders cannot repeal the laws of physics, and supply-demand still guides short-term direction most of the time. Estimate the force required to lift price to new highs or sink it below support for every setup. Whipsaws and overshoots can occur only if market interest falls below this important level.

NOISE

Questionable positions invoke wish fulfillment instead of risk management. Effective strategy must deal with expectations as well as results. Market participants love to see things that aren't there, and the daily grind gives them many opportunities. Because ranges persist most of the time, many intermediate highs and lows capture inappropriate attention and lead to bad decisions. Tape reading and Level II compound this problem with their emotional bursts of excitement and pain.

Technical noise increases in shorter time frames and decreases in longer ones. This underlying mechanism explains why many day traders bleed capital when they take too many positions. They misidentify each market wobble as an entry signal rather than waiting for cross-verification to line up. Longer time frames reduce noise because primary market forces still carry weight and guide trend development. When choosing shorter holding periods, always filter trades through broader trends to locate the most favorable setups.

Avoid Fibonacci on short-term charts except in very dynamic trends and highly liquid markets. Five-minute chart retracements work, but only after the swing trader adjusts to considerable noise and whipsaw. Narrow intraday ranges often flatten retracement signals to the point that they become useless. At the least, overlay longer-term trends on intraday charts and ignore retracement levels on less persistent price movement.

First and last hours mark intense periods of price discovery. These volatile phases invoke many imaginary trends, reversals, and shakeouts. Tighten up defensive strategies when executing positions during these times. Consider broad market forces when trying to predict short-term market direction. Step back and look at the longer-term view. Does the current action take place at a major breakout level, or are smaller forces at work? Try to avoid the first and last 15 minutes completely. The noise level spikes sharply during these intervals and most strategies become pure gambling.

THIRTY RULES FOR THE MASTER SWING TRADER

TRADE CRAFT

Each market day spawns excellent trading patterns. But many skilled participants still wash out through bad selection and poor timing. Why doesn't their experience save them from ultimate failure? The answer holds great wisdom for every trading aspirant. Simply put, long-term survival depends much more on personal discipline than on market knowledge. Sloppy execution wastes months at the guru's feet. Low self-esteem inflicts more damage than a sudden selloff. And a great stock cannot overcome a bad attitude.

Marginal players view speculation through greedy eyes. Without rules or tactics, they chase hot stocks and hope for the big score. Fate may reward these gamblers with an occasional windfall, but easy profits only reinforce a reckless attitude and open the door to eventual demise. Market professionals quickly find these lost souls and send them off to less challenging hobbies.

Opportunity waits for discovery. But modern markets demand careful planning and precise execution at all times. The road to success begins with the master pattern. Use Pattern Cycles to build powerful tactics that tap a market's vast potential. Test their real-time performance in each session and adapt a personal style that matches individual needs. Then exercise strict discipline through every phase of position management.

Read the charting landscape with great skill and select only the best setups. Execute positions based on numbers, time, and the smell of the crowd. Knowledge of the master pattern encourages detached execution and solid risk management. This science of trend allows swing traders to build systematic techniques that avoid reckless action. Take the time to explore this hidden world and become a true master of the trade.

RULES FOR THE TRADING GAME

Trade management demands simple understanding of complex market forces. Use these battle-tested rules to internalize the classic mechanics that move price and create opportunity.

MARKET WISDOM

- Forget the news, remember the numbers.

You're not smart enough to know how news will affect price. The chart already knows and reflects it in the numbers. Use the period before scheduled news to apply a convergence-divergence analysis that compares price action to current expectations. The best information comes when the chart diverges sharply from common wisdom.

- If you have to look, it isn't there.

Forget your college degree and trust your instincts. The best setups jump out from the market noise and create a sense of urgency to trade. Take a deep breath and cross-verify your numbers. Then act quickly before the opportunity disappears.

- Price has memory.

What did price do the last time it hit a certain level? Chances are it will do it again. Trend mirrors capture some of this movement, but actual experience does a better job. Watch when a favorite stock returns to a price level that turned a profit or loss in the past. The prior tape action embeds deeply in the trading subconscious and guides fresh tactics.

- Profit and discomfort stand side by side.

Look for the setup that scares you the most. That's the one you probably need to trade. Don't expect to feel comfortable until an active position finally closes out. If it feels too good, everyone else will trade it the same way and become the crowd.

- Stand apart from the crowd at all times

Trade ahead of, behind, or contrary to the crowd. Be the first in and out of the profit door. Take their money before they take yours. Always be ready to pounce on the crowd's ill-advised decisions, poor judgment, and bad timing. Your success depends on the misfortune of others.

THE SWING

- Buy the second low. Sell the second high.

Price extremes attract contrary tactics. The first test of a new high should fail. The first test of a new low should succeed. Watch for a breakout or breakdown the next time around.

- Buy the first pullback from a new high. Sell the first pullback from a new low.

Act quickly when the market gods offer a gift. Pullbacks let traders jump on board moving trains. They also provide fuel to carry a market higher or lower.

- Buy at support. Sell at resistance.

What do you do when you walk into a wall? Price has only two choices when it reaches a barrier: continue forward or reverse. Pick the right one and start counting your profits.

- Short rallies, not selloffs.

When markets drop, short sellers get ready to cover, making this a terrible time to execute new short sales. Wait until they ignite a squeeze and get shaken out at higher prices. Then jump in quietly while no one is watching.

TIME

- Trends depend on their time frame.

Trend relativity errors end trading careers. Make sure your pattern works in the period that you want to trade. Opportunity aligns to specific time segments. Profitable trades find the right ones, while losing trades chase the wrong ones.

- Manage time as efficiently as price.

Time is money in the markets. Don't waste either. Profit relates directly to the amount of time set aside for market analysis. Know your holding period for every trade. And watch the clock to become a market survivor.

- Avoid the open.

They see you coming. The best opening strategies exit old trades and wait patiently for new ones.

- The trend is your friend.

Strong stocks get stronger and weak stocks get weaker. Always surf the wave in trending markets. Save contrary thinking for pullbacks and ranges.

EXECUTION

- Expect the market to reverse as soon as you get filled.

Locate the safety net before jumping into a trade. Stand aside when the exit door is out of reach. Wait for a pullback or drop down and trade the next-lower time frame. Never toss a coin into the fountain and hope your dreams will come true.

- Match tactics to market conditions.

Shift gears quickly when trades stop working. Market inefficiency dries up as the crowd plays your game. But a new door will open as soon as the old one closes. Find it and profit until the herd heads your way.

- Trade with the TICK, not against it.

Go with the money flow. Draw trendlines and channels around TICK to predict where the next big move will occur. Then trade with the wind to your back.

- Major convergence signals the best trades.

Watch for the bull's eye. Look for the price and time that points repeatedly to a specific trade entry. The market is trying to tell you something.

- Don't confuse execution with opportunity.

Save Donkey Kong for the weekend. Pretty colors and fast fingers don't build successful careers. Understanding price behavior and market mechanics does. Learn what a good trade looks like before falling in love with the software.

OPPORTUNITY AND RISK

- The perfect opportunity rarely exists.

Learn to trade in shades of gray. Profits depend on different levels of inefficiency. Get off the sidelines and act when enough ducks sit in a row.

- Know the price that violates the pattern.

Keep both risk and reward in sight at all times. Look for trades where price must move only a short distance to show that it was a mistake. Then look the other way to find a profit target and apply this math to every opportunity. Limit execution to positions with low risk and high profit potential. Then update analysis with every new tick.

- Control risk before seeking reward.

Wear your market chastity belt at all times. Attention to profit is a sign of trading immaturity, while attention to loss is a sign of trading experience. The markets have no intention of giving money to those who do not earn it.

- Swing for percentage and distance.

Learn to hit both the single and home run. The best profits go to the swing trader with the highest AvgWIN and %WIN. Concentrate on building both sides of the market equation.

- Big losses rarely come without warning.

You have no one to blame but yourself. The chart told you leave and the news told you to leave. Learn to visualize trouble and head for safety with only a few bars of uncomfortable information.

SECRETS OF THE PRICE CHART

- Bulls live above the 200-day, bears live below.

Are you flying with the birds or swimming with the fishes? The 200-day moving average divides the investing world in two. Bulls and greed live above the 200-day, while bears and fear live below. Sellers eat up rallies below this line, while buyers to come to the rescue above it.

- The big move hides just beyond price congestion.

Enter in mild times and exit in wild times. Don't count on the agitated crowd for your trading signals. It's usually too late for an easy profit by the time they act. Execute new trades in narrow bars at support or resistance whenever possible.

- Big volume kills trends.

Blow-offs take buyers and sellers out of the market. When volume peaks too sharply or quickly, it will short circuit movement in the prevailing direction. These climax events wash out the crowd as efficiently as a flat market.

- Current price is the best indicator of future price.

What does the latest number say about the market? The answer predicts the next number, up or down. But go ahead and add a few indicators anyway just to stay out of trouble.

- Perfect patterns carry the greatest risk for failure.

Demand warts and bruises on your trade setups. Market mechanics work to defeat the majority when everyone sees the same thing at the same time. Look closely for failure when perfection appears.

- Trends rarely turn on a dime.

Reversals build slowly. Investors are as stubborn as mules and take a lot of pain before they admit defeat. Short sellers are true disbelievers and won't cover without a fight.

- Some gaps never fill.

The old traders' wisdom is a lie. Exhaustion gaps get filled. Breakaway and continuation gaps may never fill. Trade in the direction of their support when price approaches for the first time.

THE MASTER SWING TRADER

Commit yourself to a lifetime of opportunity and conflict. Professional traders still face unexpected drawdowns and missed profits, but they understand that longevity depends on shaking off their short-term demons and moving on to the next trade. And they have the confidence to expect a profit on the very next position.

Seek market knowledge but avoid the knowledge game. Books and seminars can undermine successful trade execution after a few years of experience. Realize that secondary reinforcement from sitting at the guru's feet may not build either profits or skills. True market wisdom comes only through personal trading experience.

Size doesn't matter. Avoid the bias that position size and professional responsibility must grow with trading experience. Some may find a home managing other people's assets. Others should just stay at home and watch the kids while the markets pay their lunch money. No single characteristic describes the successful swing trader. This master technician may look like a local businessman, soccer mom, or software geek.

Treat this noble profession with great respect. Combine the discipline of a saint with the tenacity of a bulldog through every trading opportunity. The markets work to fool the majority at every turn. Don't be surprised when you suddenly become part of the crowd that you're trying to avoid. Use the opportunity to peek in the mirror and see what it looks like before extricating yourself from this dangerous herd.

Enjoy the long road to market knowledge. Each twist offers a new gem to carry into the next active position. Over time, many battle scars teach a profound understanding of the modern financial markets. Neophytes become members of an exclusive club as they evolve into seasoned professionals. As their power grows, they often wonder if they can fully tame the beast and have it under their total control. Unfortunately, this popular fantasy will never come true.

Even the master swing trader must take what the market gives with humility, acceptance, and good humor.

SUPPLIERS

Active Trader Magazine
555 West Madison St., Suite 1210
Chicago, IL 60661
800-341-9384
http://www.activetradermag.com

Joe DiNapoli
Coast Investment Software, Inc.
6907 Midnight Pass
Sarasota, FL 34242
941-346-3801
http://www.fibtrader.com

Hard Right Edge
Brooke Publishers, Inc
8055 South Garfield Way
Littleton, CO 80122
303-773-6233
http://www.hardrightedge.com

Intelligent Speculator
P.O. Box 2953
Sumas, WA 98295
604-671-5456
http://www.intelligentspeculator.com

International Online Trading Expo
23456 Madero, Suite 240
Mission Viejo, CA 92691
888-411-EXPO
http://www.onlinetradingexpo.com

Investor Links
IL Data Corporation, Inc.
2350 Saddle Hollow Rd, Suite 1
Crozet, VA 22932
877-823-8182
http://www.investorlinks.com

MB Trading
214 Main Street, PMB 241
El Segundo, CA 90245
888-790-4800
http://www.mbtrading.com

Omega Research
8700 West Flagler St, Suite 250
Miami, Florida 33174
305-485-7000
http://www.omegaresearch.com

Mark Seleznov
Trend Trader
15030 N. Hayden Rd, Suite 120
Scottsdale, AZ 85260
888-328-7363
http://www.trendtrader.com

Silicon Investor
Go2Net, Inc.
999 Third Ave.
Seattle, WA 98104
206-447-1595
http://www.siliconinvestor.com

Technical Analysis of Stocks and Commodities Magazine
4757 California Ave. SW
Seattle, WA 98116
800-832-4642
http://www.traders.com

Tony Oz Enterprises
Stock Junkie
P.O. Box 3043
Laguna Hills, CA 92654
http://www.stockjunkie.com

Townsend Analytics
100 South Wacker Dr., Suite 2040
Chicago, IL 60606
800-827-0141
http://www.taltrade.com

Worden Brothers
Five Oaks Office Park
4905 Pine Cone Dr.
Durham, NC 27707
800-776-4940
http://www.tc2000.com

GLOSSARY

Abandoned baby   A three-bar candlestick reversal pattern. A single bar gaps up or down but then immediately gaps back in the opposite direction on the next bar. The shadow of the lone candle never crosses the shadow of the bar before the first gap or after the second gap.

Accumulation-distribution (acc-dis)   The underlying buying or selling pressure within a particular stock.

Adam and Eve (A&E)   Top or bottom reversal pattern noted by its sharp, volatile first high (low) and slower, rounded second high (low).

Ascending triangle   A common continuation pattern that forms from a rising lower trendline and a horizontal top resistance line.

AvgLOSS   A performance measurement that shows the total losses divided by the number of losing trades.

AvgWIN   A performance measurement that shows the total profits divided by the number of winning trades.

Axe   The market maker who exerts the most influence in a particular stock.

Bear hug   A trading strategy that finds short sale opportunities in weak markets that rally into resistance or narrow range bars on the verge of breakdown.

Bollinger Bands (BB)   Elastic support and resistance channels above and below price bars that respond to the tendency of price to draw back to center after strong movement in either direction. The Bollinger Band center band sets up at the moving average chosen for the indicator.

Breakaway gap   A classic gap, popularized in *Technical Analysis of Stock Trends,* that signals the start of a new trend after a prolonged basing period.

Bucket shops   Early 20th century stock gambling parlors that catered to short-term speculation. Fictional trader Jesse Livermore discusses his experiences in them in the classic *Reminiscences of a Stock Operator.*

Charting landscape   A 3D view that evaluates complex price action through multiple layers of information on a single price chart.

Coiled spring   A trading strategy that executes a position at the interface between a rangebound market and a trending market.

Continuation gap   A classic gap, popularized in *Technical Analysis of Stock Trends,* that signals the dynamic midpoint of an ongoing trend.

Convergence-divergence (C-D)   The tendency of two or more charting landscape features to confirm or refute an expected price outcome.

Clear air (CA)   Pockets of thin participation and ownership that often lead to wide range price bars.

Climbing the ladder   Bollinger Band pattern that indicates a strong and sustained rally.

Cross-verification (CV)   The convergence of unrelated directional information at a single price level.

Cross-verification × 4 (CV×4)   A high-probability trade in which a single price and time emerges from analysis through at least four unrelated methods.

Cup and handle (C&H)   A popular pattern that triggers a breakout through a triple top. The formation draws a long and deep base after an intermediate high. The market rallies into a double top failure that creates the "cup." It pulls back in a small rounded correction that forms the "handle" and then surges to a new high.

Cup and two handles (C&2H)   A cup and handle variation that draws two congestion zones on the right side of the pattern before price ejects into a strong breakout.

Dark cloud cover   A two-bar candlestick reversal pattern. The first bar draws a tall rally candle. The next candle gaps up but closes well within the range of the prior bar.

Descending triangle   A common reversal pattern that forms from a descending upper trendline and a horizontal bottom support line.

Dip trip   A trading strategy that buys pullbacks in an active bull market.

Doji   A one-bar candlestick reversal pattern in which the open and close are the same (or almost the same) price and the high–low range is above average for that market.

Double bottom (DB)   A common reversal pattern in which price prints a new low, reverses into a rally, and returns once to test the low before moving higher.

Double top (DT)   A common reversal pattern in which price prints a new high, reverses into a selloff, and returns once to test the high before moving lower.

Dow Theory   Observations on the nature of trend by Charles Dow in the early 20th century. It also notes that broad market trends verify when the three major market averages all move to a new high or low.

Electronic communications networks (ECNs)   Computer stock exchanges that rapidly match, fill, and report customer limit orders.

Elliott Wave Theory (EWT)   A pattern-recognition technique published by Ralph Nelson Elliott in 1939 that believes all markets move in five distinct waves when traveling in the direction of a primary trend and three distinct waves when traveling in a correction against a primary trend.

Empty zone (EZ)   The interface between the end of a quiet rangebound market and the start of a new dynamic trending market.

Execution target (ET)   The predetermined point in price, time, and risk that a trade entry should be considered.

Execution zone (EZ)   The time and price surrounding an execution target that requires undivided attention in order to decide if an trade entry is appropriate.

Exhaustion gap   A classic gap, popularized in *Technical Analysis of Stock Trends*, that signals the end of an active trend with one last burst of enthusiasm or fear.

Fade   A swing strategy that sells at resistance and buys at support.

Failure target   The projected price that a losing trade will be terminated. The price at which a trade will be proven wrong.

Farley's Accumulation-Distribution Accelerator (ADA)   A technical indicator that measures the trend of accumulation-distribution.

Fibonacci (Fibs)   The mathematical tendency of trends to find support at the 38%, 50%, or 62% retracement of the last dynamic move.

Finger finder   A trading strategy that initiates a variety of tactics based upon one-bar candlestick reversals.

First rise/first failure (FR/FF)   The first 100% retracement of the last dynamic price move after an extended trending market.

5-8-13   Intraday Bollinger Bands and moving average settings that align with short-term Fibonacci cycles. Set the Bollinger Bands to 13-bar and two standard deviations. Set the moving averages to 5-bar and 8-bar SMAs.

Five-wave decline   A classic selloff pattern that exhibits three sharp downtrends and two weak bear rallies.

Flags   Small continuation pattern that prints against the direction of the primary trend.

Foot in floor   Bollinger Band pattern that indicates short-term support and reversal.

Fractals   Small-scale predictive patterns that repeat themselves at larger and larger intervals on the price chart.

Gap echo   A gap that breaks through the same level as a recent one in the opposite direction.

Hammer   A one-bar candlestick reversal pattern in which the open-close range is much smaller than the high–low range that prints well above average for that market. The real body must sit at one extreme of the high–low range.

Harami   A one-bar candlestick reversal pattern in which the open-close range is much smaller than the high–low range and sits within the real body of a tall prior bar.

Hard right edge   The location where the next bar will print on the price chart. This also points to the spot where the swing trader must predict the future.

Head and shoulders   This classic reversal pattern forms from an extended high that sits between two lower highs. Three relative lows beneath the three highs connect at a trendline known as the neckline. Popular opinion expects a major selloff when the neckline breaks.

Head in ceiling   Bollinger Band pattern that indicates short-term resistance and reversal.

Historical volatility   The range of price movement over an extended period of time as compared to current activity.

Hole-in-the-wall   A sharp down gap that immediately follows a major rally.

Inside day   A price bar that prints a lower high and higher low than the bar that precedes it.

Inverse head and shoulders   This classic reversal pattern forms from an extended low that sits between two higher lows. Three relative highs above the three lows connect at a trendline known as the neckline. Popular opinion expects a major rally when the neckline breaks.

January Effect   The tendency of stocks to recover in January after end-of-year, tax-related selling has completed.

Mesa top   A double top reversal pattern that declines at the same angle as the initial rally.

Moving Average Convergence-Divergence (MACD)   A trend-following indicator that tracks two exponentially smoothed moving averages above and below a zero line.

Moving average crossover   The point where a moving average intersects with another moving average or with price.

Moving average ribbons (MARs)   Wide bands of mathematically related and color-coded moving averages.

Narrow-range bar (NR)   A price bar with a smaller high-low range as compared to the prior bar's high-low range.

Narrowest range of the last seven bars (NR7)   A low-volatility time–price convergence that often precedes a major price expansion. A price bar with a smaller high-low range as compared to the prior six bars' high–low ranges.

NR7-2   The second NR7 in a row. A low-volatility time-price convergence that often precedes a major price expansion.

Neckline   A trendline drawn under the support of a head and shoulders pattern or over the resistance of an inverse head and shoulders pattern.

Negative feedback   Directionless price action in which bars move back and forth between well-defined boundaries.

Noise   Price and volume fluctuations that confuse interpretation of market direction.

On Balance Volume (OBV)   A volume indicator that measures the progress of accumulation-distribution.

Oscillator   A subset of technical indicators that accurately measures flat market conditions by assigning overbought and oversold price levels.

Overbought   The evolution of price action to a state in which it runs out of buying pressure.

Oversold   The evolution of price action to a state in which it runs out of selling pressure.

Pattern analysis   Price prediction through interpretation of the crowd behavior seen in repeating chart formations.

Pattern Cycles   The tendency of markets to repeat identical price formations through different stages of development in all time frames. The master market blueprint that generates all chart patterns.

Pennant   Small continuation pattern that prints against the direction of the primary trend.

%WIN   A performance measurement that shows the total winners divided by the total number of trades.

Positive feedback   Directional price action in which bars gather momentum and move from one level to the next.

Power spike   A trading strategy that seeks high-volume events and executes positions to capitalize on their special characteristics.

Profit target   The projected price that a successful trade will be terminated. The price at which a trade faces first resistance.

Random Walk   Classic theory that chaos drives all market activity and that price movement cannot be predicted.

Rectangle   Small continuation pattern that prints sideways to the primary trend.

Relative Strength Index   A technical indicator that measures a stock's ability to close up rather than down for a specific period of time. An oscillator invented by

J. Welles Wilder that measures overbought, oversold, and divergent market situations.

Ribbon crosspoint   A horizontal support and resistance zone created by a moving average crossover.

Rising wedge   Reversal pattern that slowly rises in an uptrend until price suddenly ejects into a selloff.

Seasonality   The predictable appearance of certain market characteristics that reflect specific and repeating calendar events.

Setup   A sequence of bars, patterns, or other charting landscape features that predict the direction and timing of future price movement.

Shooting star   A one-to-three-bar candlestick reversal pattern with a small real body and tall shadow that pushes into an intermediate high before a sudden change in direction.

Signpost   Point on the charting landscape that identifies an imminent trading opportunity.

Silent alarm   A rare high-volume signal that prints a narrow range bar and flags an impending breakout.

Slippage   The difference between expected transaction costs and actual transaction costs.

Slippery slope   Bollinger Band pattern that indicates a sustained decline.

Standard deviation (std dev)   The positive square root of the expected value of the square of the difference between a random variable and its mean.

Stochastics   An overbought-oversold oscillator that compares the current bar to a preset selection of high and low prices. The indicator plots the results on a graph between 0 and 100.

Support-resistance (S/R)   Horizontal and nonhorizontal barriers that current price should not pass without the application of sufficient directional force.

Swing trading   A complex execution strategy that relies on identification of market opportunity through the charting landscape.

Symmetrical triangle   A common pattern formed from descending and rising trendlines. The formation has an equal bias of breaking out in either direction.

Technical analysis   Market prediction that studies crowd behavior through evolving price and volume activity.

3rd of a 3rd   The middle wave and most dynamic price movement within a complete Elliott five-wave rally or decline.

3rd watch   A trading strategy that executes a long position on a triple top breakout.

Trend mirrors (TM)   Past chart activity that influences the direction and development of current trend and range.

Trend relativity error   A common mistake committed when a trader prepares an analysis in one time frame but executes in another.

Trendlet   Small pocket of chart activity that appears and disappears over time.

Trendline   A line that connects a series of highs or lows. The trendline can represent support in an uptrend or resistance in a downtrend. Horizontal trendlines mark support-resistance and rangebound conditions.

Triangles   A related set of common three-sided congestion patterns.

Wave   Sustained price movement in one direction marked by clear high and low reversal boundaries.

Whipsaw   Erratic price behavior that triggers false signals and incurs trading losses.

Window dressing   Institutional buying or selling near the end of a quarter that makes reported results appear better than actual results.

BIBLIOGRAPHY

Achelis, Steven B. *Technical Analysis from A to Z.* Chicago: Probus, 1995.

Appel, Gerald. The Moving Average Convergence-Divergence Trading Method. Toronto: Scientific Information Systems, 1985.

Bernstein, Jake. *The Compleat Day-Trader.* New York: McGraw-Hill, 1995.

Connors, Laurence A., and Linda Bradford Raschke. *Street Smarts.* M. Gordon, 1995.

Crabel, Tony. *Day Trading with Short Term Price Patterns and Opening Range Breakout.* Greenville, S.C.: Traders Press, 1990.

Dalton, John M. *How the Stock Market Works.* 2nd ed. New York: New York Institute of Finance, 1993.

DiNapoli, Joe. *Trading with DiNapoli Levels.* Sarasota, Fla.: Coast Investment Software, 1998.

Douglas, Mark. *The Disciplined Trader: Developing Winning Attitudes.* New York: New York Institute of Finance, 1990.

Edwards, Robert D., and John Magee. *Technical Analysis of Stock Trends* 6th ed.. New York: New York Institute of Finance, 1992.

Elder, Alexander. *Trading for a Living.* New York: John Wiley & Sons. 1993.

Fischer, Robert. *Fibonacci Applications and Strategies for Traders.* New York: John Wiley and Sons, 1993.

Granville, Joseph E. *Granville's New Strategy of Daily Stock Market Timing for Maximum Profit.* Englewood Cliffs, N.J.: Prentice-Hall, 1976.

Hirsch, Yale. *The Stock Trader's Almanac.* Old Tappan, N.J.: Hirsch Organization, 1997 (revised annually).

LeFevre, Edwin. *Reminiscences of a Stock Operator.* New York: G. H. Doran, 1923. Reprint, New York: John Wiley & Sons, 1993.

Malkiel, Burton. *A Random Walk Down Wall Street.* (Rev. ed.). W.W. Norton, & Co., 1999.

Murphy, John J. *Technical Analysis of the Financial Markets.* New York: New York Institute of Finance, 1999.

Nison, Steve. *Japanese Candlestick Charting Techniques.* New York: New York Institute of Finance, 1991.

O'Neil, William J. *How to Make Money in Stocks.* New York: McGraw-Hill, 1994.

Oz, Tony. *Stock Trading Wizard.* Laguna Hill, Calif.: Tony Oz Publications, 1999.

Plummer, Tony. *The Psychology of Technical Analysis: Profiting from Crowd Behavior and the Dynamics of Price.* Chicago: Probus, 1993.

Schwager, Jack. *The New Market Wizards.* New York: Harper Business, 1992.

Sperandeo, Victor, and T. Sullivan Brown. *Trader Vic: Methods of a Wall Street Master.* New York: John Wiley and Sons, 1991.

Taylor, George. *The Taylor Trading Technique.* Greenville, S.C.: Traders Press, 1994.

Vakkur, Mark. "Seasonality and the S&P 500." *Technical Analysis of Stocks and Commodities Magazine* 14, no. 6 (June 1996): 241–43.

Weinstein, Stan. *Stan Weinstein's Secrets for Profiting in Bull and Bear Markets.* Chicago: Irwin Professional Publishing, 1988.

Wilder, J. Welles. *New Concepts in Technical Trading Systems.* Greensboro, N.C: Trend Research, 1978.

Williams, Larry. *The Secret of Selecting Stocks for Immediate and Substantial Gains.* Brightwaters, N.Y.: Windsor Books, 1986.

Zweig, Martin. *Martin Zweig's Winning on Wall Street.* Rev. ed. New York: Warner Books, 1994.

INDEX

ABOUT THE AUTHOR

Alan Farley is a private trader and publisher of the Hard Right Edge (http://www.hardrightedge.com) website. He is a highly acclaimed and nationally recognized educator on technical analysis and short-term trading tactics. Alan has been part of the market scene for over 14 years as a private investor, advisor, and author. He is a featured speaker and lecturer at national trading forums, where he teaches his highly original strategies for modern swing traders.

Alan has been featured in *Barron's, Smart Money, Tech Week, Active Trader, MoneyCentral, Online Investor, America-Invest,* and *TheStreet.com.* He consults with major news organizations on the difficult issues that face today's online traders and is a powerful voice for the Net revolution changing the face of the modern financial markets.